Book of *of* Mormon

BOOK of LIES

Published by 1811 Press, LLC
P.O. Box 71
McLean, Virginia 22101

First Edition Paperback 2012

ISBN-13: 978-1-939179-00-5

Front cover design: Ron Toelke, www.toelkeassociates.com
Design/production: Toelke Associates, www.toelkeassociates.com;
                    Pegasus Type, www.pegtype.com

Printed in the USA

10 9 8 7 6 5 4 3 2 1

Book *of* Mormon

BOOK of LIES

THE

BOOK OF MORMON :

AN ACCOUNT ... AND OF

MORMON ... ROM

Meredith Ray Sheets
Kendal Sheets

1811 Press, LLC

Wherefore ... and also ...
the La... e House o...
Israel ... n, and also...
by the ... p, and hi...
up unto ... by the gi...
and p... and of Moro...
ni, and ... y of Gentile...
the inter... en from til...
Book of E...

lso, which is ... of Jared, ... scattered at the tim...
the LORD ... nguage of the ... en they were building...
tower to get ... which is to shew unto ... ant of the House...

TABLE OF CONTENTS

DEDICATION

To all those who seek the truth through the exercise of enlightened criticism.

To William "Bubba" Stamm.

ACKNOWLEDGMENTS

FIRST, MY THANKS TO THE TWO LONG-AGO BUT NOT FORGOTTEN MORMON missionaries who knocked on my door one fateful day in 1987. Without their dedication and patience, I never would have been inclined to read *The Book of Mormon*, which led to this stunning discovery. For my four children, I am constantly reminded by your support through all these years of working on this project to appreciate the kindness you bestowed on me. Most of all, to my lovely wife and lifelong companion, Ladona, a talented artist, writer, teacher, and devoted mother. Thank you for all your patience and understanding through the long days and nights of my working on "the book."

—*Meredith Ray Sheets*

THIS BOOK IS THE RESULT OF THE WORK DONE BY A PROFESSIONAL, GENEROUS, and dedicated team of people, to whom I owe my deepest gratitude. Foremost is editor, mentor, and friend Laurie Rosin. For many years she championed this book as her own and shepherded it along from beginning to end. Her brilliant work and renowned reputation are eclipsed only by her kindness. Without her this book simply would not have happened. My gratitude also to editor Paul Thayer, who worked many long hours with true professional acuteness under a demanding schedule on a detailed and challenging manuscript. He carried us across the finish line of this marathon. Many thanks to proofreader Sandy Fishman. Her careful attention to overwhelming detail raised the bar for all of us. I also extend my special posthumous thanks to Trudi Martineau, who was our proofreader until she passed away in 2009. God bless your soul and thank you.

I'm very grateful to Ron Toelke of Toelke Associates and to Kenneth Benson of Pegasus Type, who turned the raw manuscript into a work of art. Many thanks to you both for the book design and the stunning and perceptive cover illustration. Ken's ingenuity in creating the numerous tables deserves special recognition. Both of you made the impossible possible. A special note of thanks to Randy Wyeth at I Do Photography. Randy's talent and ingenuity spared my rare book collection from being dismantled.

To SSAGLX for saving me, thank you. My gratitude to Joseph Zito for teaching me intellectual property litigation, VH1 for being there, Jessica Smith for graphics, JDPP, Joel Longnecker, and all my friends who encouraged me.

To my mother, an English teacher, who spent countless hours raising me to be a better writer and better person. Finally, to Soraya Nouralian, a talented dancer, artist, and businesswoman. Her kindness and patience prevailed through years of trials and triumphs, sacrifices and successes while I researched and wrote this book. She deserves more gratitude than I can express. I could not have done this without her.

—Kendal Sheets

TO THE LIBRARIANS WHO ASSISTED US WITH LOCATING SCORES OF RARE AND hard-to-find books at the Library of Congress, Smithsonian Museum, Georgetown University, Johns Hopkins University, the University of Utah, the University of Denver, George Washington University, Montgomery County College in Maryland, the University of Oklahoma, and many other sources.

For any errors in this book we take full responsibility as far as they were under our control.

—Meredith Ray Sheets
Kendal Sheets

⟫ 1 ⟪

The Source

In 1830, Edwin Budding invented the lawnmower, H. D. Hyde invented the fountain pen, and Joseph Smith Jr. invented a religion.

How does one conceive of and then market a brand-new religion to people of other faiths and beliefs? By its nature, religion creates a deep bond with its followers. They try to live according to its scripture, structure, and strictures. And yet many people abandoned—and still abandon—their religion in favor of Joseph Smith's church of Latter-day Saints. Why? What did Smith offer that prompted men and women to turn away from what they believed and how they were raised to embrace entirely new tenets?

For starters, Joseph Smith brought holiness home to America. Rather than a Bible whose stories spring from long ago and far away, *The Book of Mormon*[1] sets much of its foundation right here in the United States. We stand on hallowed ground. That alone proved seductive in a young, nineteenth-century America where anything was possible.

Smith claimed that as a teenager, he spoke with an angel who gifted him with golden plates inscribed with hieroglyphics. A self-proclaimed uneducated farm boy, he was given the ability to translate the symbols, which became *The Book of Mormon*. A miracle indeed, in Upstate New York.

Smith made sure his believers would not have to reject what was familiar to them. *The Book of Mormon* does not stray far from the Old and New Testaments. Many of the stories and events are similar. *The Book of Mormon*'s opening chapters take place in Palestine, and they acknowledge the One God and his prophets, including Moses and son Jesus. Joseph preached that *The Book of Mormon* was a restoration of lost biblical truths and rituals. The style and tone of the book reflect the Bible's, so prospective converts would not have to move outside their comfort zone.

Equally important, *The Book of Mormon* is a darned fine yarn, with lots of action and exotic adventures.

Joseph Smith knew he had a good chance of selling his religion, even though only five people organized the church in 1830 in Seneca, New York. Why? Because he also based his *Book of Mormon* primarily on a third book that had already been a success around the world.

The book on which Smith based his writing contained the essential elements he needed. All he had to do was plagiarize it—and a few others—and then conceal what he had done with soporific wordiness, minor changes, and reorganization. He counted on his followers to be an eager audience unfamiliar with the true sources of his so-called awakening and inspiration.

The Book of Mormon and Smith's other writings came primarily from *The Travels of Marco Polo, a Venetian, in the Thirteenth Century, Being a Description of Remarkable Places and Things, in the Eastern Parts of the World*, published in English in 1818.[2]

Smith did not accomplish this task himself. Joseph Smith Sr. began the project. Father and son completed *The Book of Mormon* together.

In the pages that follow, you will read the countless connections between Marco Polo's accounts of his wondrous journeys to the Smiths' *Book of Mormon*, including the adventures and customs of the nomadic Tartars of Asia. You will read the names of people and places, animals, and adventures lifted directly from *The Travels of Marco Polo* as well as material from the 1818 edition's seventy-five-page introduction by British author William Marsden.

For the basic structure of *The Book of Mormon*'s opening, the Smiths dipped into Marco Polo's memoirs of his years spent with the Tartars. Needing details for authenticity, the Smiths copied history, geography, and theory from travel books available in the early 1800s, such as Christopher Columbus's journals, which were compiled by his son Don Ferdinand, and records of New World conquests by Hernando Cortez. Their content stretches from Asia to Lapland and from the Middle East to the Americas. The Smiths recast the texts in biblical times and set them in the Holy Land, Mexico, and North America, duping an ever-expanding population of believers.

Many different religious sects follow the teachings of Joseph Smith Jr. and identify themselves as Joseph Smith's Latter-day Saints, who are commonly known as Mormons. The largest sect by member size is located in Salt Lake City, Utah, and now boasts more than twelve million members, with more than half living outside the United States. The Community of Christ, the second largest, is located in Independence, Missouri, and claims a quarter-million members worldwide.[3] Many other splinter groups have come and gone over time. The fundamentalist Latter-day Saints, who continue Smith's ordained practice of polygamy and view those who do not as apostate Mormons, remain in strong numbers in the United States but for obvious reasons keep their church rolls secret.

Mormon adherents operate at the highest level of business, government, and academia. According to some estimates, the membership of the LDS doubles approximately every fifteen years. This is due mainly to missionary efforts. It is now the fourth-largest religion in the United States and is growing much more rapidly than other religions, largely because of a young Venetian man's adventures that commenced in 1271.

Marco Polo's father, Nicolo, was a merchant, and as a boy Marco was trained to be a trader as well. He learned to read and write and how to exchange foreign currency by using his knowledge of mathematics.

In 1269, Nicolo and his brother, Maffio, traveled to eastern Asia, where they met the Mongolian ruler Kublai Khan. Before the merchants returned to Italy, the khan invited them to come back to his empire. They did and brought young Marco with them. They sailed from Venice to a port in

Palestine. At that point Joseph Smith Sr. picked up their adventures and made them his own.

When did this remarkable discovery of the Smiths' plagiarism begin? How did the investigation take shape?

In 1987 Meredith Ray Sheets, this book's coauthor, was living in Rawlings, Wyoming, when two missionaries of the Utah-based Church of Jesus Christ of Latter-day Saints knocked on his door. Sheets, a chemical engineer with a master's degree in science and forty-five years' experience in the petrochemical industry, was working for a Mormon-owned company. This was the first time he had met Mormon believers, and he spent a lot of time with them.

"Would you have any interest in *The Book of Mormon*?" one of the missionaries on his doorstep asked. "Would you like to know more about the religion?"

The question roused Sheets's natural curiosity. Since his college days, he had been involved with anthropological societies and natural-history museums. He invited the men into his home and listened to their presentation. One of their assertions was that Native Americans are descendants of the people in *The Book of Mormon*.

"Do you have any evidence of that?" Sheets asked.

"Yes, we do," they replied. "If you'd like, we'll come back in a few days and show it to you."

While they were gone, Sheets read several of the chapters of *The Book of Mormon*. He looked forward to the missionaries' return, knowing he would enjoy the discussion.

When the missionaries returned, they brought with them a slide projector and a new presentation. The slides showed ancient artifacts from Mexico and Central America unearthed by archeologists.

"These civilizations are evidence of the people in *The Book of Mormon*," one young man said. "Now look at this." The next slide showed an ancient child's toy in the shape of a llama with a roller attached.

"This is proof that the ancient people in America were using wheels on chariots, just as *The Book of Mormon* describes," he continued.

"I'm curious about the elephants in 'The Book of Ether,'" Sheets told them. "In verse nineteen in chapter nine, it says, 'they also had horses, and asses, and there were elephants and cureloms and cumoms; all of which were useful unto man, and more especially the elephants and cureloms and cumons.'"

"Yes," one of the missionaries said. "The people in the book had elephants with them, along with horses and other animals."

"Your 'facts' are incorrect," Sheets replied mildly. "I have extensive knowledge and experience investigating the ancient Americas, and the elephants in the American continents died out during the last Ice Age, approximately ten thousand years ago."

Meredith Sheets's passion was studying and collecting relics from ancient America. He had investigated Ice Age animals in America and the ancient Native Americans. Since the 1950s, he had personally discovered and excavated extinct Ice Age animals such as mammoths and saber-toothed tigers. He collected artifacts from ancient Native American sites ranging from the old American West, dating from well over 10,000 BC, and coauthored the first scholarly book published on the identification of North American Indian arrowheads.

The missionaries eventually took their leave. Were it not for those two men, Sheets might never have begun his investigation of *The Book of Mormon*.

During the next week, he read *The Book of Mormon* from cover to cover. It fascinated him but for reasons other than theology. After reading it a second time, he noticed something odd: the names, stories, and themes in *The Book of Mormon* seemed familiar. He thought about that for a few days, then pulled his favorite book from his bookshelf—*The Travels of Marco Polo*. Sheets's introduction to that book had been in secondary school, and he had read it numerous times since then.

He riffled through the pages, looking for a specific reference. The first word he recognized was *melek*, which means "king" or "ruler." The word *Melik* appears in *The Book of Mormon* as the name of a land. Now where were the other words that had sounded familiar? Besides *melek*, Meredith matched *Cumeni, Camorah, Gazalem, Sariah, Toemner, Manti,* and *Zenos* from *The Book of Mormon* with the same or similar names and words in *The Travels of Marco Polo.*

Were these corresponding appellations a wild coincidence? Could that be possible? Sheets considered that notion, even though it seemed farfetched.

Then he found the "Tree of Life" story in "The First Book of Nephi"— the first section in *The Book of Mormon.* He knew he was on to something.

The coauthor of *Book of Mormon, Book of Lies,* Meredith Sheets's son, Kendal M. Sheets, also brings specialized knowledge to this remarkable study. Both an engineer and an experienced attorney, he practices patent law and litigates intellectual property cases that include patent, trademark, and copyright-infringement lawsuits in the United States federal courts.

Neither Meredith nor Kendal Sheets has a personal agenda or prejudices against the Mormon faith. Their combined skills of critical thinking, mathematics, science, archeology, and expertise with intellectual-property infringement were all put to the test when confronting Joseph Smith Jr. and his father. In *The Book of Mormon, Book of Lies,* you will find comparisons, graphics, tables, and charts to prove that the content of *The Book of Mormon* is not original.

Meredith and Kendal Sheets devoted over twenty-five years to their investigation, and it resulted in astonishing discoveries. The men pored over many 200-year-old books and built their own library of rare volumes. Their research notebooks fill bookshelf after bookshelf.

Their investigation focused on finding the plagiarizing authors' accounts, descriptions, words, names, stories, customs, peoples, and currencies in *The Book of Mormon.* They looked back almost seven hundred years to explain who wrote the Mormon holy scriptures. The results, as you will see, are remarkable.

The Book of Mormon and the story surrounding its creation may be the greatest deception in the history of America if not the entire world. Millions of people believe the book is the divine word of God. It is, in fact, an intricate lie that has grown out of all imaginable proportions.

The purpose of *Book of Mormon, Book of Lies* is to expose the Mormon prophet, Joseph Smith, and others responsible for writing and perpetuating his fraud.

Was Joseph Smith Jr. capable of a ruse of this magnitude? Could a man write a book even though he claimed not to have a good command of the English language or possess the necessary literary skills? Just how did he do it?

Over the centuries, he claimed, the Holy Bible has been corrupted, and it is incomplete. *The Book of Mormon*, however, is the most correct book ever written. It is the original, entire message of Jesus Christ, received directly from God.

Did that get your attention?

That is how young Joseph Smith marketed his new religion. Furthermore, he said he had translated *The Book of Mormon* from hieroglyphics engraved on golden plates buried on a hillside in Palmyra, New York, about 1,600 years ago. He learned of these wondrous treasures from an angel named Moroni, who appeared when Joseph was but a teenager. Moroni told him where to unearth the gold tablets, which he did four years after the vision.

Why was Joseph Smith the chosen one to bring the "fullness" of the gospel to humankind and the restoration of God's true church to Earth?

Who was Joseph Smith Jr.?

⌘

Joseph was the fourth son of Lucy Mack Smith and Joseph Smith Sr., who had eleven children, nine of whom lived to adulthood. In his own words, with grammar copied true to the original writing, he said:

> I was born in the town of Charon in the (State) of Vermont North America on the twenty third day of December AD 1805 of goodly Parents who spared no pains to instructing me in (the) christian religion at the age of about ten years my Father Joseph Smith Siegnior moved to Palmyra Ontario County in the State of New York and being in indigent circumstances were obliged to labour hard for the support of a large Family

having nine children and as it required the exertions of all that were able to render any assistance for the support of the Family therefore we were deprived of the bennifit of an education suffice it to say I was mearly instructid in reading and writing and the ground (rules) of Arithmatic which constuted my whole literary acquirements.[4]

He was born on his grandfather's farm in Sharon, Vermont. He was a fifth-generation American, and his forebears were well-educated.

When the family farm failed, the Smiths moved to New Hampshire, then to Palmyra, New York, to work as merchants and farmers. Joseph's father was also a part-time schoolteacher.[5] The boy evidenced a flair for storytelling. He attended school in Royalton, Vermont,[6] and in New Hampshire.[7] According to his mother,

We established our second son Hyrum in an academy at Hanover; and the rest, that were sufficient age, we were sending to a common school that was quite convenient.[8]

His first vision, Joseph claimed, was of God and Jesus Christ, who appeared when he was a young teenager in the spring of 1820. He had gone into the woods to seek solitude, hoping to resolve a troubling question: which church should he join? Jesus told him not to affiliate himself with any church since they were all incorrect and their religious creeds an abomination.

Joseph Jr. was not the first in his family to have divine visions and hear the voice of God. The mother's and father's visions began in 1811, when Joseph Jr. was six years old. Not only were they similar to the visions described in *The Book of Mormon*, the circumstances surrounding the father's and son's visions were alike. As with the boy, the man was also seeking a correct version of the religion of the ancient apostles. In her book, Lucy Mack Smith wrote:

About this time (1811) my husband's mind became much excited upon the subject of religion; yet he would not subscribe to any particular system of faith, but contended for the ancient order, as established by our Lord and Saviour Jesus Christ, and his Apostles.[9]

Fervor and *enthusiasm* best describe the religious environment during Joseph's youth. No longer were believers attracted to the somber, well-educated ministers of the past. Large numbers of settlers moved quickly westward, but the scarcity of churches did not prevent them from worshiping. Traveling ministers were common. Revivals, missionary societies, and advertising were some ways that developing churches persuaded the populace to join them. Preachers held camp meetings and played to the crowd's emotions. Those emotions ran high, and shouting, weeping, falling, jumping, jerking, and even barking were common.[10]

Various denominations struggled to grow. The successful ones, however, sponsored speakers who claimed to have experienced spiritual manifestations and who preached from spirit, not from a book.[11]

For young Joseph Smith to say he spoke not *from* spirit but *with the Spirit* caused a commotion. Pastors scorned him, but his parents supported him, and local farmers and merchants were curious about him. Their interest grew when in 1832 Joseph described his visitation of September 21, 1823:

> . . . and it came to pass when I was seventeen years old I called again upon the Lord and he shewed unto me a heavenly vision for behold an angel of the Lord came and stood before me and it was night and he called me by name and he said the Lord had forgiven me my sins and he revealed unto me that in the Town of Manchester Ontario County N.Y. there was plates of gold upon which there was engravings which was engraven by Maroni & his fathers the servants of the living God in ancient days and deposited by the commandments of God and kept by the power thereof and that I should go and get them and he revealed unto me many things concerning the inhabitants of the earth which since have been revealed in commandments & revelations and it was on the 22d day Sept. AD 1822 and thus he appeared to me three times in one night and once on the next day . . .[12]

In her memoirs, Lucy Mack Smith recounted that remarkable year by saying:

> During our evening conversations, Joseph (Jr.) would occasionally give us some of the most amusing recitals that could be imagined.[13]

We thought it odd that she made no mention of Moroni's—or Maroni's—appearance or the secreted gold plates. Perhaps buried treasure and apparitions were unremarkable in the Smith household.

We can trace the genesis of Joseph's idea of digging up buried golden tablets. In 1825–26 Joseph and his father sold their services as "money-diggers" while Junior attended school with his brother Hyrum. Money-digging had much in common with Moroni's message.

In 1825 a newspaper in Palmyra, New York, where the Smiths lived from 1816 to 1827, reported:

> We are sorry to observe even in this enlightened age, so prevalent a dispo-
> sition to credit the accounts of the marvellous. Even the frightful stories
> of money being hid under the surface of the earth, and enchanted by
> the Devil or Robert Kidd, are received by many of our respectable fellow
> citizens as truths. We had hoped that such a shameful undertaking would
> never have been acted over [again in] our country.[14]

Joseph reportedly used a stone that allowed him to see in the spirit world where treasure was buried on someone's property.[15]

At this time the Smiths operated out of a farm in South Bainbridge, New York. The farmer, Josiah Stowel, had received some funding for the money-digging from the younger Smith's future father-in-law, Isaac Hale.[16]

Four years later, Joseph was tried for vagrancy in Bainbridge. He admitted using a seer stone to dig for buried treasure. The judge recorded that under examination, Smith made a statement in his own defense.

> Prisoner examined. Says that he came from the town of Palmyra, and had
> been at the house of Josiah Stowel[l] in Bainbridge most of time since;

had small part of been employed in looking for mines, but the major part had been employed by said Stowel on his farm, and going to school. That he had a certain stone which he had occasionally looked at to determine where hidden treasures in the bowels of the earth were; that he professed to tell in this manner where gold mines were a distance under ground, and had looked for Mr. Stowel several times, and had informed him where he could find these treasures, and Mr. Stowel had been engaged in digging for them. . . . that he had occasionally been in the habit of looking through this stone to find lost property for three years, but of late had pretty much given it up on account of its injuring his health, especially his eyes, made them sore; that he did not solicit business of this kind, and had always rather declined to have anything to do with this business.[17]

The judge called him a "glass looker," found him guilty, and noted that Smith had not found any treasure.

Treasure, however, is exactly what he said he had found on September 22, 1827, when he ostensibly unearthed the angel Moroni's golden tablets.

What did *treasure* mean to Joseph Smith Jr.? A rare religious artifact from antiquity or possibly fame and public adoration? Collaborating with his father in a scheme that made money-digging pale by comparison? What were they willing to do to have treasure within their grasp?

Ahuilizapan

✦ 2 ✦

STRATEGIES

What is *plagiarism*? It is the act of taking someone's words and ideas and claiming them as your own. This is bold dishonesty because if you are found out, your reputation is ruined. You lose the faith and trust of others.

Copying various texts, changing them, and passing them off as *The Book of Mormon* was a Smith family enterprise. Joseph Smith Sr. intended to create a new religion and have his namesake son gain recognition as one of God's true prophets. Both objectives require the faith and trust of others. Junior and Senior's ultimate goals was to benefit financially and provide for their future.

Had their machinations been discovered, the Smith family would have suffered severe consequences and had their dreams destroyed. They had to be very cautious in laying the groundwork and carrying out their plans. No one could discover how *The Book of Mormon* was compiled. The entire family knew that for their own survival, they could tell no one.

The Smiths made that pact. No one would ever find out that Father and his namesake converted the stories of Marco Polo and other travelers into *The Book of Mormon*. In Lucy Mack Smith's book, *Biographical Sketches of*

Joseph Smith the Prophet, and His Progenitors for Many Generations, which was published in London in 1853, she said:

> Accordingly, by sunset the next day we were all seated, and Joseph (Jr.) commenced telling us the great and glorious things which God had manifested to him; but, before proceeding, he charged us not to mention out of the family that which he was about to say to us, as the world was so wicked that when they came to a knowledge of these things they would try to take our lives; and that when we should obtain the plates, our names would be cast out as evil by all people. Hence, the necessity of suppressing these things as much as possible, until the time should come for them to go forth to the world.[18]

In her memoir Mrs. Smith concealed in hidden messages the truth that her son Joseph colluded with her husband to write *The Book of Mormon* and then sell it along with the new religion. Let's return to her recital of Joseph's knack for storytelling, where she explains that in 1823 the eighteen-year-old knew about *The Book of Mormon*'s subject matter years before he or his parents claimed to have obtained the gold plates. On page eighty-five, she said:

> During our evening conversations, Joseph (Jr.) would occasionally give us some of the most amusing recitals that could be imagined. He would describe the ancient inhabitants of this continent, their dress, particular; their mode of warfare; and also their religious worship. This he would do with as much ease, as if he had spent his whole life with them.[19]

According to what Joseph claimed later, however, he gained his extensive knowledge of ancient Native Americans from Moroni's gold plates, and these details appear in *The Book of Mormon*.

Let's look at her last sentence in the extract: "as if he had spent his whole life with them." It probably means that he *had* spent his whole life with the plagiarized sourcebooks in his father's library.

When Senior, his wife, and his son conspired to proclaim their secret manuscript to be a book from God, several conditions worked in their favor. First, while established religious leaders were in an uproar about the strange new religion, the overall environment was receptive to the Smiths' absurd claims. Upstate New York was called the "burnt-over" district because a constant parade of itinerant preachers rendered the local residents scattered and drained, for religious enthusiasm was literally being burnt out of them.[20]

Second, the Smiths had learned from their money-digging activities that some people were willing to believe in anything, no matter how preposterous, so long as the hoodwinkers were convincing and confident.

Third, Joseph Sr. gave his boy a head start on the project. He began compiling *The Book of Mormon* in 1811, when his son turned six years old. When Junior was old enough, he assisted with the project and became the front man for the conspiracy.

By the time he reached his teens, Joseph Jr. was handsome and charismatic, a talented storyteller and persuasive speaker—in other words, perfect for the job. Perhaps this is why he and not one of his siblings was his father's "chosen one."

As an underpinning of his ruse, Joseph Jr. had to portray himself as a humble, unlikely candidate to carry out God's will. If people accepted his unsuitability as a prophet, then his accomplishment would take on epic proportions. The idea of God's raising a hayseed to prophet status would be more believable than if a slick salesman claimed to be the Exalted One. The greater the disparity between his capabilities and achievements, the more intense the awe his audience would feel.

To that end, Smith passed himself off as an uneducated son of a farmer without the skills necessary to compose *The Book of Mormon* except as it came to him from God. He said his first vision occurred when "I was an *obscure boy*, only between fourteen and fifteen years of age"[21] and that he was preaching to the church as "an *unlearned boy*."[22]

His conveyance of God's message depended entirely on a translation of "reformed Egyptian," a heretofore unknown ancient language that was supposed to be engraved on the gold tablets.

From the start, before *The Book of Mormon* was published, Smith produced written sermons and instructions that he said came directly from

God to Smith himself. These divine directives made sure no one would contest his assertions. In 1830, he wrote:

> But behold, verily, verily I say unto you, no one shall be appointed
> to receive commandments and revelations in this church, excepting my
> servant Joseph, for he receiveth them even as Moses:
>
> And thou shalt be obedient unto the things which I shall give unto
> him, even as Aaron, to declare faithfully the commandments and the rev-
> elations, with power and authority unto the church.[23]

While Joseph Smith's academic ability and his flair for writing and storytelling have been documented, Marco Polo could accurately be considered unschooled. His reputation is as a great explorer and traveler, not a talented writer. *The Travels of Marco Polo*, edited and published in London by William Marsden in 1818, was available to Joseph Smith Sr. as a resource for his *Book of Mormon. Travels* is not well written; the content and the historical discovery, however, make the story timeless. Young Polo took notes during his journey, and years later he dictated his memoirs to a scribe. His accounts were vivid and detailed because he himself had lived them.

Marco Polo was the first European explorer to record traveling to the Mongolian, or more properly the Tartar, empire. Kublai Khan, grandson of the infamous Genghis Khan, ruled Tartary and Cathay (China) in 1260 AD and is considered the fifth emperor of the fierce Moghul, or Mungal, Tartars. His vast holdings extended from the southern provinces of Persia (roughly present-day Iran, Iraq, and the Arabian coast) to northern China. Polo served Kublai Khan as court administrator, which allowed him to travel freely throughout the empire for many years.

After almost two decades in Asia, Polo returned to Venice and told stories to his countrymen about wondrous and unknown lands, about a civilization greater than those in Europe, and about his service as an ambassador for the great Tartar emperor in the Far East. His accounts seemed so farfetched, the Venetians did not, could not, believe him.

In 1298, Polo, serving as a ship's captain in a regional war, was taken prisoner. Using his notes and memory, Polo described his travels to a fellow prisoner, who wrote them down. The stories described Armenia, Persia, India, Mongolia, Java, and southern China. Polo included details about the lands, civilizations, animals, foods, religions, battles, industry, resources, rulers and councils, and customs.

Throughout the centuries, different versions of Marco Polo's memoirs have surfaced in various languages, including Latin, Italian, French, and German.

Marsden's 1818 edition was unique because he was the first to perform an exhaustive study of the various Polo manuscripts and to match the material with verifiable history.[24] He compared facts and events from Polo's descriptions with modern (as of 1818) travelers' accounts and contemporary knowledge of the Middle East, China, India, and various parts of Asia (Figure 1).

The editor also included a map that showed many of the lands that Marco Polo mentioned (Figure 2).

Marsden included in his book an informative introduction, seventy-five pages long, that is relevant to *Book of Mormon, Book of Lies*, and he added numerous footnotes describing his research, which are also pertinent because they, too, proved useful to Joseph Smith.

Marsden's task was challenging for many reasons, not the least of which was the sheer number of translations and alterations from which he worked. Other hurdles for the translator included Polo's poor writing ability and his limited knowledge of his own language. Polo spoke a Venetian dialect of Italian, not formal Italian. Having departed on his historic trip when he was a young teenager, he did not have the benefit of a formal education. Furthermore, because his absence was so prolonged, he became accustomed to the language of the khan. Polo certainly did not know how to write an epic story, being an *unlearned boy* when he left home.[25]

Marsden's introduction to *The Travels of Marco Polo* states that traveler had "a deficiency of skill in literary composition," and "probably labored under the disadvantage of not possessing a ready command either of his own or any other language."[26] Polo "was therefore obliged to have recourse to the assistance of others in the preparation of his materials,"[27] and "from

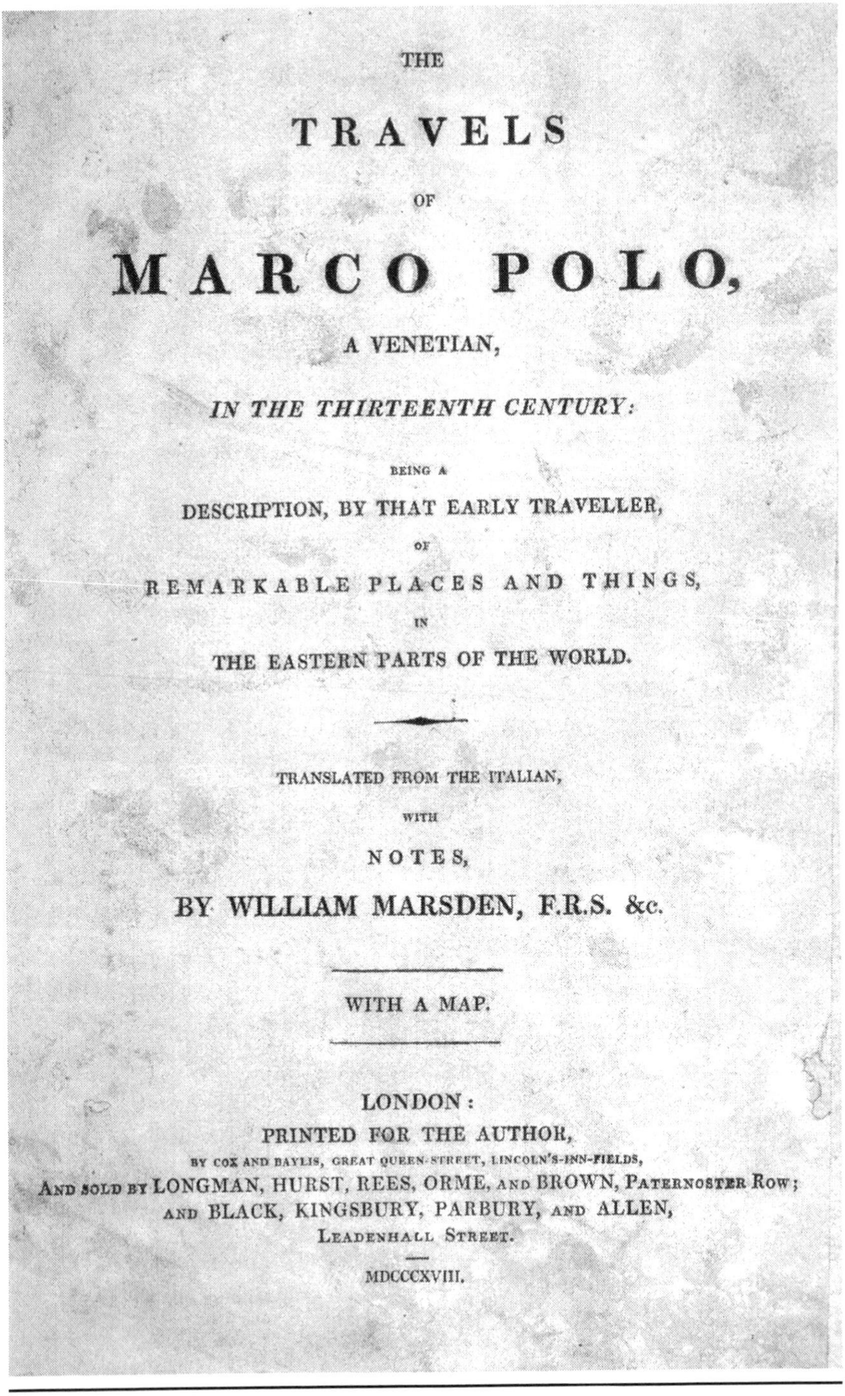

THE

TRAVELS

OF

MARCO POLO,

A VENETIAN,

IN THE THIRTEENTH CENTURY:

BEING A

DESCRIPTION, BY THAT EARLY TRAVELLER,

OF

REMARKABLE PLACES AND THINGS,

IN

THE EASTERN PARTS OF THE WORLD.

TRANSLATED FROM THE ITALIAN,

WITH

NOTES,

BY WILLIAM MARSDEN, F.R.S. &c.

WITH A MAP.

LONDON:

PRINTED FOR THE AUTHOR,

BY COX AND BAYLIS, GREAT QUEEN-STREET, LINCOLN'S-INN-FIELDS,

AND SOLD BY LONGMAN, HURST, REES, ORME, AND BROWN, PATERNOSTER ROW;

AND BLACK, KINGSBURY, PARBURY, AND ALLEN,

LEADENHALL STREET.

MDCCCXVIII.

Figure 1. Marsden, *Travels of Marco Polo*, Title Page

his verbal communications, the narrative is said to have been drawn up . . . by a person named Rustighello or Rustigielo."[28]

According to Marsden, Polo never wavered from his story, and the scribe attested to the veracity of the memoirist's words. Only after Polo displayed treasures from his journey to Asia did his medieval countrymen give credence to his adventures.

Obviously Smith seemed to have much in common with the Venetian. Both men wanted people to believe incredible stories outside the knowledge of their audience. Supposedly Smith, like Polo, lacked the literary skills necessary to communicate these tales. Polo needed the service of a scribe, and Smith depended upon a scribe as well—one who believed whatever Smith said—but for a very different reason. The self-proclaimed prophet, however, also depended upon Marco Polo—among others—to provide the magical, exciting, and exotic content of his *Book of Mormon*.

Both men's stories involve golden tablets engraved with strange symbols. Polo's tablets were twelve inches tall and three inches wide and read:

> By the strength of the eternal Heaven, holy be the Khan's name. Let him that pays him not reverence be killed.

As for Smith's? Well, no one actually saw the plates, but he claimed to have them, and he used people's willingness to believe him to work his magic. His underlying strategy was to make sure his new religion shared elements and conditions of established faiths.

Junior plotted methods to attract a large population of potential believers and convert them. Even the most bizarre tales require some realism, so he integrated facts into his book. He devised foolproof methods to silence critics and skeptics. He offered himself as the spiritual leader. The most difficult task by far was disguising the true sources for *The Book of Mormon*, but Joseph Smith Jr. made quick work of that, too.

The Book of Mormon: An Account Written by the Hand of Mormon upon Plates Taken from the Plates of Nephi, which Smith had copyrighted in 1830, is the history of the ancient Hebrews, both in the Holy Land and, later, in the Americas. It consists of fifteen chapters, called "books." *The Book of*

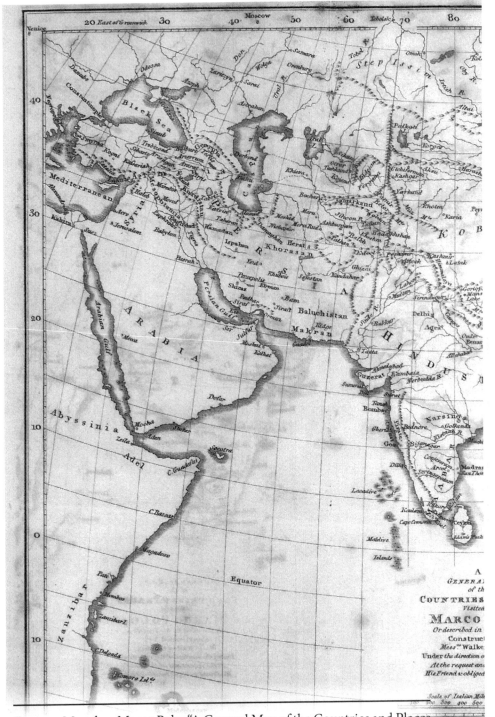

Figure 2. Marsden, Marco Polo, "A General Map of the Countries and Places Visited by Marco Polo"

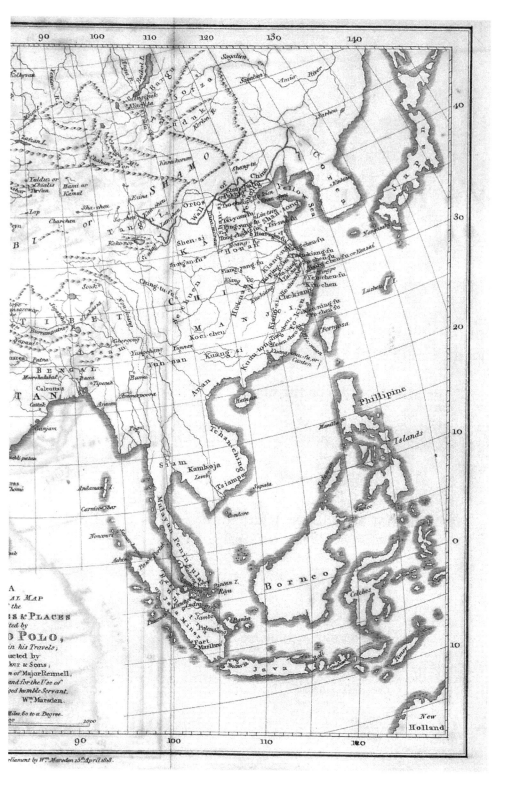

A
... MAP
... the
... & PLACES
... by
... POLO,
... in his Travels;
... by
... kar & Sons;
... n of Major Rennell.
... and for the Use of
... ged humble Servant,
W. Marsden.

... Miles 60 to a Degree.

Mormon is considered a sacred volume by the churches of the Latter-day Saints (Figure 3).

Joseph Smith wrote a letter to a Chicago newspaper describing it:

> In this important and interesting book the history of ancient America is unfolded, from its first settlement by a colony that came from the Tower of Babel, at the confusion of languages, to the beginning of the fifth century of the Christian Era. We are informed by these records that America in ancient times has been inhabited by two distinct races of people. The first were called Jaredites, and came directly from the Tower of Babel. The second race came directly from the city of Jerusalem, about six hundred years before Christ. They were principally Israelites, of the descendants of Joseph. The Jaredites were destroyed about the time that the Israelites came from Jerusalem, who succeeded them in the inheritance of the country. The principal nation of the second race fell in battle towards the close of the fourth century. The remnant are the Indians that now inhabit this country. This book also tells us that our Savior made His appearance upon this continent after His resurrection; that He planted the Gospel here in all its fulness, and richness, and power, and blessing; that they had Apostles, Prophets, Pastors, Teachers, and Evangelists; the same order, the same priesthood, the same ordinances, gifts, powers, and blessings, as were enjoyed on the eastern continent, that the people were cut off in consequence of their transgressions, that the last of their prophets who existed among them was commanded to write an abridgment of their prophecies, history, &c, and to hide it up in the earth, and that it should come forth and be united with the Bible for the accomplishment of the purposes of God in the last days.[29]

According to the story, Lehi and Nephi brought with them tablets with engraved scriptures and a history of their Jewish tribe. Nephite prophets added more metal plates over the centuries. The plates chronicle that Jesus Christ visited two peoples in the Americas, the Nephites and Lamanites, in the first century. Mormon, a military leader of the Nephites, recorded the events of his people from 327 to 385 AD. By the end of Mormon's life,

THE

BOOK OF MORMON:

AN ACCOUNT WRITTEN BY THE HAND OF MOR-MON, UPON PLATES TAKEN FROM THE PLATES OF NEPHI.

Wherefore it is an abridgment of the Record of the People of Nephi; and also of the Lamanites; written to the Lamanites, which are a remnant of the House of Israel; and also to Jew and Gentile; written by way of commandment, and also by the spirit of Prophesy and of Revelation. Written, and sealed up, and hid up unto the LORD, that they might not be destroyed; to come forth by the gift and power of GOD unto the interpretation thereof; sealed by the hand of Moroni, and hid up unto the LORD, to come forth in due time by the way of Gentile; the interpretation thereof by the gift of GOD; an abridgment taken from the Book of Ether.

Also, which is a Record of the People of Jared, which were scattered at the time the LORD confounded the language of the people when they were building a tower to get to Heaven: which is to shew unto the remnant of the House of Israel how great things the LORD hath done for their fathers; and that they may know the covenants of the LORD, that they are not cast off forever; and also to the convincing of the Jew and Gentile that JESUS is the CHRIST, the ETERNAL GOD, manifesting Himself unto all nations. And now if there be fault, it be the mistake of men; wherefore condemn not the things of GOD, that ye may be found spotless at the judgment seat of CHRIST.

BY JOSEPH SMITH, JUNIOR,

AUTHOR AND PROPRIETOR.

PALMYRA:

PRINTED BY E. B. GRANDIN, FOR THE AUTHOR.

1830.

Figure 3. Book of Mormon Title Page

the Nephites were nearly extinct, the result of horrific battles with the Lamanites. Although not clear from the text, Mormon apparently led his army across Central and North America to wage an epic battle around a hill he called Camorah.[30]

Mormon and his son, Moroni, along with the rest of the Nephites, set up tents around the hill Camorah and battled the Lamanites. The Nephite army was destroyed by the Lamanites. In the end, only Moroni survived. Before Mormon died, he gave Moroni golden plates that held the record of their civilization's history. Moroni added engravings to the plates and then hid them in a stone box in the Camorah hillside.

In the introduction to *The Book of Mormon*, Smith wrote: "I would also inform you that the plates of which hath been spoken, were found in the township of Manchester, Ontario county, New York."[31] The Latter-day Saints church sect in Salt Lake City, Utah, has built a visitors center and monument on Camorah.

The Book of Mormon opens with the "First Book of Nephi," which was supposedly engraved in metal plates by Lehi's son Nephi, starting around 600 BC. As the first book anyone would read of Smith's new gospel, the content had to seem believable and authentic. Many of the people to whom Smith was preaching were Christians. Either they were already familiar with the Old Testament, or at the very least they had read or heard Bible stories. Smith used Old Testament verses and organization as a template.

The opening paragraphs needed to inspire the reader to turn the pages. The first pages had to convince at least some of the skeptics that the book really could have been translated through "the gift and power of God." The content also needed to be similar to the Bible's, and the style had to match the Bible's. "The First Book of Nephi" had to be a page-turner.

Joseph Smith accomplished all this not by writing about miraculous events and divine preaching—although plenty of those were added later— but by referencing actual geography and history of the Middle East and a factual account that took place in part around Jerusalem.

This is the only chapter in *The Book of Mormon* set in the Holy Land and on the Arabian peninsula. Its setting includes Jerusalem and the Red Sea and the route to the fertile southern coast of Arabia. It describes familiar figures and events, such as Zedekiah, king of Judah, and the fall of Jerusalem.

Readers might think, therefore, that Smith's stories of the Holy Land could be authentic. They might also wonder how an "unlearned youth" could possibly know detailed stories about the Holy Land and Arabia when he had never traveled beyond New England. Obviously he must have found the golden plates and translated them.

Smith not only made use of content that was familiar, he added to it. He later claimed:

> The boldness of my plans and measures can readily be tested by the touchstone of all schemes, systems, projects, and adventures, truth; for truth is a matter of fact; and the fact is, that by the power of God I translated *The Book of Mormon* from hieroglyphics, the knowledge of which was lost to the world, in which wonderful event I stood alone, an unlearned youth, to combat the worldly wisdom and multiplied ignorance of eighteen centuries, with new revelation, which (if they would receive the everlasting Gospel,) would open the eyes of more than eight hundred millions of people, and make "plain the old paths."[32]

Let's look at the beginning of *The Book of Mormon*. Nephi begins with this summary of the story (Figure 4).

In brief, a Hebrew man, Lehi, sees a vision of God, Christ, and the twelve apostles. In a dream God orders Lehi to leave Jerusalem with his wife, Sariah, and their four sons. Almost immediately God tells Lehi to send his sons back to Jerusalem to recover brass plates from the powerful and wicked Laban.

When their attempts fail, Nephi's older brothers, Laman and Lemuel, vent their frustration on him. An angel saves Nephi from their beating and orders the brothers to retrieve the plates. Nephi returns alone to Laban's house while his brothers wait for him outside the city.

Nephi finds Laban passed out from drink. As directed by God, Nephi murders Laban. He disguises himself as Laban and tricks the servant Zoram into giving him the brass plates. These he takes to his brothers.

*An account of Lehi and his wife Sariah, and his four Sons,
being called, (beginning at the eldest,) Laman, Lemuel,
Sam, and Nephi.   The Lord warns Lehi to depart out of
the land of Jerusalem, because he prophesieth unto the people concerning their iniquity ; and they seek to destroy his
life.   He taketh three days' journey into the wilderness
with his family.   Nephi taketh his brethren and returns to
the land of Jerusalem after the record of the Jews.   The account of their sufferings.   They take the daughters of Ishmael to wife.   They take their families and depart into the
wilderness.   Their sufferings and afflictions in the wilderness.   The course of their travels.   They come to the large
waters.   Nephi's brethren rebelleth against him.*

Figure 4. Introduction to "The First Book of Nephi," p. 5

When Zoram realizes his mistake, he plans to flee, but Nephi persuades him to join Lehi's family in their travels.

The group travels from Jerusalem down the coastal areas of the Red Sea on the Arabian peninsula. During the journey, Lehi preaches repentance and experiences a number of miracles and visions. The Hebrew sees visions of God on his throne, a pillar of fire in the sky, and the Tree of Life.

Nephi reads the engraved plates and finds Jewish genealogy and God's laws. He sees that Joseph and his father, Jacob, are his forebears. The plates also contain the five books of Moses and writings by the prophet Jeremiah.

A golden ball that functions as a compass appears outside Lehi's tent. On it, God has written travel directions for Lehi. Eventually the travelers reach the southern seacoast and a place they call Bountiful. The ball leads them to the coast, where Nephi builds a ship. With the ball as his guide, Nephi sails the group to the Promised Land of North America.

⌘

"The First Book of Nephi" sounds authentic, and it also has all the elements of good fiction: visions, dreams, divine entities, a difficult mission, and violence; an admirable protagonist with an open heart and a hateful antagonist who schemes to steal valuables; and the cliffhanger of a biblical family about to embark for North America. Who could stop reading such a book?

The facts Smith included lent credibility to his fiction. The technique had its intended effect on his readers: if First Nephi was true, then so must be Smith's claims to have translated the words from golden plates. And if that was true, then Smith must have found the plates as a result of an angelic vision. And if that was true, then he must be the true prophet of God. And if that was true . . .

We know Smith's first trick was to use content already accepted as fact by the readers and then build on it. What was his second? What is the real "First Book of Nephi"? Just what did Joseph Smith do?

Πιιαχγαcαc

3

THE REAL
"FIRST BOOK OF NEPHI"

Imagine a plagiarist sitting with two open books before him. On his left is the original source; on the right is his work in progress. His eyes shift back and forth between the volumes. Pen in hand, he reads one book, then transfers some of its content onto the blank page of the other.

Left, right, left, right . . .

The second strategy implemented by Joseph Smith Sr. and Joseph Smith Jr. was to lend authenticity to *The Book of Mormon* by copying details of eyewitness accounts of places and events. The more specific their tales about the ancient Jews and their travels, the more factual the material would seem.

The Smiths did not have to cast about for resources or pore over countless books for the information they needed. Evidence of their clever idea to conceal the sources of their story can be found again and again between the covers of the Bible, William Marsden's *The Travels of Marco Polo*, various memoirs of European travelers, and history books.

In some instances, the Smiths copied both text and content; in others, they plagiarized content alone.

For his translation of Polo, the British editor and author Marsden had cross-referenced facts and events from the Venetian's memoir with reports written by modern travelers. These men had firsthand knowledge of the Middle East, China, India, and various parts of Asia. Marsden credited them in his introduction to *The Travels of Marco Polo*—notably John Pinkerton and Robert Kerr, who both published *Marco Polo* translations as part of their own travel volumes. The Smiths had but to locate and read Pinkerton's and Kerr's books, which were published in the early 1800s, and marry the facts from those books with the fiction of *The Book of Mormon*.

Father and son used this content as their inspiration for plot action, people, and locations in the first chapter (and elsewhere) in *The Book of Mormon* and as their guide for chronology. "The First Book of Nephi," standing alone, may appear to be a biblical story of a Jewish family traveling through the Holy Land. Place it next to *Marco Polo*, however, and we can recognize it for what it is—plagiarism.

Not only are incidents alike and in the identical sequence, they are found in approximately the same place in *The Travels of Marco Polo* and *The Book of Mormon*. This can be seen by using simple mathematics: at what percentage of text into the volume from the first page does the material appear? Now we have the Smiths' third strategy: using *The Travels of Marco Polo* as the infrastructure of *The Book of Mormon*.

If you place the 1830 *Book of Mormon* side by side with the 1818 edition of *The Travels of Marco Polo*, you will find matching names and stories on or near the *relative* page numbers in both books. Simply put, the Joseph Smiths used *Marco Polo* as the organizing principle of *The Book of Mormon* as well as the source of specific stories, names, and numbers.

The Smiths started at the beginning of *Marco Polo* and generally worked their way through the book to the end. The recurrence of this method proves it is not mere coincidence.

You can check this pattern for yourself. Here's how to go about it: Marsden's *Travels of Marco Polo* has 756 pages; *The Book of Mormon* has 588 pages. Although the actual story of First Nephi begins on page five, our percentage method still works. Open one of the books—Polo's or the Smiths'—to any page. Do a little math to find how far that page is from the beginning. Then match that percentage to a page in the other book.

To find a percentage through the text in *Marco Polo*, divide a page number where a story is printed in the text by the entire pages in the book. For example, let's say you opened *The Travels of Marco Polo* to page 683. Divide 683 by 756, the total number of pages in Marsden's translation:

$$683 \div 756 = .9034, \text{ or } 90.34\%$$

In other words, the percentage of the way through the text from beginning to end for page 683 in *The Travels of Marco Polo* is 90.34 percent.

The same method can be used for the 1830 edition of *The Book of Mormon* by dividing any page number by 588, the total number of pages. For example, you've opened the Smiths' book to page 425:

$$425 \div 588 = .7227, \text{ or } 72.27\%$$

Assume Smith *generally* copied from Marco Polo in a deliberate way. This rule is not hard and fast; Smith would have been cautious enough to deviate from it on occasion. But we should be able to find matching stories at similar percentages in both books. This astonishing discovery could do the most damage to *The Book of Mormon*'s purported authenticity.

For example, the Smiths copied a Marco Polo story about a battle at exactly 58.33 percent of the way through each book. There is less than a 1/10,000 difference between the two placements in the two books.

In an attempt to prove Smiths' copying by finding the same story near the identical percentage points in *The Book of Mormon* and *The Travels of Marco Polo*, the researchers chose a percentage number and then looked for matching stories at that point in the books. As a basic demonstration, let's begin with 33 percent, then 50 percent, and finally use 66 percent of the way through the text of each book.

We'll begin with multiplication to find a specific page number in *The Travels of Marco Polo*:

$$33.33\% \times 756 \text{ pages} = \text{page } 252$$

Now we'll do the same for *The Book of Mormon*:

$$33.33\% \times 588 \text{ pages} = \text{page } 196$$

This means a story somewhere around page 252 in *Marco Polo* should also be found at about page 196 in *The Book of Mormon*.

One-third through the Marco Polo narrative, on page 252, we find the story of a culprit being condemned, and then his corpse burned and eaten:

> They are addicted moreover to this beastly and horrible practice; that when any culprit is condemned to death, they carry off the body, dress it on the fire, and devour it.

Skim *The Book of Mormon*, starting with page 196, and look before or after that page for anyone put to death by fire. On page 190, or 32.31 percent of the way into the text, the researchers found this about a man named Abinadi who was condemned and burned to death:

> And it came to pass they took him, and bound him, and scourged his skin with faggots, yea, even unto death. And now when the flames began to scorch him, he cried unto them. . . . And now when Abinadi had said these words, he fell, having suffered death by fire. (Mosiah 9: pp. 190–191 [17:13–20])[33]

The stories occur at a difference of 1.02 percent from each other.

What can we find halfway through each book?

$$765 \text{ pages} \div 2 = \text{page } 378$$

Page 378 is 50 percent of the way through the text of *The Travels of Marco Polo*. While some curious facts are located near that page, not until page 405, or 3.6 percent farther through the text, did the researchers find a striking account of ancient engravings that seemed like something Joseph Smith might have been interested in. Italics have been added for emphasis:

It was near this capital that an *ancient inscription on stone was discovered, which, in Syriac and Chinese characters, recorded the state of Christianity in that province or kingdom,* set forth the protection and indulgence it received from different emperors, and contained a list of its bishops.

The above is Marco Polo's description of a stone with ancient writing on it, and the text is about an extinct people.

Now what do we find halfway through *The Book of Mormon?* This takes us to the chapter titled "Book of Alma."

$$588 \text{ pages} \div 2 = \text{page } 294$$

None of the above words was found on that page. Continuing to page 326, however, or 55.44 percent into *The Book of Mormon,* we find the story of twenty-four inscribed plates about a people who have been destroyed:

And now, my son Helaman, I command you that ye take the records which have been entrusted with me; and I also command you that *ye keep a record of this people,* according as I have done, upon the plates of Nephi, and keep all these things sacred which I have kept, even as I have kept them: for it is for a wise purpose that they are kept; and these plates of brass *which contain these engravings,* which have the records of the Holy Scriptures upon them, which have the genealogy of our forefathers, even from the beginning. (Alma 17: p. 326 [37:1–3])

And now behold, if they are kept, they must retain their brightness; yea, and they will retain their brightness; yea, and also shall all the plates which do contain that which is Holy Writ. (Alma 17: p. 326 [37:5])

Yea, I say unto you, were it not for these things that these records do contain, which are on these plates, Ammon and his brethren could not have convinced so many thousand of the Lamanites, of the incorrect tradition of their fathers; yea, these records and their words, brought them unto repentance; that is, they brought them to the knowledge of the

Lord their God, and to rejoice in Jesus Christ, their Redeemer. (Alma 17: p. 326–327 [37:9])

Turn a few more pages to 328, or 55.78 percent into the text, and you will read an account of the godly Jews, the Jaredites, who no longer existed:

> And now, I will speak unto you concerning those twenty-four plates, that ye keep them, that the mysteries and the works of darkness, and their secret works, or the secret works of *those people, which have been destroyed*, may be made manifest unto this people; yea, all their murders, and robbings, and their plunderings, and all their wickedness, and abominations, may be made manifest unto this people; yea, and that ye preserve these directors. (Alma 17: p. 328 [37:21])

> And the Lord said, I will prepare unto my servant Gazelem, *a stone*, which shall shine forth in darkness unto light, *that I may discover unto my people which serve me, that I may discover unto them the works of their brethren;* yea, their secret works, their works of darkness, and their wickedness and abominations. (Alma 17: p. 328 [37:23])

The difference in the location of these two stories in both books is a mere 2.2 percent:

Joseph Smith   55.8%
Marco Polo   53.6%
Difference   =   2.2%

Line up the key words and phrases from *Marco Polo* on the left with the ones from *The Book of Mormon* on the right, and the Smiths' pattern becomes obvious:

Marco Polo	*The Book of Mormon*
an ancient **inscription** . . . in Syriac and Chinese characters	And these plates of brass, which contain these **engravings**, which have

Marco Polo	The Book of Mormon
	the records of the Holy Scriptures upon them
on stone	a stone, which shall shine forth in darkness
was discovered	that I may discover
recorded the state of Christianity in that province or kingdom	Ammon and his brethren could not have convinced so many thousand of the Lamanites, of the incorrect tradition of their fathers; yea, these records and their words brought them unto repentance; that is, they brought them to the knowledge of the Lord their God, and to rejoice in Jesus Christ their Redeemer . . .
contained a list of its bishops	that I may discover unto them the works of their brethren
. . . where will be found a fac-simile of the inscription, with a literal translation of each character . . .	And now, I will speak unto you concerning those twenty-four plates, that ye keep them, that the mysteries and the works of darkness, and their secret works, or the secret works of those people, which have been destroyed,
Some suspicions were naturally excited in Europe . . . its authenticity appears no longer disputed . . .	may be made manifest unto this people.

For our final experiment, let's read what is two-thirds through *The Book of Mormon* and *The Travels of Marco Polo*. We'll reverse the procedure by finding a story in *The Book of Mormon* and then see if we can match it to a Marco Polo account.

$$588 \text{ pages} \times 66.66\% = \text{page } 392$$

On page 392 of *The Book of Mormon* is a verse that reads:

. . . therefore they took no thought concerning the city of Manti.

Two-thirds into *The Travels of Marco Polo* lands us on page 504. On page 505 (66.80 percent) is the following quote from Chapter LXVII titled "Of the Cities of Sing-gui and Va-gui:"

> . . . so prodigious is their number that they might not only subdue the whole of the province (Manji)

The name of the *southern land* of the Tartar empire, Manji, seems to have been copied by Smith as a *southern land* of Nephites, Manti. Manji/Manti are a mere 0.14 percentage points from each other in both books.

Now we'll look at one more example from the same chapter of *Marco Polo* and of *The Book of Mormon*. A story about drunken enemies is found in both books just a few pages apart. *The Book of Mormon* version is found on page 380, or 64.63 percent. The relative page number for Marco Polo's account would be around page 487.

Moving forward to 503—or 66.53 percent through Polo's text—we find a story about drunken soldiers and the captives who murder them. This reflects a 1.90 percent difference between the placement in the two books.

The content of the stories and the sequence of the words are essentially the same:

Marco Polo (66.53%)	Joseph Smith (64.63%)
walled city	wall of the city
wine	wine
fatigue	weary
drink in excess	take of the wine freely
intoxicated	drunken
people . . . perceived	men saw
fell asleep	deep sleep
murdering them	could have slain them
not suffering one to escape	took them prisoners
it was carried	took possession.

After copying all those words, Joseph Smith changed the ending of Polo's story about the drunken men. Smith had the drunken men taken prisoner rather than using Marco Polo's ending of having them murdered. Even so, Smith used the same idea of murdering them by writing on page 380:

But had they awoke the Lamanites, behold they were drunken, and the Nephites could have slain them. (Alma 14: p. 380 [55:18])

Let's begin with overall plot structure and the sequence of events. Both books begin with brothers—Nicolo and Maffio Polo and Lehi's sons Nephi, Laman, Lemuel, and Sam—and their travel adventures back and forth from Jerusalem or the coastal city of Acre, near Jerusalem. The first page establishes the date on which each group commences its journey:

It should be known to the reader that, at the time when Baldwin II was Emperor of Constantinople . . . in the year of our Lord 1250 . . . (Marsden, Marco Polo, p. 1)

For it came to pass, in the commencement of the first year of the reign of Zedekiah, king of Judah . . . (1 Nephi 1: p. 5 [1:4])

Dates and travel itineraries from primary sources were important details to the Smiths. The Book of Mormon is supposed to be a history book as well as scripture. Senior and Junior needed to know how long a journey would take, so they found out from a man who had accomplished it. Then they inserted the number of days or months into their project.

Let's take an overview of the stories, beginning with "The First Book of Nephi," Ch. 1, p. 42 [17:4], which says:

And we did sojourn for the space of many years, yea, even eight years in the wilderness.

Nicolo and Maffio Polo traveled between eight and nine years on their eastward journey to and from Asia. They left Constantinople in 1260 and returned to Acre in April 1269. Because Acre was only about ninety miles from Jerusalem, it was close enough to provide a credible basis for Lehi's travels.

(0.13%) *The Travels of Marco Polo*, translated in 1818 by Wm. Marsden Book I, Ch. I, p. 1	(1.19–1.36%) *The Book of Mormon*, 1830, 1 Nephi 1: pp. 7–8 [2:2–5]
After mature deliberation on the subject of their proceedings, it was determined, as the measure most likely to improve their trading capital,	And it came to pass that the Lord commanded my father . . .
that they should **prosecute their voyage**	that he should take his family and depart
into the Euxine or Black sea.	into the wilderness.
(The Polo family had left their homes in Venetia, then departed Constantinople.) With this view they made purchases of	And he left his house, and the land of his inheritance, and
many fine and costly jewels,	his gold, and his silver, and his precious things,
and taking	and took
	nothing with him save it were his family, and provisions, and tents, and
their departure	he departed
from Constantinople,	into the wilderness;
	and he came down by the borders near
navigated (note: the Black Sea)	the shore of the Red Sea;
to a port named *Soldadia*, from whence they	and he
travelled by land . . .	travelled in the wilderness . . .

Because of Acre's proximity to Jerusalem and the copying of the Polos' trips to Jerusalem, we can speculate with some confidence that this is why the Smiths described Lehi's home as the "land of Jerusalem" in the introduction of First Nephi instead of its biblical name, "Jerusalem."

> The Lord warns Lehi to depart out of the land of Jerusalem, because he prophesieth not the people concerning their iniquity; and they seek to destroy his life. He taketh three days' journey into the wilderness with his family. Nephi taketh his brethren and returns to the land of Jerusalem after the record of the Jews. (1 Nephi 1: p. 5)

When they were close to the Red Sea, Lehi led his wife, Sariah, and four sons into the wilderness, where they pitched a tent near a river. In *The Travels of Marco Polo*, William Marsden uses a phrase in a footnote near the same percentage location. He describes how the Chinese emperors provide for travel accommodations to Europeans:

(3.17%) *Marco Polo*, p. 23–24	(1.36%) 1 Ne 1: p. 8 (2:6)
43. The attention of the Chinese emperors to the accommodation of travellers whom they invite to their court . . . is strongly exemplified in the above journey of the Lama . . . On many occasions he was escorted by the *Kalmuck* chiefs, through whose country he passed, with numerous bodies of horse.	And it came to pass that when he had travelled three days in the wilderness,
Wherever **his tents were pitched, a** boarded platform was set up. . . .	**he pitched his tent** in a valley beside a river of water.

A better comparison, though, is found in another Marsden footnote later in the book. On pages 158–159 of the story, Marco Polo is traveling near the town of Lop, which is close to the "commencement of the great Desert." The Smiths would have gleaned much from Polo about what it was like for a group to cross a desert, which would help them create the story of Lehi's trek across Arabia:

Travellers who intend to cross the desert, usually halt for a considerable time at this place, as well to repose from their fatigues . . . (T)he stock of provisions should be laid in for a month, that time being required for crossing the desert in the narrowest part. To travel in the direction of its length would be a vain attempt, as little less than a year must be consumed, and to convey stores for such a period would be found impracticable.

. . . at the end of each day's march, you stop at a place where water is procurable; not indeed in sufficient quantity for large numbers, but enough to supply fifty or an hundred persons, together with their beasts of burthen. At three or four of these halting places the water is salt and bitter, but at the others, amounting to about twenty-eight, it is sweet and good. In this tract neither beasts nor birds are met with, because there is no kind of food for them.

Marsden added footnote 320 after the paragraph, which he used to verify some of Polo's story with modern travelers' records. In 1790, traveler John Bell of Antermony, Scotland, crossed the same desert on his way to Peking. He wrote:

On the 4th October, 1720 . . . after every man had drunk his fill of the pure and wholesome *water of the Tola*, and filled his bottle with it, we departed with some regret, as we could hope for no more *rivers or brooks* . . . In the evening we reached some pits of brackish water, where *we pitched our tents*. On the 5th we set out again, and in the evening came to some fountains of pretty fresh water.

After studying the writings of Polo, Marsden, and Bell, the Smiths felt confident enough to write about traveling a few days and making camp near rivers in the desert:

And it came to pass that when he had *travelled three days* in the wilderness, *he pitched his tent* in a valley *beside a river of water*.

Although they travel in different directions, both groups make four trips to Jerusalem with similar results. For example, the two sets of brothers make their way past the (Red or Black) Sea and take their treasures to a designated location. The Polos and Lehi's sons meet an influential man and present their gifts. Nicolo and Maffio give all their "costly jewels" to the Tartar khan; Nephi and his brothers bring "our gold and silver" to the powerful Laban, who takes it from them.

(0.13%) Marco Polo, p. 1	(1.87%) 1 Nephi 1: p. 11[3:21–23]
made purchases of many fine and costly jewels . . .	did gather together our gold, and our silver, and our precious things.
from whence they travelled by land until	And after that we had gathered these things together,
they reached	we went up again
the court of a powerful chief of the Western Tartars, named Barka . . .	unto the house of Laban.
When they had	. . . when
laid before him the jewels	Laban saw our property,
they brought with them,	and that it was exceeding great,
and perceived their beauty pleased him . . .	he did lust after it,
	insomuch that he thrust us out, and sent his servants to slay us, that he might obtain our property. . . . and
. . . they courteously presented them for his acceptance.	we were obliged to leave behind our property,
	and it fell into the hands of Laban.

Next, the khan sends the Polo brothers on a mission to the pope and to Jerusalem, and Lehi sends the brothers on a mission to Laban in Jerusalem.

(1.59%) *Marco Polo*, p. 12	(1.53%) 1 Nephi 1: p. 9 [3:2]
When he (Grand Khan) had obtained all the information that the two brothers communicated with such good sense,	I, Nephi, returned from speaking with the Lord, to the tent of my father.
he expressed himself well satisfied, and	. . . he (Lehi) spake unto me, saying: Behold
having formed in his mind	I have dreamed a dream,
the design of employing them as his ambassadors to the pope . . . on a mission to the See of Rome.	
(See: "Having heard these	in the which
commands addressed to them by the Grand Khan . . ."	the Lord hath commanded me
which appears after the following sentence.) He moreover signified his pleasure that	
upon their return they should bring with them,	that thou and thy brethren shall return
from Jerusalem,	to Jerusalem.
some of the holy oil.	

The khan charges the brothers Polo with taking letters to the pope and bringing back one hundred teachers of the Christian faith from Acre. The Venetians undertake this mission to deliver letters to the pope because they desire that Christianity be preached in Asia. Nephi and his brothers also go on a mission charged with obtaining records—a prediction that Christianity will be preached.

Smith copied the story by changing it to read that the Lord commanded, through Lehi, that the brothers bring back the records of the Jews from Laban in Jerusalem.

(1.59%)	(1.53%)
Marco Polo, p. 12	1 Nephi 1: pp. 9–10[3:4,19,20]

. . . having heard these commands addressed to them by the Grand *Khan* . . .	. . . Wherefore the Lord hath commanded me
His object . . . was to make a request to his Holiness (previous paragraph)	that thou and thy brothers should go unto the house of Laban, and seek the records, and bring them down hither into the wilderness.
that he would send to him an hundred men of learning, thoroughly acquainted with the principles of the Christian religion,	(p. 10) . . . And behold, it is the wisdom of God that we should obtain these records,
as well as with the seven sciences, and qualified to prove to the learned of his dominions,	that we might preserve unto our children . . .
by just and fair argument,	words which have been spoken
that the Faith professed by Christians is superior to . . .	by the mouth of all the holy prophets, which have been delivered unto them by the
He moreover signified his pleasure that upon their return they should bring with them, from Jerusalem, some of the holy oil from the lamp which is kept burning over the sepulcher of	
our Lord Jesus Christ, whom he professed to hold in veneration and to consider as the true God.	spirit and power of God, since the world began . . .

Nicolo and Maffio's mission involves a golden tablet; Nephi and his brothers have brass plates. Nephi, like Nicolo and Maffio, is willing to do as directed.

(1.59%) *Marco Polo*, p. 12	(1.53%) 1 Nephi 1: p. 9 [3:7]
. . . they (Polos) . . . declaring (to Grand Khan)	. . . I, Nephi, said unto my father,
their willingness	I will go
and instant readiness to perform, to the utmost of their ability,	and do the things
whatever might be the royal will.	which the Lord hath commanded . . .

(1.59–1.72%) *Marco Polo*, pp. 12–13	(1.53–1.70%) 1 Nephi 1: pp. 9–10 [3:3, 7, 9]
He likewise gave orders that they be furnished with	For behold, Laban hath the record of the Jews, and also a genealogy of my forefathers, and they are
a golden tablet displaying the imperial cipher,	engraven upon plates of brass.
according to the	I, Nephi, said unto my father, I will go and do the things which
usage established by his majesty;	the Lord hath commanded,
in virtue of which the person bearing it,	for I know that the Lord giveth no commandments
together with his whole suite, are	unto the children of men,
safely conveyed and escorted from station to station	save he shall prepare a way for them . . .
by the governors of all places within the imperial dominions . . . Being thus honorably commissioned	
they (note: the Polo brothers) took their leave	And I, Nephi, and my brethren, took our journey
of the Grand Khan, and set out on their journey	
(note: to see the pope and go to Acre and Jerusalem)	in the wilderness with our tents, to go up to the land of Jerusalem.

(1.59–1.72%)	(1.53–1.70%)
Marco Polo, pp. 12–13	1 Nephi 1: pp. 9–10 [3:3, 7, 9]
and there learned, with extreme concern, that Pope Clement the Fourth was recently dead.	
A Legate, whom (the pope) had appointed . . . was at this time	. . . Laman went in unto the
resident in Acre,	house of Laban,
and to him they gave an account	and he talked with him as he sat in his house.
of what they had in command from the Grand Khan *of Tartary*.	And he desired of Laban the records which were engraven upon the plates of brass . . .

The "command" was the items described and desired by the khan. The Smiths used these in the Nephi story by calling them the "records." Both sets of brothers attempted to obtain the records.

When the Polos reach Acre, they learn that the pope has died. They need to be patient until a new pope is named.

Note that the idea of patience in the Polos' journey—to wait and then attempt again to obtain the items of the khan's command—was copied in Nephi's case, where the khan, which means "lord," becomes the supernatural "Lord's command." The Polos return to the "pope" (which means "father") and the brothers in *The Book of Mormon* return to their father, Lehi.

(1.72%)	(1.70%)
Marco Polo, p. 13	1 Nephi 1: pp. 10–11 [3:15]
He advised them by all means	. . . I said unto them, that as the Lord liveth, and as we live,
to wait the election of another Pope . . .	we will not go down unto our father in the wilderness, until we have accomplished the thing which the Lord hath commanded us.

Between their first and second trips, the Polos visit Venice—also called Venetia—and their families. Lehi's sons want to return to their father (who is with their family) but instead go to the "land of our father's inheritance" or "land of our inheritance."

(1.72%) *Marco Polo*, p. 13	(1.70%) 1 Nephi 1: pp. 10–11 [3:16, 22]
they determined upon employing the interval in	and my brethren were about to
a visit to their family.	return unto my father in the wilderness. But behold I said unto them, that as the Lord liveth, and as we live, we will not go down unto our father in the wilderness.
They accordingly embarked at Acre in a ship bound to Negropont, and from thence went on to Venice . . .	. . . therefore let us go down to the land of our father's inheritance . . . we went down to the land of our inheritance . . .

On the third trip to Acre, the Polos return from Jerusalem with some oil from a lamp on the holy sepulcher. Their objective is to visit with the legate—a representative of the pope's and an authority in the Church—and then to return to the khan with the lamp oil. At that time, the legate gives them letters for delivery to the great khan.

Nephi and his brothers return from their successful third trip to Jerusalem with "the engravings," which are upon the plates of brass. Their goal is to take the plates back to their father.

(2.38%) Marco Polo, p. 18	(1.87%) 1 Nephi: pp. 11–12 [4:1, 4]
Under the sanction of the Legate	I spake unto my brethren, saying:
they made a visit	Let us go up again
to Jerusalem,	unto Jerusalem . . .
	. . . they did follow me up until we came without the walls of Jerusalem.

(2.38%) Marco Polo, p. 18	(1.87%) 1 Nephi: pp. 11–12 [4:1, 4]
and there provided themselves with some of the oil belonging to the lamp of the holy sepulchre, conformably to the directions of the Grand Khan.	(note: obtaining the oil from the holy sepulcher was part of the "command" given by the khan to the Polos, and the Smiths used the khan's "commands" as part of the metaphor for obtaining the "records" from Laban in Jerusalem).

The newly elected pope commands the Polos to come back to Acre, where he "then appointed two friars of the order of preachers" to accompany them to the grand khan and to do whatever might be required of them. In Joseph Smith's version, the Lord commands Lehi to bring Nephi and Nephi's brothers back to Jerusalem and to take Ishmael and his family into the wilderness. The pope and the Lord commanded. . . .

(2.51%) Marco Polo, p. 19	(2.72%–3.06%) 1 Nephi: 2, pp. 16–18 [7:2–7,16,21–22]
These letters (note: from the pope)	. . . the Lord commanded
found them (Polo brothers and Marco) still in Armenia, and	
with great alacrity they obeyed the summons	him that I, Nephi, and my brethren, should
to repair once more to Acre;	again return unto the land of Jerusalem,
	and bring down Ishmael and his family into the wilderness.

The brothers return from their fourth trip to Acre/Jerusalem:

	. . . I, Nephi,
for which purpose the King furnished them with a galley;	did again, with my brethren, go forth

sending at the same time an ambassador from himself, to offer his congrat-
ulations to the sovereign pontiff.

into the wilderness

(note: who lived at Acre near
Jerusalem).

to go up to Jerusalem.

The brothers go to the presence of the pope/Ishmael:

Upon their arrival

. . . we went up unto the house of
Ishmael, and

They are received with satisfaction:

his Holiness received them in a distinguished manner,

we did gain favor in the sight of Ishmael, insomuch that

The words of the Lord are spoken:

and immediately dispatched

them with letters papal,

we did speak unto him the

words of the Lord.

And they journey to the great khan or father:

. . . through the blessing of God,

they were conveyed

in safety

to the royal court.

(to accompany them to the great
Khan. . . .)
(from next sentence in Marsden's text)

(p. 17)

. . . they took their journey

with us down into the wilderness

to the tent of our father.

Both groups suffer many difficulties on their journey and cannot write
about all their experiences.

(0.40%)	(1.02%)
Marco Polo, p. 3	1 Nephi 1: pp. 6–7 [1:16]
Many things worthy of admiration were observed by them in the progress of their journey, but	. . . my father had read and saw many great and marvelous things . . .
which are here omitted . . .	And now I, Nephi, do not make a full account of the things
(See above "Many things . . . were observed".)	which my father hath written, for he hath written many things which he saw in visions and in dreams . . .

(1.72%)	(7.14%)
Marco Polo, p. 13	1 Nephi 5, p. 42 [17:6]
. . . notwithstanding	. . . notwithstanding
these advantages,	we had suffered
so great were the	many afflictions, and
natural difficulties	much difficulty,
they had to encounter . . .	
(See above, "Many things worthy of admiration were observed by them in the progress of their journey, but which are here omitted . . .")	yea, even so much that we cannot write them all.

The travelers become frightened for their safety or rebelled and wished to return to Jerusalem/Acre,

	(2.89%, p. 17) Laman and Lemuel, and two of the daughters Ishmael, and the two sons of Ishmael, and their
the two friars determined not to proceed further . . .	families, did rebel against us . . . in the which rebellion,
they placed themselves under the protection of the Master of the Knights Templars, and . . .	they (Ishmael's family), were desirous to

| returned directly to the coast. (note: and probably to Acre, near Jerusalem) | return unto the land of Jerusalem. |

and the brothers proceed on their journeys.

Nicolo, Maffio, and Marco, however, undismayed by perils or	(3.06%, p. 18)
difficulties (to which they had long been inured), passed the borders of Armenia, and	. . . we did again
prosecuted their journey.	travel on our journey toward the tent of our father.

Both groups travel for several years and take multiple trips to or near Jerusalem. The Polos were gone for so long that the khan felt concern for them, as did Nephi's parents for their sons.

(1.72%) *Marco Polo*, p. 13	(7.14%) 1 Nephi: 5, p. 42 [17:4]
. . . and three years elapsed	And we did sojourn for the space of many years,
before they (the Polo brothers) were enabled to reach a sea-port town in the lesser Armenia named *Giazza* . . . they arrived at *Acre* in the month of April 1269 . . .	yea, even
(0.66%, p. 5, n. 3) . . . Müller and Bergeron . . . introduce into their texts the date of 1269, which was	
eight years	eight years
after the expulsion of the Emperor Baldwin, and was, in fact, the year in which they (Polo brothers) returned to Syria	
from their first Tartarian journey.	in the wilderness.

This next comparison covers Marco Polo's comments on the khan's concern for the welfare of the Venetian travelers on their journey to visit the pope and Jerusalem and his showing "great pleasure" at their upcoming arrival. Joseph Smith's writing shows that Nephi's mother, Sariah, was concerned for the welfare of the brothers on their trip to visit Jerusalem and that Sariah and Lehi were "exceedingly glad" for their return.

(3.17%) Marco Polo, p. 24	(2.38%) 1 Nephi 1: p. 14 [5:1–2]
Upon their arrival	. . . that after we had came down into the wilderness
they were honourably and graciously received by the Grand Khan,	unto our father, behold he was filled with joy, and
in a full assembly of his principle officers.	also my mother, Sariah,
When they drew nigh to his person, they paid their respects by prostrating themselves on the floor.	
He immediately commanded them to rise,	was exceedingly glad,
and relate to him the circumstances of their travels.	for she truly had mourned because of us; for she had supposed that we had perished in the wilderness.

After the two sets of brothers are greeted, they make their presentations. The Polos hand over the "letters and presents" (the letters and credentials and the oil from Jerusalem) from the pope to the grand khan, and Lehi's sons give the "plates of brass" to him. These plates from Jerusalem contain the "record," which Smith used as a substitute for the pope's letters, gifts, and Christian teachers.

Although the story in *Marco Polo* does not state that the Polos traveled with the golden tablet on their return to the grand khan, Smith carries the theme of using metal tablets/plates with inscriptions to the Nephi journey back to his father as "brass plates."

(3.17%)	(2.55%)
Marco Polo, p. 24	1 Nephi 1: p. 15 [5:10, 19]

. . . they paid their respects (to the Grand Khan) by prostrating themselves on the floor.	And after that they had given thanks unto the God . . .
The letters . . . and the presents	(see "records" below)
from Pope Gregory	my father Lehi
were then laid before him,	took the records
	which were engraven upon the plates of brass,
and upon hearing the former read,	and he did search them from the beginning.
he bestowed much commendation on the fidelity, the zeal, and the diligence of his ambassadors; and	
receiving with due reverence the oil from the holy sepulchre	Wherefore
he gave directions that	he said that these plates of brass
it be preserved	should never perish;
with religious care.	neither should they be
(Note that the khan moreover signified his pleasure that upon their return they should bring with them, from Jerusalem, some of the holy oil from the lamp which is kept burning over the sepulcher of our Lord Jesus Christ)	dimmed. . . .

Let's take one more look at the Smiths' undeniable plagiarism in the chart below, from the first pages through the four trips the Polos and Lehi's sons took to Acre and Jerusalem, respectively. We show the page numbers and percentages for each story part in each book.

Parts of the Stories	The Travels of Marco Polo Pub. 1818 Book I, Ch. I	The Book of Mormon Pub. 1830 "The First Book of Nephi"
Documentation of a date	1 (0.13%)	5 (0.85%) (actually page 1 of First Nephi)
Brothers journey past Red Sea or Black Sea.	1 (0.13%)	7 (1.19%)
Polo brothers take "costly jewels" to Tartar khan; Nephi brothers take "our gold and our silver" to Laban.	1 (0.13%)	11 (1.87%)
Polo brothers meet Tartar chief Barka; Nephi brothers meet Laban.	1 (0.13%)	11 (1.87%)
Polos give jewels; Laban takes Nephi's gold and silver.	2 (0.26%)	11 (1.87%)
Polo brothers are sent on a mission, charged with delivering letters, desiring that "Christianity" be preached; Nephi's brothers sent on mission, charged with obtaining records, a prediction that "Christianity" would be preached.	12 (1.59%)	9 (1.53%)
The Polo brothers willing to make the mission; brothers of Nephi murmur about mission.	12 (1.59%)	9 (1.53%)
Both groups say they will do as khan or lord commands.	12 (1.59%)	9 (1.53%)
Polos' golden tablet and Nephi's plates of brass; Polo brothers return to pope ("father"); Nephi brothers return to father.	13 (1.72%)	10 (1.70%)
Many difficulties on their journeys; cannot write about all of their experiences.	3 (0.40%) 13 (1.72%)	6 (1.02%) 42 (7.42%)

Parts of the Stories	The Travels of Marco Polo Pub. 1818 Book I, Ch. I	The Book of Mormon Pub. 1830 "The First Book of Nephi"
Brothers travel for several years.	13 (1.72%) 5 note 4	42 (7.14%)
Brothers take multiple trips to or near Jerusalem.	13–20 (1.72–2.65%)	10–18 (1.70–3.06%)
First of four trips.	13 (1.72%)	10 (1.70%)
In between first and second trips, brothers visit their family.	13 (1.72%)	10 (1.70%)
Second of four trips.	18 (2.38%)	11 (1.87%)
Third of four trips.	18 (2.38%)	11–12 (1.87–2.04%)
Fourth of four trips.	19 (2.51%)	16–18 (2.72–3.06%)
Polo brothers make presentation of "letters and presents" from the pope to the Grand Khan; brothers give the "plates of brass" to Lehi.	24 (3.17%)	15 (2.55%)

Nicolo and Maffio Polo were the primary traveling merchants, and they invited young Marco to accompany them on their return trip to the khan's court. This feature of adding a traveling companion (whose name will surprise you) shows up in "The First Book of Nephi." When Nephi and his brothers returned to the tent of their father, they took with them Zoram, the manservant of the slain Laban. *Zoram* is similar to the backward spelling of *Marco*, with the C removed and a Z added at the beginning. Even the medieval travelers' name was fair game for the Smiths.

The Smiths substituted the items that the khan charged the Polo brothers with obtaining from Acre/Jerusalem for the "records" that were "engraven/engravings/written" on the "plates of brass." Smith transformed into "plates of brass" the engraved "tablets of gold" that the Polo brothers received. Smith created Nephi's sons' safe arrival at the "tent" of their father from the Polo family's eventual return to Asia.

(2.38%–2.65%) *Marco Polo*, pp. 18–20	(2.38%) 1 Nephi 1: p. 14 [4:35,38]
. . . they judged it expedient to return to Acre; and on this occasion they took with them young Marco Polo.	Now Zoram was the name of the servant . . . that he would go down into the wilderness unto our father.
. . . they made a visit to Jerusalem,	And it came to pass that we took
and there provided themselves with some of the oil belonging to the lamp of the holy sepulchre,	the plates of brass
conformably to the directions of the Grand Khan. (p. 19) Upon their arrival his Holiness received them in a distinguished manner, and dispatched them with letters papal, accompanied by two friars of the order of Preachers . . . men of letters and science, as well as profound theologians. He also charged them with valuable presents . . .	(which contained the "record" that Joseph Smith used as a metaphor for the items shown that the Polo brothers were obtaining from Acre/Jerusalem to take back to the Khan, e.g., the oil, the friars, the letters from the pope, the gifts).
. . . young Marco Polo.	and the servant of Laban (Zoram),
After	and
crossing several deserts . . . and passing many dangerous defiles,	departed into the wilderness, and
they advanced so far, in a direction between north-east and north, and at length they gained information of the Grand *Khan*, who then had his residence in a large and magnificent city named Cle-men-fu. By these means, and through the blessing of God,	
they were conveyed in safety to the royal court.	journied unto the tent of our father.

Left, right, left, right . . . The four trips to Jerusalem were copied text and context; the return trip to Asia was copied text only.

In the next chapter we will look at two momentous experiences for Lehi's family. The first is their coming upon the Tree of Life, and the second is their arrival in a place called Bountiful. There they prepare for their astonishing voyage from the Middle East, across the ocean, to the Americas. We will also learn about the Smiths' fourth strategy for hiding their conspiracy from prospective followers and critics alike.

THE TREE OF LIFE

. . . and I also beheld that the tree of life was a representation of the love of God. (1 Nephi 3: p. 25)

In "The First Book of Nephi," Nephi's father, Lehi, has a dream in which he sees a vision of the glowing Tree of Life, whose fruit is "desirable to make one happy." Like most religions and myths that include a Tree of Life as an important symbol, the one in Lehi's vision figures large in *The Book of Mormon* and the gospel of the churches of the Latter-day Saints.

Joseph Smith Sr. needed to make a good first impression on his prospective followers in order to establish the divine originality of his scripture. While his stories were rich and fresh, he also made sure they sounded like the Old Testament. From First Nephi, page 16 (Figure 5).

The Smiths' audience was sure to be familiar with the Garden of Eden story, which is anything but happy. Reading a more pleasing account would certainly have appealed to the curious. The concept of God's presenting of an exotic white fruit that is desirable and whose sweet taste can make someone happy is a welcome contrast to the fruit that drove Adam and Eve from the Garden of Eden. Compare the disparate views of God: In the

And it came to pass that after I had prayed unto the Lord, I beheld a large and spacious field. And it came to pass that I beheld a tree, whose fruit was desirable, to make one happy.

And it came to pass that I did go forth, and partake of the fruit thereof; and I beheld that it was most sweet, above all that I ever had before tasted. Yea, and I beheld that the fruit thereof was white, to exceed all the whiteness that I had ever seen. And as I partook of the fruit thereof, it filled my soul with exceeding great joy; wherefore, I began to be desirous that my family should partake of it also; for I knew that it was desirous above all other fruit.

Figure 5. 1 Nephi 1: p. 19.

Old Testament, he is wrathful and punishing. In *The Book of Mormon* he is benevolent and generous. Which God would you prefer watching over you?

This illustrates the Smiths' fourth strategy: Begin with a well-known story and add to it.

After Lehi partakes of the white fruit, he wants to share it with his loved ones, just as God has shared it with him. Lehi beckons to his wife and sons Nephi and Sam, and they enjoy the sweetness, too. Laman and Lemuel, however, do not accept their father's invitation.

Next Lehi says,

And I beheld a rod of iron; and it extended along the bank of the river, and led to the tree by which I stood. And I also beheld a strait and narrow path, which came along by the rod of iron, even to the tree by which I stood; and it also led by the head of the fountain, unto a large and spacious field, as if it had been a world; and I saw numberless concourses of people; many of whom were pressing forward, that they might obtain the path which led unto the tree by which I stood. (1 Nephi 2, p. 19–20 [8:19–21])

Lehi fears for Laman and Lemuel, thinking that God might cast them off, and exhorts them to follow his counsel and keep the commandments.

Many people appear and taste the fruit. Rather than pleasing them, it makes them feel ashamed, and they avert their eyes from Lehi's gaze. People in finery point in derision at the people eating the pale fruit. Some of the gathering feel their way to a "great and spacious building" on the other side of the river, while others drown in the "fountain." Still others disappear from view, "wandering in strange roads."

Nephi asks God for a vision similar to his father's and for its interpretation:

> And it came to pass that the spirit saith unto me, look! and I looked and beheld a tree; and it was like unto the tree which my father had seen; and the beauty thereof was far beyond, yea, exceeding of all beauty; and the whiteness thereof, did exceed the whiteness of the driven snow. (1 Nephi 3: p. 24 [11:8])

The symbolism becomes clear to him:

> And it came to pass that I beheld that the rod of iron which my father had seen, was the word of God, which led to the fountain of living waters, or to the tree of life; which waters are a representation of the love of God; and I also beheld that the tree of life was a representation of the love of God. (1 Nephi 3, p. 25 [11:25])

Nephi learns in the vision that the great and spacious building represents the pride of the world and watches it fall down.

At this point the Smiths transform their *Book of Mormon* into the Bible's prequel, which predicts events with which even the most rustic New York country bumpkin would be familiar. These include the birth, ministry, and death of Jesus Christ; Christopher Columbus's traversing the Atlantic Ocean; the American War of Independence; and the scattering of the "seed of my brethren," the American Indians.

So clever are Joseph Smith Sr. and his namesake that they even predict *The Book of Mormon*—a record made by the ancestors of the Indians—and what is believed to be the founding of their Church of Christ, as it was first known. It is not named in "The Book of Nephi," although the events described there suggest the nascence of the church, the restoration of text missing from the Bible, and the outbreak of battles of extinction.

Nephi's vision includes his own progeny as well as the future generations of Laman's and Lemuel's. Nephi's offspring will have the gospel but be destroyed for their iniquity; Laman's and Lemuel's progeny will not know the gospel but will survive for generations and be taught by *The Book of Mormon* and the future church.

The Spirit will not permit Nephi to record these events because John the Apostle will accomplish that task. That won't happen for another six hundred years, however.

What is this wonderful white fruit from the Tree of Life? Where did the Smiths come up with that idea? Before we make those connections with John Pinkerton (1811) and William Marsden (1818), let's look at the plagiarists' fifth strategy, comprised of two closely related concepts. One is *tautology*, the conscious use of meaningless repetition, and the other is *prolixity*, or undue length. So effective was this scheme that we have to eliminate the repetition and wordiness before making our comparisons.

Here is an example of their ploy as it appears across only two pages in First Nephi, although it is prevalent throughout the Smiths' prose:

Smiths' Use of "It Came to Pass" in a Short Story

Page Lines	"The First Book of Nephi" pp. 40–41, Continuous in lines "1" through "86"
5	And it came to pass that as I, Nephi went
9	And it came to pass that we did return
12	And it came to pass that Laman . . . did murmur
18	Now it came to pass that I, Nephi, having
22	And it came to pass that I, Nephi, did speak
25	And it came to pass that I, Nephi, did make
29	And it came to pass that he did inquire

Page Lines	Smiths' Use of "It Came to Pass" in a Short Story
	"The First Book of Nephi" pp. 40–41, Continuous in lines "1" through "86"
32	And it came to pass that the voice of the Lord
34	And it came to pass that the voice of the Lord
37	And it came to pass that when my father
41	And it came to pass that I, Nephi, beheld
50	And it came to pass that I, Nephi, did go forth
52	And it came to pass that I did slay
54	And it came to pass that I did return
56	And it came to pass that they did humble
59	And it came to pass that we did again
64	And it came to pass that Ishmael died
65	And it came to pass that the daughters

The Smiths also employed long adverbs, such as *exceedingly, consummately, immeasurably,* and so on, to mask the plagiarism and, they may have thought, to sound similar to the Old Testament.

Page Lines	Smiths' Use of "Exceedingly" or "Exceeding" in the Short Story
	"The First Book of Nephi" pp. 40–41, in lines "1" through "62"
13	did begin to murmur exceedingly
16	they were all exceeding sorrowful
20	began to be exceedingly difficult
39	he did fear and tremble exceedingly
66	did mourn exceedingly

They also used filler words and copied the same word or word forms.

Smiths' Filler Words:
Nephi Getting Food and Suffering

Page Lines	"The First Book of Nephi" pp. 40–41
5	I, Nephi, went forth to slay food
8	loss of my bow, for we did obtain no food
9	we did return without food for our families
11	they did suffer much for the want of food
21	insomuch, that we could obtain no food
9	Whither shall I go, to obtain food
53	insomuch, I did obtain food for our families
56	they beheld that I had obtained food
11	they did suffer much
14	because of their suffering and afflictions
18	I, Nephi, having been afflicted
67	because of their afflictions
71	and we have suffered much affliction
72	after all these sufferings

Let's clean up the Smiths' prose about the Tree of Life incident from First Nephi. By deleting unnecessary phrases, we reduce the number of words from ninety to fifty-seven:

. . . after I had prayed . . . I beheld a large and spacious field.

. . . I beheld a tree, whose fruit was desirable, to make one happy.

. . . I did . . . partake of the fruit . . . and . . . it was most sweet, above all that I ever had before tasted.

. . . and . . . the fruit . . . was white, to exceed all the whiteness that I had ever seen.

juice runs again as it did at first.[1218]   Some trees naturally yieldit of a reddish, and others of a pale colour.[1219]   The Indian nuts also grow here, of the size of a man's head, containing an edible substance that is sweet and pleasant to the taste, and white as milk.   The cavity of this pulp is filled with a liquor clear as water, cool, and better flavoured and more delicate than wine or any other kind of drink whatever.[1220] The inhabitants feed upon flesh of every sort, good and bad, without distinction.[1221]

Figure 6. Marsden, Marco Polo, 607

Now let's turn to *The Travels of Marco Polo*, chapter 13, page 607 of William Marsden's 1818 translation.[34] In it the desirable fruit is called "Indian nuts" (Figure 6).

Compare these extracts side by side:

Copying the Tree of Life

The Travels of Marco Polo Book III, Chapter XIII, Page 607, of the Third Kingdom, Called Samara	*The Book of Mormon* first Nephi: 2, pg. 19 [8:10–11]
Some trees . . .	. . . I beheld a **tree**,
The Indian nuts also grow here . . . containing an **edible substance** that	whose **fruit**
[. . . The cavity of this pulp is filled with liquor clear as water, **cool, and better flavoured and more delicate than wine or any other kind of drink whatever** . . .]*	was **desirable**, to make one happy.
	. . . it was
is **sweet**	most **sweet**,
and pleasant to the	above all that I ever before
taste,	**tasted**.
and	. . . and the fruit was

Copying the Tree of Life

The Travels of Marco Polo Book III, Chapter XIII, Page 607, of the Third Kingdom, Called Samara	The Book of Mormon first Nephi: 2, pg. 19 [8:10–11]
white as milk.	white, to exceed all the whiteness
	that I had ever seen.

*This quote is in the next sentence, but it gives qualitative descriptions of an edible substance in the nuts.

In Lehi's vision, the white, sweet fruit might seem mysterious and otherworldly because it has no name. When the secret of the white fruit is brought to light, however, it is merely Marco Polo's description of coconuts. The Smiths appropriated the coconut palm in Marco Polo and used it as the Tree of Life to begin *The Book of Mormon*. Smith's key words from Polo's story give it away. Below, Marco Polo's text is on the left, and *The Book of Mormon*'s is on the right—all from the same story and in the same sequence:

sweet	most sweet
taste	tasted
nuts containing an edible substance	fruit
white as milk	white to exceed all whiteness

Now let's return to Lucy Mack Smith's memoir. In it she claimed that in 1811 her husband had a vision of the Tree of Life. (Joseph Smith Sr. was in very good company, sharing a vision with Lehi and Nephi!) Mrs. Smith described what he saw:

Its beautiful branches spread themselves somewhat like an umbrella, and it bore a kind of fruit, in shape much like a chestnut bur, and as white as snow, or, if possible, whiter.[35]

Later, Joseph Sr. calls the burs "shells":

. . . the burs or shells commenced opening . . .[36]

CURIOUS AND REMARKABLE VOYAGES AND TRAVELS

OF

MARCO POLO, A GENTLEMAN OF VENICE,

Who in the Middle of the thirteenth Century paſſed through a great part of Aſia, all the Dominions of the Tartars, and returned Home by Sea through the Iſlands of the Eaſt Indies.

[Taken chiefly from the accurate Edition of Ramuſio, compared with an original Manuſcript in His Pruſſian Majeſty's Library, and with moſt of the Tranſlations hitherto publiſhed.]

Figure 7. Pinkerton, Vol. 7, *Marco Polo*, 101.

This description of Senior's vision differs both from the story of the Tree of Life in *The Book of Mormon* and from the coconut tree in the 1818 edition of *The Travels of Marco Polo*. In that same edition, a different story about a "tree of the sun" reads:

> There is [in the province of Timochain . . . on the borders of Persia] . . .
> a species of tree called the tree of the sun, and by Christians arbor secco,
> the dry or "fruitless tree." Its nature and qualities are these. It is lofty, with
> a large stem, having its leaves green on the upper surface, but white or
> glaucous on the under. It produces husks or capsules like those in which
> the chestnut is enclosed, but these contain no fruit. (Marsden, p. 109)

There is one compatible original text, however, and that is the 1811 edition of *The Travels of Marco Polo* by John Pinkerton (Figure 7).[37]

Polo tells a story about a "Tree of the Sun," which produced a "prickly shell" that was "like those of chestnuts."

Both Lucy Mack Smith and Pinkerton's *Marco Polo* used the same words to describe the fruit—or seeds—on the tree of the sun. Here is copy taken from the 1811 old English-style Pinkerton text (Figure 8).

("It produceth prickly husky shells, like those of chestnuts . . .")[38]

The word *shells* is *not* in Marsden's 1818 version. That description says that the sun tree has "capsules." But it *is* written in Pinkerton's 1811 version.

plain, in which a great tree grows, called the Tree of the Sun, which the Chriftians call the Dry Tree. This tree is very thick, and hath leaves which on the one fide are white, and on the other fide green. It produceth prickly hufky fhells, like thofe of chefnuts, but nothing in them. The wood is folid and ftrong, in colour yellow, like box. There

Figure 8. Pinkerton, Vol. 7, *Marco Polo*, 114

How remarkable that Mrs. Smith's memoir states that her husband had this vision in the same year Pinkerton's book was issued, 1811—the vision that mirrors the Tree of Life story in *The Book of Mormon* (1 Nephi 2: p. 19). The description of "dazzling white" fruit by Joseph Sr. echoes "white, to exceed all the whiteness that I had ever seen" in *The Book of Mormon*. Joseph Sr. eats the fruit and finds it "delicious beyond description"; Lehi finds it "most sweet, above all that I had ever before tasted" in *The Book of Mormon*.

How can we help but think that Joseph Sr. acted alone in composing this section of First Nephi—at the very least—because his namesake son was only six years old in 1811? Clearly the father was inventing *The Book of Mormon* tales years before the son could have had any involvement.

The Tree of the Sun story appears in both *Marco Polo* versions, 1811 and 1818, so why would Lucy Mack Smith's memoir pinpoint her husband's vision as taking place in 1811? *The Book of Mormon* is dated 1830. Was tying her husband to the plagiarism and absolving her son of wrongdoing done inadvertently, or did she do it on purpose? You will find the answer in a later chapter.

When Lehi was looking for his sons Laman and Lemuel, in the vision he saw a "rod of iron." The rod "extended along the bank of the river and led to the tree by which I stood," according to page 19. He also saw

> . . . a straight and narrow path, which came along by the rod of iron, even to the tree by which I stood; and it also led by the head of the fountain (which means "river") and led to the tree by which I stood.

At first glance, a rod of iron and sweet white fruit seem an odd combination. What could be the connection? Returning to the same paragraph those of the lungs and of the spleen.[1217]   When these shoots that have been cut are perceived not to yield any more juice, they contrive to water the trees, by bringing from the river in pipes or channels, so much water as is sufficient for the purpose ; and upon this being done, the juice runs again as it did at first.[1218]   Some trees naturally yield it of a

Figure 9. Marsden, *Marco Polo,* 607

of the "Indian nut" sentence on page 607 of the 1818 *Travels of Marco Polo,* the medieval traveler described how date-bearing trees in the country of Samara are irrigated with water through pipes and ditches from a river leading to the trees (Figure 9).

Placing the two texts side by side yields this comparison:

1818 *Travels of Marco Polo*	1830 *Book of Mormon*
When these shoots that have been cut are perceived not to yield any more juice, they contrive to water the trees, by bringing from the river in	And I beheld a
pipes or	rod of iron; and it extended
(see above: "to water the trees, by bringing from the river")	along the bank of the river, and led to the tree by which I stood.
	And I beheld a
channels,	straight and narrow path,
	which came along by the rod of iron, even unto the tree by which I stood;
so much water [bringing from the river] as is sufficient for the purpose.	and it also led by the head of a fountain . . . (1 Nephi 2, p. 19)

The odd combination comes from the way that date palms were watered from a nearby river. The mysterious "rod of iron" isn't really the "word of God," it's just an irrigation pipe leading from a river to water the trees. The "straight and narrow path" leading to the tree isn't metaphorical wisdom; it is an irrigation ditch, or "channel," plain and simple.

Atotonilco

✠ **5** ✠

Names and Numbers

In "The First Book of Nephi," Lehi's sons take four trips to Jerusalem. The objective of their fourth journey is to meet Ishmael and persuade him to leave that city with his family and join their great adventure sanctioned by God.

On the way back to camp, however, Laman, Lemuel, and some members of Ishmael's family decide to return to Jerusalem. Nephi, hoping to change their mind, reminds them of the prophecies:

> And if it so be that we are faithful in him, we shall obtain the land of promise; and ye shall know at some future period, that the word of the Lord shall be fulfilled, concerning the destruction of Jerusalem; for all things which the Lord hath spoken concerning the destruction of Jerusalem, must be fulfilled. (1 Nephi 2: p. 17 [7:13])

> Now, behold, I say unto you, that if ye will return unto Jerusalem, ye shall also perish with them. And now, if ye have choice, go up to the land, and remember the words which I speak unto you, that if ye go, ye will also perish; for thus the spirit of the Lord constraineth me that I should speak. (1 Nephi 2: p. 17 [7:15])

Laman and Lemuel, the perfect villains, become enraged, bind Nephi with ropes, and leave him to die in the desert. The young man manages to free himself and then hurries to catch up with his brothers' group. Laman and Lemuel try again to harm him, but Ishmael's daughters intervene, and the wayward brothers ask for forgiveness. Lehi's sons marry the women who have softened the men's hearts.

Now that the group is together, the journey is under way. Lehi and his entourage will ultimately trek overland through Arabia, or the "wilderness," from somewhere near Jerusalem, southward along the Red Sea, and finally eastward to the southern Arabian coast. How will they get to their destination? God provides.

And it came to pass that the voice of the Lord spake unto my father, by night, and commanded him, that on the morrow, he should take his journey into the wilderness.

And it came to pass that as my father arose in the morning, and went forth to the tent door, to his great astonishment, he beheld upon the ground a round ball, of curious workmanship; and it was of fine brass. And within the ball were two spindles; and the one pointed the way whither we should go into the wilderness. (1 Nephi 5: p. 39 [16:9–10])

Using the director, the group treks south-southeast in a direction that parallels the shore of the Red Sea. No typical brass ball shows the way; it is a miraculous instrument created by God, who writes inscriptions on it for Lehi. Looking on the ball, the travelers discover a message that causes them to "fear and tremble exceedingly."

And it came to pass that I, Nephi, beheld the pointers which were in the ball, that they did work according to the faith, and diligence, and heed, which we did give unto them. (1 Nephi 5: p. 40 [16:28])

And there was also written upon them, a new writing, which was plain to be read, which did give us understanding concerning the ways of the Lord; and it was written and changed from time to time, according to the faith and diligence which we gave unto it: And thus we see, that by small means, the Lord can bring about great things. (1 Nephi 5: p. 40 [16:29])

As long as the members of Lehi's group remain faithful unto God, the ball will lead them through the most fertile parts of the land. If they are not, it will not function properly, and they will be left to find their own way through the wilderness.

This brass ball is an important symbol in *The Book of Mormon*, and it appears in more than one chapter and time period. While the brass director has no specific name in First Nephi, in "The Second Book of Nephi," it is called a "compass." No surprise there. Later, however, in "The Book of Alma," it is called a "liahona."

Imagine needing to come up with a marvelous name for an important artifact. Where would you begin? Ideally the word would be unique, sound exotic and ancient, and have some connection to distance and direction.

The Smiths had a challenge: Marco Polo did not mention a compass in his history. Problem solved: William Marsden *did* mention a compass, albeit a Chinese one.

At 38.8 percent into *The Travels of Marco Polo*, you will find a footnote written by Mr. Marsden in 1818 with the word *compass*. On either side of that word, you will find "li" and "Hoang." He explains that a *li* is a Chinese mile. *Hoang-ching* is a Chinese compass. This footnote is from page 293 of the 1818 edition (Figure 10).

Note the seventh line from the top: "gives eighteen *li* for the compass of the *Hoang-ching*."

To build a new name for a compass, move *li* and *Hoang* together. The result? "Lihoang." That word might seem difficult to trace, but the Smiths wanted to make absolutely certain. To hide the source, they changed the *g* to an *a*, giving them "lihoana." If they moved the first *a* forward two letters, between the *i* and the *h*, the word would be more melodious and a bit more hidden from its origin.

So let's look again at what the Smiths did:

lihoang ➡ *lihoana* ➡ *liahona*

" de tour.   Cette muraille est *crenelée* le long de la courtine....C'est là propre-
" ment ce qui s'appelle le palais, parce que cette enceinte renferme les apparte-
" mens de l'empereur et de sa famille."   T. i. p. 116.   The Chinese *li* or *ly* being
equal to 296 French toises or 1776 feet, and the French foot being to the English
in the proportion of 1068 to 1000 (or about 16 to 15) it follows that the *li* should
contain 1897, or, for the sake of round numbers, 1900 English feet, and consequently twelve *li*, 22,800 such feet; which differs only by a $\frac{1}{11}$ part from the number of feet (21,120) in four English miles.   It must be remarked, however, that
De L'isle's Plan gives eighteen *li* for the compass of the *Hoang-ching*, originally
designed by *Yong-lo* for the boundary of his palace, but which has been contracted by his successors, to what is termed the *Kong-ching* or *Tse-kin*, and
measures only six *li* or 11,400 feet.

Figure 10. Marsden, *Marco Polo*, 293

Liahona, according to the Joseph Smiths, is a *compass* in *The Book of Mormon*. Although it was introduced in the beginning of Lehi's travels, the authors waited until 57 percent through *The Book of Mormon*, Alma 17: p. 329 [37:38], to offer the explanation (Figure 11).

So the derivation of this exotic name is not a mystery. It is yet another excellent example of the Smiths' dipping into William Marsden's editorial footnotes to compose *The Book of Mormon*.

Liahona is one word of hundreds the Smiths needed to devise for their tale, and *The Travels of Marco Polo* offered a mother lode. As we move through a list of names, you will see how closely the words correspond as well as many of their percentages. Starting with page one, we note the percentages where names appear in the same place in *The Book of Mormon* relative to *The Travels of Marco Polo*. Although Joseph Sr. and Joseph Jr. took precautions to hide their plagiarism, they weren't enough. The copying is transparent.

And now my son, I have somewhat to say concerning the thing which our fathers call a ball, or director ; or our fathers called it liahona, which is, being interpreted, a compass ; and the Lord prepared it.

Figure 11. Alma 17: p. 329 [37:38]

CHAPTER III.

Of the province called Turkomania, where are the cities of Kogni, Kaisariah, and Sevasta, and of its commerce.

Figure 12. Marsden, *Marco Polo*, 45

For instance, consider the name *Sariah*, Lehi's wife and Nephi's mother. Her name is obviously close to the biblical *Sarah*, but it's an unusual spelling that is closer to *sariah*, found on pages forty-one, forty-four, and forty-five of the 1818 *Travels of Marco Polo* as part of the name of the city Kaisariah (Figure 12).

We learn in the footnote on page 44 that *Kaisariah* is a Turkish language pronunciation of the ancient city of Caesarea, which still exists in modern Turkey (Figure 13).

A variation of the word also appears in Latin as "Sarai" earlier, in a footnote on page seven (Figure 14).

Another name known to all Mormons is Camorah, the hill in New York State where, the Smiths say, two epic battles of extinction raged in ancient times and where Joseph Jr. claimed to have uncovered the golden plates in their stone box centuries later.

88. The Turkomans of *Karamania* were a race of Tartars settled in Asia minor, under the government of the *Seljuk* princes, of whom an account will be found in the following note. *Kaisariah* or Cæsarea, and *Sevasta* or Sebaste, the Sebastopolis Cappadociæ of Ptolemy and *Siwas* or *Sivas* of the present day, were cities belonging to the same dynasty, that had been conquered by the Moghuls in the year 1242. *Karamania* is described by Büsching as comprehending the ancient provinces of Cilicia, part of Cappadocia, Lycaonia, Isauria, Pamphylia, Lycia, Pisidia, and a part of the greater Phrygia.

Figure 13. Marsden, *Marco Polo*, 44

BOOK OF MORMON, BOOK OF LIES

" Sarai, a qua distat plus viginti diætis." Geographia (Büsching) p. 265. *Assara* is the city of *Sarai*, with the definitive article prefixed. " Sarai," says the same geographer, " urbs magna, sedes regia Tartarorum. . . . . . .Apud eam fluit

Figure 14. Marsden, *Marco Polo*, 7

In approximately 600 BC, Lehi's ship sailed to the North American continent. There the travelers' split into two groups, one following Nephi and the other following his elder brother, Laman. Their numbers grew over two centuries, and the populace called themselves the Nephites and the Lamanites. The former were descendants of Nephi and the latter of Laman. These supposedly pre-Colombian factions were often at war. Their final clash, a battle of extinction, took place on the hill Camorah.

In the confrontation, the leader of the Nephites, Mormon, dies, along with two hundred forty thousand of his soldiers, plus their women and children. Before Mormon perishes, he gives the sacred engravings of his people's history on the plates to his son, Moroni, along with the responsibility to protect them.

Moroni, the lone survivor of the Nephites, abridges and re-engraves the records of his nation's history, then buries them in a stone box on the hill Camorah. There they remained, undiscovered, for fourteen hundred years. In the nineteenth century, Moroni returns to Earth as an angel and appears before Joseph Jr. to reveal the gold tablets' existence and location.

The Book of Mormon contains a chapter called "Book of Mormon." In it is the first mention of Camorah:

> And I, Mormon, wrote an epistle unto the king of the Lamanites, and
> desired of him that he would grant unto us that we might gather together
> our people unto the land of Camorah, by a hill which was called Camo-
> rah, and there we could give them battle.
>
> And it came to pass that the king of the Lamanites did grant unto me the
> thing which I desired.

And it came to pass that we did march forth to the land of Camorah, and we did pitch our tents round about the hill Camorah; and it was in a land of many waters, rivers and fountains; and here we had hope to gain advantage over the Lamanites.

And when three hundred and eighty and four years had passed away, we had gathered in all the remainder of our people unto the land Camorah. (Mormon 3: p. 529 [6:2–6:5])

The Smiths gave that hill another name, *Ramah*, in a different chapter. Seemingly against all odds, it is again the site of an epic battle between factions of a prior group of Jewish immigrants before Lehi and his tribe reached the shores of North America. They were called the Jaredites.

"The Book of Ether" describes how the Jaredites set out for the Western Hemisphere after the fall of the Tower of Babel. To them, the hill Camorah was known as "Ramah."

Moroni writes "The Book of Ether" from a set of plates that bears the Jaredites' history. He states (Figure 15).

In this battle, millions of Jaredites were killed. Here we have another improbable coincidence: as with Moroni and his small group, only a small number of Jaredites survive the conflict, and one lived on to record the history of his people on metal plates. His name was Ether.

What does all this have to do with Marco Polo? Skimming the text of the 1818 publication, the reader comes across these passages on page 683 (Figure 16).

Marco Polo visited a place called "Kumari." Marsden, having studied the Latin version of Polo's manuscript, added footnote 1378, which explains

> And it came to pass that the army of Coriantumr did pitch their tents by the hill Ramah; and it was that same hill where my father Mormon did hide up the records unto the Lord, which were sacred.—

Figure 15. Ether 6: p. 571 [15:11]

CHAPTER XXVI.

Of Kumari.

KUMARI [1378] is a province where a part of our northern constellation, BOOK III.
invisible at *Java* and to within about thirty miles of this place, may CHAP. XXVI.
be just seen, and where it appears to be the height of a cubit above the
horizon.[1379]   The country is not much cultivated being chiefly covered
with forests, which are the abode of a variety of beasts, especially apes,
so formed and of such a size as to have the appearance of men.[1380]
There are also long-tailed monkies, very different from the former in
respect to magnitude.   Tigers, leopards, and lynxes abound.

NOTES.

1378. *Kumari* or, as it appears in the Latin version, *Comari,* is the correct
name of the extreme southern promontory of India, mentioned by Ptolemy as the
Κομαρια ἀκρον promontarium Komariæ, and called by modern Europeans Cape
Comorin.   In the course of our author's route from the eastern to the western
coast of the peninsula, this place ought to have been noticed before the city of
Koulam, an inacuracy that may have arisen from the transposition of detached
materials.

Figure 16. Marsden, *Marco Polo,* 683

that the Latin version of *Kumari* is "Comari" and also called by Europeans
"Cape Comorin." Comari is a land in the extreme south of India.

Camorah and *Comorin* are pronounced and spelled similarly. Furthermore, both *Camorah* and *Comari* are names for an area of land.

Here is a test: Had the Joseph Smiths copied Marco Polo's text, then
the unusual names *Camorah* and *Ramah* should logically appear together
somewhere in *The Travels of Marco Polo*; after all, they are the name of
the same hill in *The Book of Mormon*, and if they were plagiarizing *The
Travels of Marco Polo*, what would be more convenient than copying two
names that are close together? In other words, if Senior and Junior changed

> 1380. The worship of *Hanuman,* a rational and very amusing ape, of the Hindu mythology, who, with an army of his own species, assisted *Rama* in the conquest of Ceylon, after having rescued his wife *Sita* from the power of *Ravana,* its tyrant, by whom she had been carried off, has produced a feeling of veneration for the whole race, but particularly for those of the larger class, whose form approaches nearest to the human. The consequence of this superstition is, that the breed, being unmolested, multiply exceedingly, to the great annoyance of the inhabitants of villages. It has been conjectured with much plausibility, that the monkies of *Rama's* army were in fact the half-savage mountaineers of the country near Cape Comorin.

Figure 17. Marsden, *Marco Polo,* 684

Comari to *Camorah,* then *Ramah* should appear near the word *Comari* and relate to Marco Polo's description of the Indian land "Kumari."

Let's see if that is the case. We turn to the next page to 684 in *The Travels of Marco Polo*—the page after Marsden's quote regarding "Comari," where we find footnote 1380 (Figure 17).

Here, Marsden describes "The worship of Hanuman, a rational and very amusing ape, of the Hindu mythology." This mythical ape has "an army of his own species . . . [that] assisted *Rama* in the conquest of Ceylon."

He continues with his description:

> . . . the monkies of *Rama's* army were in fact the half-savage mountaineers of the country near Cape Comorin.

The Smiths poached these names and used them together to name a hill.

Rama was a leader of an army from Comari. The plagiarists simply used a person's name for a place name. They also borrowed the relationship of Rama's army as a military theme. "Ramah" in Joseph Smith's version is the site of a horrific battle.

As their plagiarism continued, the father and son became more brazen. They altered the spelling slightly (Comari/Camorah); they left the words nearly unchanged (Rama/Ramah); they swiped words in close proximity in the original text (Comari/Rama); and they retained the general theme (an army of mountaineers/the location of a battle on a hill).

As with *Ramah*, some words added to *The Book of Mormon* have different meanings, such as Polo's *Melik* for "king" and the Smiths' *Melek* for "land." Other words have the same meaning, such as the name of an army commander or ruler (Tiemour/Teomner, Moron/Moron) and a land to the south (Manji/Manti). Some copied words are almost identical to the originals—for example, Cumani/Cumeni and Zeno/Zenos.

Others are more difficult to decipher, such as Guzzerat/Deseret. A few are reversed spellings of their source words (Marco/Zoram), and some are a combination of all the above (Pharaon/Pahoran).

One general pattern that prevails is that the first few letters or the phonetic beginning of a Mormon name from *Marco Polo* or other literature source is unchanged. The first table that follows below displays words from *Marco Polo* and *The Book of Mormon*. The column on the left lists the similar words, with *The Book of Mormon* names in italics.

The second table reflects names from pre-1830 sources other than *The Travels of Marco Polo*. The names and words are in the left column, the sourcebook is in the center column, and the definitions are on the right. Again, words from *The Book of Mormon* are italicized. The percentages shown for some words indicate that not only the stories but the names used in the Mormon copy can be found at a similar relative placement in both books.

Table of Names from the 1818 *Travels of Marco Polo*

Amu	province of idolators, p. 456 (60%)
Amulet	charm or jewel worn, *p. 570 (75%)*
Amulek	*Missionary, p. 245 (42%)*
Comari, Comorin	land, p. 683 (90%)
Camorah	*land, hill, p. 529 (90%)*
Coromandel	area of India, p. 608 (80%)
Corom	*Jaredite king, p. 539 (92%)*

Table of Names from the 1818 *Travels of Marco Polo*

Cumani	race of people, p. 53 (7%)
Cumeni	*Lamanite city, p. 383 (65%)*
Pacumeni	*Nephite, son of Pahoran, p. 407 (69%)*
Guzzerat	kingdom along Indian sea, p. 690 (91%)
Deseret	*honeybee, p. 541 (92%)*
Ghazan	name, son of Argun, king of Persia, p. 34 (5%)
Gazelem	*name, servant of God, p. 328 (56%)*
Ismaelians	followers of Mahomet—Shi'a sect, p. 115 (15%)
Ishmael	*Hebrew man, joined Lehi's trek, p. 16 (3%)*
Jacobites	Christian people, p. 146 (19%)
Jacobites	*Christian people, p. 124 (21%)*
Kisi, Kisch	island in Persian Gulf, p. 65 (9%)
Kish	*corrupt Jaredite ruler, p. 553 (94%)*
Akish	*wilderness area, p. 569 (97%)*
Korum	city, p. 188 (25%)
Corom	*king, p. 539 (92%)*
Laban	Arabic for "milk," p. 731 (97%)
Laban	*man in Jerusalem possessing brass plates p. 9 (2%)*
Lama	type of priest, esp. in Tibet, p. 241 (32%)
Laman	*brother of Nephi, p. 5 (1%)*
Alma	*prophet, p. 190 (32%)*
Leang	money = 10 grossi, p. 356 (47%)
Leah	*money = half a shiblum, p. 252 (43%)*
Li . . . Hoang-ching	Chinese measurement for distance, p. 293 (39%)
Liahona	*compass, also called "ball" or "director," p. 329 (56%)*
Mahomet	prophet of the Mahometans, p. 706 (93%)
Mahah	*son of prophet Jared, p. 549 (93%)*
Manji	southern land of China, p. 40 (5%), p. 264 (35%), p. 300 (40%), p. 475 (63%), p. 487 (64%)
Manti	*hill, southern land, p. 222 (38%), p. 286 (48%), p. 342 (58%), p. 392 (67%)*

Table of Names from the 1818 *Travels of Marco Polo*

Melik	lord or chief, p. 55 (7%)
Melek	*land in Zarahemla, p. 242, (41%)*
Mulehet	district of Mohametan Alo-eddin, the place of heretics, p. 112 (15%)
Mulek	*Nephite city, p. 369 (63%)*
Panchin lama	holy man in Tibet, rules with Dalai lama, p. 415 (55%)
Paanchi	*rebel leader of Nephites, p. 407 (69%)*
Pacauca	prayer of naked king, p. 631 (83%)
Pachus	*king of dissenters, p. 401 (68%)*
Pharaon	name of Egyptian rat/vermin, p. 743, (98%)
Pahoran	*Nephite chief judge, p. 366 (62%)*
Rama	military commander, p. 684 (90%)
Ramah	*hill, p. 571(97%)*
Kaisariah	city of Caesarea, p. 45 (6%)
Sarai	Tartar city, p. 7 (1%)
Sariah	*wife of Lehi (1–8%)*
Shähhr/Sahar	city in S. Arabia, p. 730 (97%)
Shazer	*place in S. Arabia, p. 39 (7%)*
Shiraz	city in Persia, p. 74 (10%)
Sherrizah	*tower, p. 584 (77%)*
Sihon	river in Giazza, p. 43 (6%)
Sidon	river in Zarahemla, p. 225 (38%)
Si-ning	market, p. 226 (30%)
Sinim	*land, p. 55(9%)*
Tiemour	the Tartar ruler "Timur," p. 287, n. 533 (38%)
Teomner	*man, officer in Nephite army, p. 391 (67%)*
Zennar	sacred thread worn by brahmans, p. 666 (88%)
Zemnarihah	*military chief "hanged," p. 461 (78%)*
Zeno	man, literature investigator: "in the words of Apostolo Zeno," Marsden intro. pp. i, xxi, xxxiv, liv, lvi, lviii, lx, lxviii.
Zenos	*prophet: "according to the words of Zenos," p. 51 (9%)*
Zenock	*prophet: "according to the words of Zenock," p. 51(9%)*

Often the discovery of a name taken from *Marco Polo* leads to other related stories about that name or gives us an insight into why Joseph Smith copied that particular name or word. This made our investigation all the more exciting because we could access the thoughts and motives behind the plagiarism.

The name *Alma* is a good example. Alma was a Nephite prophet who figures prominently in *The Book of Mormon*. In Zarahemla, he was a priest under King Noah at a time when the Nephites had fallen away from God and become corrupted. Abinadi (the one who "suffered death by fire") preached to King Noah, but it was Alma who was won over to Christianity. He traveled throughout the land of Zarahemla preaching, and he baptized the Nephites who listened to the message of Jesus Christ.

The Smiths transformed the spelling of *lama* to create *Alma*. A "lama" is a Tibetan priest whose followers practice "Lamaism." Our Latter-day authors introduced Alma for the first time at a point (32 percent to be exact) where Marco Polo wrote about a Christian kingdom within Tartary, and editor William Marsden discussed the beliefs that a lama practiced a corrupted form of Christianity:

lama	*Marco Polo*	"Christian priests"	31.48–31.75%, pp. 238–240
Alma	*Book of Mormon*	Priest, Christian leader, etc.	32.31–32.65%, Mosiah 9, p. 190 [17:2–3].

Let's look into the reasons behind using the Tibetan *lama* for the character Alma. Marco Polo recalled that in Tenduk, "The king now reigning is a descendant of Prester John, and named George. He is both a Christian and a priest; the greater part of the inhabitants being also Christians." (Marsden, 236). Alma was placed in the Nephite kingdom under King Noah: "But there was one among them, whose name was Alma, he also being a descendant of Nephi." (Mosiah 9: p. 190).

Marsden noted:

If then it be admitted that at an early period some of the Tartar tribes, with their chiefs, were converted to Christianity . . . there can be no special reason for excepting the prince named Ung-khan, whose particular tribe, it may be observed, bore the appellation of Krit, Kera-it, or Kerrit . . . which in the East is a common mode of pronouncing the words of Christ and Christian. (Marsden, 239).

And Alma preached Jesus to the Jews:

And not it came to pass that Alma, who had fled from the servants of king Noah, repented of his sins and iniquities, and went about privately among the people, and began to teach the words of Abinadi; yea, concerning that which was to come, and also concerning the resurrection of the dead, and the redemption of the people, which was to be brought to pass through the power, and sufferings, and death of Christ, and his resurrection and ascension into Heaven. (Mosiah 9: p. 191).

Marsden revealed, regarding the area of Tibet inhabited by people who were Christians yet subjects to the grand khan:

. . . that their chief was at the same time a *lama*, he may not have been willing to divest himself of the priestly character. . . . The belief of an early spreading of the Gospel in these parts derives some additional strength from an opinion entertained by some of the best informed missionaries, that the *lama* religion itself is no other than a corrupted species of Christianity. (Marsden, 239). It is an old notion, that the religion of Thibet is a corrupted Christianity. (Marsden, 240). The appellation of Prester John, was no other than the supreme *lama* of the Tartars. (Marsden, 241).

This means there was some thought behind turning the "lama" priest of Tibet into a Nephite priest named "Alma," who preached Christianity to the Nephites. A lama, thus Alma, was a priest of corrupted Christianity. This gives us insight into what the Smiths really thought about religion.

Let's continue. Alma goes down to a river to live, preach, and baptize the Nephites:

... as many did believe [Alma], did go forth to a place which was called Mormon, having received its name from the king, being in the borders of the land ... Now there was in Mormon a fountain of pure water, and Alma resorted thither ... he did baptize every one that went forth ... in the waters of Mormon. (Mosiah 9: pp. 191–192 [18:4,5,16])

A "fountain" in this case means a "river," and guess who else lived near a river—the lama.

This name of *Argon* appears to be the *Orgon* of the Jesuits. ... The river so called runs through the part of Tartary here described ... on the north-western bank of the *Orgon* we find, in modern times, the *urga* or station of the grand *lama* of the Mungals ... forming a boundary between the dominions of China and Russia. (Marsden, 241–242).

The ingeniousness behind the Smiths' plan for *The Book of Mormon* was not only the re-creation of stories. It was also how they hid their nefarious work from being found out. They combined elements of other modern publications by travelers and explorers (as of the early nineteenth century) into their *Marco Polo*-based faux Nephite history and set it all back centuries before the actual events took place. We'll get into all that in future chapters, but for now let's examine some names from other books that were in print and available for the Smiths to use to create their record:

Names from Other Pre-1830 Literature Sources

Name	Source	Definition
Bountiful	*Modern Traveller, Arabia* (1825)[39]	"Medinah and Tayif [in Arabia] are represented 'on a bountiful land, with plenty of water, and covered with gardens and plantations" ... "excellent fruits" (p. 289)
Bountiful	*Book of Mormon*	*Fertile land in Arabia: "the land which we called Bountiful, because of its much fruit" (p. 42)*

Names from Other Pre-1830 Literature Sources

Name	Source	Definition
Cumana	*Modern Traveller, Mexico* (1825)	land in South America (p. 169)
Cumeni	*Book of Mormon*	*Lamanite city (p. 383)*
Mare erythraeum	*Travels of Verthema* (R. Kerr. 1812)[40]	Red Sea, called by the ancients, was of much more extended dimensions (Vol. 7, p. 66)
Irreantum	*Book of Mormon*	*Sea, being interpreted, is many waters (p. 42)*
Ismael	C. Niebuhr (Pinkerton 1811)[41]	traveller with Niebuhr along Red Sea (p. 50)
Ishmael	*Book of Mormon*	*traveller with Lehi along Red Sea (p. 16)*
Moron	*Conquest of Mexico* by Bernal Diaz (R. Kerr 1812)[42]	conquistador: soldier and "expert horseman" in Cortes's army (Vol. 4, pp. 6–7)
Moroni	*Book of Mormon*	*commander or "chief captain" of Nephite army (p. 341)*
Moron	*Book of Mormon*	*Jaredite king (p. 562)*
Molech	Pococke (Pinkerton 1811)	pagan god of the Ammonites (Vol. 10, p. 424)
Mulek	*Book of Mormon*	*Son of Zedekiah, p. 430 (73%)*
Moriah	H. Maundrell (Pinkerton 1811)[43]	mountain near Jerusalem (Vol. 10, p. 359)
	Pococke (Pinkerton 1811)[44]	mountain in Holy Land (Vol. 10, p. 415)
Mosiah	*Book of Mormon*	*Nephite King (p. 167)*
Morianton	*Book of Mormon*	*Nephite land (p. 365)*
Moriantum	*Book of Mormon*	*land (p. 584)*
Nehhm	*Modern Traveller Arabia* (1825)	territory in S. Arabia near Red Sea (p. 7)
Nehhm	C. Niebuhr (Pinkerton 1811)	area in S. Arabia near Red Sea (Vol. 10, p. 99, 104)
Nahor Hussine	H. Maundrell (Pinkerton 1811)[45]	deep river near Tyre (Vol. 10, p. 314)
Nahom	*Book of Mormon*	*area in southern Arabia near Red Sea (p. 41)*

Names from Other Pre-1830 Literature Sources

Name	Source	Definition
Nephthali	Pococke (Pinkerton 1811)	Jewish tribe near Acre (Vol. 10, p. 445)
Nephtuim	Clavigero (C. Cullen 1806, 1817)	grandnephew of Noah, first settlers in Mexico (p. 378)
Nephites	*Book of Mormon*	*people of Nephi (Jews from "land of Jerusalem")(pp. 5, 72, 116)*
Mamam el Pharaone	R. Clayton (Pinkerton 1811)[46]	baths of Pharao (Vol. 10, p. 404)
Berke el Pharaone	R. Clayton (Pinkerton 1811)	lake of Pharao (Vol. 10, p. 404)
Pahoran	*Book of Mormon*	*Nephite chief judge (p. 366)*
Sidon	Pococke (Pinkerton 1811)	land with river near Tyre
Sidon	*Book of Mormon*	*River in "Zarahemla" (p. 225)*
Wilderness	*Modern Traveller Arabia* (1825)	"Desert"—"Arabia" conjectured to derive from Hebrew *orebeh*, meaning "a wilderness or desert" (p. 2)
Wilderness	*Book of Mormon*	*General term for land in Arabia travelled by Lehi*
Zemarites	H. Maundrell (Pinkerton 1811)	ancient people in Holy Land (Vol. 10, p. 316)
Zemnarihah	*Book of Mormon*	*captain of robbers*
Ziph	*Modern Traveller Arabia* (1825)	sea near Arabia (p. 118)
Ziff	*Book of Mormon*	*metal ore (p. 178)*
Zeno	Pococke (Pinkerton 1811)	"great philosopher" born in Cyprus (Vol. 10, p. 576)
Zenos	*Book of Mormon*	*prophet: "according to the words of Zenos," p. 51*

Numbers in *The Book of Mormon*

Not to be overshadowed by unusual names and exciting stories from Marco Polo, the numbers that Joseph Smith used in *The Book of Mormon* are equally impressive. Marco Polo gained the nickname in Venice of "Messer

Millioni" because of the mind-bogglingly large numbers he used to describe armies, people, cities, and money in the Tartar empire.

Smith used some of Polo's numbers but hid them just enough so that *he* could still recognize them but, he hoped, nobody else could. Many of the numbers are identical or very similar but are used to count different things. For example, a number of people counted by Polo may be used as a number for years by Smith.

Being degreed engineers and educated in advanced mathematics, the researchers found this to be a very interesting element of *The Book of Mormon* mythology. The Smiths could have calculated any numbers that they wanted for counting people, soldiers, years, days, etc. Numbers, unlike names, aren't unique in their spelling. Numbers don't necessarily arouse suspicion of plagiarism. The only way to find certain matching numbers is to determine the percentage-through-the-text placement of similar numbers.

For whatever reasons, this is the course the Smiths took. They derived or outright copied Polo's numbers to use throughout *The Book of Mormon.* Why? Perhaps these numbers were used as some type of placeholders or reference points for the Smiths within the text. Or perhaps the Smiths hoped to create something they could pass off as believable history. By using numbers from Marco Polo, they would not have to worry about something's seeming inaccurate or counterfeit.

We already know about the *four* trips to Acre by the Polo brothers and likewise *four* trips to Jerusalem by Nephi and his brothers. Another example comes from the first time that Joseph Smith would have encountered the number 600. In *The Travels of Marco Polo*, the explorer described "about six hundred persons" lost by the death of the crews on the sailing voyage to Persia. This appears on page thirty-four, which is at about 4.50 percent into the text. The Joseph Smiths used this *same number* as "six hundred years" in First Nephi on page twenty-two, at 3.74 percent of the way through the text. This is a mere 0.76 percent, or less than a 1 percent difference in placement from *Marco Polo.* Smith could have made up any number he wanted, but instead he used the number from Marco Polo and inserted it at the same place. Let's look at Nephi's writing about his father, Lehi:

Yea, even six hundred years from the time that my father left Jerusalem, a Prophet would the Lord God raise up among the Jews; yea, even a Messiah; or, in other words, a Saviour of the world. (1 Nephi 3: p. 22 [10:4])

A second way that Smith used Polo's numbers was to count the number of people or things out of the stories themselves. For example, if people were traveling somewhere in one part of Polo's book, Smith could use the same number of people or number of trips in his composition. This way, numbers are copied but are embedded in the story. Here's an example with which we are already familiar. Marco Polo didn't say "two brothers went to Jerusalem four times." Instead, "[The Polo brothers] judged it expedient to return to Acre. . . . They took along with them young Marco Polo." This was transformed into "I, Nephi, did again, with my brethren, go forth into the wilderness to go up to Jerusalem."

This table shows some of the numbers, with *Marco Polo* on the top and *The Book of Mormon* on the bottom. Percent-through-the-text is included as full percent numbers, with *The Book of Mormon* percentages ordered from lowest to highest.

Number: Marco Polo, Book of Mormon	Percent Through Text (page)	Description
4	1–3%	brothers' trips to Acre
4	2–3%	brothers' trips to Jerusalem
2	2% (p. 18)	brothers in Venice
2	3% (p. 17)	sons, daughters
3	Intro (p. 18)	men visited Jerusalem
3	3% (p. 17)	other daughters
600	4% (p. 34)	persons died on ships
600	5% (p. 22)	years until a prophet would the Lord God raise up, even a Messiah
3, 4	7% (p. 50)	3 days' journey, 4 islands in lake
4	7% (p. 39)	days travel, cross river

Number: Marco Polo, Book of Mormon	Percent Through Text (page)	Description
600	8% (p. 58)	years before his time, monastery founded
600	9% (p. 51)	years before God of Israel comes
40	29% (p. 220)	days journey
40	29% (p. 168)	days wandered
24 & 47	29% (p. 217)	strokes as punishment
24 & 43	29% (p. 172)	43 people take journey, 24 plates with engravings
2 & 2	28% (p. 210)	two days and two nights on horseback
2 & 2	36% (p. 213)	two days and two nights fasting
200	33% (p. 251)	silken cords supporting building
204	33% (p. 192)	souls baptized in waters of Mormon
3	34% (p. 254)	days' journey
3	32% (p. 190)	days after brought before him
30 & 60	35% (p. 264)	troops are distance of 30, 40, and even 60 days' journey
33 & 63	38% (p. 221)	Mosiah died in 30 and 3rd year of his reign, being 60 and 3 years old
6,000	41% (p. 311)	Chen-ku's men
6,562	38% (p. 226)	Nephites slain
12,000	41% (p. 312)	Kogatai's guard
12,532	38% (p. 226)	Amlicites slain
2000	64% (p. 486)	garrison of at least 2,000 men (note for "many troops are stationed in this part of the country." p. 485)
2000	64% (p. 376)	Helaman did march at the head of his 2,000 stripling soldiers
2,200 & 200	66% (p. 443)	2,200 miles men travel; 200 monks in temple
2,060 & 200	66% (p. 385)	200 men out of 2,060
30,000	86% (p. 651)	30,000 Tartars attacking Zipangu, who remained on the island after wreck
30,000	88% (p. 519)	Nephites gathered together, exceed 30,000, a number of battles

Number: Marco Polo, Book of Mormon	Percent Through Text (page)	Description
240,000	76% (p. 577)	number of Tartar soldiers invading Japan,
240,000	90% (p. 529–530)	total number of Nephite soldiers slain at Hill Camorah by Lamanites
8	94% (p. 707)	Paces in length
8	92% (p. 543)	Vessels/barges
16	94% (p. 707)	Paces
16	92% (p. 543)	Small stones

The Nephites suffered a terrible end to their kingdom at the hands of the Lamanites. We learn that tens of thousands were killed at the epic battle of Camorah. Although the story (90 percent) is not placed at the same percentage (75 percent) as an equally tragic defeat of the Tartars, the number of slain soldiers is exactly the same. First, a summary of the Nephites:

pp. 529–530 (90%)	10,000	. . . which were with me . . .
	10,000	. . . of my people . . .
	10,000	. . . lead by my son of Moroni . . .
	10,000	. . . of Gidgiddonah had fallen . . .
	10,000	Lamah had fallen with his . . .
	10,000	Gilgal had fallen with his . . .
	10,000	Limhah had fallen with his . . .
	10,000	Joneam had fallen with his . . .
	60,000	Camenihah, Moronihah, Antionum, Shiblom, Shem, and Josh.
	100,000	. . . ten more . . . with their ten thousand each . . .
	240,000	total fallen

Keep your eye on that final total of Nephites felled in battle. Since William Marsden's footnote 1144 on page 577 (76 percent) may be too unbelievable for some readers, we copied the text (Figure 18).

By Kæmpfer we are furnished, from the annals of the Japanese, with their account of the fate experienced by these invaders. "*Gouda* succeeded his father "in the year of *Synmu* 1935, of Christ 1275." "In the ninth year of his reign "(1283 or 1284), the Tartar general *Mooko* appeared upon the coasts of Japan "with a fleet of 4,000 sail, and 240,000 men. The then reigning Tartarian "emperor *Sijsu (Chi-tsou* or *Shi-tsu),* after he had conquered the empire of China "about the year of Christ 1270 (1280) sent this general to subdue also the em- "pire of Japan. But this expedition proved unsuccessful. The *Cami,* that is "the gods of the country, and protectors of the Japanese empire, were so "incensed at the insult offered them by the Tartars, that on the first day of the "seventh month, they excited a violent and dreadful storm, which destroyed all "this reputed invincible armada. *Mooko* himself perished in the waves, and "but few of his men escaped." Vol. i, p. 187. When we thus find the native

Figure 18. Marsden, *Marco Polo,* 577

It is the same number: two hundred and forty thousand.

This story also reveals a source of the Smiths' use of troop divisions of ten thousand and one hundred thousand men. Marco Polo recalled the tragic invasion of Japan by the Tartars. In retreat, two chiefs on ships "whose rank entitled them to command an *hundred or ten thousand men,* directed their course homewards, and returned to the Grand khan." A third connection silences any doubts. Some Tartars were stranded after the battle. Polo said:

> Those of the Tartars who remained upon the island where they were wrecked, and who amounted to about *thirty thousand men,* finding themselves left without shipping, abandoned by their leaders . . ." (Marsden, 570–571).

Looking back to a few pages before the huge battle at the hill Camorah, we read that a preliminary confrontation took place.

> Now the Lamanites, and the Lemuelites, and the Ishmaelites, were called Lamanites, and the two parties were Nephites and Lamanites. And it came to pass that the war began to be among them, in the borders of

Zarahemla, by the waters of Sidon. And it came to pass that the Nephites had gathered together a great number of men, even to exceed the number of *thirty thousand*. (Mormon 1: p. 519 [1:9–11])

With Polo on the left and Smith on the right, the numbered connections for the battles are:

10,000 Tartar soldiers	*10,000* Nephite soldiers
100,000 Tartar soldiers	*100,000* Nephite soldiers
240,000 Tartars sailed	*240,000* Nephites fallen
30,000 Tartars stranded	Exceed *30,000* Nephites gathered

The Kolob

Now let's examine the name *Kolob*. First we will offer some brief background that concerns Joseph Smith Jr. and his attraction to ancient Egypt.

A few years after they published *The Book of Mormon* in 1830, the Smiths purchased four Egyptian mummies and authentic Egyptian papyri with hieroglyphics. Joseph put the mummies and papyri on display at a museum in Nauvoo, Illinois, and guided tours for guests to view them.[47]

Smith said that the ancient papyri were a long-lost book of the Old Testament prophet Abraham, and he claimed to have translated the pictographs into English by the grace of God, just as he had translated *The Book of Mormon* from "reformed Egyptian." Smith titled his translation *The Book of Abraham*.

This was a risky assertion because the Frenchman Jean-François Champollion had deciphered Egyptian hieroglyphics on the Rosetta Stone in 1822.[48] Junior may not have been aware of Champollion's work even after its publication in 1837. Smith's claim violated his own strategy of "enlightened criticism" that he would have learned from William Marsden. This meant including only material in his sacred book that could not be proved or disproved. In the introduction to *Marco Polo*, Marsden wrote of Polo's story:

Nearly the whole of what he had to tell was new, and consequently strange, and no reference could then be made, as in later times, to the corroborating experience of others, nor could he venture to appeal to the internal evidence of truth and consistency, where there was no exercise of enlightened criticism. (Marsden, xxxiv–xxxv).

Since no other person had experienced what Polo had written about, it was:

1. impossible to corroborate Polo's stories,
2. impossible to look at the internal evidence of the story to find the truth, and
3. impossible to look at internal consistency of Polo's stories.

Smith's cavalier attitude to violate such principles would have inescapable consequences regarding his integrity.

The hieroglyphics on Smith's papyri have since been translated by modern scientists. Not surprisingly, their content was not a book about Abraham, but contained Egyptian funeral documents that were debunked by a reverend and group of learned professors as early as 1912.[49] That seems not to have bothered the believers in *The Book of Mormon*. (Why that is, is inexplicable.) Rather, the Egyptian papyri have been embraced by the various churches of the Latter-day Saints. The Mormons in Utah at the Church of Jesus Christ of Latter-day Saints include *The Book of Abraham* as part of the *Pearl of Great Price*, a collection of sacred books, and are in possession of the original funeral papyri owned by Smith.

A curious name popped up in chapter three of Smith's papyrus translation: *Kolob*. It refers either to a planet near God or to where God resides:

And thus there shall be the reckoning of the time of one planet above another, until thou come nigh unto Kolob, which Kolob is after the reckoning of the Lord's time; which Kolob is set nigh unto the throne of God, to govern all those planets which belong to the same order as that upon which thou standest. (*Book of Abraham*, 3:9)

Let's turn now to James Duncan's *Modern Traveller, Arabia*, published in London in 1825. You will become better acquainted with Duncan's book in the next chapter (Figure 19).

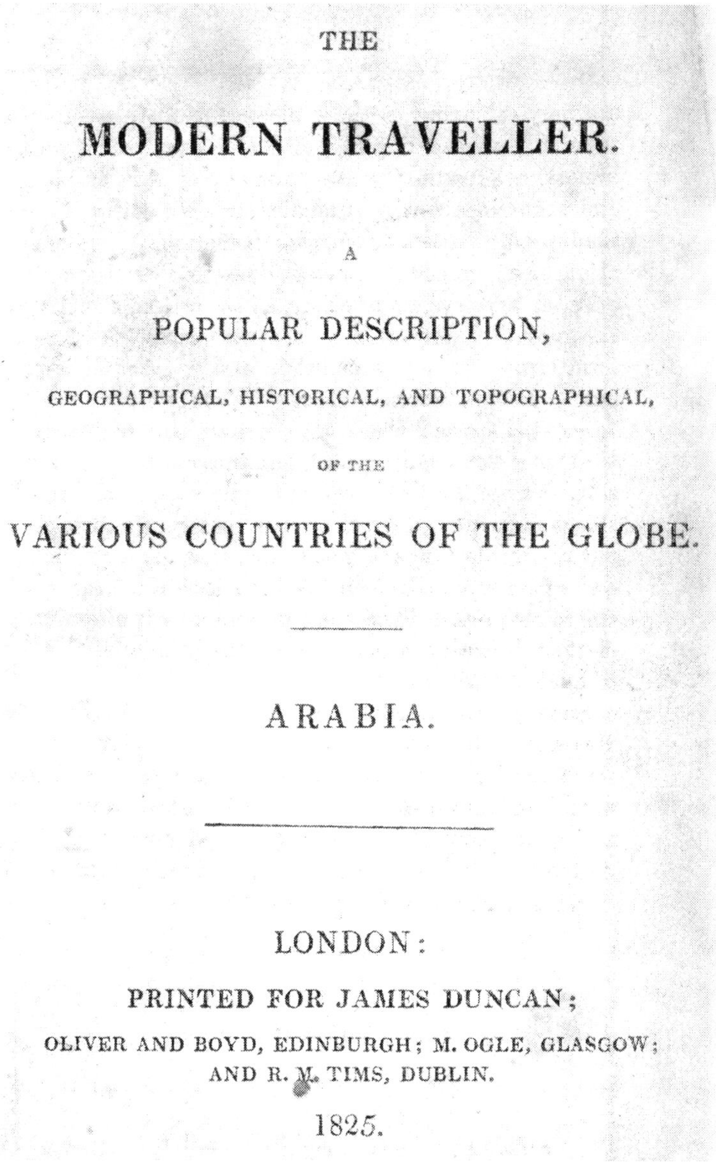

THE

MODERN TRAVELLER.

A

POPULAR DESCRIPTION,

GEOGRAPHICAL, HISTORICAL, AND TOPOGRAPHICAL,

OF THE

VARIOUS COUNTRIES OF THE GLOBE.

ARABIA.

LONDON:

PRINTED FOR JAMES DUNCAN;

OLIVER AND BOYD, EDINBURGH; M. OGLE, GLASGOW;
AND R. M. TIMS, DUBLIN.

1825.

Figure 19. Duncan, *Modern Traveller, Arabia*, Title Page

MOUNT SINAI & CONVENT.

Published by J. Duncan, 37, Paternoster Row, Sep 1825.

Figure 20. Duncan, *Modern Traveller, Arabia*, Plate 2, "Mount Sinai & Convent"

The following paragraph, from page 145, comes in the middle of a discussion about the Christian Convent of Mount Sinai near Jerusalem. Duncan included an engraved plate of the convent and Mount Sinai (Figure 20).

Again we find the most unusual word *Kolob*. If you want to know how unusual, search it on the Internet (Figure 21).

Duncan's book reads:

> They are under the presidence of a Wakyl or prior, but the Ikonomos ... whom the Arabs call the *Kolob*, is the *true head of the community, and manages all its affairs.* The order of Sinai monks dispersed over the East, is *under the control of an archbishop*, in Arabic called the Reys. He is chosen by a council of delegates from Mount Sinai and from the affiliated convent at Cairo, and he is confirmed, pro forma, by the Greek patriarch of Jerusalem.[50]

We'll compare the *Modern Traveller, Arabia* and *The Book of Abraham* to yield some fascinating connections.

In Duncan, Kolob is "the true *head of the community*, and *manages its affairs*" and "the *order* of the Sinai monks."

In *The Book of Abraham*, Smith used Kolob to name a star or planet that is "the great one" that is "to *govern* all those which belong to the same *order*."

" At present, there are only twenty-three monks in the convent. They are under the presidence of a Wakyl or prior, but the Ikonómos (Οἰκονόμος), whom the Arabs call the Kolob, is the true head of the community, and manages all its affairs. The order of Sinai monks dispersed over the East, is under the control of an archbishop, in Arabic called the Reys. He is chosen by a council of delegates from Mount Sinai and from the affiliated convent at Cairo, and he is confirmed, *pro formâ*, by the Greek patriarch of Jerusalem. The archbishop can do nothing as to the

Figure 21. Duncan, *Modern Traveller, Arabia*, 145

This constitutes a simple rewrite of pages 145–146 of *The Modern Traveller, Arabia*. In context:

Joseph Smith: And the name of *the great one is Kolob*, because it is near unto me, for I am the Lord thy God: I have set this one to govern all those which belong to the same order as that upon which thou standest. (Abr. 3:9)

James Duncan: They are under the presidence of a Wakyl, or prior, but the Ikonomos (Oinovauos), whom the Arabs call the *Kolob*, is the true *head of the community*, and *manages all its affairs*. The *order* of Sinai monks dispersed over the East, is under the control of an archbishop, in Arabic called the Reys. (Duncan, *Arabia*, 145).

Joseph Smith: And thus there shall be the reckoning of the time of *one planet above another*, until thou come nigh unto Kolob, which Kolob is after the reckoning of the Lord's time; which Kolob is set nigh unto the throne of God, to *govern all those planets* which belong to the same order as that upon which thou standest. (Abr. 3:19)

James Duncan: but it is generally believed to have consisted in the adoration of "*the host of heaven*," and the worship of images . . . the temple of Mecca is said to have been consecrated to Zohal, or Saturn . . . *thus as to the stars and planets*, the tribe of Hamyar chiefly worshipped the sun. (Duncan, *Arabia*, 146).

Smith also used the exact word—*intelligences*—and its meaning as did James Duncan, who defined *intelligences* on page forty-six as the angels the Muslims worshipped. Smith describes them as beings in heaven with Abraham.

Joseph Smith: I came down in the beginning in the *midst of all the intelligences* thou has seen . . . (Abr. 3:21) Abraham, the *intelligences that were organized* before the world was; and among these were many of the noble and great ones. (Abr.3:22)

James Duncan: Of the *angels, or intelligences*, which they worshipped, the Koran makes mention of only three. (Duncan, *Arabia*, 46).

Smith continued to skip around Duncan's pages, looking for names. In *The Book of Abraham*, chapter one, you will find the gods *Elkenah* and *Korash*. On page forty-six of *The Modern Traveller, Arabia* are two tribes, *Kenanah* and *Koreish*.

We introduce this remark for the purpose of connecting it with the fact, that, at the time of Mohammed's appearance, there prevailed two leading and distinct dialects-the Hamyaritic and the *Koreish*. . . . The latter dialect is that which Mohammed himself spoke, and in which the Koran is written. (Duncan, Arabia, 43).

Al Uzza, i.e., the most mighty, is said to have been worshipped by the tribes of *Koreish*, Kenanhah, and Salin: the acacia, or Egyptian thorn, appears to have been dedicated to her. (Duncan, Arabia, 45).

The state of the eastern churches, more especially of the Arabian, were in a deplorable state of declension and ignorance when the *Koreishite* imposter first conceived the bold project of uniting the jarring creeds of Jew, Christian, and Magian, in a new religion adapted to the clime and the people. (Duncan, *Arabia*, 52–53).

Smith refers to *kokoeuban*, meaning "stars in heaven." Duncan mentions the *Sultan of Kaukeban* on page forty-three. Kaukeban is a province.

Other similarities in these paragraphs include (Smith/Duncan): Mahmackrah/Manah, Egypt/Egyptian.

Below you will find those words in context:

Joseph Smith: For their hearts were set to do evil, and were wholly turned to the god of *Elkenah*, and the god of Libnah, and the god of *Mahmackrah*, and the god of *Korash*, and the god of Pharaoh, king of *Egypt*. (Abr. 1:6)

James Duncan: *Al Uzza*, i.e. the most mighty, is said to have been worshipped by the tribes of *Koreish*, *Kenanah*, and Salim: the acacia, or *Egyptian* thorn, appears to have been dedicated to *Manah*, the goddess of the tribes of Hodhail and Khozaah. (Duncan, *Arabia*, 46–47)

Joseph Smith: And the Lord said unto me: Abraham, I show these things unto thee before ye go into Egypt, that ye may declare all these words.

If two things exist, and there be one above the other, there shall be greater things above them; therefore Kolob is the greatest of all the *Kokaubeam* that thou has seen, because it is nearest unto me. (Abr.3:15–3:16)

James Duncan: II. Inland Districts. 9. Yemen Proper, including . . . (4.) The principality of the Sultan (or Seid) of *Kaukeban*. (Duncan, *Arabia*, 6–7).

Can any doubt yet exist about the Joseph Smiths' use of *The Travels of Marco Polo* and other pre-1830s resources while composing *The Book of Mormon*?

If yes, then let's turn to the next chapter in the Smiths' composition, which discusses Lehi's journey through the wilderness. Here the plagiarists were forced to put *The Travels of Marco Polo* aside because the Venetians did not follow the same route as Lehi.

Fortunately for them, they found a replacement.

✳ 6 ✳

INTO THE WILDERNESS

Let's return to the narrative in the "The First Book of Nephi." Lehi's sons have completed four trips to Jerusalem. The brass plates are in Lehi's possession, and Ishmael's family has agreed to join the group. Another traveler is Zoram, who had been servant to the evil Laban.

As you will recall, the Joseph Smiths copied the Polos' four trips to Acre and transformed them into Nephi's four trips to Jerusalem.

Now the tale takes a turn, both literally and figuratively. After the Polos leave Acre and Lehi's companions depart Jerusalem, the two groups head in different directions. The Venetians go northeast to the Black Sea and to Asia; Lehi treks west from Jerusalem to the Red Sea, then heads southeast near the Red Sea and then along the southern Arabian coast.

This presented a big problem to the plagiarists. From this point in Lehi's story, they could no longer steal solely from *The Travels of Marco Polo*. Yes, while writing their *Book of Mormon* the father and son could continue to extract names and stories and methods from the medieval traveler, but now they needed to find geographical data and details necessary for authenticity. The plagiarists had to find firsthand accounts by explorers who had traveled across Arabia. Once the Smiths located three source-books that provided the text required, they set aside *The Travels of Marco*

Polo. This chapter focuses on those reference materials, which bring Lehi's band across the Arabian desert to the Red Sea and beyond.

Their first resource is editor John Pinkerton's *Voyages and Travels* in Asia, which was published in 1811 (Figure 22).[51]

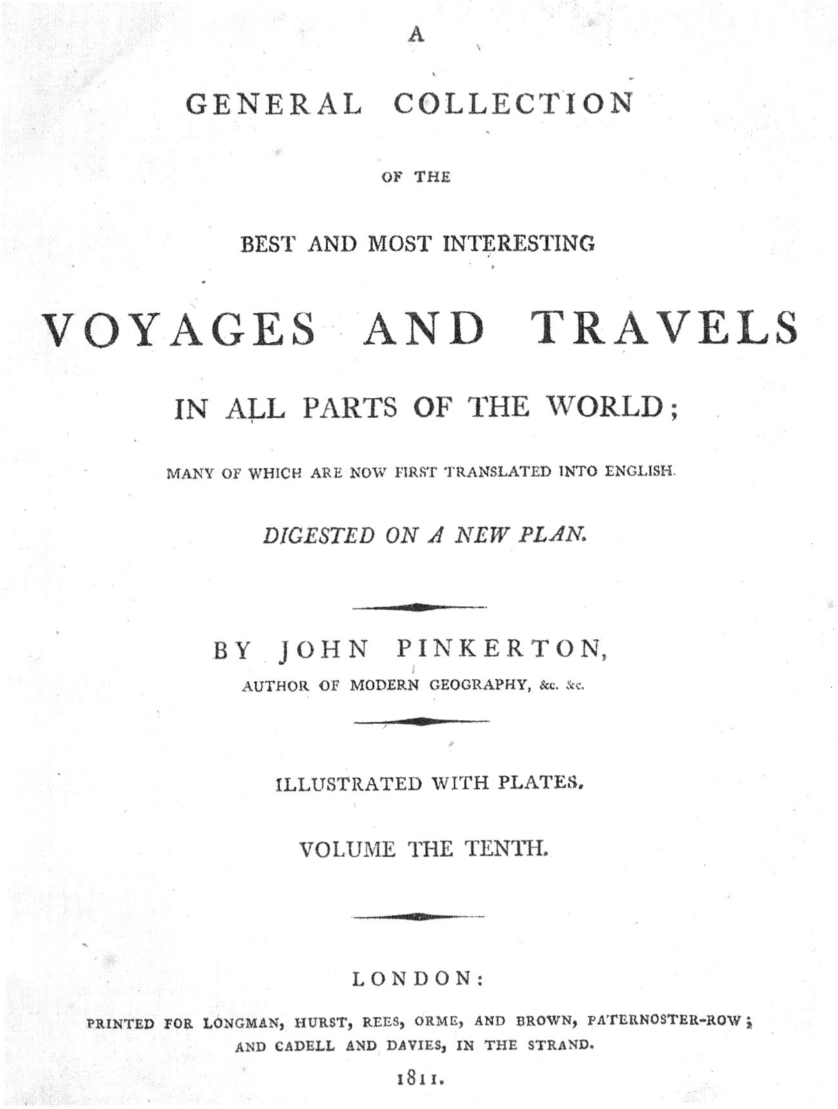

A

GENERAL COLLECTION

OF THE

BEST AND MOST INTERESTING

VOYAGES AND TRAVELS

IN ALL PARTS OF THE WORLD;

MANY OF WHICH ARE NOW FIRST TRANSLATED INTO ENGLISH.

DIGESTED ON A NEW PLAN.

BY JOHN PINKERTON,

AUTHOR OF MODERN GEOGRAPHY, &c. &c.

ILLUSTRATED WITH PLATES.

VOLUME THE TENTH.

LONDON:

PRINTED FOR LONGMAN, HURST, REES, ORME, AND BROWN, PATERNOSTER-ROW; AND CADELL AND DAVIES, IN THE STRAND.

1811.

Figure 22. Pinkerton, *Voyages and Travels*, Vol. 10, Title Page

The first traveller record in the book is that of Carston Niebuhr (Figure 23).[52]

A

GENERAL COLLECTION

OF

VOYAGES AND TRAVELS.

ASIA

TRAVELS IN ARABIA.

BY

CARSTEN NIEBUHR.

ABRIDGED FROM THE ORIGINAL WORK.

JOURNEY FROM CAIRO TO SUEZ AND MOUNT SINAI.

CHAP. I. — *Preparations for our departure.*

ALTHOUGH the chief object of our voyage was to vifit Arabia, we were unwillingly detained in Egypt for nearly a year. Several circumftances obliged us to this involuntary delay.

On account of the pretended fanctity of the Pilgrims, Chriftians are prohibited from travelling to Arabia by land, with the caravan for Mecca. They are under a neceffity, therefore, of waiting till the feafon when the Red Sea becomes navigable, and veffels fail from the harbour of Suez for Jidda.

While we waited thefe opportunities, we found it equally impoffible to vifit mount Sinai, or Jibbel-el-Mokatteb, the celebrated hill of infcriptions, both of which we defigned to examine. The Egyptians had been at war, during all the laft year, with a fmall tribe of Arabs who dwelt in the environs of Tor, which rendered fuch a journey impracticable before the return of the caravan from Mecca, the conductor of which had been commiffioned to negotiate a peace with the offended Arabs.

This fkirmifhing war had arifen from the intemperate rapacity of the Arabs, who gain their livelihood by hiring out camels, and carrying goods between Suez and

VOL. X.   B   Cairo.

Figure 23. Pinkerton, *Voyages and Travels*, Vol. 10, 1

The Dutchman Carsten Niebuhr was one of the most well-known explorers of that part of the world at the time. In his collection, Pinkerton included explorers in Volume Ten such as Robert Clayton, Richard Pococke, and others, all of whom had their own adventures in Arabia.

Niebuhr's journey in 1762 took him by caravan from Cairo to Suez, on to Mt. Sinai, and then to Jidda (Jeddah) and Mecca. The column continued south along the Red Sea to Mokkha, then headed eastward into Yemen, traveled between the mountains and on to Saana. Niebuhr described the overland journey in Arabia close to the seas and oceans. He discussed the food, clothing, customs, language, religion, commerce, science—including astronomy—and natural history. He provided all the details the plagiarists required, but they didn't stop with Niebuhr.

Their second reference book was *Voyages and Travels, Volume 7*, of editor and translator Robert Kerr's travel series, published in 1812.[53]

It included a personal account of an unknown explorer, Ludivico Verthema. Like the Polos, Verthema was Italian.[54] In 1502–03 he traveled overland from Damascus to the Red Sea and down the coast to Mecca, and then by boat to Aden on the southwestern coast. For Lehi and his troop, the long road to the imaginary land of Bountiful really begins at Damascus, not Jerusalem, and this is where the story of Verthema became crucial to *The Book of Mormon*.

The third sourcebook is editor James Duncan's *The Modern Traveller, a Popular Description, Geographical, Historical, and Topographical, of the Various Countries of the Globe, Arabia*, published in 1825 in London (Figure 24).[55]

Duncan included some of Niebuhr's story but not Verthema's. Instead he added the exploits of Domingo Badhia, a Spaniard who sailed down the Red Sea to the port of Djidda in 1807. This gentleman passed himself off as "Ali Bey." He, like Verthema, trekked through Arabia along the Red Sea and visited mosques at nearby Mecca. He wrote detailed accounts of seeing the pilgrimages by Muslims. Duncan included the following engraved plate called "Mosques at Mekka and Medinah," which Ali Bey would have seen on his trip (Figures 25a and 25b).

A

GENERAL

HISTORY AND COLLECTION

OF

VOYAGES AND TRAVELS,

ARRANGED IN SYSTEMATIC ORDER:

FORMING A COMPLETE HISTORY OF THE ORIGIN AND PROGRESS

OF NAVIGATION, DISCOVERY, AND COMMERCE,

BY SEA AND LAND,

FROM THE EARLIEST AGES TO THE PRESENT TIME.

BY

ROBERT KERR, F. R. S. & F. A. S. EDIN.

ILLUSTRATED BY MAPS AND CHARTS.

VOL. VII.

EDINBURGH:

Printed by George Ramsay and Company,

FOR WILLIAM BLACKWOOD, SOUTH BRIDGE STREET,

AND JOHN BALLANTYNE AND CO. HANOVER-STREET, EDINBURGH:

J. MURRAY, ALBEMARLE-STREET; R. BALDWIN, AND GALE,

CURTIS, AND CO. PATERNOSTER-ROW, LONDON:

AND J. CUMMING, DUBLIN.

1812.

Figure 24. Kerr, *Voyages and Travels*, Vol. 7, Title Page

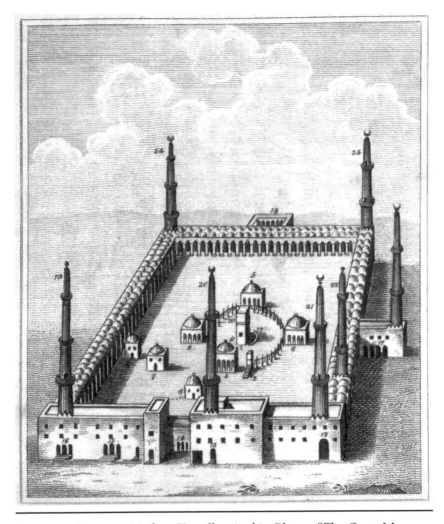

Figure 25a. Duncan, *Modern Traveller, Arabia*, Plate 3, "The Great Mosques at Mecca and Medina"

Until partway through chapter five in "The First Book of Nephi," the Smiths plagiarized Kerr's *Voyages and Travels* and Duncan's *Modern Traveller* back and forth, back and forth. Then, when Lehi and Nephi turn east to travel along the southern shore of Arabia, the Smiths added excerpts from Pinkerton's *Voyages and Travels* to the mix.

Figure 25b.

People who accept *The Book of Mormon* as truth marvel at Lehi's turning to the east. If not for the golden plates, how would Joseph Jr., an uneducated farm boy in Palmyra, New York, know the route to the sea? "The First Book of Nephi," which he had translated into English, must have informed him of that route.

105

In truth, the Smiths had a map opposite the cover page of James Duncan's *Modern Traveller*, which illustrated the direction to follow. Tiny lines marked the roads and water wells between the cities; one was from Jerusalem down the coast of the Red Sea to Mecca. Dark, thick wavy lines indicated mountains. Thin wavy lines were rivers or, as they are known in Arabia, *wadis*, which flow to the sea only during the rainy season. A few rivers flow year-round, however, and the modern travelers noted them in their writings, too.

The guidebooks also said that all roads turn from the desert to the east, toward the sea. The route was called the "Incense Trail" (Figure 26).

So much material was copied from Pinkerton, Kerr, Duncan, and *The Travels of Marco Polo* that an entire book could be devoted to just this one topic. For our purposes, however, the table below will make the point.

Asia/Arabia in *The Book of Mormon*

Book of Mormon Subject	1811, 1818 Polo	1812 Verthema	1811 Clayton	1811 Niebuhr	1811 Pococke	1825 Duncan
Personal Record	▪	▪	▪	▪	▪	▪
"Wilderness" in Arabia						▪
Desert in Arabia		▪	▪	▪	▪	▪
Travel near Red Sea		▪	▪	▪		▪
Metal plates/tablets	▪					▪
Brass Engraving				▪		▪
Compass in Arabia		▪		▪		
Mountains in Arabia		▪	▪	▪		▪
Rivers to Red Sea			▪	▪		▪
Animals in Arabia	▪	▪	▪	▪	▪	▪
Mounds of Stones	▪	▪	▪	▪	▪	▪
Place Called Nahom (Nehhm, Nahor)				▪		▪

Asia/Arabia in *The Book of Mormon*

Book of Mormon Subject	1811, 1818 Polo	1812 Verthema	1811 Clayton	1811 Niebuhr	1811 Pococke	1825 Duncan
Fertile region in S. Arabia "Bountiful"		▪		▪		▪
Steel in Arabia		▪		▪		▪
Pitched tents		▪	▪			▪
Forests in S. Arabia	▪	▪	▪	▪	▪	▪
Metal ore in S. Arabia	▪			▪		▪
Fruit, honey, trees	▪	▪		▪		▪
Shipbuilding in S. Arabia	▪			▪		

The next table illustrates how the Smiths used their reference books: the men opened with Verthema traveling down the Red Sea to Aden, taken from volume seven of Robert Kerr's collection. Then they switched to Niebuhr in volume ten of John Pinkerton's series. The descriptions to the east of Nahom depend upon the memoir of Carsten Niebuhr, who provided details of life and geography in the southern Arabian provinces of Yemen, Hadramaut, and Oman. When Lehi reaches his destination at Bountiful, the plagiarists stopped using all three books. Joseph Smith, Jr. and his father had all the information they needed about Arabia to concoct Lehi's adventures:

First Nephi	Sourcebook
"Wilderness" is the desert	James Duncan, *Modern Traveller Arabia*
Compass used overland in desert toward Red Sea	Robert Kerr (L. Verthema)
Overland to Red Sea	L. Verthema
Fertile area by Red Sea	L. Verthema
Fight with arrows and slings	L. Verthema

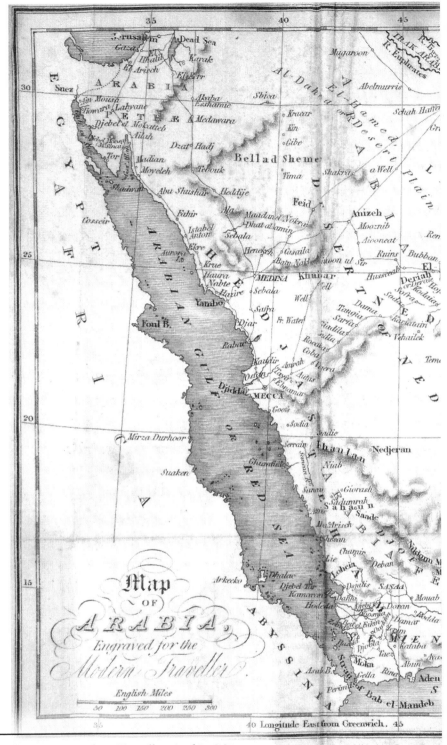

Figure 26. Duncan, *Modern Traveller, Arabia,* Map

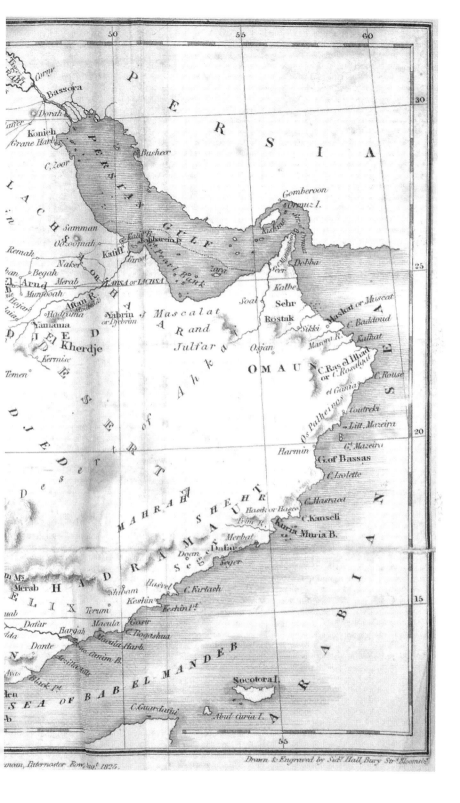

First Nephi	Sourcebook
Ishmael traveled with Lehi	Pinkerton (C. Niebuhr: Ismael traveled with Niebuhr)
Nahom	C. Niebuhr (Nehhm, Nahor)
East along S. Coast	C. Niebuhr
"Bountiful"	*Modern Traveller* & C. Niebuhr
Fruit/Honey/Meat	L. Verthema & C. Niebuhr
Go up a mountain to talk to God	L. Verthema
Iron ore	*Modern Traveller* & C., Niebuhr
Timbers/forests	C. Niebuhr
Build ships	C. Niebuhr/Marco Polo

Let's accompany Lehi and his fellow travelers into the desert. Providing the journey's authenticity will be Niebuhr, Verthema, and Ali Bey.

Lehi was commanded by the Lord "even in a dream, that he should take his family and depart into the wilderness." (1 Nephi 1: p. 7 [2:2]) On page two of James Duncan's *Modern Traveller*, the translator called the desert in Arabia a "wilderness," a probable derivative of the Hebrew *orebeh*, meaning a "wilderness" or "desert."

Before Lehi leaves Jerusalem, he prays for guidance because many prophets have foretold of that city's destruction.

And it came to pass as he prayed unto the Lord, there came a *pillar of fire* and dwelt upon a rock before him; and he saw and heard much; and because of the things which he saw and heard, he did quake and tremble exceedingly. (1 Nephi 1: p. 6 [1:6])

James Duncan reported:

A very singular phenomenon also occurred, which has been taken notice of by the ancients;—the sun set like a *pillar of fire*, having totally lost its usual round form,—a splendid testimony in favour of Agatharchides, who says, the sun rose like a *pillar of fire*. (*Modern Traveller, Arabia*, 326)

Having obeyed God's bidding in Jerusalem, Lehi sets out on a momentous journey across the desert. Heeding the Lord, his band gathers its possessions and provisions, collapses the tents, and crosses the river Laman. They travel south-southeast for four days, then make camp in Shazer.

> And it came to pass that we did take our bows and our arrows, and go forth into the wilderness, to slay food for our families; and after that we had slain food for our families, we did return again to our families in the wilderness, to the place of Shazer. (1 Nephi 5: p. 39 [16:13])

Meredith and Kendal Sheets scoured the three sourcebooks for *Shazer*, but the name was in none of them. They found something interesting, however, in *The Travels of Marco Polo*, located in the chapters about southern Arabia. Polo visited "Escier." William Marsden's footnote 1472 on page 730 tells of the city of "Sheher" or "Sahar" near the sea:

> ... there is little room for doubt that Escier must be the Schähhr of Niebuhr, (or Sheher in our orthography), the Sahar of D'Anville, and the Seer of Ovington's voyage. If pronounced with the Arabic article, Al-sheher, or, more correctly, As-sheher, it would approach still more nearly to the Italian pronunciation of Escier.

Now we'll look at another detail that would have amazed Joseph Smith Jr.'s believers in 1830: as Lehi's travelers trek south along the Red Sea coast, the liahona leads them to a "fertile" area. Most people would have supposed that the Arabian wilderness was endless sand stretching in all directions. Yet Nephi wrote:

> And we did go forth again, in the wilderness, following the same direction, keeping in the most *fertile parts* of the wilderness, which was in the *borders near the Red Sea*. (1 Nephi 5, p. 39 [16:14])

And it came to pass that we did travel for the space of many days, slaying food by the way, and with our bows and our arrows, and our stones, and our slings; and we did follow the directions of the ball, which led us in the more *fertile parts* of the wilderness. (1 Nephi 5, pp. 39–40 [16:16])

Smith's adherents would assume that a desert is not fertile, so how could their prophet have known of these lush areas unless the golden plates had so stated? Well, he learned it from Ludivico Verthema. The Venetian had written that near the shores of the Red Sea lies a fertile area having fruits and animals to eat. In fact, Verthema called it an "earthly paradise":

The inhabitants are all Mahometans; the soil around the town is very unfruitful, as it wants water; yet this town, which stands on the *shore of the Red Sea, enjoys abundance.* . . . After six days sailing from Juddah, we came to a city named Gezan . . . This city is *close to the sea*, and stands in a *fertile district* resembling Italy, having plenty of pomegranates, quinces, peaches, Assyrian apples, pepons, melons, oranges, gourds, and various other fruits, also many of the finest roses and other flowers that can be conceived, *so that it seemed an earthly paradise.* It has also abundance of flesh.[56]

The wondrous brass sphere, the liahona, leads them on. Sailors using a compass to navigate the seas would have been common knowledge in the 1830s. Even Columbus had one on his famous voyage. But who would have thought of using a compass for an overland journey across Arabia? Such an innovative idea must have come from Joseph Smith Jr.'s golden tablets, right?

No. In his 1812 translation of Ludovico Verthema's travel adventures, Robert Kerr tells us on pages fifty-seven and fifty-eight that the Italian had a guide to lead him on a camel through the deserts from Damascus to Mecca. This fellow used a compass to find the way across the desert just as a sailor uses one on the ocean.

Verthema wrote (Figures 27 and 28).

at ten paces distance. For this reason those who travel across
the sea of sand are enclosed in wooden cages on the backs of

58   *Travels of Verthema*   PART II. BOOK III.

camels, and are guided by experienced pilots by chart and
compass, as mariners on the ocean. In this journey many pe-

Figures 27 & 28. Kerr, Voyages and Travels, Vol. 7, 57 & 58

Robert Kerr wrote another book, this one about Hernando Cortes, who used a compass to find his way through the jungles of Mexico[57]:

> The resources of Cortes were quite inexhaustible, as he guided our
> way by a mariners compass, assisted by his Indian map.

This book, since it was part of the same series collection with Verthema, would have been available to the Smiths at the time of their plagiarism.

Nephi stated that Lehi's compass—the brass ball with two spindles, or "directors"—was of "curious workmanship." Verthema used the exact same phrase "curious workmanship" to describe a fountain in Damascus. From page forty-eight, ten pages before his mention of the compass, Verthema described fountains in Damascus:

> A fine clear river runs past the city, which is so well supplied with water
> that almost every house has a fountain of *curious workmanship*, many of
> them splendidly ornamented with embossed or carved work.

Next, what of the compass's design? Did the Smiths use their imagination to invent the object? You decide: in John Pinkerton's book Carsten Niebuhr describes an "astrolabe," an early type of compass used in Arabia.[58] It, too, was made of brass. It, too, describes the compass's two-dimensional representation of the round "sphere of the Earth."

> **A**
>
> *ASTROLABE* is a mathematical inftrument that can fcarce be ufed in the ocean by reafon of the waves. There are two forts of them. The firft are made ufe of by Eaft-India mafters, at a time when the fea is as fmooth as the face of a looking-glafs. This fort is ferviceable in taking the height of the fun, by the means of two little pins, which are bored fo as to have two dioptrick perforations, that ferve to conduct the rays of light to that luminary. The latter are fuch as the mathematicians commonly make ufe of for aftronomical obfervations, and are furnifhed with azimuths, almucantaras, loxodromick tables, and the concentrick and excentrick tables of the fphere.

Figure 29. Pinkerton, *Voyages and Travels*, Vol. 13, 371

Let's open another volume of Pinkerton's *Voyages and Travels* for a definition of an astrolabe[59] (Figure 29).

The Joseph Smiths would have learned that an astrolabe has "two little pins." This matches what is stated in First Nephi, where it says, "And within the ball were two spindles; and the one pointed the way whither we should go into the wilderness." (1 Nephi 5, p. 39 [16:10])

After many days, Lehi's group pitches its tents so they can rest and replenish their provisions.

And it came to pass that as I, Nephi, went forth to slay food, behold, *I did break my bow, which was made of fine steel;* and after that I did break my bow, behold, my brethren were angry with me, because of the loss of my bow, for we did obtain no food.

And it came to pass that we did return without food to our families. And being much fatigued, because of their journeying, they did suffer much for the want of food. (1 Nephi 5: p. 40 [16:18–19])

Nephi's "steel bow" is noteworthy. Steel armor for military use is not mentioned in the source books as existing in Arabia pre-1830. Joseph Smith would have learned, however, that it had been in Arabia for many centuries—not as bows but as armor for horses.

Describing a military exhibition for him in Mokkha, Carsten Niebuhr stated,

> Two of the horses had frontlets, or regular head-armour of polished steel. Now there can be little doubt that these were old heir-looms, fashioned long centuries ago; and without any great stretch of the imaginations, we may suppose them to have glittered in the van of the Arabian armies. (Duncan, *Modern Traveller, Arabia*, 319–320).

Now read Marco Polo's story on page 82 about Kierman, where the Venetian remarks upon "veins of steel" and "bows" (Figure 30).

Either Polo made a mistake in his account, or Marsden did in his translation. "Steel" is not found in veins as, for example, is gold. Steel is an end product of blended metals. To be more correct, the book should have read "veins of iron ore." Apparently the Smiths assumed from the misinformation that the Tartars made their bows of steel.

Hungry and tired, Nephi's father and brothers complain against the Lord, and before rearming himself, Nephi talks with them about their hardened hearts. Lehi, chastened, hears God speak to him. The Lord says to look

KIERMAN is a kingdom on the eastern confines of Persia,[180] which was formerly governed by its own monarchs, in hereditary succession; but since the Tartars have brought it under their dominion, they appoint governors to it at their pleasure. In the mountains of this country are found the precious stones that we call turquoises.[181] There are also veins of steel,[182] and of antimony[183] in large quantities. They manufacture here in great perfection all the articles necessary for warlike equipment, such as saddles, bridles, spurs, swords, bows, quivers, and every kind of arms in use amongst these people. The

Figure 30. Marsden, *Marco Polo*, 82

at the brass ball's directors and inscriptions. The travelers' obedience and faith are restored, and the compass functions properly.

> And it came to pass that I, Nephi, did go forth up into the top of the mountain, according to the directions which were given upon the ball. (1 Nephi 5: p. 41 [16:30])

Is it remarkable that the Smiths knew about mountains in the Arabian desert? Not really, once you know what he was reading:

> The whole peninsula, Niebuhr says, may be considered as an immense pile of mountains, encircled with a belt of flat, arid, sandy ground. This belt, to the whole of which he gives the name Tehama, begins at Suez, and extends round the whole peninsula to the mouth of the Euphrates, being formed, towards the north, by the Syrian desert and Arabia Petraea. Its breadth varies: that of the plain adjacent to the Red Sea is generally about two days' journey from the sea-shore to the rise of the hills.... The principal chain of mountains runs nearly parallel with the Red Sea, at a distance of from thirty to eighty miles. It increased in elevation as it extends southward, and sends out a branch in line parallel to the shore of the Arabian Sea [Indian Sea] as far as Omaun, terminating in the point called *Ras al Had*.[60]

And from Marco Polo, let's take a look at the full quote from above— the one about the warlike equipment:

> There are also veins of steel, and of antimony in large quantities. They manufacture here in great perfection all the articles necessary for warlike equipment, such as saddles, bridles, spurs, swords, bows, quivers, and every kind of arms in use amongst these people.... In the mountainous parts are bred the best falcons that any where take wing... and their flight is so swift that no bird can escape them. Upon leaving *Kierman*, you travel for eight days along a plain, by a pleasant road, and rendered still more delightful by the abundance of partridge and other game.

What if we arrange the corresponding phrases from the above extracts so they appear side by side? Eight different plagiarized words or phrases emerge:

Key Connecting Words Shown in Sequence		
	Marco Polo	Joseph Smith
1	of steel	of fine steel
2	manufacture here	did make out of wood
3	bows	bow
4	quivers (arrows go in a quiver)	an arrow
5	in the mountainous parts	into the top of the mountain
6	no bird can escape them	did slay wild beasts
7	abundance of game	return . . . bearing the beasts
8	more delightful	how great was their joy

The Smiths had another source to describe the wild beasts in the mountains. From page seventeen of Duncan's *Modern Traveller*:

> Among the other carnivorous animals are the *nemer*, or panther . . . the *fath* or ounce, the jackal . . . wolves, foxes, and wild boars. The hare is seen in some mountainous parts.

Now Lehi's band begins the final leg of their trek across the wilderness, moving in the same direction as before and, at intervals, making camp and resting.

During this time Ishmael dies and is buried in *Nahom*, an area in southern Arabia by the Red Sea. This event brings us back to Carsten Niebuhr. In Duncan's 1825 *Modern Traveller*, the Dutchman refers to a place named *Nehhm*, an area in southern Arabia near the Red Sea.[61] Upon his arrival at Mokha, Niebuhr stayed at the house of a friend, Seid Salak, whose son's name was *Ismael*.

Ismael accompanied Niebuhr while sailing down the Red Sea from Jidda to Loheia, just as Ishmael accompanied Lehi down the coast of the

Red Sea. Neibuhr's Ismael didn't die, but a few pages after his introduction on page fifty, one of Niebuhr's other companions, Mr. Von Haven, died and was buried in Mokha.

Ishmael's daughters, grief-stricken and worn out from the tribulations of a desert journey, wish to return to Jerusalem. Ishmael's sons as well as Laman and Lemuel plot to murder Lehi and Nephi. The Lord intervenes and provides the travelers with food. The journey recommences:

> And it came to pass that we did again take our journey in the wilderness; and we did travel nearly eastward, from that time forth. And we did travel and wade through much affliction in the wilderness; and our women did bear children in the wilderness.

> And so great were the blessings of the Lord upon us, that while we did live upon raw meat in the wilderness, our women did give plenty of suck for their children, and were strong, yea, even like unto the men; and they began to bear their journeyings without murmurings.

> And thus we see that the commandments of God must be fulfilled. And if it so be that the children of men keep the commandments of God, he doth nourish them, and strengthen them, and provide means whereby they can accomplish the thing which he has commanded them; wherefore, he did provide means for us while we did sojourn in the wilderness.
>
> (1 Nephi 5: p. 42 [17:1–4])

Wait a minute. "We did live upon raw meat"? In a hot climate, eating raw meat might not be such a great idea. Even in temperate climes, the thought of doing that is unappetizing. We can count on New Englanders in the 1830s to eat their meat cooked, right? So why would the Smiths concoct such a weird story? Most likely because they had read it in the 1818 edition of *The Travels of Marco Polo*, specifically in a section about the customs in Asia, where one practice is the eating of raw meat. Here, from pages 434–435 are the details (Figures 31 and 32).

These people have the following singular usage. As soon as a woman has been delivered of a child, and rising from her bed, has washed and

swathed the infant, her husband immediately takes the place she has left, has the child laid beside him, and nurses it for forty days. In the mean time the friends and relations of the family pay to him their visits of congratulation, whilst the woman attends to the business of the house, carries victuals and drink to the husband in his bed and suckles the infant at his side.[856] These people eat their meat raw or prepared in the manner that has been described, and along with it eat rice· Their wine is manufactured from rice, with a mixture of spices, and is a good beverage.

Figures 31 & 32. Marsden, *Marco Polo*, 434 & 435

Where else in literature are eating raw meat *and* nursing an infant found in the *same paragraph?*

Read side by side, this information in *The Book of Mormon* and *The Travels of Marco Polo* matches remarkably well. Polo's account apparently had a positive impact on the Smiths' opinion of eating raw meat. In Asia it was customary; in *The Book of Mormon* it was a blessing from God.

The Smiths changed the Polo recollection somewhat. Rather than the husband's becoming like the mother of the child by staying in bed with the infant for forty days, they said that the women became *"strong . . . like unto the men."*

The Travels of Marco Polo Of the province of Kardandan and the city of Vochange, pp. 434–435	*The Book of Mormon* *1 Nephi 5: p. 42*
Proceeding	And it came to pass we
	did again
five days journey	take our journey in the wilderness; and we

The Travels of Marco Polo Of the province of Kardandan and the city of Vochange, pp. 434–435	The Book of Mormon 1 Nephi 5: p. 42
in a westerly direction from Karazan, you enter the province of Kardandan. . . . These people have the following singular usage. As soon as a	did travel nearly eastward, from that time forth.
woman has been delivered of a child,	. . . our women did bear children
and rising from her bed, has washed and swathed the infant, her husband immediately takes the place she has left, has the child laid beside him, and nurses it for forty days. In the mean time the friends and relations of the	in the wilderness. And so
family pay to him their visits of congratulation,	great were the blessings of the Lord upon us, that while
whilst the woman attends to the business of the house, carries victuals and drink to the husband in his bed	
and suckles the infant	(see "suck for their children" below)
at his side. These	
people eat their meat raw	we did live upon raw meat
or prepared in the manner that has been described, and along with it eat rice.	in the wilderness, our women did give plenty of
(See "suckles the infant" above.)	suck for their children,
[See above: "whilst the woman attends to the business of the house, carries victuals and drink to the husband in his bed"]	and were strong, yea, even like unto the men; and they began to bear their journeyings without murmurings.
In this district they have neither temples nor idols, but	And if it so be that the children of men
pay their worship to the elder or ancestor of the family, from whom, they say, as	keep the commandments of God,
they derive their existence, so to him	he doth nourish them . . .
they are indebted for all that they possess.	he did provide means for us while we did sojourn in the wilderness.

Is there any question about how the Smiths plagiarized not only *The Travels of Marco Polo* but other books as the need arose? That they stumbled by copying the errors in their sourcebooks into *The Book of Mormon*? That they included the bizarre only because it appeared in the source materials?

In the next chapter, we will watch Lehi's band reach their destination, Bountiful, with the able assistance of Niebuhr, Verthema, and the Spaniard Ali Bey.

Tehuillojocan

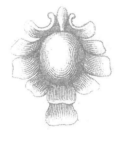

7

A PLACE CALLED BOUNTIFUL

In the final chapters of "The First Book of Nephi," the spindles on the miraculous brass compass direct Lehi's party along the Red Sea coast to their final destination before departing for the Americas. The travelers have endured a journey of eight years, just as the Polos spent eight years going to and from Kublai Khan's empire.

The Joseph Smiths' work continued as they gleaned information from various guidebooks available to them. These resources provided the routes, the number of days necessary to traverse specific distances, and the wild beasts an adventurer would hunt, along with the weapons used for that purpose.

Mormons believe that "The First Book of Nephi" tale proves that Lehi's band traveled through the Holy Land, across the Arabian Peninsula, and to the southern coastline. Does that "proof" still stand up if First Nephi mirrors *The Travels of Marco Polo* and other memoirs?

Senior and Junior needed to find a location suitable for shipbuilding, which was the Lord's next task for Nephi. The ideal setting would yield timber and the materials necessary to make tools for Nephi's purpose. It would also have a harbor from which Lehi's party could set sail for the Promised Land. These criteria might seem impossible to meet, but Joseph Smith Sr.

and his namesake son were up to the task, poring over the guidebooks of their time and extracting, then altering, precisely what they required.

The plagiarists did a spectacular job of pulling together bits and pieces of various resources to build a cohesive story that was part lie, part fact. The only data they lacked were instructions for constructing a vessel capable of crossing an ocean.

The Smiths also wanted to keep their readers engaged, so they created conflict among their characters. God's command to Nephi to build a ship exacerbates the tension between Lemuel and Laman on the one hand and Nephi and Lehi on the other. The murderous scoundrels scheme to kill Nephi and their father. God rebukes them, causing Lemuel and Laman to change their mind. This is another good example of dramatic suspense; readers must wonder how long the wayward brothers' repentance will last. Tension is a clever device to introduce when the plot action in *The Book of Mormon* slows with a desert crossing.

How did the Smiths go about researching this part of the story? They knew that travelers along the Incense Trail would come upon fertile areas and harbors where ships could be built and commerce would be brisk, but the father and son needed specifics—those details that would make *The Book of Mormon* seem authentic. So let's travel with Lehi and his band now, tracing his route and his creators' inspiration.

Lehi turns south-southeast to follow the coast of the Red Sea. The Smiths knew which way to go perhaps from Domingo Badhia (Ali Bey), who headed that way when he was near Mecca:

Duncan, *Arabia*, p. 273	1 Nephi 5: p. 39 [16:13]
Here Ali Bey was soon followed by a detachment of Wahhabees, mounted upon dromedaries . . . Saoud himself, the Wahhabite sultan, arrived, and his tents were pitched at a short distance . . . the whole camp set out	And it came to pass that we travelled for the space of four days, nearly a
in a direction S.E. by E.	south, southeast direction, and we did pitch our tents again . . .

During this leg of their journey, the trekkers have plenty to eat, their sustenance provided by God; the Smiths had an abundance of details, provided by Verthema. Both the Lord and Verthema send Nephi up a mountain to slay beasts for food, using a sling.

> And it came to pass that we did travel for the space of many days, slaying food by the way, with our *bows and our arrows, and our stones, and our slings* . . . (1 Nephi 5: p. 39 [16:15])

> And it came to pass that I, Nephi, did make out of wood a bow, and out of a straight stick, an arrow; wherefore, *I did arm myself with a bow and an arrow, with a sling, and with stones.* And I said unto my father, Whither shall I go to obtain food? (1 Nephi 5: p. 40 [16:23])

> And it came to pass that *I did slay wild beasts, insomuch, that I did obtain food for our families.* (1 Nephi 5: p. 41 [16:31])

In Verthema's account, we learn that people by the Red Sea use slings:

> In war they use round targets of buffalo hide, strengthened by some light bars of iron, having a wooden handle, and short broad-swords. At other times they use vestures of linen and divers colours. . . . In war every man carries a sling, when he casts stones, after having whirled them frequently round his head.[62]

Nephi and his party also fend off wild creatures inhabiting the hills. Let's compare the story of Nephi's hunting expedition with Verthema's account:

Travels of Verthema R. Kerr. vol. 3, p. 76	"The First Book of Nephi"
I returned in three days journey to Aden, passing in the mid way by an	And it came to pass that I, Nephi, did go forth up into the top of the

exceedingly large and high mountain, on which there **are many wild beasts,** and in particular the whole mountain is	mountain, according to the directions which were given upon the ball. (1 Nephi 5: p. 41[16:30])
as it were covered with monkeys. There are also many lions, so that it is by no means safe to travel that way unless in large companies of at least a hundred men. I passed this way along with a numerous company, yet we were in much danger	And it came to pass that **I did slay wild beasts,** insomuch, that I did obtain food for our families. (1 Nephi 5: p. 41 [16:31])
from the **lions** and other **wild beasts** which followed us, insomuch that we were forced to fight them with	14 And it came to pass that we did take our
darts, slings, and arrows,	bows and our arrows,
using also the aid of dogs, and after all	and go forth into the wilderness, to slay food for our families; and after that we had slain food for
we escaped with some difficulty.	our families we did return again to our families. (1 Nephi 5: p. 39 [16:14])

Now Lehi turns east, as did Marco Polo. Both groups cross rivers and proceed for many days. Father and son basically described Marco Polo's eastward journey but changed some of the details.

(0.26%) *The Travels of Marco Polo*	(6.63%, 7.14%) "The First Book of Nephi"
(p. 2) it was recommended to	(p. 42), [17:1]
them, as the only practicable mode of reaching Constantinople, to proceed in an	we did travel
easterly direction	nearly eastward
Leaving that place,	(p. 39) [16:12–13] we did . . . take our tents, and depart
and advancing still further,	into the wilderness,
They crossed the Tigris	across the river Laman

VIEW OF MOOSA.

Figure 33. Duncan, *Modern Traveller*, Arabia, Plate 4, "View of Moosa"

Carsten Niebuhr was the Smiths' primary southern-Arabia "consultant." His travels brought him along the Red Sea coastal areas in Yemen.

Duncan also included an abridgement of Niebuhr's record, such as this page describing travels to Mocha and then on to Moosa and Sanna.[63] In a plate showing the "View of Moosa," notice the mountains shown in the background. Were these the mountains Nephi climbed and hunted within (Figure 33)?

An overland route along the eastward turn by Lehi at Nahom/Nehhm, near Yemen province, took his group to the provinces of Haudraumat and Oman on the southern Arabian coast. Take note of the geographical details from Niebuhr's observations:

> Haudramaut is bounded on the west by Yemen, on the south-east by
> the ocean, on the north-east by Oman, and on the north by a great desert.
> It comprehends a wide extent of country, especially if, with the Arabians,
> we include in it the district of Mahhra. Mahhra seems to be like Tehama, a

sandy plain, extending in breadth, from the shores of the ocean backward to where the hill country commences. These plains have probably once been covered by the sea.

Such being the state of the coast, and of the Highlands, Hadramaut, like Yemen, exhibits great diversities of soil and surface. Some parts of it are dry and desert; but the hills are extremely fertile, and are intersected by well watered vales.[64]

Niebuhr's material about the province of Oman sets the stage for the glorious place that our travelers dubbed "Bountiful," where Lehi will complete the grueling overland trip:

> The province of Oman is bounded on the east by the ocean; on the north by the Persian Gulph; on the west and south by extensive deserts. I visited no part of it, but the environs of Muskat; and, therefore, do not speak concerning it from personal observation. . . . The rivers continue to flow throughout the year . . . *the country affords plenty of cheese, barley, lentiles, with several different sorts of grapes. Of dates such abundance is here produced.*[65]
>
> The most important and best known city in the dominions of this Imam is Maskat. . . . It stands at one end of a beautiful plain; beside a small gulph; encompassed with steep rocks, *forming an excellent harbour, in which the largest vessels may find shelter.* This harbour is likewise protected by forts; and the city thus fortified by both art and nature.[66]

The Smiths made no mention of distance until the old man and his companions reach Bountiful. Now, at last, they arrive at the land of fruit and honey.

> And we did sojourn for the space of many years, yea, even eight years in the wilderness. And we did come *to the land which we called Bountiful, because of its much fruit, and also, wild honey;* and all these things were prepared of the Lord, that we might not perish. *And we beheld the Sea, which we called Irreantum which being interpreted, is, many waters.*
> (1 Nephi 5: p. 42 [17:4–50])

Believers in *The Book of Mormon* would have been awestruck by Joseph Smith's detailed knowledge of the Red Sea coastline. Let's explore a few sources.

Reference Books	First Nephi
Medinah and Tayif are represented as situated "on a **bountiful land**."(Duncan, *Modern Traveller, Arabia,* 289)	"And we did come to the land which we called **Bountiful,**
"Tayif," Niebuhr says, "... this city supplied Djidda and Mekka with excellent **fruits,** particularly **raisins, and carries on a considerable trade in almonds,** which grow in great **plenty** in its territory." (Duncan, *Modern Traveller, Arabia,* 289)	because of its **much fruit,**
Of the Territories of Shan and Khaulan. They live upon meat, **honey,** milk, and some vegetables. (Pinkerton, *Voyages and Travels,* Vol. 10, 97)	and also, wild **honey . . .**

Marco Polo's story comes into play here, his arrival on pages 83–94 (10.98%) being less than four percentage points from First Nephi, page 42 (7.14%).

(p. 83) Upon leaving Kierman, you travel for eight days along a plain, by a pleasant road, and rendered still more delightful by the abundance of partridge and other game. You also frequently meet with towns and castles . . . until at length you arrive at a considerable descent . . . Fruit trees are found there in great numbers . . .

(p. 94) At the extremity of the plain beforementioned as extending in a southern direction to the distance of five days journey, there is a descent for twenty miles . . . This declivity conducts you to another plain, very beautiful in its appearance, two days journey in extent, and is called the plain of *Ormus.* Here you cross a number of handsome streams, see a country covered with date-palms, amongst which are found the francoline partridge, birds of the parrot kind . . . At length you reach the border of the ocean, where, upon an island . . . stands a city named *Ormus*, whose port is frequented by traders . . .

Now look at the connecting keywords for these two sections:

travel eight days	sojourn eight years
along a plain	in the wilderness land
conducts you to another plain	we did come to the land
very beautiful	Bountiful
Fruit trees covered with date-palms	much fruit
reach . . . the ocean	we beheld the Sea

Ludivico Verthema also lent a hand with geography and a generous helping of fruit:

Departing Dante, I came in two days journey to the city of Almacharam, on the top of a very high mountain of very difficult ascent, by a way so narrow that only two men are able to pass each other. On the top of this mountain is a plain of wonderful size, and *very fertile, which produced abundance* of every thing necessary to the use of man. It has also plenty of water, insomuch that at one fountain only there is sufficient water to supply a hundred thousand men. . . . The country around is *fertile in all things, except wood.*[67]

Three days journey from thence I came to another city named Zivith or Zabid, half a days journey from the Red Sea. This is a well built city, *abounding* in many good things, particularly in white sugar and various kinds of *delicious fruits.*[68]

Once again from Niebuhr, quoted by James Duncan:

Fruits are very plentiful at Saana. Here are more than twenty different species of grapes, which, as they do not all ripen at the same time, continue to afford delicious refreshment for several months. . . . The Jews make a little wine, and might make more, if Arabs were not such enemies of strong liquors.[69]

On page forty-two, Nephi gives the sea an odd name, "Irreantum," which he interpreted to mean "many waters." How did the Smiths invent that word? This is a question quickly answered: In Robert Kerr's *Voyages and Travels*, "Travels of Verthema," Volume 10, he tells us in footnote six that *Mare erythraeum*—an ancient word for "Red Sea"—used to be much larger. Like a sea with "many waters," perhaps? The entire footnote reads:

> The *Mare erythraeum* of the ancients *was of much more extended dimensions*, comprising *all the sea* of India from Arabia on the west to Guzerat and the Concan on the east, with the coasts of Persia and Scindetic India on the north; of which sea the *Red Sea* and the Persian gulfs were considered branches or deep bays.[70]

After spending many days in Bountiful, Nephi hears the voice of God:

> Arise, and get thee into the mountain. And it came to pass that I arose and went up into the mountain, and cried unto the Lord. (1 Nephi 5: p. 42 [17:7])

This is Nephi's second mountain-climbing expedition; the first occurred when he slew the wild beasts. Ludovico Verthema also climbed a mountain for a spiritual reason; imprisoned as an infidel, he feigned insanity, hoping to win his freedom from the Arabs in Aden. After convincing his captors that he was a madman because he had been touched by God, Verthema was set free to pay homage to a man "who was reputed to be a saint."[71]

Verthema meets with the holy man; Nephi speaks to God. The spiritual guide "heals" Verthema, who is then ready to sail on a merchant ship to India. God prepares Nephi for his voyage to the Americas:

> Thou shalt construct a ship, after the manner which I shall shew thee, that I may carry thy people across these waters. (1 Nephi 5: p. 42 [17:8])

Few readers would be surprised by God's instructions to build a ship. This idea illustrates the Smiths' strategy of using a familiar Old Testament story—Noah's ark—and embellishing it. We have a second connection to the Old Testament here, this one with Moses. When Nephi returns to camp and begins building the ship to carry his family to the Promised Land, Laman and Lemuel mock him for trying to do the impossible. Nephi expresses his confidence that God makes impossible things possible, and he refers often to Moses' bringing his people out of Egypt and into the Promised Land:

And it came to pass that I, Nephi, spake unto them, saying: Do ye believe that our fathers, which were the children of Israel, would have been led away out of the hands of the Egyptians, if they had not hearkened unto the words of the Lord?

Yea, do ye suppose that they would have been led out of bondage, if the Lord had not commanded Moses that he should lead them out of bondage?

Now ye know that the children of Israel were in bondage; and ye know that they were laden with tasks, which were grievous to be borne; where-fore, ye know that it must needs be a good thing for them, that they should be brought out of bondage.

Now ye know that Moses was commanded of the Lord to do that great work; and ye know that by his word the waters of the Red Sea were divided hither and thither, and they passed through on dry ground.

But ye know that the Egyptians were drowned in the Red Sea, which were the armies of Pharaoh; and ye also know that they were fed with manna, in the wilderness; yea, and ye also know that Moses, by his word, according to the power of God which was in him, smote the rock, and there came forth water, that the children of Israel might quench their thirst; and not-withstanding they being led, the Lord their God, their Redeemer, going before them, leading them by day, and giving light unto them by night, and doing all things for them which was expedient for man to receive, they hardened their hearts and blinded their minds, and reviled against Moses and against the true and living God. (1 Nephi 5, p. 44 [17:23–30])

In case there was any doubt concerning the deep bond between the Old Testament and *The Book of Mormon*, the Smiths added:

And he loveth them which will have him to be their God. Behold, he loved our fathers; and he covenanted with them, yea, even Abraham, Isaac, and Jacob; and he remembered the covenants which he had made; wherefore, he did bring them out of the land of Egypt . . . (1 Nephi 5: p. 45 [17:40])

And they did harden their hearts from time to time, and they did revile against Moses, and also against God; nevertheless, ye know that they were led forth by his matchless power into the land of promise. (1 Nephi 5: p. 45 [17:42])

No question about how the readers of 1830—and today—would liken Nephi to Moses, and Laman and Lemuel to the faithless hordes.

Repeatedly in "The First Book of Nephi," Laman and Lemuel repent for their violent schemes and acts and their lack of faith. Repeatedly God and Nephi forgive them. Forgiveness is a major theme in this chapter in *The Book of Mormon*, and here it serves again as a source of dramatic tension. Now the readers must worry about Lehi, his wife, Sariah, and the others being trapped on a ship in the middle of the ocean with these homicidal adversaries. If the Smiths intended to write a page-turner, they succeeded.

Nephi needs four things before he can undertake God's request: iron ore and a fire, a bellows so he can melt the iron and forge tools, and timber for constructing the ship.

And I saith, Lord, whither shall I go, that I may find ore to molten, that I may make tools to construct the ship, after the manner which thou hast shewn unto me?

And it came to pass that the Lord told me whither I should go to find ore, that I might make tools. (1 Nephi 5: p. 43 [17:9–17:10])

Carsten Niebuhr's book told Joseph Smith Sr. and his namesake son where to find iron mines in the mountains of southern Arabia:

The Arabs call the mountainous tract between Haschid-u-Bekil and Hedjas, Sahan. This tract of country is of considerable extent, and produces an abundance of fruit of all kinds. *Iron mines have also been discovered in it,* but for want of wood have not been wrought. From this circumstance, the iron in Yemen is both dear and bad.[72]

A ship can't float without wood, and forests are rare in the region's sea of sand.

Wood for the carpenter's purposes is in general extremely dear through all Yemen; and wood for the fire at Sana is no less so. *All the hills near the city [Sana] are bleak and bare, and wood is therefore brought hither from the distance of three days* journey; and a camel's burthen commonly costs two crowns.[73]

Fortunately, Carsten Niebuhr provided the information and the details the plagiarists needed:

The country is rich ... in indigenous trees ... and forests are to be seen in the high lands, though they are rare. .... Indian fig-tree ... the date-tree, the cocoa-palm, and the fan-leaved palm ... the plantain or banana ... the almond; the apricot-tree; the pear-tree; the apple-tree; the quince-tree; the orange-tree.[74]

After constructing his bellows of animal skins, forging iron tools, and cutting wood, Nephi needed a place to build a ship. Here is Niebuhr's description of a harbor and ships in Oman Province:

The inhabitants of Oman, although not fond of sea fights, are nevertheless the best mariners in all Arabia. *They have several good harbours,* and employ many small vessels in the navigation between Jidda and Basra. *To this last town there come annually fifty such vessels, called Traenkis;* the structure of which I described in the account of our passage from Jidda to Lohaia. *They are sewed together without nails, the planks being bound with cords.*[75]

A vessel sewn together with cords rather than with planks secured by nails would not be seaworthy, so the Smiths could not plagiarize its construction for *The Book of Mormon*. Marco Polo also mentioned building ships, but his remarks proved no more helpful to the Smiths for Nephi's own vessel:

The vessels built at Ormus are of the worst kind, and dangerous for navigation. . . . Their defects proceed from the circumstance of nails not being employed in the construction; the wood being of too hard a quality, and liable to split or crack like earthenware. When an attempt is made to drive a nail it rebounds, and is frequently broken. The planks are bored, as carefully as possible, with an iron augre, near the extremities; and the wooden pins or trenails being driven into them, they are in this manner fastened (to the stem and stern).[76]

Now this, from page thirteen of John Pinkerton's *Voyages and Travels, Arabia*, Volume 15:

The vessels most used in the Red Sea, though ships of all sizes may be met with there, are gelves. . . . these are the more convenient, because they will not split, if thrown upon banks, or against rocks. These gelves have given occasion to the report that out of the cocoa-tree alone, a ship may be built, fitted out with mast, sails, and cordage. . . . This indeed cannot be done out of one tree, but may be out of several of the same kind. *They saw the trunk into planks, and sew them together with thread which they*

spin out of the bark, and which they twist for the cables; the leaves stitched
together make the sails.

This is not an ocean-worthy ship, either. Marco Polo must have disappointed the Smiths terribly; when referring to vessels that would fare well
on long voyages, he chose not to detail the construction, saying:

At the same time preparations were made for the equipment of fourteen

ships, each having four masts, and capable of being navigated with nine

sails, *the construction and rigging of which would admit of ample descrip-*

tion, but, to avoid prolixity, it is for the present omitted. (Marsden, 29)

If usable shipbuilding details were not available to the Smiths, what
could they have done? Only one thing: gloss over the subject. First, this:

Marco Polo, p. 29	1 Nephi 5: p. 42 [17:8]
[the *Khan*] addressed them with much kindness and condescension . . . requiring from them a promise . . . they would return to him once more . . .	the Lord spake unto me, saying:
construction and rigging of	Thou shalt construct a ship, after the manner
which would admit of ample description.	which I shall shew thee,

Then this from *The Book of Mormon*:

And it came to pass that they did worship the Lord, and did go forth with

me; and we did work *timbers of curious workmanship.* And the Lord did

shew me from time to time, after what manner I should work the timbers

of the ship.

Now I, Nephi, *did not work the timbers after the manner which was learned by men, neither did I build the ship after the manner of men; but I did build it after the manner which the Lord had shewn unto me; wherefore, it was not after the manner of men.* (1 Nephi 5: p. 47 [18:1–18:2])

And it came to pass that *after I had finished the ship according to the word of the Lord, my brethren beheld that it was good, and that the workmanship thereof was exceeding fine;* wherefore, they did humble themselves again before the Lord. (1 Nephi 5: p. 47 [18:4])

"Curious workmanship"? Do you remember that phrase from chapter six, when Ludivico Verthema used it to describe fountains in Damascus?

After Nephi and his brothers finish building their ship, the voice of the Lord commands Lehi to load his family and supplies onto the vessel.

And it came to pass that on the morrow, after that we had prepared all things, much *fruits* and *meat* from the wilderness, and honey *in abundance*, and provisions, according to that which the Lord had commanded us. (1 Nephi 5: p. 47 [18:6])

Writing this section was simple because in all the personal memoirs the Smiths consulted, the modern adventurers wrote about how to provision a ship for a long voyage: plentiful water, and abundant fruits, nuts, olive oil, and other foodstuffs. Let's look at the connections between the text of *The Travels of Marco Polo* and *The Book of Mormon*.

(3.84%) *Marco Polo*, p. 29	(7.99–8.16%) 1 Nephi: 5, pp. 47–48 [18:5–6]
He [*Khan*/lord] also gave directions	the voice of the Lord came unto my father, that we should arise and go down into the ship.

(3.84%) *Marco Polo*, p. 29	(7.99–8.16%) 1 Nephi: 5, pp. 47–48 [18:5–6]
that the ships should be furnished with stores	after we had prepared all things, much fruits and meat from the wilderness, and honey in abundance,
and provisions for two years.	and provisions,
[see above "He [khan] gave directions"]	according to that which the Lord had commanded us,
On them [ships] were embarked	we did go down into the ship
	with all our loading and our seeds, and whatsoever thing we had brought with us, every one according to his age;
the ambassadors, having the queen (wife to be) under their protection, together with Nicolo, Maffio, and Marco Polo.	wherefore, we did all go down into the ship, with our wives and our children.

In chapter five of the 1830 edition of *The Book of Mormon*, "The First Book of Nephi" story of Bountiful ends with Lehi's group setting out for the Promised Land. Will the group have a safe voyage? Will the brass sphere's directors guide them across the ocean? What evil schemes will Lemuel and Laman dream up, and will the brothers be successful in carrying them out? Will the provisions last for the duration of the trip?

What New Englander of the 1830s would not want to know the answers to these tantalizing questions? Their natural curiosity would surely draw them forward to chapter six of "The First Book of Nephi."

8

NEW WORLD, OLD TRICKS

In the first chapters of *The Book of Mormon*, Joseph Smith Jr. and his father depended largely on *The Travels of Marco Polo*[77] as their source for storyline, structure, and details. When Lehi set out across Arabia, where Polo did not travel and therefore could not provide details, the plagiarists switched to the memoirs of adventurers who had and who could.

The Smiths faced the same situation when Lehi's family and companions sail for the Promised Land, but Niebuhr, Verthema, Bey, and the other memoirists in Arabia had never crossed the ocean to get to the Western Hemisphere. The plagiarists needed a new storyline and specifics to integrate into *The Book of Mormon*. Only a seafarer who had written about his voyage to the New World would do, so whose adventures could they steal?

The tricksters did not have to look far. They found exactly what they needed in *History of the Discovery of America, by Christopher Columbus; Written by his Son Don Ferdinand Columbus.*

Kendal Sheets came across Don Ferdinand's biography while searching for pre-1830s editions of *The Travels of Marco Polo*. *The Discovery of America, by Christopher Columbus* appears in Robert Kerr's *A General History and Collection of Voyages and Travels*, published in 1811 in Edinburgh and London[78] and in John Pinkerton's seventeen-volume set *Voyages and Travels*, published in 1812.[79]

How might the Smiths have known that Pinkerton's and Kerr's traveller collection sets contained the story of Christopher Columbus sailing to America? Simple: these two collections of voyages and travels were so well known that William Marsden mentioned them in footnotes of the 1818 *Travels of Marco Polo*, which had been their primary source for "The First Book of Nephi."

What a perfect reference book was *The Discovery of America, by Christopher Columbus*! The story of crossing the Atlantic Ocean and populating the Promised Land in *The Book of Mormon* corresponds to the illustrious explorer's sailing to the New World in Don Ferdinand's biography of his father.

A Genoan by birth, Christopher Columbus discovered the West Indies in 1492 while sailing under the Spanish crown. The admiral carried aboard ship a copy of *The Travels of Marco Polo*, and his goal was to find a passage to Tartary and India, which the medieval adventurer had described in his memoirs, by sailing west. When Columbus reached the island of San Salvador in the Bahamas, he thought he was in India, so he called the natives "Indians." He believed he had landed at the Tartar empire visited by Marco Polo.

The Joseph Smiths did not wholly abandon *The Travels of Marco Polo* in favor of Don Ferdinand's biography. They continued to plunder Polo's memoirs because they believed John Pinkerton's theory of the origin of Mexican Indians, which claimed that the Aztec empire had originated with Tartar warriors whose ships had blown off course on its way to Japan. Proceeding under that assumption, the Smiths knew Polo's stories of Asia would seem plausible when set in ancient America.

Lehi's voyage takes place at the conclusion of "The First Book of Nephi," but the Smiths dipped into *The Discovery of America, by Christopher Columbus* well before that point in the story. Yes, they based their ocean crossing on Don Ferdinand's biography, but they also borrowed much from the author's opening paragraphs, in which he introduces himself and the book he is writing about his father (Figure 34).

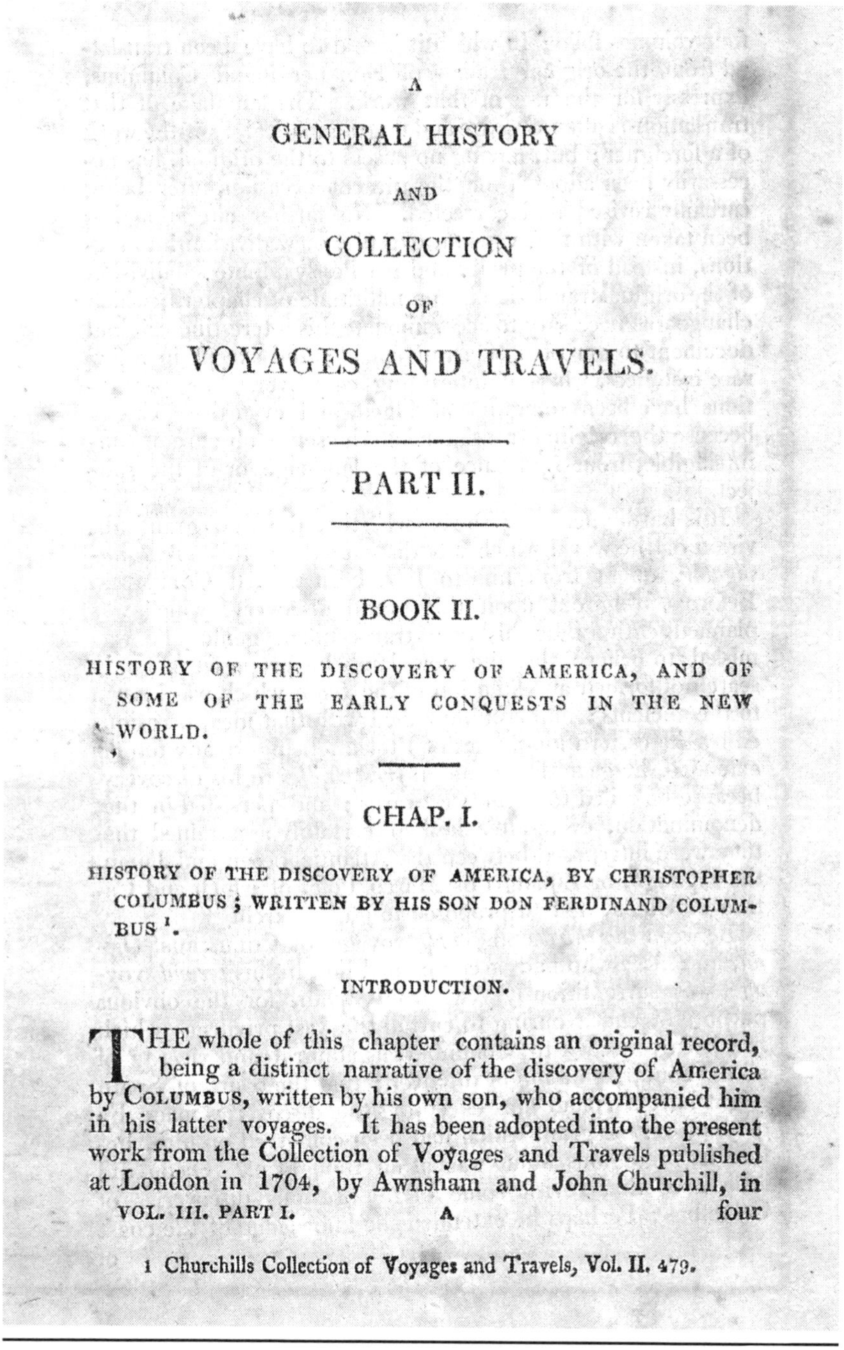

A

GENERAL HISTORY

AND

COLLECTION

OF

VOYAGES AND TRAVELS.

PART II.

BOOK II.

HISTORY OF THE DISCOVERY OF AMERICA, AND OF
SOME OF THE EARLY CONQUESTS IN THE NEW
WORLD.

CHAP. I.

HISTORY OF THE DISCOVERY OF AMERICA, BY CHRISTOPHER
COLUMBUS ; WRITTEN BY HIS SON DON FERDINAND COLUM-
BUS [1].

INTRODUCTION.

THE whole of this chapter contains an original record,
being a distinct narrative of the discovery of America
by COLUMBUS, written by his own son, who accompanied him
in his latter voyages. It has been adopted into the present
work from the Collection of Voyages and Travels published
at London in 1704, by Awnsham and John Churchill, in

VOL. III. PART I.   A   four

---

1 Churchills Collection of Voyages and Travels, Vol. II. 479.

Figure 34. Kerr, *Voyages and Travels*, Vol. 3, "History of the Discovery of
America, 1

The early pages of "The First Book of Nephi" and Ferdinand Columbus's Preface correspond in many ways. Other material from Don Ferdinand's chapters also found its way into *The Book of Mormon*: an original "record," a voyage over deep and unknown waters under God's protection to spread the gospel, the mutiny of the crew (as well as the very same word to describe their insubordination), a malfunctioning compass, and divine intervention to save the day. Both texts are described as abridgments. Both fathers suffered scorn despite doing great service. Lehi and Christopher Columbus undertook glorious adventures as visionaries and prophets of God's word. Both books refer to Jewish progenitors.

The Discovery of America, by Christopher Columbus serves as a template for Nephi's first words straight through to Lehi's reaching the Promised Land in First Nephi, with Polo, Pinkerton, and Kerr in between. This points to premeditation; the Smiths had gathered all their sourcebooks in advance of their composition so they could be ready whenever the need arose for a story, a word, or a detail.

Don Ferdinand and Nephi both recorded the events of their father's life, but perhaps this connection seems too insignificant to point out. After all, countless sons have written about their father. You will, however, see so much shared content that you will not doubt that these two books are bound as tightly together as the cords Laman and Lemuel wound around Nephi's wrists and ankles.

In Kerr's Volume 3, Part II, Book II, pages seven to nine, Don Ferdinand wrote in his preface (Figure 35).

Because Admiral Don Christopher Columbus, *my father, was a person most worthy* to be held in eternal remembrance, it seems reasonable that *I his son, who sailed some time along with him,* should to my other performances add this my chiefest work: *The history of his life and of the wonderful discovery of the West Indies.*

In consequence of *his great and continual sufferings, and the diseases he long laboured under,* my father had not the time *to reduce his own notes and observations* into historical order; and *these having fallen to me,*

THE AUTHORS PREFACE.

Because admiral DON CHRISTOPHER COLUMBUS, my father, was a person most worthy to be held in eternal remembrance, it seems reasonable that *I his son*, who sailed some time along with him, should to my other performances add this my chiefest work: *The history of his life, and of his wonderful discovery of the West Indies.*

In consequence of his great and continual sufferings, and the diseases he long laboured under, my father had not time to reduce his own notes and observations into historical order; and these having fallen to me, enable me to execute the present undertaking. Knowing that many others had undertaken to execute this task, I long delayed its performance. But, having read those other narratives, I found that they exaggerated many circumstances, had passed lightly over other matters of importance, and had even entirely omitted much that was deserving of particular notice. From these considerations I have been induced to publish this work; thinking it more becoming that I should undergo the censure of wanting skill, rather than to permit the truth respecting my noble father to remain in oblivion. Whatever may be the faults in this performance, these will not be owing to my ignorance of the truth; for I pledge myself to set down nothing which I do not find in his own papers or letters, or of which I have not actually been a witness.

In the following work, the reader will find a faithful record of all the reasons which induced the admiral to enter upon his great and glorious and successful enterprize, and will learn how far he personally proceeded in his *four* several voyages to the New World. He will see what great and honourable

Figure 35. Kerr, Voyages and Travels, Vol. 3, 7

enable me to execute the present undertaking. . . . and *he* most *unworthily and inhumanly treated after performing such unparalleled services* . . .

In the following work, the reader will find a *faithful record* of all the reasons which induced the admiral to enter upon *his great and glorious and successful enterprize* . . .

. . . *his own son, who possessed every advantage derivable from a liberal education* . . .

But considering *that my father seemed to have been particularly cho-sen by the Almighty for the great work which he performed and may be considered in some measure as an apostle of the Lord by carrying the gospel among the heathen; and that other apostles were called upon from the sea* and the rivers and not from courts and palaces, by him *whose progenitors were of the royal blood of the Jews,* yet were pleased that they should be in a low and unknown estate.

Now, from *The Book of Mormon,* compare the italicized phrases in both Don Ferdinand's preface above and those from the first page of "The First Book of Nephi," below.

I, Nephi, having been born of *goodly parents,* therefore *I was taught some-what in all the learning of my father;* and *having seen many afflictions* in the course of my days-nevertheless, *having been highly favored of the Lord in all my days;* yea, having had a great knowledge of the goodness and the mysteries of God, therefore *I make a record of my proceedings in my days;* yea, *I make a record in the language of my father, which consists of the learning of the Jews and the language of the Egyptians. And I know that the record which I make, to be true; and I make it with mine own hand; and I make it according to my knowledge.* (1 Nephi: 1, p. 5 [1:1–3])

Let's enumerate the shared elements. Don Ferdinand and Nephi open by introducing themselves: "I his son" and "I, Nephi." Both accounts are personal narratives told from the point of view of a father's son. Nephi and Don Ferdinand allude to the "noble" and "goodly" heritage of the parent; they acknowledge God's favor and their own education. Don Ferdinand refers to the admiral's "great and continual sufferings" and Nephi relates Lehi's "many afflictions."

The Discovery of America, by Christopher Columbus and "The First Book of Nephi" both refer a number of times to "the Jews." In the Colum-bus story, Don Ferdinand writes "by him *whose progenitors were of the royal blood of the Jews,*" and in First Nephi 2: p. 16 [6:1–2] you'll find:

AND now I, Nephi, do not give the genealogy of my fathers in this part of my record; neither at any time shall I give it after upon these plates which I am writing; for it is given in the record which has been kept by my father; wherefore, I do not write it in this work. *For it sufficeth me to say, that we are a descendant of Joseph.*

Don Ferdinand says, "that those Indian nations which he discovered might become citizens and inhabitants of the heavenly Jerusalem" (pages nine and ten). Nephi claims:

For the fullness of mine intent is that I may persuade men to come unto the God of Abraham, and the God of Isaac, and the God of Jacob, and be saved. (1 Nephi 2: p. 16 [6:4])

Don Ferdinand's motivation for writing his biography is setting the record straight. He wants the readers to know the truth about his father:

But having read those other narratives, I found that they exaggerated many circumstances, had passed lightly over other matters of importance, and have entirely omitted much that was deserving of particular notice. *From those considerations I have been induced to publish this work.*[80]

Nephi's motivation is the same: he wants to inform the readers about Lehi:

Therefore, *I would that ye should know* that after the Lord had shewn so many marvelous things *unto my father Lehi*, yea, concerning the destruction of Jerusalem, behold he went forth among the people, and began to prophesy and to declare unto them concerning the things which he had both seen and heard. (1 Nephi 1: p. 7 [1:18])

The content of *The Discovery of America, by Christopher Columbus*— sailing to the Americas and colonizing the land—corresponds with the underlying premise of *The Book of Mormon*: that Jews sailed from the

Middle East to "the [North American] continent, which they populated and, by so doing, became the *"forefathers of our western Tribes of Indians"*.[81]

Both sons attest to the veracity of their "record." Don Ferdinand accompanied his father on his fourth voyage to the New World.

> In the following work, the reader will find *a faithful record* . . . Whatever be the faults in this performance, these will not be owing to my ignorance of the truth, for *I pledge myself to set down nothing which I do not find in his own papers or letters, or of which I have not actually been a witness.* (Kerr, *Voyages, Vol. 3*, 8).

Nephi states:

> *And I know that the record which I make, to be true; and I make it with mine own hand; and I make it according to my knowledge.* (1 Nephi 1: p. 5 [1:3])

The admiral's son admits to *"the faults* in this performance," (page seven), and Nephi says, "And now, *if I do err*, even did they err of old. Not that I would excuse myself because of other men, but because of the weakness which is in me, according to the flesh, I would excuse myself." (1 Nephi 5: p. 50 [19:6])

What further comparisons can we make? Both Lehi and Christopher Columbus leave the familiar (the Middle East and Europe) for unknown destinations. Both men are voyagers and prophets who experience glorious events. In *The Book of Mormon*, Lehi has visions and communicates with God; in *The Discovery of America*, Christopher Columbus is devoutly religious and has dreams of discovering a new land. In both volumes, the men's dreams become reality.

Next, both accounts are *abridgments*, a condensed form of an original text. In Kerr's 1811 edition, the translator states that the full writings of Christopher Columbus, recorded by his son, were *by necessity* abridged. The editor explains practical reasons why he took that liberty. *The Book of Mormon* emphasizes through Nephi that his story is an abridgement. We are left to draw the conclusion, however, that "The First Book of Nephi" is but a part of a larger, even more wondrous story. The table below compares the verbiage.

The Discovery of America	The Book of Mormon
p. 2. change was necessary to accommodate this interesting original document to our plan of arrangement; and except in a few rare instances, where uninteresting controversial argumentations have been somewhat abridged, and even these chiefly because the original translator left the sense obscure or unintelligible, from ignorance of the language or of the subject.	1 Ne. 2: p. 16 [6:3] And it mattereth not to me that I am particular to give a full account of all the things of my father, for they cannot be written upon these plates, for I desire the room, that I may write of the things of God.
p. 7. my father had not time to reduce his own notes and observations into historical order; and these having fallen to me, enable me to execute the present undertaking.	1 Ne. 1, p. 6–7 [1:17–18] And now I, Nephi, do not make a full account of the things which my father hath written, for he hath written many things which he saw in visions and in dreams; and he also hath written many things which he prophesied and spake unto his children, of which I shall not make a full account;
pp. 43–44. Yet as I conceive that the relation of these particulars might now be tiresome to the readers, I shall only give an account of what appears to me necessary and convenient to be known.	but I shall make an account of my proceedings in my days—Behold, I make an abridgment of the record of my father, upon plates which I have made with mine own hands; wherefore, after I have abridged the record of my father, then will I make an account of mine own life. (1 Nephi 2: p. 16 [6:5]) Wherefore, the things which are pleasing unto the world, I do not write, but the things which are pleasing unto God and unto those who are not of the world.

Next we find numerous similarities in the men's exploits. Here Don Ferdinand says of his father:

He was incontestably the first bold and scientific mariner who ever dared to launch out into the *trackless ocean, trusting only in the guidance of the needle and the stars.* (Kerr, *Voyages, Vol. 3,* 4)

Thus as St. Christopher received that name because he carried Christ *over the deep waters* with great danger to himself; so the admiral Christopher Colonus, imploring the protection of Christ, carried himself and his people over the unknown ocean, that those Indian nations that he discovered might become citizens and inhabitants of the heavenly Jerusalem. (Kerr, *Voyages, Vol. 3,* 9–10).

Lehi, too, sets out across the trackless, unknown ocean, trusting only in the guidance of his miraculous compass's needles and in his faith that God would protect him and lead him to the Promised Land:

And it came to pass that after we had all gone down into the ship, and had taken with us our provisions and things *which had been commanded us, we did put forth into the sea,* and were driven forth before the wind, towards the promised land ... (1 Nephi 5: p. 48 [18:8])

For neither Columbus nor Nephi is the voyage smooth. Columbus's crew is edgy and frightened of the danger; Lemuel, Laman, and Ishmael's children are rude and frightened. According to Don Ferdinand:

All the people in the *squadron being utterly unacquainted with the sea they now traversed, fearful of their danger* at such an unusual distance from any relief, and seeing nothing around them but sky and water, *began to mutter among themselves,* and anxiously observed any appearance. (Kerr, *Voyages, Vol. 3,* 47).

And now Nephi:

... and after we had been driven forth before the wind, for the space of many days, behold, my brethren, and the sons of Ishmael, and also their wives, began to make themselves merry, insomuch that they began to dance, and to sing, and *to speak with much rudeness, yea, even that they did forget by what power they had been brought thither; yea, they were lifted up unto exceeding rudeness.* (1 Nephi 5: p. 48 [18:9])

... wherefore, they knew not whither they should steer the ship, insomuch, that there arose a great storm, yea, *a great and terrible tempest;* and we were driven back upon the waters for the space of three days; *and they began to be frightened exceedingly, lest they should be drowned in the Sea.* (1 Nephi 5: p. 48 [18:13])

When the crew's rebelliousness targets the admiral and when Laman, Lemuel, the sons of Ishmael, and their wives turn against Nephi, Columbus and Nephi must stand alone to face their adversaries.

That the admiral was a foreigner who had no favour at court; and as so many wise and learned men had already condemned his opinions and enterprize as visionary and impossible, *there would be none to favor or defend him.* (*The Discovery of America, by Christopher Columbus,* p. 49)

Nephi says,

Now, my father, Lehi, had said many things unto them, and also unto the sons of Ishmael; but, behold, *they did breathe out much threatenings against anyone that should speak for me;* and my parents being stricken in years, and having suffered much grief because of their children, they were brought down, yea, even upon their sick beds. (1 Nephi 5: p. 49 [18:17])

Christopher Columbus was scorned by those for whom he wished to do extraordinary service.

[The readers] will see what great and glorious articles were conceded to him, before going upon his great discovery by King Ferdinand and Queen

Isabella, *how basely all these were violated, and he most unworthily and inhumanly treated.* (pp. 5–6)

Lehi's similar treatment in First Nephi echoes the admiral's:

And it came to pass that the Jews did mock him because of the things which he testified of them; for he truly testified of their wickedness and their abominations; and he testified that the things which he saw and heard, and also the things which he read in the Book, manifested plainly of the coming of a Messiah, and also the redemption of the world.

And when the Jews heard these things, they were angry with him; yea, even as with the prophets of old, whom they had cast out and stoned and slain; and they also sought his life, that they might take it away. (1 Nephi 1, p. 7 [1:19–20])

Both Columbus and Lehi were scorned because they were visionaries. Their ability to think beyond the realm of possibilities didn't set well with their colleagues and family. For Columbus, the crew was working toward a mutiny, more so every day. During the trip, neither Columbus's reputation nor his being a foreigner in the Spanish court would help him maintain control of his crew. They knew the criticism he had received at court from being a *visionary*:

That the admiral was a foreigner who had no favour at court; and as so many wise and learned men had already condemned his opinions and enterprize *as visionary* and impossible.... Thus they went on day after day, *muttering, complaining,* and consulting together. (Kerr, Vol. III, p. 49)

For Lehi, he was likewise accused in the same words by his rebellious sons, even before they set sail:

Now this he spake because of the stiffneckedness of Laman and Lemuel;
for behold, they did *murmur* in many things against their father, *because
he was a visionary man* . . . (1 Nephi 1: p. 8 [2:11])

Next, both the crew and Nephi's family act aggressively toward the
admiral and Nephi, respectively. Admiral Columbus tries to reason with his
mutinous crew. Nephi attempts to speak sense to his brothers and brothers-
by-marriage. According to Don Ferdinand:

> . . . and though the admiral was not fully aware of the extent of their
> cabals, *he was not without apprehensions* of the inconstancy in the pres-
> ent trying situation, and of *their evil intentions towards him.* He therefore
> exerted himself to the utmost to quiet their apprehensions and to sup-
> press their evil design, sometimes using fair words, and at other times
> fully resolved to expose his life rather than abandon the enterprize; he put
> them in mind of the due punishment they would subject themselves to if
> they obstructed the voyage. (Kerr, Vol. III, p. 49)

In First Nephi 5: p. 47 [18:10], we have:

> And I, Nephi, *began to fear exceedingly,* lest the Lord should be angry with
> us, and smite us, because of our iniquity, that we should be swallowed up
> in the depths of the Sea; wherefore, I, Nephi, began to speak to them with
> much soberness; but, behold, *they were angry with me,* saying: We will not
> that our younger brother shall be a ruler over us.

Lemuel and Laban would not suffer Nephi to "be a ruler over us," and
Columbus's crew asserted that the admiral "was desirous to make himself a
great lord at the expence of their danger." (Kerr, *Voyages*, Vol. 3, 49).

The situation aboard ship becomes dire for Christopher Columbus and
Nephi. The crew wants to harm the admiral and return to Spain. (Earlier in
First Nephi, Lemuel and Laman want to harm Nephi and return to Jerusa-
lem.) (First Nephi 2: p. 16 [7:15–7:16])

Let's look at the crew's plans for Christopher Columbus:

Some even proceeded so far as to propose, in case the admiral should refuse to acquiesce in their proposals, that *they might make a short end of all disputes by throwing him overboard.* (*The Discovery of America, by Christopher Columbus*, p. 49)

And now Nephi:

And it came to pass *that Laman and Lemuel did take me and bind me with cords, and they did treat me with much harshness* . . . (1 Nephi 5: p. 48 [18:9])

Next, in both accounts, the seafarers' compass fails to give proper directions. From Don Ferdinand's biography:

It was likewise noticed that the compass varied a whole point to the N. W. at nightfall, and came due north every morning at day-break. (Kerr, Vol. 3, p. 51)

In *The Book of Mormon*, Nephi's being bound caused their divine liahona to malfunction:

And it came to pass that after they had bound me, insomuch that I could not move, *the compass, which had been prepared of the Lord, did cease to work* . . . (1 Nephi 5: p. 48 [18:12])

The tension aboard the ships is not quickly resolved. Columbus's men continue "to murmur," and Nephi's foes will not loosen the cords binding his wrists and ankles.

They still continued however to murmur, alleging that *this south-west wind was by no means a settled one.* . . . In spite of every argument used by the admiral, assuring them that the alterations in the wind were occasioned by the vicinity of land . . . *they were still dissatisfied and terrified.* (Kerr, *Voyages*, Vol. 3, 48).

The unsettled wind in Columbus's biography becomes a tempest in First Nephi:

> ... wherefore, they knew not whither they should steer the ship, inso-much, that *there arose a great storm, yea, a great and terrible tempest*; and we were driven back upon the waters for the space of three days; and they began to be frightened exceedingly, lest they should be drowned in the Sea; *nevertheless, they did loose me not.* (1 Nephi 5: p. 48 [18:13])

On Nephi's ship, when the liahona stopped working, the tempest got worse, because the *unsettled wind* in Columbus's account didn't sound dramatic enough to satisfy the Smiths. To add more action, they adapted another story of Columbus, who sailed through a storm after he reached the West Indies.

Discovery of America Kerr, Vol. 3, p. 68–69	*The Book of Mormon* 1 Nephi 5, p. 48 [18:14–15]
[as the wind and sea were then **very tempestuous** . . .]	a great and **terrible tempest;** and
although the **wind was adverse,** the admiral set sail immediately . . .	we were **driven back** upon the waters
owing to contrary currents, was unable to reach the coast of Hispaniola until the next day . . .	
and **three** of the Indians who had been brought from the other islands, with **three** Spaniards . . .	for the space of **three days** . . .
After traveling about **four leagues** they found a sort of town or village . . .	And on the **fourth day** which we had been **driven back,** the **tempest** began to be exceeding sore.
he found one man alone in a small canoe, which they all wondered was	And it came to pass that we were about to be
not swallowed up by the waves, as the wind and sea were then very tempestuous.	**swallowed up** in the depths of the Sea.

By using a simple story about sailing on rough seas, we can now understand a little better how plagiarism using multiple reference books can be accomplished, and we can see the methods the Smiths used to write their tale regardless of which traveler or explorer they copied from. From this story:

very tempestuous	great and terrible tempest
wind was adverse, contrary currents	driven back upon the waters
three Indians	three days
four leagues	fourth day
swallowed up by the waves	swallowed up in the depths of the sea

Our sailors' compasses weren't broken; they malfunctioned. *The Discovery of America* and "The First Book of Nephi" each offer an explanation.

It was likewise noticed that the compass varied a whole point to the N.W. at nightfall, and came due north every morning at day-break. As this unheard-of circumstance confounded and perplexed the pilots, who apprehended danger in these strange reasons and at such unusual distance from home, the admiral endeavoured to calm [the pilots'] fears by assigning a cause for this wonderful phenomenon: He alleged *it was occasioned by the polar star making a circuit round the pole, by which they were not a little satisfied.* (*Kerr, Vol. 3*, p. 51)

As for the liahona:

And it came to pass after they had loosed me, *behold, I took the compass, and it did work whither I desired it.* And it came to pass that I prayed unto the Lord; and after I had prayed, the winds did cease, and the storm did cease, and there was a great calm. (First Nephi 5: p. 49 [18:21])

Divine intervention spares both men from their enemies. According to *The Discovery of America, by Christopher Columbus:*

On this the people were again ready to mutiny and resumed their murmurs and cabals against him. *But it pleased God to aid his authority by fresh indications of land. (Kerr, Voyages, Vol. 3, p. 52)*

It would have been impossible for the admiral to have much longer withstood the numbers which now opposed him; *but it pleased God that such manifest tokens of being near land appeared. (Ibid. 54)*

As for Nephi:

. . . and there was nothing, save it were the power of God, which threatened them with destruction, could soften their hearts. (1 Nephi 5: p. 49 [18:20])

Columbus's and Nephi's tormentors beg forgiveness. The crew repents when they are on terra firma. And the brothers? When the sea becomes calm. First, *The Discovery of America, by Christopher Columbus*:

All the Christians present . . . *implored [the admiral's] forgiveness* of the many affronts he had received from them through their fears and want of confidence. (p. 56)

Next, *The Book of Mormon*:

. . . wherefore, when they saw that they were about to be swallowed up in the depths of the sea, *they repented of the thing which they had done, insomuch that they loosed me.* (1 Nephi 5: p. 49 [18:20])

Admiral Columbus and Lehi reach their destination:

Being now very much on their guard, they still *held on their course* until about two in the morning of Friday the twelfth of October, when the *Pinta* which was always far a-head, owing to her superior sailing, made the signal of seeing land . . . *The admiral went on shore* with his boat well-armed. (*The Discovery of America, by Christopher Columbus*, p. 55)

In *The Book of Mormon*:

> *And it came to pass that I, Nephi, did guide the ship, that we sailed again towards the promised land.*
>
> *And it came to pass that after we had sailed for the space of many days, we did arrive to the promised land; and we went forth upon the land,* and did pitch our tents; and we did call it the promised land. (1 Nephi 5: p. 49 [18:21–23])

Let's consider a couple of words. You may have noticed Don Ferdinand's frequent use of *murmur* and also *mutter* when describing the unrest among the members of his father's crew. This is the same word the Smiths used repeatedly when Lemuel and Laman conspired against their father and Nephi. All the references below are from "The First Book of Nephi."

> ... for behold, they did *murmur* in many things against their father, because he was a visionary man. (p. 8 [2:11])
>
> And thus Laman and Lemuel, being the eldest, did *murmur* against their father. And they did *murmur* because they knew not the dealings of that God who had created them. (p. 8 [2:12])
>
> And now, behold thy brothers *murmur*, saying: It is a hard thing which I have required of them. (p. 9 [3:5])
>
> And after the angel had departed, Laman and Lemuel again began *to murmur*, saying, how is it possible that the Lord will deliver Laban into our hands? Behold, he is a mighty man, and he can command fifty, yea, even he can slay fifty; then why not us? (p. 11 [3:31])
>
> Now when I had spoken these words, they were yet wroth, and did still continue to *murmur*; Nevertheless they did follow me up until we came without the walls of Jerusalem. (p. 12 [4:4])

And now, my brethren, if ye were righteous, and were willing to hearken to the truth, and give heed unto it, that ye might walk uprightly before God, then ye would not *murmur* because of the truth, and say thou speakest hard things against us. (pp. 38–39 [16:3])

And it came to pass that Laman and Lemuel, and the sons of Ishmael, did begin to *murmur* exceedingly, because of their sufferings and afflictions in the wilderness; and also, my father began to *murmur* against the Lord his God; yea, and they were all exceeding sorrowful, even that they did *murmur* against the Lord. (p. 40 [16:20])

You will find the word *murmur* or some form of it eight more times in First Nephi. In the subsequent chapter, Second Nephi, you will find Don Ferdinand's other "complaining" word, *mutter*, in the story:

And when they shall say unto you, Seek unto them that have familiar spirits, and unto wizards that peep, and mutter: should not a people seek unto their God? (2 Nephi 9: p. 94 [18:19])

When they reached the New World, Columbus and crew went ashore carrying the royal flags. They were so emotional that they all kneeled and kissed the ground:

The admiral went on shore with his boat well armed, and *having the royal standard of Castile and Leon* displayed, accompanied by the commander of the other two vessels ... carrying the particular colours which had been allotted for the enterprize, which were white with a green cross and the letter F. on one side, and on the other the names of Ferdinand and Isabella crowned.

The *whole company kneeled on the shore and kissed the ground for joy, returning God thanks for the great mercy they had experienced* during their long voyage through seas hitherto unpassed, and their now happy discovery of an unknown land. (Kerr, Vol. 3, p. 55–56)

These acts of the crew became transformed into prophecies from the voice of God in First Nephi:

> Thus saith the Lord God, Behold, I will lift mine hand to the Gentiles, *and set up my standard to the people*: and they shall bring thy sons in their arms, and thy daughters shall be carried upon their shoulders.
>
> And kings shall be thy nursing fathers, and their queens thy nursing mothers: they *shall bow down to thee with their face towards the earth, and lick up the dust of thy feet; and thou shalt know that I am the Lord . . .*
> (1 Nephi 6: pp. 55–56 [21:22–23])

The phrases *Carrying the royal standard* versus *set up my standard*, and *kneeled on the shore and kissed the ground* versus *they shall bow down and lick up the dust of thy feet* read like storybook endings to such great adventures.

The plagiarists have worked their trickery yet again. Nephi's biography of his father is taken from Don Ferdinand's book about his own. Lehi's ocean crossing is Admiral Christopher Columbus's voyage. Lemuel and Laman play the same role as Columbus's rebellious crew. Nephi and Lehi are patterned after the famous explorer. Lehi's voyage is derived from *The Discovery of America, by Christopher Columbus*, step by step.

Taking into account all the evidence set out thus far, is the plagiarism of Joseph Smith Sr. and his namesake not obvious?

Now we will move on to the Joseph Smiths' next story, whose foundation is Hernan Cortes's conquest of Mexico.

✤ 9 ✤

THE RISE
OF THE NEPHITES

In fewer than fifty-five years since leaving Jerusalem, Lehi, the leader of the chosen group of Jews, dies. His two youngest sons, Nephi and Sam, succeed him and remain loyal to the ways of God. The elder sons, Laman and Lemuel, continue to "murmur" about their brother Nephi's trying to "rule over" them by preaching to them from the brass plates. Their feelings turn so callous that the elder brothers plot to murder their younger sibling while they're all still living in tents at base camp.

The Lord warns Nephi to flee, so he and his loyalists escape into the wilderness to a place they name Nephi. He has the sword of Laban, the liahona, and the brass plates with him. He builds a temple after the design of Solomon. God tells Nephi to make new plates for engraving their history. His brothers' people, now called the Lamanites, are their enemies. To prepare for a Lamanite attack, Nephi readies the army by making each soldier a new sword based on the design of the sword of Laban.

In *The Book of Mormon*, these events are recorded in "The Second Book of Nephi." A series of smaller "books" follows Second Nephi: the Books of Jacob, Enos, Jarom, Omni, and "The Words of Mormon." Next comes "The Book of Mosiah," in which the Nephites' king discovers the people and land of Zarahemla, where the two groups live together.

Over the next ten centuries, Zarahemla becomes home to a variety of interesting people: Prophets, nobility, warriors, epic heroes, and villains are all part of the populous land:

> Now those which were in favor of kings, were those of high birth; and they sought to be kings; and they were supported by those which sought power and authority over the people. (Alma 23: p. 367 [51:8])

How could a promising group of Jews from the Holy Land arrive with nothing but their tents and yet build an advanced civilization in just a few centuries?

Let's search for the answer by examining the narrative in the "Second Book of Nephi." After prompting by God to escape into the wilderness, Nephi becomes a king:

> And it came to pass that I, Nephi, did cause my people that they should be industrious, and that they should labor with their hands. And it came to pass that they would that I should be their King. But I, Nephi, was desirous that they should have no King; nevertheless, I did do for them according to that which was in my power. (2 Nephi 4: p. 72 [5:17])

> For behold, they had hardened their hearts against him, that they had become like unto a flint; wherefore, as they were white, and exceeding fair and delightsome, that they might not be enticing unto my people, therefore the Lord God did cause a skin of blackness to come upon them. And thus saith the Lord God, I will cause that they shall be loathsome unto thy people, save they shall repent of their iniquities. And cursed shall be the seed of him that mixeth with their seed: for they shall be cursed even with the same cursing. And the Lord spake it, and it was done. And because of their cursing which was upon them, they did become an idle people, full of mischief and subtlety, and did seek in the wilderness for beasts of prey.

Figure 36. 2 Nephi 4: p. 73

The Tartars whom he carried thither, and who were men of a light complexion, mixing with the dark Indian women, produced the race to whom the appellation of *Karaunas* is given, signifying in the language of the country, a mixed breed; [203] and these are the people who have since been in the practice of committing depredations, not only in the country of *Reobarle*, but in every other to which they have access. In India they acquired the knowledge of magical and diabolical arts, by means of which they are enabled to produce darkness, obscuring the light of day to such a degree, that persons are invisible to each other, unless within a very small distance. [204] Whenever they

Figure 37. Marsden, *Marco Polo,* 87

The Nephites' God cursed a rebellious faction of Lamanites left behind at camp by turning their skin black and making them "loathsome." "And he caused the cursing to come upon them, yea, even a sore cursing, because of their iniquity," Nephi recorded. The rest of the original verse is from 2 Nephi: 4, p. 73 [5:21–24] (Figure 36).

How could the Smiths have written such a thing? Read this paragraph from page 87 of the 1818 *Marco Polo*, where Polo encountered the "Karaunas" (Figure 37).

If at first the *Marco Polo* paragraph doesn't sound like the same Mormon story about cursed Lamanites, read on.

Joseph Smith's Use of *Marco Polo* to Develop a Tale About People with "A Skin of Blackness"

The text from *Marco Polo* occurs at 11.51 percent, and the Smith story from the "Second Book of Nephi" is found at 12.41 percent, resulting in a difference of only 0.9 percent (meaning, for our purposes, they are at the same location in each book).

11.51% *Travels of Marco Polo* Book I, Ch. XIV, p. 87	12.41% *Book of Mormon* 2 Nephi 4: p. 73 [5:21, 23, 24]
The Tartars . . . who were	And he [the Lord] caused the cursing to come upon them [the Lamanites], yea, even a sore cursing, because of their iniquity. For behold, they had hardened their hearts against him, that they had become like unto a flint; wherefore, as
men of a light complexion,	they were white, and exceedingly fair and delightsome, that they might not be enticing unto my people, therefore
mixing with the	[see "mixeth with their seed," below] the Lord God did cause a
dark Indian women,	skin of blackness
produced the race . . . of *Karaunas* . . .	to come upon them . . .
signifying in the language of the country,	And thus saith the Lord God, I will cause that they shall be loathsome unto thy people, save they repent of their iniquities. And cursed shall be the seed of him that
a mixed breed;	mixeth with their seed:
[see "mixing with the," above]	for they shall be cursed with the same cursing. And the Lord spake it and it was done.
and these are the people	they did become an idle people,
who have since been in the practice	
of committing depredations,	full of mischief and subtlety,
not only in the country of *Reobarle*, but in every other to which they have access.	and did seek in the wilderness for beasts of prey.

The key words are:

Marco Polo	"Second Nephi"
men of light complexion	they were white
dark Indian women	skin of blackness mixing with the dark

162

Indian women (mixed breed)	mixeth with their seed
these are the people	an idle people
committing depredations	full of mischief and subtlety
in the country	in the wilderness

Smith continues with this Polo theme of cursed, dark-skinned people in a later chapter called the "Book of Alma." In Alma Chapter 1, page 228 [3:6], the Lamanites had dark skin, which was a "curse" (Figure 38).

Reading forward in *Marco Polo*, we learn about a sacred religious marking of the Hindus. This transferred into *The Book of Mormon* as a mark for a band of godless people called the Amlicites, Lamanite allies who followed wicked King Amlici. They wore the mark *and* were cursed with dark skin.

The Travels of Marco Polo Book III, Ch. XXII p. 663, 87.70%	The Book of Mormon Alma 1: p. 228–229 38.78% [3:4–18]
They also burn the bones of oxen, reduce them to powder, and with this make an unguent for the purpose of	. . . the Amlicites, for they also had a mark set upon them; yea, they set the mark upon themselves, yea, even a
marking various parts of the body,	**mark of red upon their foreheads.**
which they do in a reverential manner. If they meet a person with whom they are upon cordial terms, **they smear the centre of his**	. . . Behold, the Lamanites have I cursed; and I will set a **mark** upon them . . . Now the Amlicites knew not that they were fulfilling the words of God, when they began to **mark them-selves in their**
forehead	foreheads;
with some of the prepared ashes.	nevertheless they had come out in open rebellion against God; therefore it was expedient that the curse should fall upon them.

"The Second Book of Nephi" continues with a story that Meredith Sheets located by using the percentage-through-the-text procedure. The placement is an exact match. We begin with a story about promises of

> And the skins
> of the Lamanites were dark, according to the mark which was
> set upon their fathers, which was a curse upon them because
> of their transgression and their rebellion against their brethren,

Figure 38. Alma 1: p. 228 [3:6]

paradise—meaning heaven—and free milk and wine for those who enter there. Joseph Smith copied this story, strangely enough, from Marco Polo's record of the "old man of the mountain," a Muslim leader in Persia and head of a cadre of well-trained assassins. We found the matching *Book of Mormon* story by using our percentage method. Smith wrote his version at a relative page number that is less than a one percent difference from Polo's story.

Our Polo story is from thirteenth-century Persia and a chief named Alo-eddin, who terrified the inhabitants of neighboring countries and kingdoms. Alo-eddin set up an independent kingdom within mountainous areas of the Kurdistan region of Persia, along with fortress-like castles. He was deemed an "Ismaealian" and a heretic by other "Mahometans" for following the Shia sect of Islam, but he commanded a great deal of respect among his fearful accusers. Polo wrote: "There was no person however powerful, who having become exposed to the enmity of the old man of the mountain, could escape assassination."

According to Polo, the chief would attract or capture young men from the area and bring them as recruits to his castle. He would promise them paradise if they served him and obeyed Mahomet's will. Their captor would give the group a strong, intoxicating drink until they were in "a deep sleep." While asleep, they would be carried into a garden prepared in a hidden area of the castle. This garden had beautiful women, wine, food, and lush scenery. When the men awoke, they thought they had gone to paradise and that all Alo-eddin had promised them was true. After a few days of revelry, they were drugged again and carried unconscious to the chief, to whom they declared that they had visited paradise, just as he had promised them. Duped, the young men would serve him dutifully, giving their life in exchange for the promises of paradise.

The original 1818 Marco Polo text[82] appears below (Figure 39).

This was a useful story for the Joseph Smiths. They wasted few Marco Polo words to describe a wonderful land of milk and honey for the faithful, if they would only "remember the words of your God" (Figure 40).

Placing these two stories side by side in a comparison table shows how the Smiths came to Marco Polo's streams of wine and milk and took freely from them. Here the words of the Muslim prophet Mahomet become the words of the prophet *Jacob* speaking to the Nephites.

CHAPTER XXI.

Of the old man of the mountain ; of his palace and gardens; of his capture and his death.

Having spoken of this country, mention shall now be made of the old man of the mountain.[236]   The district in which his residence lay, obtained the name of *Mulehet,* signifying in the language of the Saracens, the place of heretics, and his people that of *Mulehetites* [237] or holders of heretical tenets ; as we apply the term of *Patharini* to certain heretics amongst Christians.[238]   The following account of this chief, Marco Polo testifies to his having heard from sundry persons. He was named *Alo-eddin*,[239] and his religion was that of Mahomet.   In a beautiful valley enclosed between two lofty mountains, he had formed a luxurious garden, stored with every delicious fruit and every fragrant shrub that could be procured.   Palaces of various sizes and forms were erected in different parts of the grounds, ornamented with works in gold, with paintings, and with furniture of rich silks.   By means of small conduits contrived in these buildings, streams of wine, milk, honey, and some of pure water, were seen to flow in every direction. The inhabitants of these palaces were elegant and beautiful damsels, accomplished in the arts of singing, playing upon all sorts of musical instruments, dancing, and especially those of dalliance and amorous allurement.   Clothed in rich dresses they were seen continually sport-

Figure 39. Marsden, *Marco Polo*, 112

Come, my brethren, every one that thirsteth, come ye to the waters; and he that hath no money, come buy and eat; yea, come buy wine and milk without money and without price. Wherefore, do not spend money for that which is of no worth, nor your labor for that which cannot satisfy. Hearken diligently unto me, and remember the words which I have spoken; and come unto the Holy One of Israel, and feast upon that which perisheth not, neither can be corrupted, and let your soul delight in fatness. Behold, my beloved brethren, remember the words of your God; pray unto him continually by day, and give thanks unto his holy name by night. Let your hearts rejoice, and behold how great the covenants of the Lord, and how great his condescensions unto the children of men; and because of his greatness, and his grace and mercy, he hath promised unto us that our seed shall not utterly be destroyed, according to the flesh, but that he would preserve them; and in future generations, they shall become a righteous branch unto the House of Israel.

Figure 40. 2 Nephi 6: p. 83 [9:50–53]

14.81% *The Travels of Marco Polo* Book I, Ch. XXI, p. 112–113	14.12% *The Book of Mormon* 2 Nephi 6: p. 83 [9:50–53]
By means of small conduits contrived in these buildings,	Come, my brethren, every one that thirsteth,
streams of	come ye to the waters;
	and he that hath no money, come buy and eat; yea, come buy
wine, milk, honey,	wine and milk
and some of pure water, were seen to flow in every direction.	without money and without price.
. . . Mahomet having promised	. . . Hearken diligently unto me, and remember the words which I have spoken;
to those who should obey his will	and come unto the Holy One of Israel, and
the enjoyments of Paradise,	feast upon that which perish not,

166

14.81% *The Travels of Marco Polo* Book I, Ch. XXI, p. 112–113	14.12% *The Book of Mormon* 2 Nephi 6: p. 83 [9:50–53]
where every species of	neither can be corrupted, let your soul
sensual gratification	delight in fatness.
should be found	
The chief [Alo-eddin] thereupon addressing them, said:	Behold, my beloved brethren,
"we have the assurances of our Prophet	remember the words of your God;
that he who defends his lord shall inherit paradise,	pray unto him continually........Let your hearts rejoice,
and if you shew yourselves devoted to the	and behold how great the
obedience of my orders,	covenants of the Lord,
	... he hath promised to us that our seed shall not utterly be destroyed ...
that happy lot awaits you."	they shall become a righteous branch unto the house of Israel.

After reading page 112 of *Marco Polo*, Meredith Sheets calculated the percentage location of page 112, which was 100 × 112 ÷ 756 = 14.81 percent through the book. With this in mind, the best place to start looking for the same story in *The Book of Mormon* would be at 588 pages multiplied by 14.81% (588 × .1481), which resulted in page eighty-seven. Then he searched *The Book of Mormon* around page eighty-seven for the key words *wine, milk, honey,* and *pure water*. It is no random occurrence that this was exactly where he found the tale in *The Book of Mormon*. The difference between the appearances of these two stories, with the following key words, is 0.69 percent.

	Marco Polo, 14.81%	Joseph Smith, 14.12%
1	streams	waters
2	wine, milk	wine and milk
3	Mahomet having promised	remember the words

4	enjoyments of paradise	feast upon that which perish not
5	sensual gratification	delight in fatness
6	The chief addressing them	Behold my beloved brethren
7	assurances of our Prophet	words of your God
8	obedience of my orders	covenants of the Lord

The King's Son Who Would Not Take the Crown, or Buddha and the Sons of Mosiah[83]

Marco Polo said this about the island of Zeilan and the story about whom we in the West call "Buddha" (Figures 41 and 42).

The story of Buddha explains that he was a son of a king who would not accept the crown. He fled and ascended (went up to) the lofty mountain to live the rest of his austere life "in the observance of celibacy and strict abstinence." His father the king could not persuade the prince to return and rule the people.

In "The Book of Mosiah," on pages 215 and 216, Joseph Smith described the sons of King Mosiah, who also refused the crown. Let's compare these two stories, which could not involve two more seemingly different religions. The one about *Sogomon-barchan* (the Buddha) in Marco Polo's book appears at 88.49 to 88.62 percent (pp. 669–670), and the other, about the sons of Mosiah in *The Book of Mormon*, is on page 36.73 percent (p. 216). While the percentages take us to different places in the books, whatever differs from the Buddha is absorbed by the king of Mosiah.

Some initial observations: Instead of observing celibacy and strict abstinence like the Buddha, Mosiah's sons were the "very vilest of sinners" like Buddha's father; however, the sons eventually devoted themselves to "prayer, and fasting." The sons went "up to the land" of Nephi to "preach the word." In the same story, Mosiah had "plates of gold," which had ancient records engraved on them. Smith's story spills over into the next chapter, called the "Book of Alma." There the high priest of Zarahemla, named Alma, happens to run into Mosiah's sons while on his own journey. Like the island king's son, Mosiah's sons would not accept the crown of the kingdom.

I AM unwilling to pass over certain particulars which I omitted when before speaking of the island of *Zeilan,* and which I learned when I visited that country in my homeward voyage.[1352]   In this island there is a very high mountain, so rocky and precipitous that the ascent to the top is impracticable, as it is said, excepting by the assistance of iron chains employed for that purpose.   By means of these some persons attain the summit, where the tomb of *Adam,* our first parent, is reported to be found.   Such is the account given by the Saracens.[1353]   But the idolaters assert that it contains the body of *Sogomon-barchan,* the founder of their religious system, and whom they revere as a holy personage.[1354]   He was the son of a king of the island, who devoted himself to an ascetic life ; refusing to accept of kingdoms or any other worldly possession, although his father endeavoured, by the allurements of beauty and every other imaginable gratification, to divert him from the resolution he had adopted.[1355]   Every attempt to dissuade him was in vain, and the young man fled privately to this lofty mountain, where, in the observance of celibacy and strict abstinence, he at length

terminated his mortal career.[1356]   By the idolaters he is regarded as a saint.   The father, distracted with the most poignant grief, caused an image to be formed of gold and precious stones, bearing the resemblance of his son, and required that all the inhabitants of the island should honour and worship it as a deity.   Such was the origin of the worship of idols in that country ; but *Sogomon-barchan* is still regarded as superior to every other.   In consequence of this belief, people flock from various distant parts, in pilgrimage to the mountain on which he was buried.   Some of his hair, his teeth, and the bason he made use of, are still preserved, and shewn with much ceremony.   The Saracens, on the other hand, maintain that these belonged to the prophet Adam, and are in like manner led by devotion to visit the mountain.[1357]

Figures 41 & 42. Marsden, *Marco Polo,* 669 & 670

Later, Smith added to the story. He waited until he was receiving "revelations" after publication of *The Book of Mormon,* which you can find in the *Doctrine and Covenants,* to show that men can become gods or attain deity (which will be discussed in this book in the chapter on religion.) That addition to Smith's story brought his religious doctrine more in line with the worship of Buddha.

The Travels of Marco Polo Chapter XXIII of the island of Zeilan, pp. 669–670	The Book of Mormon Mosiah 12: pp. 215–216, and Alma 12: pp. 269–270
[King's Son or Sons]	
He was the son of a king . . . his father	. . . sons of Mosiah . . . returned to their father, the king . . .
[Fled to Mountain/Go "Up" to a Land]	
young man fled privately to this lofty mountain	. . . they [sons] did plead with their father many days, that they might go up to the land of Nephi.
[King's Son Abstinent and Smiths' King's Sons Devoted]	
who devoted himself to an ascetic life	. . . they had given themselves to much prayer, and fasting, therefore they had the spirit of prophecy . . .

Since the Smiths rearranged the words and phrases of Marco Polo's story, we copied the medieval traveler's account in the order that it appears. They also changed some of the details, such as Buddha's climbing a mountain and Mosiah's sons' going into the "wilderness."

[King Did Not Want Son To Go Up to the Land/Mountain]	
his father endeavored, by the allurements of beauty and every other imaginable gratification, to divert him from the resolution he had adopted. Every attempt to dissuade him was in vain. . . .	that they did plead with their father many days, that they might go up to the land of Nephi
[Son Traveled to the Mountain/Wilderness]	
the young man fled privately to this lofty mountain	. . . Mosiah granted that they might go . . . and they took their journey into the wilderness

[King's Son or Sons Refused To Be King]

refusing to	Now king Mosiah had no one to confer the kingdom upon, for there was not any of his sons which would
accept of kingdoms	accept of the kingdom . . .
or any other worldly possession.	(Mosiah 12: p. 216 [28:10])
(see above, "refusing to accept of kingdoms")	. . . having refused the kingdom
	which their father [Mosiah] was desirous to confer upon them . . .
	(Alma 12: p. 269 [17:6])

[Endured Hardships]

in the observance of celibacy and strict abstinence	. . . ye shall be patient in long suffering and afflictions . . . that ye may shew forth good examples . . . (Alma 12: p. 270 [17:11])

[Gold and Precious Stones]

caused an image to be formed of	. . . and their hearts were set upon riches, or upon
gold and precious stones	gold, and silver, and precious stones . . . (Alma 12: p. 270)

[Son Revered as Holy Saint/Sons Bretheren in the Lord]

. . . . . . the idolaters assert . . . the	. . . . . . Alma was journeying. . . . . . he met with the sons of Mosiah . . . to his joy,
founder of their religious system, and whom they revere as a holy personage.	they were still his brethren in the Lord; yea, and
By the idolaters he is regarded as a saint.	they had waxed strong in the knowledge of the truth . . . they might know the word of God.

[Worship Idols]

Such was the origin of the	. . . thus they were a very indolent people, many of whom did
worship of idols.	worship idols. (Alma 12: p. 270)

An unexpected reference is common to both stories: The original Adam, as in Adam and Eve, is completely unrelated to the Buddha or to the internal theme of princes refusing to accept the kingship. Polo said that the Saracens on Zeilan believed that the body buried on the mountain was not Buddha's but Adam's, and the Smiths also copied a reference to Adam into their story.

By the means of these some persons attain the summit, where the tomb of	. . . and they were scattered abroad upon the face of all the earth, yea, even from that time until the
Adam, our first parent,	creation of Adam.
is reported to be found . . . the Saracens . . . maintained that these belonged to the prophet Adam.	(Mosiah 12: p. 216)

An example of attaining a more sophisticated level of plagiarism comes when the Smiths integrated parts of the footnotes from the 1818 *Marco Polo* book into Mosiah. Editor William Marsden wrote the footnotes in or shortly before the year 1818; they are not the work of Marco Polo in medieval times. Recall from our comparison of Buddha's traveling to the mountain with Mosiah's sons' going into the "wilderness." From that discrepancy, you might think you're reading two unrelated stories. In footnote 1356 on page 672, however, the difference in words falls away. Marsden writes a historical account of the Buddha regarding the son's leaving the king, which contains the quote below:

[Son Traveled to the Mountain/Wilderness]	
"The king, reflecting &c. said, 'O Son . . . What dost thou in this wilderness?'"	Mosiah granted that they might go . . . and they took their journey into the wilderness

The Smiths further demonstrate advanced skills when they mention a "seer." After King Mosiah learns that his sons will not accept the kingdom, he begins to translate writings on gold plates by means of "those two stones which were fastened into the two rims of a bow." (Mosiah 12: p. 216) The story says that ". . . whosoever has these things, is called seer, after the manner of old times." The word *seer* is found elsewhere in Marco Polo's book ("kings of Seer" on page 734), but within the Buddha story is another footnote from William Marsden. This one reads:

> 1354. By the holy personage here described is meant *Buddha*, the founder of the religious system of the Singalese, who amongst a number of appellations given to him, from his supposed attributes, is most commonly known by that of *Saka* or *Sakya-muni*, signifying the "astute sage." . . . he was styled *Saka-muni-burcham*, here corrupted to *Sogo-mon-barchan* . . . There is another great god . . . whom they call *Buddou*, unto whom the salvation of the souls belong.[84]

The idea of an "astute sage" in the Buddha story inspired the Smiths to insert the "seer" into the same story. Smith claimed to receive a revelation in 1831 that the president of the Church is to be a "Seer a revelator a translator and a prophet" as part of his gifts from God.[85] Joseph's self-title of "Seer" and his prolific use of a magic stone to see gold would have been further motivated by Carsten Niebuhr's encounter with the Arab's occult practices of "Sihhr" and the use of a "philosopher's stone," which was used to turn metal into gold.[86]

Pay the Fifth

In his collection of travellers' books, Editor Robert Kerr included the account of the conquest of Mexico written by one of Cortes's captains, Bernal Diaz.[87] In the opening chapters, Cortes is moving inland from the coast and visiting an Indian tribe that paid tribute to Montezuma. Hearing that the tribe's "cacique" was upset about the high tribute he had to pay, Cortes concocted a plot to gain the loyalty of the oppressed tribe by taking prisoner Montezuma's tax collectors.

At ten o'clock the following morning, we entered the fortified town of Chiahuitztla. . . . We advanced to the middle of the city . . . fifteen persons in rich dresses came to meet Cortes . . . received notice of the cacique of Chempoalla . . . in a litter, in which he was carried by his principal nobles. On the arrival *he and the chiefs of Chiahuitztla, made bitter complaints of the tyranny of Montezuma* over the whole district of Totonacas, which contained thirty towns, having engrossed all the gold, and *oppressed them by heavy tributes* by taking away their sons for sacrifices to idols and their daughters as slaves. . . .[88]

The Smiths convert the Mexican tax collectors into Ammon, a Lamanite, and the three Lamanite brothers seized by the king. "The Book of Mosiah" switches the characters around a bit, such as where Ammon complains to the king about high taxes, but the local chief of Chempoalla complained to Cortes. The Chempoallans become sworn to follow Cortes and the king of Spain. They gain the advantage of stopping payment of "heavy tributes" to Montezuma, whereas Ammon swears allegiance to the Nephite king and declares it is better to be a Nephite slave than to pay tax to the Lamanites.

The Conquest of Mexico, by Bernal Diaz, (Kerr, pp. 488–490)	"Book of Mosiah" Ch. 5: pp. 168–170 [7:6–18]
. . . and while they were thus conferring, notice was brought that five Mexican collectors of the tribute had just arrived. This intelligence greatly alarmed the natives	And Ammon took three of his brethren, and their names were **Amaleki, Helem, and Hem,** and they went down into the land of Nephi;
. . . they sent for the fat cacique of Chempoalla and the chiefs of Chiahuitztla, whom they severely reprimanded for having received and entertained us.	and behold, they met the king of the people, which was in the land of Nephi, and in the land of Shilom;
(p. 489) But Cortes made them to be seized, and ordered them to be fastened by the neck to some large staves and collars, like a pillory, so that they	and they were surrounded by the king's guard, and was taken, and was bound, and was committed to prison.

The Conquest of Mexico, by Bernal Diaz, (Kerr, pp. 488–490)	"Book of Mosiah" Ch. 5: pp. 168–170 [7:6–18]
were unable to move, even ordering one of them to be soundly beaten, who proved refractory . . . placing them under a	
guard of our soldiers.	[see "king's guard," above]
(p. 490) He made	And it came to pass when they had been in prison
two of them be	two days, they were again
brought before him [Cortes] at midnight, whom	brought before the king, and
he caused to be unbound; and, pretending ignorance of what happened,	their bands were loosed; and they stood before the king, and was permitted, or rather commanded that
he asked who they were and why they had been made prisoners.	they should answer the questions which he should ask them.
	And now, when Ammon saw that he was permitted to speak . . . for I am assured that if ye had known me, ye would not have suffered that I should have worn these bands. For I am Ammon, and am a descendant of Zarahemla,
They answered that they were Mexican officers,	and have come up out of the land of Zarahemla, to inquire concerning our brethren, whom Zeniff brought up out of that land.
who had been made prisoners by the chiefs of that town by his encouragement.	
(p. 489) On his arrival [the fat cacique of Chempoalla] he and the chiefs of Chiahuiztla, made bitter complaints of the	
tyranny of Montezuma over the whole district of Totonacas . . . having engrossed all the gold, and	For behold, we are in bondage to the Lamanites, and are

The Conquest of Mexico, by Bernal Diaz, (Kerr, pp. 488–490)	"Book of Mosiah" Ch. 5: pp. 168–170 [7:6–18]
oppressed them by heavy tributes, but particularly by taking away their sons for sacrifices to the idols, and their daughters as slaves.	taxed with a tax which is grievous to be borne.
[The Chempoallans] likewise at this time entered into	And now, behold, our brethren will deliver us out of our bondage, or out of the hands of the Lamanites, and
promise of allegiance to the king of Spain, of which a formal instrument was drawn upon before	we will be their slaves:
the royal notary . . . to the great joy of the natives for being relieved from the vexatious exactions of the Mexican officers.	for it is better that we be slaves to the Nephites, than to pay tribute to the king of the Lamanites.
(p. 490) He [Cortes] pretended to know nothing of the matter, and expressed sorrow for what had befallen them.	
[He promised likewise to set their companions free, and to reprimand the caciques for their conduct.]	And now, king Limhi commanded his guards that they should no more bind Ammon, nor his brethren, but caused that they should go to the hill which was north of Shilom, and bring their brethren into the city, that thereby
Then ordering food to be given them, he treated them kindly, and desired them to inform Montezuma, that he was exceedingly desirous of becoming his friend and servant, and that he was much displeased with the Totonacas for having used them ill.	they might eat, and drink, and rest themselves from the labors of their journey; for they had suffered many things: they had suffered hunger, thirst, and fatigue.
With a cheerful countenance,	. . . when they had gathered themselves together, that he spake
Cortes assured them that	unto them in this wise . . . the time is at hand, or is not far
he and his valiant companions would defend them from all attacks of the Mexicans; and the caciques, in return,	distant, when we shall no longer be in subjection to our enemies, notwithstanding our many strugglings, which

The Conquest of Mexico, by Bernal Diaz, (Kerr, pp. 488–490)	"Book of Mosiah" Ch. 5: pp. 168–170 [7:6–18]
engaged to support us with all their forces.	have been in vain; yet I trust there remaineth an effectual struggle to be made.

Taxation issues seem to be important in the Nephite kingdoms. In the line of rulers in the land of "Nephi," Zeniff conferred his kingdom to Noah, one of his three sons. King Noah turned from God and indulged in "many wives and concubines" and caused the people to commit "whoredoms and all manner of wickedness." To underwrite this lavish lifestyle, he levied a tax. During his research, Kendal Sheets discovered that once again the Smiths turned to the story of the conquest of Mexico and Captain Diaz for this topic. It was General Cortes who kept the king's law of paying a fifth of the bounty back to the Spanish monarch as a tax. The plagiarists also found the "pay the fifth" tax mentioned in *Modern Traveller* by James Duncan, which matches better to the payment of gold and silver:

The Modern Traveller, Mexico and Guatemala, by James Duncan (1825)	"Book of Mosiah" Ch. 5: pp. 178 [11:3]
A fifth of the whole was set apart as the tax due to the king. Another fifth was allowed to Cortes as commander. (p. 57)	And [King Noah] laid a tax of one fifth part of all they possessed;
[The Spaniards then collected all the treasure . . . and having melted the gold and silver . . .]	a fifth part of their gold and of their silver,
Conquest of Mexico by Bernal Diaz (Robert Kerr, 1811)	
When they came to pay the **fifth** for the **copper axes** (. . . Kerr, Vol. 3, 431) On making the division, Cortes in the first place, **caused a fifth to be laid** aside for his majesty; secondly, a **fifth** for himself, as had been agreed upon . . . (Kerr, Vol. 4, 72)	and a **fifth** part of their ziff, and of their **copper**, and of their brass and their iron; and a **fifth** part of their fatlings; and also a **fifth** part of all their grain.

Kings and Judges

Both Zarahemla and Mexico (prior to the conquest) were ruled by a king or dictator who rose to power in a special type of election. In "The Book of Mosiah," King Mosiah wanted the people to choose his successor:

> Now when Mosiah had done this, he sent out throughout all the land, among all the people, desiring to know their will concerning who should be their king. And it came to pass that the voice of the people came, saying: We are desirous that Aaron, thy son, should be our king, and our ruler. (Mosiah 8: p. 217 [29:2])

"The Book of Helaman" reads "For as their laws and governments were established by the voice of the people . . ." (Helaman 2, p. 417 [5:2]) In *The Modern Traveller*, Duncan wrote "Montezuma II . . . acceded to the throne by unanimous election in 1502," and "Up to 1352, the Mexicans were governed by a species of aristocracy; but a monarch was then elected, whose whole dominions, however, were comprehended in the city."[89]

During King Montezuma's imprisonment by the Spanish soldiers, Cortes kept using him to quell the rebellions that were continually arising in the empire against the invaders. After about six months, the nobles in the empire gave up on the idea of rescuing their emperor and elected a new ruler. After Montezuma was killed, Bernal Diaz noted that "About this period, Cuitlahuitzin, who had been elected sovereign of Mexico in place of his brother Montezuma, died of the small-pox, and Quaubtemotzin, or Gautimotzin, was chosen in his stead, a young man of twenty-five years of age, of fine appearance, exceedingly brave, and so terrible to his subjects that every one trembled at his sight."[90]

The land of Zarahemla was ruled by kings, including Mosiah, Benjamin, and Noah, and also by "judges." Alma was the first judge:

> And it came to pass that Alma was appointed to be the chief judge; he being also the high priest; his father having conferred the office on him,

and had given him the charge concerning all the affairs of the church. (Mosiah 13: p. 220 [29:42])

Much is written in *The Book of Mormon* about Zarahemla's judges, but the two types of governments—civil and dictator or military rule—are basically what happened in Mexico before and after the Spanish conquest. Montezuma had his own judges in his court and also at the market, but they never ruled the empire:

> Four ancient nobles, who were his relations and served as councillors and judges, stood beside the throne.[91]

Montezuma had his own judges at the market as well:

> In the midst of the great square is a house which I shall *call l'Audiencia, in which ten or twelve persons sit constantly for determining any disputes* which may arise respecting the sale of goods. There are other persons who mix continually with the crowd, to see that a just price is asked.[92]

After the conquest, Cortes was a de facto ruler for a time, after which the Spanish crown set up a civil government ruled by a governor and a "tribunal" with judges:

> While Cortes remained in Spain, the members of the court of royal audience arrived in Mexico. Of this court, Nuno de Guzman, who had been governor of Panuco, was president; the *four oydors or judges being the* licentiates. . . . These magistrates had greater powers than had hiterhto been confided to any officers in New Spain."[93]

The Modern Traveller tells us:

> Cortes continued to exercise all the powers of a governor till, in 1522, he was invested with that appointment by the emperor. The court

of Spain manifested, however, their distrust of his loyalty, and jealousy of his abilities, by the most ungenerous and vexatious proceedings. In 1528, Cortes eluded a commission of inquiry only by returning to Spain; and though he succeeded in re-instating himself in the emperor's favour, and obtained as the reward of his services the title of marquess, the order of St. Jago, . . . he came back to Mexico, in 1530, with diminished authority. The *civil jurisdiction was now separated from the military command* . . . and while he was allowed to retain the situation of commander-in-chief, the *civil affairs* were henceforth administered by the *audienza real*."[94]

The rising Nephite kingdom mimics this form of government by using civil-law judges to rule alongside prophets, monarchs, or military commanders. The Smiths even textually copied Bernal Diaz's notes of having "wise, just" men as judges:

Conquest of Mexico Kerr, Vol. IV, p. 305	"Book of Mosiah" Ch. 13: pp. 217–218 [29:11, 28]
In consequence of the injustice of the former court of audience, his majesty was pleased to suppress it, and to cancel all its grants, and to	Therefore I will be your king the remainder of my days; nevertheless, let us **appoint judges**, to judge this people according to our law, and we will
appoint a new one consisting of	**newly arrange** the affairs of this people; for we will **appoint**
wise and upright men.	**wise men to be judges,**
Of this new tribunal . . . the oyders or judges . . . the new judges were wise and just,	
regulating their conduct entirely	that will judge this people
according to the will of God . . .	according to the commandments of God.

The judicial system for New Spain included the right of appeal to a higher court in the mother country. The Nephite law also provided for an appeals court:

Conquest of Mexico Kerr, Vol. IV, p. 305	"Book of Mosiah" p. 219 [29:11, 28]
He was accordingly summoned to appear, which he did not think proper to do, and it was judged proper to refer the whole affair for the present to the supreme court in Spain.	And now if ye have judges, and they do not judge you according to the law which has been given, ye can cause that they may be judged of a higher judge . . .

Abinadi and the Rise of the Prophets

One of the well-known stories to Latter-day Saints is of Abinadi, a prophet who lived during King Noah's reign. King Noah ruled the land of Nephi while King Mosiah and King Benjamin ruled Zarahemla. Abinadi went forth among the Nephites and began to prophesy:

> . . . Behold, thus saith the Lord, and thus hath he commanded me, saying, Go forth and say unto this people, thus saith the Lord: Wo be unto this people, for I have seen their abominations, and their wickedness, and their whoredoms; and except they repent, I will visit them in mine anger. (Mosiah 7: p. 179 [11:20]).

A few pages later Abinadi upsets King Noah by preaching against the king's hypocrisy. Abinadi was imprisoned after the king ordered, ". . . Away with this fellow, and slay him: for what have we to do with him, for he is mad." (Mosiah 7: p. 183 [13:1]). This accusation of madness by a ruler of an imprisoned prophet sounded very familiar. But it didn't come out of any source books for the Americas. Remember Ludovico Verthema, the Italian in Arabia whom Lehi mimicked in the trek along the Red Sea? The Smiths switched back to that sourcebook for the tale of Abinadi.

When Verthema reached Aden on the southwest coast of Arabia, he was thrown into prison by the local Muslim sultan for the crime of being a Christian. He plotted his escape by pretending to be a Mohametan and feigning madness. The story of Abinadi is copied from Robert Kerr's 1812 book. The plot skips around a bit in chapter seven of the "Book of Mosiah," so we added some narrative between the scenes and included citations after each quote.

Voyages and Travels in . . . Arabia . . . by Ludovico Verthema Kerr Vol. 7, pp. 68–73	"The Book of Mosiah" Ch. 7, pp. 179–182
The day after our arrival at Aden, the Mahometans **took me prisoner**, and put shackles on my legs in consequence of	. . . he [Abinadi] went forth among them, and began to prophesy, saying, Behold, thus saith the Lord, and thus hath he commanded me . . . (p. 179) . . . when **king Noah** had heard of the words . . . he was
an idolater calling after me that I was a Christian dog.	also wroth; and he saith, Who is Abinadi . . . or who is the Lord . . . (p. 180)
Upon this the Mahometans laid hold of me, and	. . . **they were angry with him**; and they **took him** and
carried me before the lieutenant of the sultan, who assembled his council, to consult with them	**carried him bound before the king,** and saith unto the king, Behold, we have brought a man before thee which has prophesied evil concerning thy people . . . (p. 181)
if I should be put to death as a Christian spy.	. . . they were wroth with him, and sought to **take away his life;**
The sultan happened to be absent from the city, and as the lieutenant had not hitherto adjudged any one to death, **he did not think fit to give sentence against me** till my case were reported to the sultan. **By this means, I escaped the present danger,** and remained in prison 55 days . . .	
. . . But **God assisted me,** for the master of the prison made fast its gates, that these outrageous men might not offer me violence.	but the **Lord delivered him out of their hands.** [p. 180 [11:26–27])
On the **second day** of my confinement . . .	. . . after the space of **two years,** that Abinadi came among them in disguise, that they knew him not . . . (p. 180 [12:1])

Voyages and Travels in . . . Arabia . . . by Ludovico Verthema Kerr Vol. 7, pp. 68–73	"The Book of Mosiah" Ch. 7, pp. 179–182
many Mahometans went in great rage to the lieutenant to demand that I should be put to death as a Portuguese spy.	["they were wroth with him, and sought to take away his life" (p. 180 [11:26–27])]
Only a few days before, these men had difficulty escaped from the hands of Portuguese by swimming, with loss of their foists and barks, and therefore greatly desired to be revenged of the Christians, outrageously affirming that I was Portuguese and a spy.	. . . this man hast lied concerning you, and he hath prophesied in vain. And behold, we are strong, we shall not come into bondage, or be taken captive by our enemies . . . . Behold, here is the man, we deliver him into thy hands . . . (p. 181 [12:15–16])]
The sultan happened to be absent from the city . . . I . . .	. . . king Noah caused that Abinadi should be
remained in prison 55 days . . .	cast into prison;
carried me before the lieutenant of the sultan, who	and he commanded that the priests should gather themselves together, that he might
assembled his council . . .	hold a council with them what he should do with him. (pp. 181–182 [12:17]) . . . they saith unto the king, Bring him hither, that we may question him. And the
At the end of fifty-five days,	
the sultan sent for me into his presence; so I was placed on the back of a camel with my shackels . . . When I was brought before the sultan,	king commanded that he should be brought before them.
he asked me what I was:	And they began to question him, that they might cross him, that thereby they might have wherewith to accuse him;
on which I answered that I was a Roman, and had professed myself a Mahometan and Marmeluke at Babylon in Egypt, or Cairo . . . that I was	but he answered them boldly, and withstood all their questions, yea, to their astonishment: for he did withstand them in all their

Voyages and Travels in . . . Arabia . . . by Ludovico Verthema Kerr Vol. 7, pp. 68–73	"The Book of Mosiah" Ch. 7, pp. 179–182
no Christian spy, but a true Mahometan, and his devoted slave.	questions, and did confound them in all their words.
That from motives of religion, and in discharge of a vow, I had made the pilgrimage to Medinathalhabi, to see the body of Nabi or holy prophet, and . . . the sultan . . . and I now gave thanks to God and his prophet that I had attained my wish . . .	And now Abinadi said unto them, Are you priests, and pretend to teach this people, and to understand the spirit of prophesying, and yet desire to know of me what these things mean? (p. 182)
The sultan then commanded me to say Leila illala Mahumet resullah, which words I could never well pronounce, either that it so pleased God, or because I durst not, from some fear or scruple of conscience. Where, seeing me silent, the sultan committed me again to prison . . . (p. 70)	And they said, We teach the law of Moses. (p. 182)
Wherefore, seeing me silent, the sultan committed me again to prison	And now when the king had heard these words, he said unto his priests, Away with this fellow, and
. . . and it was agreed one of us	slay him: for what have we to do with him,
should counterfeit madness . . . as they consider mad men to be holy . . . until such time as the hermits might determine whether	
I were holy mad, or raging mad . . .	for he is mad.
When it was rumoured abroad that I had lived two days and nights	. . . after Abinadi had spoken these words that the people of king Noah
without meat or drink, some began to believe that I was a holy madman . . .	durst not lay their hands on him; for the Spirit of the Lord was upon him . . . (p. 183)
but the queen saw all this from her window, and laughed heartily at it among her maids, saying,	But there was one among them, whose name was Alma, he also being a descendant of Nephi. And he was a young man, and he

Voyages and Travels in . . . Arabia . . . by Ludovico Verthema Kerr Vol. 7, pp. 68–73	"The Book of Mosiah" Ch. 7, pp. 179–182
"By the head of Mahomet this is a good man."	believed the words which Abinadi had spoken, for he knew concerning the iniquity which Abinadi had testified against them:
When the president of the city heard that the queen took so much delight in my mad frolic,	Therefore he began to plead with the king that he would not be angry with Abinadi,
he gave orders that I might go at liberty about the palace.	but suffer that he might depart in peace. (p. 190)

In the original story, the "madman" Verthema escaped to India on a merchant ship after visiting many holy hermits in the mountains around Aden. Abinadi, however, suffered a different although odd-sounding fate. He was "scourged" with "faggots [sic]." There is another story where Christians died from "faggots," which appears in the 1825 *Modern Traveller, Arabia*. In this account, Christians were thrown into a trench and burned alive:

In consequence . . . of their having subsequently slain some Jews, because they would not turn Christians, Zu Nowauss, himself a Jew, invaded their territory with a	. . . the king caused that his guards should surround Abinadi, and take him; and they bound him and cast him into prison.
powerful army, and having taken their city, massacred 6,000 of the Christians of Nedjeraun, by throwing them in a trench filled with burning faggots and other combustibles.(Duncan, *Modern Traveller*, Arabia, 38)	And it came to pass that they took him and bound him, and scourged his skin with faggots, yea, even unto death. (Mosiah 9, pp. 190–191 [17:13])

The story about the rise of the Nephites was inspired by a variety of explorers: Columbus, Polo, Cortes, and Verthema. But the path to Zarahemla has only one route: the road to Mexico.

Chalco

✦ 10 ✦

THE ROAD TO MEXICO

Welcome to Mesoamerica.

Lehi's family left Jerusalem in approximately 600 BC and some years later arrived in the Promised Land. Centuries passed, and civilizations flourished and then died. Now our players in *The Book of Mormon* are the Nephites and the Lamanites, the descendants of Nephi and his brother Laman, respectively.

After starting out in the Holy Land, Joseph Smith Sr. and Joseph Smith Jr. needed a new backdrop for their story. How would they decide where to set this section of *The Book of Mormon*? The father's and son's narrative could have taken place anywhere; the whole Western Hemisphere was open to them. They might have decided on Upstate New York, for example, near Camorah Hill, where the angel Moroni ostensibly buried the plates found by Joseph Smith Jr. Or the locale could have been, say, Florida or Virginia or Massachusetts.

Where to go? Where to go . . . ?

Using three prerequisites, they whittled down their geographical options. First, they needed details of the area for authenticity; second, these details had to come from personal accounts so the eyewitnesses' adventures could be applied to the Smiths' plot action; and third, the reference books had to be available to them but unknown to their followers.

Exactly as they had done for Lehi's travels across Arabia, the Smiths researched pre-1830s books about the ancient Americas—books they felt certain their followers would not have read. The result? The plagiarists plunked their characters down in Mexico.

Combining historical facts and personal accounts, the Smiths invented a land and a city called "Zarahemla." The land of Zarahemla appears in the inner chapters of *The Book of Mormon*—the Books of Omni, Mosiah, Alma, Helaman, Third Nephi, Fourth Nephi, Mormon, and Ether.

According to the plagiarists, the city of Zarahemla was the capital of the Nephites from approximately 280 BC to 350 AD. When the Nephites first arrived there in 280 BC, they found a more ancient Hebrew tribe, the Mulekites, already living in the city. These Jews had left Jerusalem at the time when Zedekiah, the king of Judah, was captured and made prisoner in Babylon.

According to "The Book of Ether," another people had lived on the site, *well* before the "people of Zarahemla." The Jaredites—who supposedly came to the land of promise at the time of the destruction of the Tower of Babel—had resided there.

The people of Zarahemla joined with the Nephites and swore allegiance to their king, Mosiah.

The name *Zarahemla* may stem from *zara*, which is Arabic for "desert" (so noted in the 1825 edition of the *Modern Traveller, Arabia*) and from Xaragua, Hispaniola, a Spanish settlement mentioned in Robert Kerr's 1811 *History of the Discovery of America, by Christopher Columbus; Written by his Son Don Ferdinand Columbus*—another sourcebook for the Smiths.

The Smiths used the facts of their day to write stories of the vast civilization of Zarahemla and wars between the Nephites and the Lamanites. The inspiration for the Nephites and Lamanites was the Spanish conquistadores and the Aztec Indians. Hernan Cortes's small army, all devout Christians, battled the idol-worshipping and human-sacrificing Aztecs.

The Smiths transformed that into the Christian Nephites battling the idol-worshipping and human-sacrificing Lamanites. As the Smiths' story unfolded and the need arose, the roles changed back and forth; the good guys became the bad guys, and the bad guys became the good guys.

In preaching Jesus to the Lamanites, the Nephites take on the role of Cortes and the Spanish Catholic priests who proselytized the Indians. To construct this fictional civilization, including such details as roads, buildings, and cities, the Smiths used the Mexican and Tartar societies as the models for the Nephites. During battle, the Nephites and Lamanites become a mix of the Tartar, Spanish, and Mexican armies.

This chapter focuses on the geographical similarities between *The Book of Mormon*'s Zarahemla and the reference books available to Joseph Smith Sr. and Joseph Smith Jr. before they composed *The Book of Mormon*. As in the previous chapters, we will see that the Smiths employed their favorite modus operandi, this time using the journals and letters written by men who vanquished the indigenous people of Mexico in the 1500s and by travelers who explored Mexico and Latin America in the centuries after. Numerous books published before 1830 offered factual information about the Aztecs and the history of Mexico. Some books included maps of Tenochtitlan—present-day Mexico City—which the Smiths would have found extremely useful.

The Joseph Smiths had had good luck with two travel series while writing Lehi's travels across Arabia. They had plumbed editor Robert Kerr's *General History and Collection of Voyages and Travels, Volume III*. Other books in Kerr's collection, Volumes III–IV, contained the firsthand account of Captain Bernal Diaz, who traveled across Mexico in the 1500s. Kerr's books were published in Edinburgh in 1811 and 1812[95] (Figure 43).

While writing about Lehi's journey through the wilderness, the plagiarists had found eminently usable information in William Marsden's *The Travels of Marco Polo* and in editor James Duncan's *Modern Traveller, Arabia*. Another volume in Duncan's series included summaries of historical writings about Mexico and Guatemala. John Pinkerton, another familiar name from the Smiths' Arabia material, made a contribution to Senior's and Junior's decisions.

Kerr's book contained a marvelous, original eyewitness account of Hernan Cortes's march inland from Mexico's eastern shore to Tenochtitlan.

A
GENERAL HISTORY
AND
COLLECTION
OF
VOYAGES AND TRAVELS.

PART II.

BOOK II. CONTINUED.

CHAPTER V.

HISTORY OF THE DISCOVERY AND CONQUEST OF MEXICO, WRITTEN IN THE YEAR 1568, BY CAPTAIN BERNAL DIAZ DEL CASTILLO, ONE OF THE CONQUERORS.—*Continued.*

SECTION VI.

The Spaniards commence their March to Mexico; with an account of the War in Tlascala, and the submission of that Nation.

EVERY thing being in readiness for our march to Mexico, we were advised by our allies of Chempoalla to proceed by way of Tlascala, the inhabitants of that province being in friendship with them and constantly at war with the Mexicans; and at our requisition, we were joined by fifty of the principal warriors of the Totanacas [1], who likewise gave us

VOL. IV. PART I.   A   200

---

1 Clavigero says that Cortes had some troops of the Totanacas, among whom were forty nobles, serving at the same time as auxiliaries, and as hostages for the fidelity of their nation.—Clavig. II. 30.

Figure 43. Kerr, *Voyages and Travels*, Vol. 4, 1

Captain Bernal Diaz was an officer in Cortes's small army of 508 conquistadores. You were introduced to his memoir of the *Conquest of Mexico* in the account of Cortes and the tax collectors.

Diaz's detailed descriptions of the Aztec empire's land and people were precisely what the Smiths wanted. His writings became the blueprint for *The Book of Mormon*'s Zarahemla.

Most followers of the Mormon churches believe the land of Zarahemla was located somewhere in Latin America. This is mainly due to the fact that years after *The Book of Mormon* was published, Joseph Jr. himself wrote in a church newspaper that ancient cities discovered in Mesoamerica were the cities of the Nephites.

James Duncan's book *The Modern Traveller, A Popular Description, Geographical, Historical, and Topographical, of the Various Countries of the Globe. Mexico and Guatimala*, Volumes I and II, was published in 1825, which was years prior to the completion of the Smith's *Book-of-Mormon* manuscript.[96] Duncan frequently referenced Bernal Diaz's story of the conquest of Mexico as well as other Spanish and American authors. His compilation included a map of Mexico. The cover page and table of contents are reproduced below (Figures 44 and 45).

Duncan also included a map of Mexico and Mesoamerica, which would have proved very helpful to the Smiths (Figure 46).

Despite the wealth of information available to the Smiths, there is some confusion regarding the geography of the area. *The Book of Mormon* offers no landmarks as points of reference for Zarahemla, and conflicting statements are perplexing. For example, Junior wrote in *The Book of Mormon* that Camorah Hill was part of the land of Zarahemla. How could that be possible when the prophet pinpointed the location of Camorah in Upstate New York? The geography of Zarahemla seems to be, for lack of a better term, all over the map ... except that no map exists in *The Book of Mormon*.

Why did the father and son decide against including a map of Zarahemla in their sacred book? Did they not want followers to compare their own maps and drawings to those of Kerr, Duncan, and others? If so, why not? Because they would have been identical to their sourcebooks?

THE

MODERN TRAVELLER.

A

POPULAR DESCRIPTION,

GEOGRAPHICAL, HISTORICAL, AND TOPOGRAPHICAL,

OF THE

VARIOUS COUNTRIES OF THE GLOBE.

MEXICO AND GUATIMALA.

VOL. I.

LONDON:

PRINTED FOR JAMES DUNCAN;

OLIVER AND BOYD, EDINBURGH; M. OGLE, GLASGOW;
AND R. M. TIMS, DUBLIN.

1825.

Figure 44. Duncan, *Modern Traveller*, Mexico, Title Page

CONTENTS

OF THE FIRST VOLUME.

MEXICO.

Figure 45. Duncan, *Modern Traveller*, Mexico, Contents Page

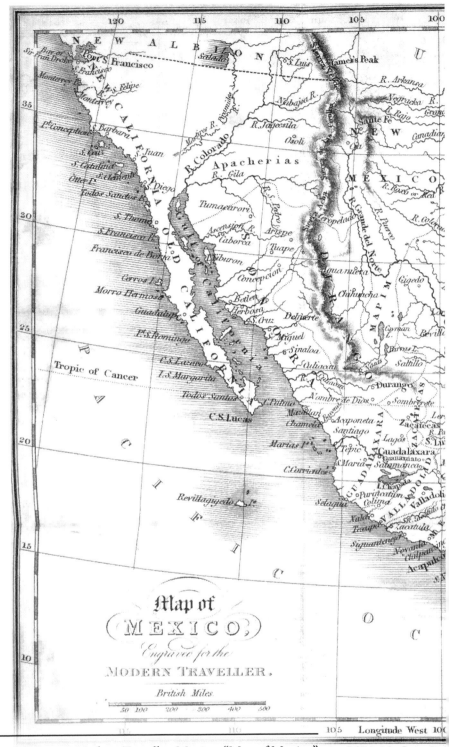

Figure 46. Duncan, *Modern Traveller*, Mexico, "Map of Mexico"

194

Or could it be that stealing stories is relatively simple to accomplish, but providing a map can create huge problems for a plagiarist? Pinpointing one specific location relative to another requires consistency and logic. Being vague sidesteps these issues.

Then there is this: if the Smiths had only elementary drawing ability, they could have copied rudimentary symbols but not maps (more about this later in the book). Under those circumstances, creating a map of Zarahemla would have forced them to engage the services of an artist. Very likely the Smiths couldn't risk bringing another man into their scheme, no matter how fine his artistic ability or sincere his promises of secrecy. Making use of scribes, as Joseph Smith Jr. did to write down his dictated *Book of Mormon*, presented no risk. One can speak words from one side of a curtain, and a scribe on the other side can commit them to paper. There is, however, no way a man hidden behind a curtain can describe to an artist how to draw a map.

Let's examine the Smiths' obfuscation a little more. Their geography for Zarahemla is vague except where it matches Tenochtitlan. This is another example of their strategy of "enlightened criticism"—including in their scriptures only material that could not be proved or disproved. Their writing encompasses pre-1825 reference materials about which their followers would know nothing. Books published after 1830, when *The Book of Mormon* was published, however, could be used as evidence to corroborate the Smiths' assertions. Next is a prime example.

In their story, Senior and Junior alluded to a "narrow neck" of land, a river named Sidon, and east and west seas. A number of other geographical elements are named, such as a land called Desolation located north of other general areas, an area to the south called Bountiful, and a wilderness. So where is the all-important Zarahemla in relation to those? Difficult to say, as the aforementioned sites have no landmarks, either.

We find the first references to Zarahemla in "The Book of Omni," Chapter 1 (p. 149 [1:12–1:13]):

Behold, I am Amaleki, the son of Abinadom. Behold, I will speak unto you somewhat concerning Mosiah, which *was made king over the land of Zarahemla*: for behold, he being warned of the Lord that he should flee out of the land of Nephi, and as many as would hearken unto the voice of the Lord, should also depart out of the land with him, into the wilderness.

And they were admonished continually by the word of God; and they were led by the power of his arm, through the wilderness, *until they came down into the land which is called the land of Zarahemla.*

So our first clue about its location is this: If travelers leave the land of Nephi and go through the wilderness, they will come *down* into the land of Zarahemla. It could therefore be located at the bottom of a mountain or in a valley or low-lying area. But how long did the journey take? A few days? A month? Years? We have no idea. We don't even know in which direction they traveled.

Editor Robert Kerr provides some help with an engraved plate of a map of the whole "Viceroyalty of Mexico" so the reader could follow the Spanish army's march across the Aztec empire (Figure 47).

The conquistador Diaz descended from a mountain into the Vale of Mexico where Tenochtitlan was built, so the Spaniard and the Smiths agree the journey takes them down from the heights. Should the Smiths' travelers turn around, they would trek through the wilderness and again find themselves in the land of Nephi. From Omni 1, p. 151 [1:27–1:29]:

And now I would speak somewhat *concerning a certain number which went up into the wilderness, to return to the land of Nephi*: for there was a large number who were desirous to possess the land of their inheritance; *wherefore, they went up into the wilderness.* And their leader being a strong and mighty man, and a stiffnecked man, wherefore, he caused a contention among them; and they were all slain, save fifty, in the wilderness, *and they returned again to the land of Zarahemla.*

And it came to pass that they also took others, to a considerable number, *and took their journey again into the wilderness.*

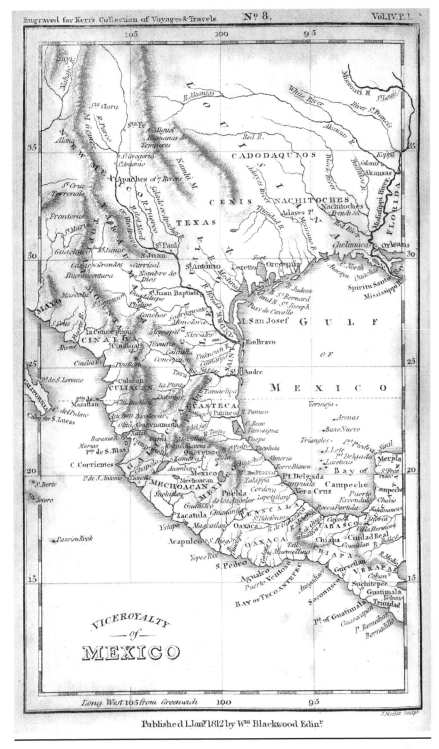

Figure 47. Kerr, *Voyages and Travels*, Vol. 4, "Viceroyalty of Mexico"

Forward and back: the land of Nephi → the wilderness → Zarahemla. Then Zarahemla → the wilderness → the land of Nephi. No specifics about direction or duration. That doesn't tell us anything.

The action returns to the land of Zarahemla in "The Book of Mosiah," with its many references to the land and the people. Using just the first four mentioned as examples (because extracting others will not deepen our understanding in any way) we find but one clue about Zarahemla's location.

And now there was no more contention in all the land of Zarahemla, among all the people who belonged to king Benjamin, so that king Benjamin had continual peace all the remainder of his days. (Mosiah 1, p. 153[1:1])

My son, I would that *ye should make a proclamation throughout all this land, among all this people, or the people of Zarahemla, and the people of Mosiah, which dwell in the land,* that thereby they may be gathered together: for on the morrow, I shall proclaim unto this my people, out of mine own mouth, that thou art a king, and a ruler over this people, which the Lord our God hath given us. (Mosiah 1, p. 154 [1:10])

And now, it came to pass that Mosiah went and did as his father had commanded him, and *proclaimed unto all the people which were in the land of Zarahemla, that thereby they might gather themselves together,* to go up to the temple, to hear the words which his father should speak unto them. (Mosiah 1, p. 155 [1:18])

. . . and also, that they might give thanks to *the Lord their God, who had brought them out of the land of Jerusalem,* and who had delivered them out of the hands of their enemies, and had appointed just men to be their teachers; and also, a just man to be their king, who had *established peace in the land of Zarahemla,* and who had taught them to keep the commandments of God, that they might rejoice, and be filled with love towards God, and all men. (Mosiah 1, p. 155–156 [2:4])

And so on. What is the clue? That the Lord their God brought the people out of the land of Jerusalem, and then they settled peacefully in Zarahemla. That means Zarahemla is not in the land of Jerusalem, but you probably could have guessed that.

In spite of all the resources available to the Smiths, Junior claimed to have learned about Zarahemla and its ancient civilizations through the angel Moroni:

> I was also informed concerning the aboriginal inhabitants of this country and shown who they were, and from whence they came; a brief sketch of their *origin, progress, civilization, laws, governments*, of their righteousness and iniquity, and the blessings of . . . *The angel appeared to me three times the same night and unfolded the same things.* After having received many visits from the angels of God unfolding the majesty and glory of the events that should transpire in the last days, on the morning of the 22nd of September, a.d. 1827, *the angel of the Lord delivered the records into my hands.*[97]

Later, as proof of his vision and translation, Joseph Smith Jr. displayed a book written by John Lloyd Stephens, which was given to him in 1841, eleven years after *The Book of Mormon* was published. Stephens, an early nineteenth-century world traveler, wrote several popular books about his explorations. His publications of *Incidents of Travels in Central America, Chiapas, and Yucatan* and *Incidents of Travel in Central America* provided descriptions of ancient Mayan ruins, accompanied by drawings done by Stephens's traveling companion, Frank Catherwood, an architect and draftsman.[98]

The *Times and Seasons*, the church newspaper of which Joseph Smith Jr. was the editor, printed that the ruins and ancient cities in Stephens's book were those of the Nephites instead of the Mayan Indians. Smith was saying that *Incidents in Travel in Central America* confirmed his miraculous writings in *The Book of Mormon*. This was a clever strategy: extract information from early books his followers were sure not to have read and then use books published later as evidence that his claims were true.

The self-styled prophet wrote extensively about how the ruins in Central America described by Stephens were the lost cities of the Nephites. He claimed that before 1830, very little was known about "ruined cities and dilapidated buildings," which was just pure dissembling. His double meaning was that his *readers* knew nothing about the ancient civilizations. From *Times and Seasons* (3:921–3:922):

> *Every day adds fresh testimony to the already accumulated evidence on the authenticity of the Book of Mormon. At the time that book was translated, there was very little known about ruined cities and dilapidated buildings.* The general presumption was that no people possessing more intelligence than our present race of Indians had ever inhabited this continent; and the accounts given in the Book of Mormon concerning large cities and civilized people having inhabited this land were generally disbelieved and pronounced a humbug. . . . *Stephens, in his "Incidents of Travels in Central America," has thrown in a flood of testimony, and from the following statements it is evident that the Book of Mormon does not give a more extensive account of large and populous cities than those discoveries demonstrate to be even now in existence.*[99]

Editor John Pinkerton had an idea about where the Indians originated. He posited in his *Voyages and Travels*, Volume XIII, page 643, that the Aztecs were descendants of ancient Tartars. He suggested that the Tartars came—or were blown off course—to the Americas while attempting to reach Japan.

> Montezuma, began to reign in the year 1270, when Kublai Khan, the conqueror of all China and of Japan, was on the throne, and in whose time happened, *I believe, the first abortive expedition to Japan, which I mentioned above, and probably furnished North America with civilized inhabitants. There is if I am not mistaken, a great similarity between the figures of the Mexican idols and those which are usual among the Tartars,* who embrace the doctrines and religion of the Dalai Lama, whose religion Kublai Khan first introduced among the Monguls, or Moguls.

Pinkerton's book was published in London in 1812. His assertion would have inspired the Smiths to weave stories from *The Travels of Marco Polo* into those of the Aztecs to create the Mormon scriptures. After all, if the Tartars were the progenitors of the Aztecs and if those Tartars were of the same tribe encountered by Marco Polo, then the plagiarists could safely copy Marco Polo's travels as if they had happened in Mesoamerica. That much would seem obvious.

Blend that scenario with *pre-1830* journals and geography and history books about the area, and you have the recipe for the land and adventures of Zarahemla. With so many different sources at their disposal, the plagiarists' wiles would have been difficult to recognize.

Because the city of Zarahemla was based on the famous Aztec city of Tenochtitlan, the land of Zarahemla in *The Book of Mormon* refers to the cities and lands surrounding Tenochtitlan that were part of the Aztec empire. Some of the region belonged to other empires and indigenous tribes.

Let's begin with the geography of the area. How do the descriptions of Tenochtitlan by a Spanish officer and Zarahemla by the Smiths correspond? In the 1500s, Cortes would have found a basin with three lakes: the Salt Lake of Mexico and the Lake of Xochimilco, both saltwater, and the Fresh Lake of Chalco. (Map from Kerr's *Voyages and Travels*, Vol. III, pub. 1812, below.) You will see that a narrow neck of land separates the Salt Lake of Mexico from the Lake of Xochimilco, and you will notice a narrow strip of land that separates the Lake of Xochimilco from the Lake of Chalco.

The awe-inspiring city of Tenochtitlan was strategically placed in the midst of the Salt Lake of Mexico. It was an island connected to the mainland by causeways.

Do we think the Smiths saw the maps and drawings from the books of editors Robert Kerr, James Duncan, and others? Yes, the illustrations were probably laid out on the table next to the manuscript the Smiths were composing. The drawing of Tenochtitlan, provided on an engraved plate from Robert Kerr, certainly would have assisted them greatly in conceptualizing the city of Zarahemla (Figure 48).

Captain Bernal Diaz described his first sight of Tenochtitlan:

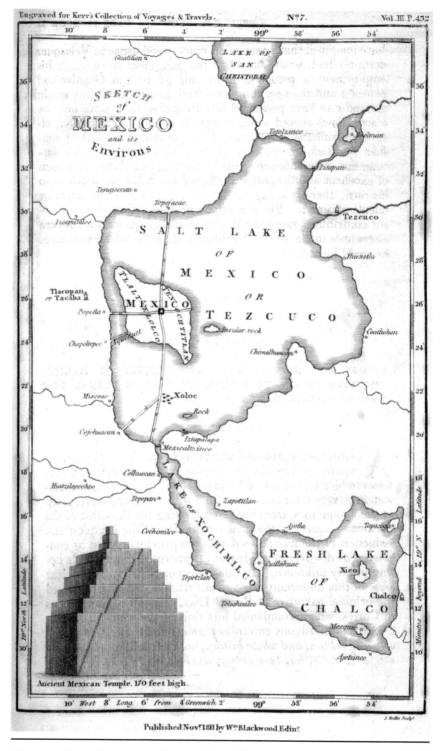

Figure 48. Kerr, *Voyages and Travels*, Vol. 3, "Sketch of Mexico and the Environs"

We then set forwards in our usual array for Mexico, *the road being crowded on both sides with innumerable multitudes of natives,* and soon arrived at the causeway of Iztalpalapan, one of those which leads to the capital.[100]

And now a look at Zarahemla:

And they did preserve the land southward for a wilderness, to get game. *And the whole face of the land northward was covered with inhabitants.* (Ether 3, p. 560 [10:21])

Diaz tells us:

The city was everywhere surrounded by water, and approachable only by long moles or causeways interrupted in many places by cross cuts, which were only to be passed by means of bridges, the destruction or removal of any of which would effectually prevent the possibility of retreat.[101]

The Smiths say this:

. . . *and the land of Zarahemla, was nearly surrounded by water;* there being a small neck of land between the land northward, and the land southward. (Alma 13, p. 288 [22:32])

The Joseph Smiths, talking about the Jaredites:

And they built a great city by *the narrow neck of land,* by the place where the sea divides the land. (Ether, 4, p. 560 [10:20])

The captain states:

Near the south-west angle of the salt lake of Mexico, it communicated by a *narrow neck or strait* with the fresh water of lake Chalco; and at their junction a mount or causeway had been constructed across, to prevent admixture of the salt and fresh lakes, having a town called Mexicaltzinco at the eastern extremity of this mound.[102]

In both Duncan's volume and Kerr's, the conquistador describes a lake that he likens to a sea:

On the 29th of October, Cortes advanced towards Mexico. . . . In descending from the mountains of Chalco, the vast plain of Mexico opened to their view. When they first beheld this prospect, one of the most striking and beautiful on the face of the earth; when they observed fertile and cultivated fields stretching further than the eye could reach; *when they saw a lake resembling a sea in the extent*, encompassed with large towns, and discovered the capital city rising upon an island in the middle, adorned with its temples and turrets; the scene so far exceeded their imagination, that some believed the fanciful descriptions of romance were realised, and that its enchanted palaces and gilded domes were presented to their sight; others could hardly persuade themselves that this wonderful spectacle was anything more than a dream.[103]

The great city of Tenochtitlan is situated in the midst of a salt water lake, *which has its tides like the sea.*[104]

Senior and Junior:

And now it was only the distance of a day and a half's journey for a Nephite, on the line Bountiful, and the land Desolation, *from the East to the West sea; and thus the land of Nephi, and the land of Zarahemla, was nearly surrounded by water; there being a small neck of land between the land northward and the land southward.* (Alma 13, p. 288 [22:32])

The comparisons for geography are both *textual*, meaning direct plagiarism of the reference books, and *contextual*, meaning the ideas or facts behind the sourcebooks were used for *The Book of Mormon*. So many intersections are available, that it would be difficult track them in only a single chapter.

Let's zero in on a phrase from the above quote, which is contextual plagiarism: ". . . it was only the distance of a day and a half's journey for a Nephite, on the line Bountiful and the land Desolation, from the east to the west sea."

Here we have an unusually specific reference—the length of a journey from one place to another. Study the two maps in this chapter, one a close-up of Tenochtitlan and Salt Lake, and the other of Mexico itself. What possibilities present themselves as east and west seas in "The Book of Alma"?

Some might assume that Alma speaks of the Atlantic and Pacific oceans on either side of the Isthmus of Darien in present-day Panama. Could that be correct? Here is what *The Modern Traveller* said of the borders of the Mexican empire: ". . . its dominion extended from the north to the south sea," meaning the Atlantic and Pacific oceans. Could a Nephite traverse the territory between oceans in a day and a half? Not likely. Even for local Indians in the eighteenth century, covering so great a distance took at least two days on foot and over water.

Then to what does Alma refer? Most likely traveling from the Salt Lake of Mexico to the freshwater Lake of Chalco. Remember, Cortes described the saltwater lake as having tides like the sea, so we can use *lake* and *sea* interchangeably. During the siege of Mexico City, Cortes was constantly adjusting troop movements for battles on the land around the salt lake. For example, he sent one officer to the "south sea" area:

As the best way to rid himself of troublesome demands, Cortes resolved to send off colonies to make settlements at convenient situations. Sandoval was sent off for this purpose to occupy Coatzaculaco and Tzapotecapan, the south-eastern provinces of the Mexican Empire. Juran Valesquez to Colima, and Villa Fuerte to Zcatollan, the most westerly provinces *on the south sea.*

But the Atlantic and Pacific are to the east and west of the Isthmus of Darien. Are there bodies of water to the north and south? Yes, the Salt Lake of Mexico to the north and the lake of Chalco to the south.

Once we take into account this geographic description, "The Book of Alma" gains clarity in respect to its reference texts. A city by the "narrow neck" of land, built "round about on the borders of the seashore" (Alma 13, p. 287 22:27) and where Zarahemla was "nearly surrounded by water" (Alma 13, p. 288 [22:32]) must mean around the borders of the Salt Lake of Mexico, which surrounded Tenochtitlan.

Traveling from the saltwater lake to the freshwater would be a reasonable journey of a day and a half for someone on foot, as one could certainly tell by looking at a map of the area. Or one could read about it from someone who had already traveled that route.

Before the final siege of Mexico City, Cortes had to secure the areas around the border of the Salt Lake against the Mexicans and their allies. His plan was to attack the island city by ship across the lake as well as fight along the causeways. His headquarters was set up in Tezcuco, which is on the northeast border of the Salt Lake, according to Kerr's map of the area. Cortes then marched south to a city on Lake Chalco, which was an overnight march down to the freshwater lake:

> Leaving the command in Tezcuco to Sandoval, *Cortes marched for Chalco on Friday the 5th of April 1521*, at the head of 300 infantry, including twenty crossbow-men and fifteen musketeers, with thirty cavalry . . . meaning to clear the district of Chalco and the environs of the lake from the Mexicans. . . . *We halted during the first night* at Tlalmanalco, and *reached Chalco the next day*, when Cortes convened all the chiefs of that state. . . . We continued our march the next day to Chimalhuecan . . . a town in the province of Chalco, where above twenty thousand warriors had assembled to join us.[105]
>
> The object of our next march was against Xochimilco, *a large city on the fresh water lake of Chalco, in which most of the houses are built.*[106]

Maps of the Mexican Empire depict rivers, and the stories of Cortes's conquest offer details about the lakes and rivers he crossed. That the Smiths wrote of rivers in Zarahemla does not point to plagiarism. Note this, however: on the border of Zarahemla runs the river Sidon.

> And it came to pass that the *Amlicites came upon the hill Amnihu, which was east of the river Sidon, which ran by the land of Zarahemla,* and there they began to make war with the Nephites. (Alma 1: p. 225 [2:15])

> And it came to pass that the king sent a proclamation throughout all the land, amongst all his people which was in all his land, which was in all the regions round about, *which was bordering even to the sea, on the east, and on the west, and which was divided from the land of Zarahemla by a narrow strip of wilderness, which ran from the sea, east, even to the sea west, and round about on the borders of the sea shore, and the borders of the wilderness which was on the north, by the land of Zarahemla, through the borders of Manti, by the head of the river Sidon,* running from the east towards the west; and thus were the Lamanites and the Nephites divided. (Alma 13, pp. 287–288 [22:27])

> *And it came to pass that the war began to be among them, in the borders of Zarahemla, by the waters of Sidon.* (Morm. 1: p. 519 [1:10])

Sidon is not found in Mexico's history or geography books or in journals. The name, however, is found in the John Pinkerton volume on Asia. In the chapter where Richard Pockocke visits the Holy Land in 1745, the *city* Sidon had a *river* near it, to the south:

> This seems to be the river mentioned by Strabo, as falling into the sea near Tyre ... having *the river to the south, and the hills to the north, between which there is a narrow pass into the plain where the famous city of Sidon stands.*[107]

Now from *The Book of Mormon*, which also places Sidon to the south:

And Alma returned and said unto them: Behold, *the Lamanites will cross the river Sidon in the south wilderness, away up beyond the borders of the land of Manti.* (Alma 11, p. 267 [16:6])

What other Zarahemla names can we find in the Smiths' reference books? Notice in the above quote that "the land of Manti" is in the *south*. In *The Travels of Marco Polo*, the land in southern China is *Manji*. (Marsden, p. 300)

Names for the Nephite northern city *Desolation* and southern city *Bountiful* both spring from names and descriptions for locales in Arabia.

And also there was many Lamanites on the east by the seashore, whither the Nephites had driven them. And thus the Nephites were nearly surrounded by the Lamanites; nevertheless the Nephites had taken possession of all the northern parts of the land, bordering on the wilderness, at the head of the river Sidon, from the east to the west, round about on the wilderness side; on the north, even *until they came to the land which they called Bountiful.* (Alma 13, p. 288 [22:29])

You will recall that "bountiful" was the description of the fertile *southern* coastline in *The Modern Traveller, Arabia*, published in 1825, on page 289: "Medinah and Tayif are represented as situated "on a *bountiful land*, with plenty of water, and covered with gardens."

The Smiths chose the name *Desolation* for a land in the north:

And it bordered upon the land which they called Desolation; it being so far northward that it came into the land which had been peopled, and been destroyed, of whose bones we have spoken, which was discovered by the people of Zarahemla; it being the place of their first landing. (Alma 13, p. 288 [22:30])

And they came from there up into the south wilderness. *Thus the land on the northward was called Desolation, and the land on the southward was called Bountiful;* it being the wilderness which was filled with all manner of wild animals of every kind; a part of which had come from the land northward, for food. (Alma 13, p. 288 [22:31])

In *The Modern Traveller, Arabia, desolation* described the area *north* of the "bountiful" area. Page 161 reads *"sea of desolation.* It would seem," Duncan says, "as if Arabia Petraea had once been an ocean of lava."
The Nephite land of *Desolation* lacked timber.

And it came to pass as *timber was exceedingly scarce in the land northward,* they did send forth much by the way of shipping. (Hel. 2, p. 412 [3:10])

Captain Bernal Diaz said in his travels with Hernan Cortes, "we entered upon the vast open plains, *in which not a tree* was to be seen."[108]
Near Desolation was the Jaredite land of Moron and an individual named Moron (not to be confused with *Moroni*).

And when he had gathered together an army, he came up unto the *land of Moron where the king dwelt,* and took him captive, which brought to pass the saying of the brother of Jared, That they would be brought into captivity.

Now the land of Moron where the king dwelt, was near the land which is called Desolation by the Nephites. (Ether 3, pp. 550–551 [7:5–7:6])

And it came to pass that he did overthrow Moron and obtain the kingdom; wherefore Moron dwelt in captivity all the remainder of his days; and he begat Coriantor. (Ether 4, p. 562 [11:18])

Where would the Smiths have found inspiration for an individual and a land with the name *Moron*? Perhaps it came from a reference to one of Cortes's cavalrymen who was killed by the Tlascalan Indians.

. . . a number of [the Tlascalan's] strongest warriors, armed with tremendous two-handed swords, made a combined attack on *Pedro de Moron,* an expert horseman. . . . *Moron died soon after of his wounds.*[109]

The Smiths' ideas for Zarahemla were clever. They kept the geography vague so they wouldn't have to bother with logic and consistency. They used numerous sources, so their plagiarism was not easily discernible. But in the geography they made a fatal mistake: all their details describe Tenochtitlan in the 1500s. Now that the Nephites had a home, they could build their empire in the land of Zarahemla.

Quauhtinchan

11

THE LAND
OF ZARAHEMLA

The Smiths described the land of Zarahemla as home to an advanced civilization. Roads led to magnificent cities with palaces and towering architecture. Gold from local mines adorned dazzling temples. The educated people communicated with a hieroglyphic writing system. From humble beginnings, the Nephites spread their Jewish civilization across the land:

> And I [Nephi] did teach my people to build buildings, and to work in all manner of wood, and of iron, and of copper, and of brass, and of steel, and of gold, and of silver, and of precious ores . . . And I, Nephi, did build a temple . . . after the manner of the temple of Solomon . . . (p. 72) . . . king Noah built many elegant and spacious buildings . . . and he also built him a spacious palace, and a throne in the midst thereof, all of which was of fine wood, and was ornamented with gold, and silver, and with precious things. (p. 178) . . . there were many cities built anew, and there were many old cities repaired; and there were many highways cast up, and many roads made, which led from city to city, and from land to land, and from place to place. (p. 465) . . . the whole face of the land had become

covered with buildings, and the people were as numerous almost, as it were the sand of the sea. (p. 519)

But Zarahemla was only a fairytale world derived from the stories and records of the Spanish conquerors and clerics in the New World. This chapter will reveal how the Smiths used pre-1830 published books about ancient Mexico and even anecdotes from *The Travels of Marco Polo* to create the land of Zarahemla. Reference material was readily available in books by James Duncan, Robert Kerr, John Pinkerton and others whose records described and engraved plates illustrated the ancient inhabitants of this continent, along with their cities, temples, war, and religion.

Upon the conquistadores' arrival at the vale of Mexico, Captain Diaz, an officer in Hernan Cortes's army, observed:

> When we contemplated the number of populous towns so closely situated to each other, some on the water, and others on the firm ground, we could not help comparing this wonderful country to the enchanted scenes we read of in Amadis de Gaul, so magnificent were the towers and temples and other superb edifices of stone and lime, which seemed everywhere to rise out of the water. Many of us were disposed to doubt the reality of the scene before us, and to suspect we were in a dream . . . as never had any one seen, heard, or even dreamt of any thing which could compare to the magnificence of the scene we now beheld.[110]

This is *not* the Nephites' Zarahemla.[111] This beautiful place belongs to the indigenous population the Spanish soldiers and priests encountered.

The Cities

Over the centuries, according to *The Book of Mormon*, the Jaredites, and then the Nephites, remained industrious and built many cities:

> But behold, our armies are small, to maintain *so great a number of cities* and so great possessions. (Alma 26: p. 392 [58:32])

[Shez's] father *did build up many cities.* (Ether 4: p. 558 [10:4])

One need only look at the maps from Robert Kerr and James Duncan—or this one published in 1806 and 1817 by attorney and historian Charles Cullen—to find a great number of cities in the Mexican Empire. We counted fifty-five just around the lakes of Mexico (Figure 49).

Eyewitness Captain Diaz is a prime resource regarding the development of the area:

> The whole fertile vale of Mexico or Anahuac, around these two lakes, and some others to the north of the great lake, was thickly planted with cities, towns, and villages, and highly cultivated, containing and giving subsistence to a prodigious population.[113]

The Roads of Zarahemla

Landlocked cities need roads for communication and commerce, and this was the case in and around the Mexican empire. One road connected Tlascala and Mexico City even though the two kingdoms were sworn enemies.

> Montezuma, it seems, had couriers posted at convenient distances along the principal roads, by which means intelligence was transmitted to the capital with astonishing rapidity.[114]

> The road to Mexico then lay for three days over bare and rugged mountains.[115]

We have no doubt the Smiths had those pages in front of them when they wrote:

> . . . there were many cities built anew, and there were many old cities repaired; and there were many *highways* cast up, and many *roads* made, *which led from city to city, and from land to land,* and from place to place. (3 Nephi 3, p. 465 [3 Nephi 6:8]).

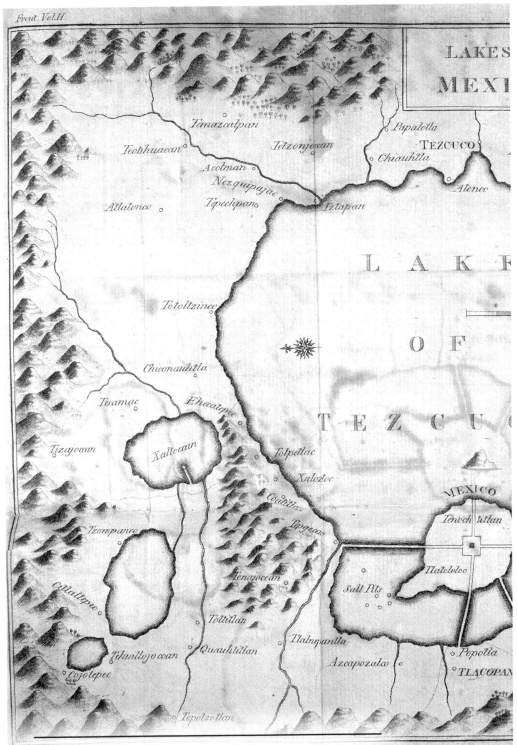

Figure 49. Cullen, *History of Mexico*, Map of "Lakes of Mexico"

The Buildings

Buildings need construction material. The Aztecs used stone, brick, and cement, and these mundane construction details found their way into *The Book of Mormon*. Humboldt, describing the temple of Mexico, wrote:

> . . . the pavement was beautifully laid with jasper stones of all colours: the rails, which went round in nature of a balustrade, were of a serpentine form, and both sides covered with stones resembling jet, placed in good order, and joined with *white and red cement*, which was a very great ornament to the building."[116]

The Smiths wrote about materials for the Nephites' homes:

> And there being but little timber upon the face of the land, nevertheless the people which went forth, became exceeding *expert in the working of cement*; therefore they did build houses of cement, in which they did dwell. (Hel. 2: p. 412 [3:7])

Handsome and Spacious Buildings

The palaces of Montezuma were impressive to the Spanish conquistadores:

> On approaching Iztapalapan, we were received by several of the highest nobles of the Mexican Empire, relations of Montezuma, who conducted us to the lodgings appointed for us in that place, which were magnificent palaces of stone, the timber work of which were cedar, having spacious courts and large halls, furnished with canopies of the finest cotton. After contemplating the magnificence of the buildings, we walked through splendid gardens, containing numerous alleys planted with a variety of fruit trees, and filled with roses. . . . In these gardens there was a fine sheet of clear water, communicating with the great lake of Mexico by a canal. . . . The apartments of the palace were everywhere ornamented with works of art, admirably painted, and the walls were

beautifully plastered and whitened. . . . When I beheld the delicious scenery around me, I thought we had been transported by magic to the terrestrial paradise.[117]

You will see similarities between Montezuma's palace and the Smiths' material. The plagiarists also turned to Marco Polo's description of the khan's palace near the city of Kanbalu on pages 287 to 290 in *The Travels of Marco Polo* and to the description of the palace at Shandu, called the khan's "beautiful palace in the city of Shandu," on pages 250 and 251.

The Smiths added two palaces to *The Book of Mormon*, one in "The Book of Mosiah" and the other in "The Book of Alma." The only detailed description of a palace is in "The Book of Mosiah." It was built by King Noah:

> And it came to pass that king Noah built many *elegant and spacious buildings*; and he ornamented them with fine work of wood, and of all manner of precious things, of gold, and of silver, and of iron, and of brass, and of ziff, and of copper; and he also built him a spacious palace, and a throne in the midst thereof, all of which was of fine wood, and was ornamented with gold, and silver, and with precious things. (Mosiah 7: p. 178 [11:8–9])

Compare King Noah's palace with on-site reporting in Mexico from James Duncan's Traveller's history:

James Duncan, *Mexico*, p. 43	Mosiah 7: p. 178
The grandeur and magnificence of his [Montezuma's] palaces, houses of pleasure . . . were correspondent to this majesty . . . Besides this palace he had others, both within and without the capital.	King Noah built many elegant and spacious buildings
The beams were of cedar, cypress, and other excellent woods, well finished and carved.	he ornamented them with fine work of wood

James Duncan, *Mexico*, p. 43	Mosiah 7: p. 178
Some of the apartments had walls of marble and other **valuable kinds of stone.**	and all manner of **precious things**
The **palace of his** usual resident was a **vast edifice of stone and lime,** which had twenty doors to the public squares and streets; three great courts . . . several halls, and more than a hundred chambers.	a spacious **palace** and a
In taking leave, no person ever turned his back upon the **throne.**	**throne** in the midst thereof . . .

Using the reports of Montezuma's palace as their guide, the Smiths next lifted the textual description of "elegant and spacious buildings" from "handsome and spacious building" in Marco Polo. The next table compares these phrases and also provides the percentage-into-the-text statistics to show the close match in the two books—less than eight percent apart.

Comparison of the Khan's Palaces at Kanbalu and Shandu With a Palace Built by King Noah

37.96% *The Travels of Marco Polo* Ch. VI. *Of the great and admirable palace of the Grand khan, near to the city of Kanbalu.* pp. 287–90	30.27% *The Book of Mormon* "The Book of Mosiah" Ch. 7: p. 178–179 [starting 11:10]
The Grand *khan* . . .	And it came to pass **that king Noah**
In the middle of each division of these walls is a	**built many**
handsome and spacious building,	**elegant and spacious buildings;**
and consequently within the enclosure there are **eight such buildings.**(p. 288)	

"Ornamented" With Woodwork and Gold

The sides of the great halls and the apartments are	**and he**

Comparison of the Khan's Palaces at Kanbalu and Shandu
With a Palace Built by King Noah

37.96% *The Travels of Marco Polo* Ch. VI. *Of the great and admirable* *palace of the Grand khan, near to the* *city of Kanbalu.* pp. 287–90	30.27% *The Book of Mormon* "The Book of Mosiah" Ch. 7: p. 178–179 [starting 11:10]
ornamented with	ornamented them with
dragons in carved work and	fine work of wood, and of all manner of
gilt, (p. 289) (which means metal *covered with* gold) . . . or his treasure	precious things, of
in gold	gold,
and silver	and of silver,
bullion, precious stones, and pearls, and also his vessels of gold and silver plate.	("precious things," above)
The stream discharges itself at the opposite extremity of the piece of water, and precautions are taken to prevent the escape of the fish, by placing gratings of	and of
copper or iron	iron . . . and of copper
at the places of its entrance and exit. (p. 290)	

Polo recorded that near the khan's palace was a hill or mound of earth. The Smiths divided the description of the single earthen mount, topped with an "ornamental pavilion" to the north, into two stories about two different towers, one on a hill north of the land and one near the temple. The khan's "royal park" was transformed into the Smiths' "resort" for the people. We split the Polo story because that is how the Smiths organized their reproduction.

Tower on *North Hill* Built by King Near Temple
and A Pavilion on a *North Mound of Earth* Built by Khan Near Palace

The Travels of Marco Polo pp. 287–90 (37.96%)	"The Book of Mosiah" Ch. 7: p. 178–179, [11:10 et seq.] (30.27%)
Not far from the palace . . . is an artificial mount of earth.	And it came to pass that he built a tower near the temple; yea, a very high tower, even so high that
The view of this altogether, the mount itself, the trees, and the building, form a	he could stand upon the top thereof and overlook the land of Shilom, and also the land of Shemlon, which was possessed by the Lamanites; and
delightful and at the same time a wonderful scene.	he could even look over all the land round about.
["and the building," above]	And it came to pass that he caused many buildings to be built in the land Shilom; and he caused
an artificial mound of earth, the height of which is an hundred paces, and the circuit at the base, about a mile.	["the hill," below]
On its summit is erected an ornamental pavilion . . . on the	a great tower to be built on the hill
northern side,	north of the land Shilom,
and about a bow-shot distance from the surrounding wall	
(p. 250: palace at *Shandu*) Departing from the city last mentioned and proceeding three days journey in a northeasterly direction, you arrive at a city named *Shandu*, built by the Grand *khan*.	["north," above]
Within the bounds of the	which had been a
royal park . . .	resort . . .

Nephite Nobility

The ancient Indian tribes Cortes encountered lived in various degrees of feudalism, with distinctions made between the patrician and plebian classes.[118] This was no more vividly displayed than on Cortes's first entry into Tenochtitlan.

> Proceeding along the broad causeway of Iztapalapan, we came to a place called *Xoloc*. . . . We were met by a numerous train of the court nobles in the richest dresses, who were sent before Montezuma to compliment us on our arrival, after which Cacamatzin and the other nobles who had hitherto attended us, went to meet their sovereign, who now approached in a most magnificent litter, which was carried by four of his highest nobles.[119]

The noble class and ruling monarchs were a topic of much discussion in the Mexican conquest. Bernal Diaz observed that "The priests were said to be all of noble families."[120]

In Cullen's *History of Mexico*, plate 24 illustrates "A Noble" and "A Woman of Rank" (Figure 50).

Figure 50. Cullen, *History of Mexico*, Plate 24, "A Noble, A Woman of Rank"

Would any 1830s New Englander have imagined that kings and nobility of such extreme pomp and grandeur existed in the jungles of ancient America? How could the Smiths have come up with such a notion? And yet *The Book of Mormon* is filled with stories of kings, which would have enthralled their followers.

The noble class in *The Book of Mormon* begins chronologically with a long line of Jaredite kings with names like Jared, Orihah, Kib, Corihor, Noah, Shiz, and even King "Moron." The Nephites and Lamanites had multiple kings with different dominions. King Mosiah was followed by Benjamin and the second Mosiah as rulers of Zarahemla. King Zeniff was followed by Noah and Limhi, who all ruled in the land of "Nephi." Lamanite king Laman was followed by Lamoni and Anti-Nephi-Lehi, who ruled in the land of Nephi. The time frame for the reign of Nephite and Lamanite kings in the Nephite calendar translates to about 200 BC to 77 BC in the Gregorian calendar.

Egyptians and the Nephite Calendar

The Nephites kept a calendar . . . or two. The information available about the Aztec calendar in the early 1800s would have inspired the Smiths to create some type of dating system for the Nephites. More importantly, it connected the Aztecs and hence the Nephites to the ancient Egyptians.

The Nephites calculated their dates in years since Lehi left Jerusalem. At the end of "The Book of Mosiah," we read:

> And it came to pass that Mosiah died also, in the thirty and third year of his reign, being sixty and three years old; making in the whole, five hundred and nine years from the time Lehi left Jerusalem; and thus ended the reign of the kings over the people of Nephi; and thus ended the days of Alma [the First], who was the founder of their church. (Mosiah 13: p. 221)

After Jesus Christ was born, the Nephites switched to a new counting system. "The Book of Nephi, The Son of Nephi, Which Was the Son of

Helaman," records the death of Jesus as "in the thirty and fourth year, in the first month, in the fourth day of the month." (3 Nephi 1: p. 452)

We learn from Charles Cullen's book that the ancient Indians also had a type of calendar adjustment:

> Boturini affirms, that a hundred and more years before the Christian era, the Toltecas adjusted their calendar, by adding one day every four years. To represent a month they painted a circle or wheel, divided into twenty figures signifying days, as appears in the plate we have given, which is a copy from one published by Valades. . . . To represent the year they painted another, which they divided into eighteen figures of the eighteen months, and frequently painted within the wheel the image of the moon.[121]

Cullen's plate below clearly illustrated the Mexican calendar (Figure 51).

Shown next is another Aztec calendar of the "Mexican Century," courtesy of Mr. Cullen. He explains,

> The century was represented by a wheel divided into fifty-two figures, or rather by four figures, which were thirteen times designed. The wheel which we here present, is a copy of two others, one of which was published by Valades, and the other by Gemelli, within which we have represented the sun, as was generally done by the Mexican[122] (Figure 52).

The historian Clavigero used the Aztec calendar to link the Mexicans to the Egyptians and noted that the Aztecs had calendar connections back to the time of the Tower of Babel. The Smiths would have picked up on this assertion and used it for their own purposes, creating a new plotline and characters dating back to the Tower of Babel. The plate below is a reproduction of ancient Aztec artwork and hieroglyphics illustrating that history:

> Respecting the symbols of the Mexican months and year, they discover ideas *entirely conformable with those of the ancient Egyptians.* The latter distinguished, as appears from their monuments, each month or art of the

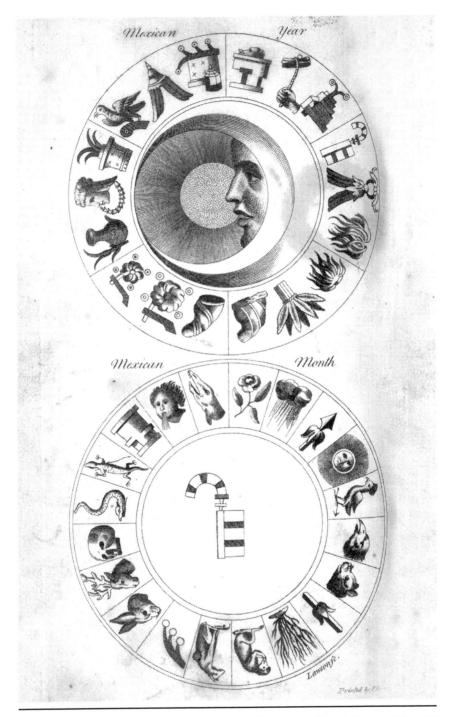

Figure 51. Cullen, *History of Mexico*, Plate 13, "Mexican Year, Mexican Month"

Figure 52. Cullen, *History of Mexico*, Plate 14, "Mexican Century"

zodiac, where the sun stood, with characteristical figures of that which happened in every season of the year.[123]

Here is a fact connected with the Mexican calendar, relative to *the building of the tower of Babel and the confusion of the tongues*[124] (Figure 53).

Cullen included Clavigero's writings about the origins of the Mexicans. Read the following quote, where Clavigero disagrees with another author's theory of Mexican origins.

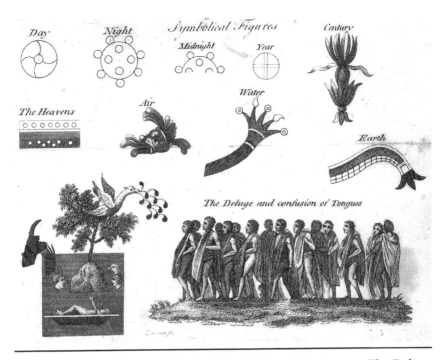

Figure 53. Cullen, *History of Mexico*, Plate 8, "Symbolic Figures, The Deluge and Confusion of Tongues"

. . . how could Siguenza imagine these pyramids anterior to the deluge, if he believed the population of America posterior to the deluge, *and the first settlers descendants of Nephtuim*, grand nephew of Noah, as Boturnini attests, who saw some of the works of Siguenza?

A name of descendants of the first settlers of Mexico converts easily from *Nephtuim* to *Nephite*. Another mystery of *The Book of Mormon* is solved, at least. Clavigero continues with the timing of the settlers stating:

"No Indian historian," says this traveller, "has been able to investigate the time of the erection of the pyramids of America; but D. Carlos Siguenza imagined them very ancient, and built a little time after the Deluge." Nor has Gemelli properly explained the opinion of Siguenza . . . amongst other of that which he wrote upon the peopling of America, says, that in that *work he fixed the first peopling of the new world* paulo post Babylonicam confusionem, that is, a little after the time which Gemelli mentioned.[125]

The Latin *Paulo post Babylonicam confusionem* for our purposes means that the plagiarists copied the idea that the first settlers in Mexico came after the fall of the Tower of Babel. The Smiths named those settlers "Jaredites." Copied below is a quote from the title page of *The Book of Mormon*:

Also, which is a Record of the People of Jared, which were scattered at the time the Lord confounded the language of the people when they were building a tower to get to Heaven.

Another mystery solved. There are many more questions to answer, such as "Where did all the animals in Zarahemla come from?"

Animals of Zarahemla

Columbus and Captain Diaz provided onsite reports about the animals in the New World.

Next day, being the 8th of November 1519, we set out on our way into the city of Mexico along the grand causeway . . . both sides of the causeway being everywhere crowded with spectators, as were all the towers, temples, and terraces in every part of our progress, eager to behold such men *and animals as had never been seen in that part of the world.*[126]

The *Modern Traveller* tells the story of an early battle between the conquistadores and a native tribe near the seashore:

In the decisive action, De Solis attributes no small effect to the horses, the strangeness of which, he says, terrified the Indians, who had never seen any before, and imagined them to be fierce monsters, half man and half beast.[127]

Yet the Smiths included horses in the land of Zarahemla. Even modern paleontology proves that this was an error on the Smiths' part. There were *no* horses living in the New World. The Native Americans had never seen such creatures. Ice Age horses in America became extinct thousands of years before the time of the Tower of Babel.

Where did the Smiths find the animals for the land of Zarahemla? For the text, they used animals from the lands Marco Polo visited. In percentage comparisons, at 96.43 percent versus 94.56 percent in the same sequence (a difference of only 1.87 percent), we find *The Book of Mormon* horses.

The Travels of Marco Polo (96.43%) (p. 729)	The Book of Mormon (94.56%) (Ether, p. 556 [9:18–19])
they accustom their	also all manner of
cattle,	cattle, of oxen, and
cows,	cows, and of
sheep,	sheep . . .
camels, and	and also many other kinds of animals . . . and they also had
horses	horses . . .

This was their tactic: the Smiths clearly copied the animals from the Far East, the Tartars' territory. Why shouldn't they write about the animals of China? After all, author John Pinkerton conjectured that the Aztecs were descendants of Tartars.[128] Who could prove it wrong? the plagiarists would have reasoned. Even James Duncan reported "The zoology of Mexico is imperfectly known."[129]

Let's investigate what *was* known. The next table compares animals mentioned by Polo, those in *The Book of Mormon*, and those in the reference books of Mexican history such *Modern Traveller* and records like *History of the Conquest of Mexico by Bernal Diaz* in the Robert Kerr book.

The animals with an asterisk are cumoms and cureloms. They were mysterious Nephite creatures in *The Book of Mormon*. In a later chapter exposing "The Book of Ether" we will show how the Smiths invented

230

these animals from those in *The Travels of Marco Polo* and *why* the Smiths believed that ancient people of America had domesticated elephants.

Table of Animals

Animal	Travels of Marco Polo	Book of Mormon	Documented History of Mexico by 1830
Apaxa (Mexican stag)			■
Ass	■	■	
Bear	■	■	■
Buffalo/Bison	■		■
Cattle	■	■	
Chicken/Rooster	■	■	■
Camel	■		
Cow	■	■	
Cumoms	■	■	
Cureloms	■	■	
Deer	■	■	■
Dog (in Mexico *techichi*)	■	■	■
Elephant	■	■	
Goat	■	■	
Horse	■	■	
Lamb	■	■	
Llama			■
Leopard	■	■	
Lion/Tiger (including jaguar or American tiger and *mitzli/puma*)	■	■	■
Ox	■	■	■
Swine/Hog	■	■	■
Wolf (in Mexico *xoloitzcuintili* and *cocyotie*)	■	■	■

Although we discovered dozens of examples of copying animals into *The Book of Mormon*, a few comparisons below are all we have room for:

Sheep, Lamb, Goat, and Kid

16.80% vs. 16.67% = Difference of 0.13%

33.47% vs. 31.63% = Difference of 1.84%

96.43% vs. 96.43% = Difference of 0.00%

(16.80%, p. 127, n. 260)	(16.67%, 2 Nephi 9: p. 98 [21:6–8])
Sheep and	. . . the lamb (young sheep) and the leopard shall lie down with the
goats	kid (young goat)
being afterwards spoken of by our author as wild animals abounding in this part of the country	. . . bear shall feed . . . lion shall eat . . . hole of the asp . . . cockatrice's den
(33.47%, p. 253)	(31.63%, Mosiah 8: p. 186 [14:7]):
These baksis (idolaters) . . . when the day arrives, they	he is brought as a
sacrifice the sheep	lamb to the slaughter, and as a sheep before her shearers is dumb . . .
(96.43%, p. 729)	(96.43%, Ether 6: p. 567 [13:11])
they accustom their . . . sheep . . . to feed upon dried fish	washed in the blood of the Lamb

Leopards and Lions

16.53% vs. 16.67% = Difference of 0.14%

44.71% vs. 44.90% = Difference of 0.19%

(16.53%, p. 125, n. 255)	(16.67%, 2 Nephi 9: p. 98 [21:6])
lions amongst the wild animals of Persia . . ./. . . des lions . . . leopards	. . . and the leopard . . . and . . . lion . . . together
(44.71%, p. 338) . . . khan has many leopards . . .	(44.90%, Alma 10: p. 264 [14:29])
for . . . chasing deer, and also many	. . . as a goat fleeth . . . from

lions,   two lions . . .

which are larger than the Babylonian
lions . . .

Wolves

44.71% vs. 40.48% = Difference of 4.23%

(44.71%, p. 338)   (40.48%, Alma 4: p. 238 [5:60])

His Majesty (the khan) has eagles also,   . . . he (the Lord) commandeth you
which are trained to stoop   that ye suffer no

at wolves,   ravenous wolf

and such is their size and strength, that   to enter among you, that ye may not be
none . . . can escape from their talons.   destroyed.

Detailed Descriptions of Money

For commerce, any advanced civilization needs a medium of exchange. The Smiths found a system for Zarahemla that appealed to them, not in the annals of Cortes but in the records of Marco Polo. Money appears in *The Book of Mormon* at 42.86 percent (page 252). Using the percent-through-the-text method, we find that Tartar currency appears in Marsden's 1818 edition of *Marco Polo* at 46.69 percent (page 353), a 3.83 percent difference between the two descriptions.

Travels of Marco Polo	46.69%
The Book of Mormon	−42.86%
Difference	3.83%

Marco Polo's recollection of the "mint of the Grand khan" appears on page 353 (Figure 54).

A summary of the values is:

"Smallest" = denier tournois

"The next" = Venetian silver groat

"others" = one besant of gold

= two besants of gold

= three besants of gold

= as far as ten besants of gold

CHAPTER XVIII.

Of the kind of Paper-money issued by the Grand khan, and made to pass current throughout his dominions.

In this city of *Kanbalu* is the mint of the Grand *khan*, who may truly be said to possess the secret of the alchymists, as he has the art of producing money by the following process.[671] He causes the bark to be stripped from those mulberry trees, the leaves of which are used for feeding silk-worms, and takes from it that thin inner rind which lies between the coarser bark and the wood of the tree. This being steeped and afterwards pounded in a mortar, until reduced to a pulp, is made into paper,[672] resembling (in substance) that which is manufactured from cotton, but quite black.[673] When ready for use he has it cut into pieces of money of different sizes, nearly square, but somewhat longer than they are wide. Of these, the smallest pass for a denier *tournois*; the next size, for a Venetian silver groat; others for two, five, and ten groats; others for one, two, three, and as far as ten *besants* of gold.[674] The coinage of this paper-money is authenticated with as much form and ceremony, as if it were actually of pure gold or silver; for to each note, a number of officers, specially appointed, not only subscribe their names, but affix their signets also; and when this has been regularly done by the whole of them, the principal officer, deputed by his majesty, having dipped into vermilion the royal seal committed to his custody, stamps with it the piece of paper, so that

Figure 54. Marsden, *Marco Polo*, 353

The Smiths did not copy the Tartar system word for word; they were more subtle in converting the numbering systems to money for the Nephites. They copied some of the names of money from Polo but also followed the numeric decimal systems recorded by Polo. This table shows the description of the Nephite coins:

The Book of Mormon, Alma 8: p. 252 [Alma 11:5–20]				
Gold			**Silver**	
Senine		=	Senum	
Seon	= 2 Senines		Amnor	= 2 Senums
Shum	= 2 Seons		Ezrom	= 4 Senums
Limnah	= Senine + Seon + Shum		Onti	= Senum + Amnor + Ezrom
			Shiblon	= 1/2 Senum
			Shiblum	= 1/2 Shiblon
			Leah	= 1/2 Shiblum
Antion		=	3 Shiblons	

Next, the equivalent values of the "senum":

$$
\begin{aligned}
\text{senum} &= 1/7 \text{ limnah} \\
&= 1/7 \text{ onti or } 0.1429 \text{ onti} \\
&= 1/4 \text{ shum} \\
&= 1/2 \text{ seon} \\
&= 2/3 \text{ antion or } 0.667 \text{ antion} \\
&= 2 \text{ shiblon} \\
&= 4 \text{ shiblum} \\
&= 8 \text{ leah}
\end{aligned}
$$

A brief investigation of the *names* chosen for Nephite money shows that they, too, came from names or words in *Marco Polo*:

The Travels of Marco Polo Names or Words	The Book of Mormon Names for Money
Si-ning (p. 226)	Senine
Sinensis (p. 303) or Sensim (p. 254)	Senum
Soung (p. 574)	Seon
Amoy (p. 583)	Amnor
Shibbergaun (p. 123)	Shiblon
Toman (implies 10,000: p. 214, 545) (Toman of gold = 80,000 Saggi)	Antion
Leang (money = 10 grossi)	Leah (money = 1/2 shiblum)
p. 356	p. 235, 44.3%

Cortes and King Montezuma vs. Ammon and King Lamoni

The story of Cortes and his officers' imprisoning the emperor Montezuma is concealed within "The Book of Alma" (Figure 55).

Montezuma pretended to his people that he was a god, and he and the rest of the Aztecs thought General Cortes was a god—Quetzalcoatl, who was prophesied to return and rule the Mexican kingdom.

Cortes did not disavow this notion until he met Montezuma, and they admitted to each other that both were just mortals.

This incident is in "The Book of Alma," chapter twelve. In Alma, the Lamanite king, Lamoni, plays the role of Montezuma, and Ammon represents the Christian soldier Cortes. Ammon, a Nephite, leaves the safety of the Nephite lands, travels through the wilderness to enter the Lamanites' kingdom, and gains the favor of King Lamoni. King Lamoni thinks that Ammon is "the Great Spirit," just as Montezuma thought Cortes was the returning god Quetzalcoatl.[130]

A number of keywords or similar situations are present, such as feeding horses, being "astonished," reading each other's thoughts, admitting "I am a man" and not a god, fear of being put to death, and the shock that Montezuma felt after he was arrested by Cortes.

Figure 55. Cullen, *History of Mexico*, Plate 5, "Montezuma Xocojotzin"

Robert Kerr, Volumes III and IV, *The History of the Conquest of Mexico* by Bernal Diaz	"The Book of Alma" Chapter 12
Some able Mexican painters accompanied the two chiefs on this occasion, who drew accurate representations of Cortes and the other Spanish officers. . . . Our presents, and intelligence of all that had passed at this interview, were conveyed with amazing rapidity to Montezuma by this officer. (Vol. III, pp. 477–479)	And it came to pass that king Lamoni caused that his servants should stand forth and testify to all the things which they had seen concerning the matter. And when they had all testified to the things which they had seen, and he had learned of the faithfulness of Ammon in preserving his flocks, and also of his great power in contending against those who sought to slay him . . . (p. 273)

Both Montezuma and King Lamoni ask their visitor if he is indeed the god of the prophecies who could perhaps read their thoughts:

Montezuma was particularly struck with the appearance of the helmet, as it impressed him strongly with the opinion that we were destined by heaven to acquire the rule over his empire. (Vol. III, p. 477)	(King Lamoni) was astonished exceedingly, and saith, Surely, this is more than a man. Behold, is not this the Great Spirit which doth send such great punishments upon this people, because of their murders?
	And they answered the king, and said, Whether he be the Great Spirit or a man, we know not (p. 273)
Our allies also advised them to be aware of practising any thing against us, as we could read their hidden thoughts, and recommended them to conciliate our favour by a present. (Vol. IV, p. 3)	And it came to pass that Ammon, being filled with the Spirit of God, therefore he perceived the thoughts of the king. (p. 274)

Below, King Lamoni again expresses his opinion that Ammon is the "Great Spirit," while King Montezuma has a similar opinion about the Spaniards:

it impressed [Montezuma] strongly with the opinion that we were destined by heaven to acquire the rule over his empire. (Vol. III, p. 477)

And now, when the **king** heard these words, he said unto them, **Now I know that it is the Great Spirit**; and he hath come down at this time to preserve your lives, that I might not slay you as I did your brethren.

Now that we were actually arrived in his dominions, he was happy to offer every favour in his power to grant, being convinced

Now this is the

we were those men predicted by the gods to his ancestors,

Great Spirit of which our fathers have spoken. (p. 273)

who, coming from that part of the world in which the sun rises, were to acquire the government of this country. (Vol. IV, p. 40)

The conquistadores fought off thousands of Tlascalan warriors without a single Spanish fatality. The seeming inability of mortal men to kill them concretized the Spaniards' reputation as gods.

This idea is captured in Alma by the priests' telling King Lamoni that Ammon cannot be killed and by Diaz's commenting on how their reputation was ruined:

since they found they could be killed like other men. (Vol. IV, p. 54)

that he **cannot be slain** by the enemies of the king; neither can they scatter the king's flocks when he is with us, because of

[Montezuma] reproached his captains for not having overwhelmed the whole of that small number of Spaniards with their numerous forces; but they alleged that a supernatural being fought against them, assisting and encouraging the Spaniards, and struck terror into their men. (Vol. IV, p. 55)

his expertness and great strength; therefore, we know that he is a friend to the king. (p. 273)

before this, we were in possession of wealth, and were considered invulnerable, and almost like demigods; (Vol. IV, p. 54)

And now, O king, we **do not believe that a man hath such great power, for we know that he cannot be slain.** (p. 273)

At their first meeting on the causeway leading to Mexico City, Cortes and Montezuma exchanged warm greetings and also admitted that they were not gods but men. Ammon repeats the statement twice.

which reported that **we were furious teules, who carried thunder and lighting along with us, that our horses ate men**, and other foolish stories. That he now saw we were valiant and wise men, for which he highly esteemed us . . . your new friends the Tlascalans have informed you that	King Lamoni did open his mouth, and said unto him, Who art thou? Art thou that Great Spirit, which knows all things?
	Ammon answered . . .
I am like a god . . . but you now see that	I am not.
I am like other men. (Vol. IV, pp. 41–42)	I am a man, and am thy servant; therefore, whatsoever thou desirest which is right, that will I do. (p. 274)

After some Spaniards are finally mortally wounded during the rebellion at Villa Rica, their divine status vanishes.

the Tlascalans had arrived secretly with letters from Villa Rica . . . Escalente and **Six Spaniards had been slain in a battle with the Mexicans** . . . the Mexican captains reported the whole of this affair to Montezuma, to whom they brought the head of Arguello. (Vol. IV, pp. 54–55)	And he said unto him, Is it because **thou hast heard** that I defended thy servants and thy flocks, **and slew seven** of their brethren with the sling, and with the sword, and smote off the arms of others, in order to defend thy flocks and thy servants; behold, is it this that causeth thy marvellings? (p. 274)

After the battle at Villa Rica, the Mexicans revolt. Cortes prepares his cavalry and infantry and asks his war council to devise a plan. Ammon, too, readies his horses (and chariots in this case). The next keywords focus on horses.

Montezuma then departed . . . after giving orders that we should be amply provided with every thing we needed . . .

and to supply us with plenty of grass for our horses. (Vol. IV, p. 40)

And it came to pass that king Lamoni inquired of his servants, saying: Where is this man that hath such great power? And they saith unto him, Behold,

he is feeding thy horses. Now the king had commanded his servants previous to the time of the watering of their flocks, that **they should prepare his horses** and chariots, and conduct him forth to the land of Nephi: (p. 273–274)

Our cavalry and infantry were all ordered to be in readiness for instant action. (Vol. IV, p. 55)

Now when king Lamoni heard that Ammon was preparing his horses and his chariots,

Cortes addressed Montezuma . . .

He was astonished

he was more astonished,

that so brave and magnanimous a monarch, who had

because of the faithfulness of Ammon, saying: Surely there has not been any servant among all my servants,

shewn so much friendship for us on all occasions, should have clandestinely

that has been so faithful as this man; for even he doth

given orders to his troops in Toton-acapan to make an attack upon the Spaniards. (Vol. IV, p. 56)

remember all my commandments to execute them. (p. 274)

Cortes and others deemed it necessary for their safety to arrest Montezuma. They knew the Mexicans would not attack their own sovereign.

Both prevaricators go to see the king—Montezuma and Lamoni. Montezuma was immobilized with fear, and in *The Book of Mormon*, King Lamoni fell "as if he were dead."

Our general, and we who were with him, immediately went to the royal apartment . . .

Cortes addressed Montezuma . . . in order to prevent the ruin of the city of

he went in unto the king,

Mexico, that it was necessary that his majesty should go immediately to our quarters, assuring him if he gave the smallest alarm, or made

any resistance, the officers and soldiers then present would put him instantly to death. On hearing this proposal	And now when he said this, he fell unto the earth, as if he were dead. (p. 276)
Montezuma was so petrified with terror and amazement that he seemed to have lost all sensation for a time. (Vol. IV, p. 55)	and he saw that the countenance of the king was changed; therefore he was about to return out of his presence; (p. 274)

In this next table, both kings delay in responding for a half hour or a full hour.

he declined the proposal of quitting the palace with disdain . . . Cortes endeavored to explain the necessity of his immediate compliance, and the king persisted in his refusal, so that the conversation drew to considerable	therefore Ammon turned himself unto the king, and said unto him, What wilt thou that I should do for thee, O king? And the king answered him not for the
length, half an hour at least having elapsed. (Vol. IV, p. 56)	space of an hour, according to their time, for he knew not what he should say unto him. (p. 274)

Why would Joseph Smith (or anyone else, for that matter) assume that ancient Americans measured time in one-hour increments? Because he plagiarized Captain Diaz, who noted the Spaniard's one-hour time clock, which was not an Aztec measurement of time.

In the material that follows, the number two, wives, sons, and family are connections between the two texts:

Montezuma then offered to put his legitimate son and	And it came to pass that his servants took him and carried him
	in unto his wife, and laid him upon a bed; and he lay as if he were dead, for
two daughters	the space of two days and two nights;

in the hands of Cortes, as hostages, and earnestly entreated that he might not be exposed before his subjects as a prisoner . . . His magnificent state litter was now brought for his accommodation, and he proceeded to our quarters in his accustomed pomp, attended by his guards, where he was received and entertained with every mark of respect . . . Thus we accomplished the seizure of the

great Montezuma . . . his wives, family, and officers being constantly with him. (Vol. IV, p. 57)	and his wife, and his sons, and his daughters mourned over him, after the manner of the Lamanites, greatly lamenting his loss. (p. 276)

The imprisonment of their sovereign by outsiders, whether demigods or not, shocked the Mexicans for a time, but then rage took hold. They plotted a rebellion. In Zarahemla, the people "murmur."

secretly informed by our Tlascalan allies that they had noticed several indications of evil intentions towards us among the Mexicans.(Vol. IV, p. 53)	And now the people began to murmur among themselves; some saying, That it was a great evil that had come upon them, or upon the king and his house, because he had suffered that the Nephite should remain in the land. (p. 278)
several of the Mexican chiefs who were along with Cacamatzin expressed their scruples about entering into war without their legitimate sovereign and proposed to send for his instructions.	And it came to pass that there was many among them, who said that Ammon was the Great Spirit, and others said he was sent by the Great Spirit;
Cacamatzin was enraged at this proposal	but others rebuked them all,
He then sent a message to Montezuma, representing the disgrace into which he had fallen, by joining himself to wizards and magicians, and declaring a resolution to destroy us all. (Vol. IV, pp. 66–67)	saying, That he was a monster, which hath been sent from the Nephites to torment us; (p. 279)

The story in "The Book of Alma" revisits the seizure of Montezuma as Ammon issues death threats against King Lamoni. Lamoni begs for his life, while Montezuma, hoping to survive, accedes to his captors' demands.

De Leon exclaimed in his rough voice to Cortes: "Why, Sir, do you waste so many words? Tell	Now when the king saw that Ammon could slay him,
him, that if he does not instantly yield himself our prisoner, **we will plunge** our	he began to plead with Ammon, that he would spare his life. But Ammon
swords into his body: Let us now assure our lives or perish." Montezuma was much struck in the manner in which De Leon expressed himself,	raised his sword, and said unto him, Behold, I will smite thee, except thou wilt grant unto me that my bretheren may be cast out of prison.
Notwithstanding these assurances,	
Montezuma was in	Now the king,
great fear of being put to death. (Vol. IV, p. 59)	fearing that he should lose his life, said,
At last he was obliged to consent saying, "I trust myself with you, let us go! let us go! since the gods will have it so." (Vol. IV, p. 57)	If thou wilt spare me, I will grant unto thee whatsoever thou wilt ask, even to half of the kingdom. (p. 281)

Montezuma remained captive for months while Cortes used him to quell rebellions (and to buy time to plunder the empire). In *The Book of Mormon*, Montezuma returned later in the persona of a converted Lamanite prophet named Samuel. In the meantime, trouble had only just begun for General Cortes—and for the Nephites in the land of Zarahemla.

⋙ **12** ⋘

PREPARING
FOR BATTLE

To send their characters to the battlefield, Joseph Smith Sr. and Joseph Smith Jr. needed to outfit their warriors with weapons. Generally the Smiths referenced armaments used by the Tartars in *The Travels of Marco Polo*. Of note is the Smiths' mention of elephants, which inhabited Asia (*The Travels of Marco Polo*) but not Mesoamerica except in the form of mastodons, extinct since the Ice Age.

They also wrote horses and chariots into the plot. We learned in the previous chapter that the horse was also unknown in the Americas until the conquistadores' arrival.

Where did the Smiths get the idea of Nephite horses and *chariots*? Obviously the Indians didn't have them; they didn't even use wheels for transportation. The Spanish didn't bring any chariots. Yet, they are there in Zarahemla:

[The Nephites] had taken their horses, and their chariots, and their cattle . . . and did march forth by thousands, and by tens of thousands . . . to defend themselves against their enemies. (3 Nephi 2: p. 459 [3:22])

Chariots might be appropriate for the Aztecs if they were the descendants of Tartars, as Mr. Pinkerton suggested. Tartars could have come to the New World on their ships and brought chariots with their horses or built them once they had settled there. The Asians in *The Travels of Marco Polo* used chariots. In footnote 1356, on page 672 in Book III, chapter XXIII, of William Marsden's 1818 edition of *The Travels of Marco Polo*, the Smiths found pay dirt with the mention of elephants, horses, and a chariot.

o Son! I will bestow upon thee the elephant-drivers, the charioteers, the horsemen, and arrayed footmen, with delightful horses.

Thus the Tartar horse and chariot became tools of war for the Nephites. Weapons used by Tartars also became the armaments of the Nephites and Lamanites.

Let's look at William Marsden's *The Travels of Marco Polo*, Book I, Chapter XIII, page 82, which describes the manufacture of metals and weapons (Figure 56).

Meredith Sheets searched *The Book of Mormon*, using the keywords *steel, antimony, manufacture, warlike equipment, saddles, bridles, spurs, swords, bows*, and *quivers*. He found these words on page 147. The original is shown below (Figure 57).

Let's compare the verbiage from these stories, written by authors separated by centuries in real life, using the table below. Highlighted keywords emphasize the commonalities.

are found the precious stones that we call turquoises.[181]   There are also veins of steel,[182] and of antimony[183] in large quantities. They manufacture here in great perfection all the articles necessary for warlike equipment, such as saddles, bridles, spurs, swords, bows, quivers, and every kind of arms in use amongst these people. The

Figure 56. Marsden, *Marco Polo,* 82

fortify our cities, or whatsoever place of our inheritance. And we multiplied exceedingly, and spread upon the face of the land, and became exceeding rich in gold, and in silver, and in precious things, and in fine workmanship of wood, in buildings, and in machinery, and also in iron, and copper, and brass, and steel, making all manner of tools of every kind to till the ground, and weapons of war; yea, the sharp pointed arrow, and the quiver, and the dart, and the javelin, and all preparations for war; and thus being prepared to meet the Lamanites, they did not prosper against us. But the word of the Lord

Figure 57. Jarom 1: p. 147

Parallel Comparison Table on Metals and Weapons

The Travels of Marco Polo Chapter XIII Page 82	*The Book of Mormon* Jarom, Chapter 1 Page 147 [1:8]
There are also veins of	in iron, and copper, and brass, and
steel,	steel,
and of antimony in large quantities. They	
manufacture	making
here in great perfection	
all the articles necessary	all manner of tools of every kind
for	to till the ground, and
warlike equipment,	weapons of war;
such as	yea,
saddles, bridles,	
spurs, swords,	the sharp pointed
bows,	arrow, and the
quivers,	quiver,
	and the dart, and the javelin,
and every kind of arms in use amongst these people.	and all preparations for war.

Observe how Senior and Junior even used the *identical sequence* as Polo, with either the same words or words altered slightly or replaced by synonyms. For example, Smith used *making* rather than *manufacturing*; *all manner of tools of every kind* instead of *all the articles necessary*; and *weapons of war* rather than *warlike equipment*.

The Spanish had steel swords with straight blades, which were copied as the steel swords of the Nephites (like the sword of Laban from "The First Book of Nephi"). In Cortes's battles:

> ...where we too were attacked by large bodies of the Indians, whom we soon obliged to retreat by means of our muskets and crossbows, and the superiority of our good swords.[131]

The Lamanites had swords, too, which we will assume meant the two-handed stone war clubs with razor-sharp edges of the Mexicans and Tlascalan Indians. In Charles Cullen's translation of *The History of Mexico by Abbé D. Francesco Saverio Clavigero*, engraved copperplate number ten illustrates an ancient Mexican Indian warrior with a bow and arrows (and we can assume the arrows are in a quiver since they are bunched together on his back), shield, sling, and a wooden sword (Figure 58).

The Spanish were impressed by the ferocity of the Indians and their fighting clubs, or what Captain Diaz called "two-handed swords":

> [The Tlascalans] now retreated to some uneven ground, where the whole army of the state of Tlascala, 40,000 in number, were posted under cover.... While closely environed in this manner, a number of their strongest warriors, armed with tremendous two-handed swords, made a combined attack on Pedro de Moron, an expert horseman.[132]

This next plate shows a Mexican sword as it could be used in combat; the engraving is of "A Gladiatorian Sacrifice" in ancient Mexico. According to Cullen, this was a fight to the death of a slave against a series of Mexican warriors. If the slave won each fight, he would gain his freedom (Figure 59).

Figure 58. Cullen, *History of Mexico*, Plate 10, "Mexican Warrior"

Figure 59. Cullen, *History of Mexico*, Plate 12, "A Gladiatorian Sacrifice"

The Book of Mormon mentions weapons of steel and iron elsewhere in action in Mesoamerica:

> Wherefore, he came to the hill Ephraim, and he did moulten out of the hill, and *made swords out of steel* for those which he had drew away with him; and after that he had armed them with swords, he returned to the city Nehor and gave battle unto his brother Corihor, by which means he obtained the kingdom, and restored it unto his father Kib. (Ether 3: p. 551 [7:9])

And I did teach my people, that they should build buildings; and that they should work in all manner of wood, and of *iron*, and of copper, and of brass, and of *steel*, and of gold, and of silver, and of precious ores, which were in great abundance. (2 Nephi 4: p. 72 [5:15])

This is interesting, since firsthand accounts of the ancient Mexican Indians reported they did not have steel swords. According to Diaz, the Indians' swords were inferior to the Spaniards'. The only steel the Mexicans wielded was on the ends of lances made from swords taken from fallen conquistadores.

Why did the Indians not have fine steel weapons? Because, according to Diaz, "there was then no wheat in Mexico, wine, oil, vinegar, pork, *iron*, and other necessaries. . . ."[133]

So where did the Smiths get iron and steel if not from their reference books?

Another befuddlement: In *The Book of Mormon*, the Nephites and Lamanites wielded a "cimeter" (today commonly spelled "scimitar"). The *cimeter* is a heavy sword with a curved blade. What was the Smiths' source-book for this weapon? According to A. V. B. Norman's *Arms and Armor* and *History of War and Weapons, 449–1660 AD*, the cimeter was reportedly first used in the seventh century AD in Japan.[134] If Norman is correct, how did the Lamanites and Nephites get their hands on this weapon in 70 BC?

. . . arm them . . . with swords, and with cimeters. (Mosiah 6: p. 175 [9:16])

. . . arm them with swords, and with cimeters. (Alma 27: p. 395 [60:2])

We surmise it was from Marsden again, footnote 878, on page 451, Chapter XLIV, in Book II.

This laudable respect shewn by the Tartar tribes to the sanctity of the grave, has been the occasion of the Russians discovering in the burial places of these people a great number and variety of undisturbed articles, as well as large deposits of the precious metals, which former conquerors had not presumed to violate. "In these tombs" says Strahlenberg "are found all sorts of vessels, urns, wearing-apparel, ornaments and trinkets, *cimetars*, daggers, horse-trappings, knives, all sorts of little idols, medals of gold and silver, chess-boards, and chess-men of gold; as also large golden plates on which the dead bodies have been laid."

In a later chapter we'll investigate Marsden's note about the Tartars having "large golden plates."

Possibly the Smiths were confused about the meaning of *cimeter*, mistaking it for a *mace*, which is a heavy staff or club, often spiked, composed wholly or partially of steel. It was used especially in the Middle Ages for breaking armor.

If the Smiths were unfamiliar with the term, which has no contextual clues about its meaning in Polo's above extract, perhaps they looked it up in *Webster's Dictionary*, the 1817 edition for use in schools.[135] There, the word is spelled *cimeter* rather than Polo's *cimetar*, and the Smiths used the former, just as in their modern Webster's dictionary.

In the following, Polo mentions iron maces:

> Their arms are bows, *iron maces*, and in some instances, spears; but the first is the weapon at which they are the most expert, being accustomed, from children, to employ it in their sports.[136]

Often the medieval traveler used the phrase *sword and mace.*

> . . . *swords, and maces* shod with iron; and such was the slaughter.[137]

> . . . the men grasped their *swords and iron maces.*[138]

Why do we suspect that the Mormon authors mistakenly substituted *cimeter* for *mace* from Marco Polo's story? Because in "The Book of Alma," page 346 [44:8] you'll find a story where the Lamanite warrior Zerahemnah

> . . . came forth and delivered up his *sword and his cimeter.*

This means that Zerahemnah was carrying two heavy swords, which is highly unlikely. A sword and mace may be wielded by one man, but Zerahemnah would clearly be overburdened by the weight.

What about the Aztecs? Indians carrying two heavy metal swords is contrary to the facts as reported on-the-ground by the conquistadors. In his *History of the Conquest of Mexico*, Captain Bernal Diaz documents the Spanish armaments and those of the Mexicans and other Indians.

> Montezuma had an army of an hundred thousand warriors.... They described the arms of the Mexicans as consisting of double-headed darts, which were projected by a kind of slings, lances having stone heads, an ell in length, and both edges sharp as a razor, and two-handed swords, edged likewise with sharp stones, besides shields and other defensive armour.[139]

After defeating the Tlascalans and negotiating a peace treaty with their chiefs, Cortes marched into Mexico along with a two thousand-man infantry regiment of Tlascalans, which functioned as a kind of Praetorian Guard for Cortes. He and his men were given a tour of Mexico City, which included the storage places for weapons and defensive armor:

> Connected with the palace of Montezuma there were two large buildings filled with every kind of arms, both offensive and defensive, some of which were richly ornamented with gold and jewels; such as large and small shields, some of the latter being so contrived as to roll up in a small compass, and to let fall in action so as to cover the whole body; much defensive armour of quilted cotton, ornamented with various devices of feather work; helmets or casques for the head made of wood and bone, adorned with plumes of feathers; immense quantities of bows, arrows, darts, and slings; lances having stone heads or blades six feet long, so strong as not to break when fixed in a shield, and as sharp as razors; clubs or two-handed swords, having edges of sharp stones; and many other articles which I cannot enumerate.[140]

Nephite army captain Moroni—not to be confused with the angel Moroni with the gold plates—was an exceptional military commander. The Smiths based his character on Hernan Cortes. His name may also be derived from one of Cortes's officers: Pedro de *Moron*.

Now how did the plagiarists work this information into *The Book of Mormon*? In about 70 BC, Captain Moroni's objective was to free his countrymen from the Lamanites. His forces had an enormous advantage over their enemy; the Nephites wore defensive body armor, but the Lamanites had none.

> And it came to pass that [Chief Captain Moroni] met the Lamanites
> in the borders of Jershon, and his people were armed with swords, and
> with cimeters, and all manner of weapons of war. And it came to pass, that
> when the armies of the Lamanites saw that the people of Nephi, or that
> *Moroni had prepared his people with breast-plates*, and with *arm-shields*;
> yea, and also *shields to defend their heads*; and also they were dressed with
> *thick clothing*.
>
> Now *the army of Zerahemnah was not prepared with any such thing*. They
> had only their swords, and their cimeters, their bows and their arrows,
> their stones and their slings; but they were naked, save it were a skin
> which was girded about their loins. (Alma 20: p. 341–342)

This plot element was lifted from *Marco Polo*, too. The Tartars were a brutal and successful warrior tribe. They conquered a vast area of Asia by savagely fighting on horseback, using their unmatched skill with a bow and arrow. If the Mexicans are their descendants, their use of the same weapons as the Tartars would please the Smiths. While the Tartars used armor, their enemies did not. According to Marco Polo:

[The Tartars] wear defensive armour made of the thick hides of buffaloes and other beasts, dried by the fire, and thus rendered extremely hard and strong.[141]

The castle [on the elephant] contained many cross-bowmen and archers, and the top of it was hoisted the imperial standard ... of the sun and moon.[142]

... the Tartars by their consummate skill in archery, were too powerful for them, and galled them the more *exceedingly*, from *their not being provided with such armour as was worn by the former*.[143]

Both the Mexicans and the Spanish wore thick, quilted cotton as armor. Fortunately, we can see examples in an engraved plate from Cullen, "Mexican Armour," with "Shields" and a "Sword" (Figure 60).

Arrows in My (Cotton) Armour

The Spanish conquerors encountered some expert archers in the Mexican Empire. Captain Diaz wrote that after one battle he had seven arrows sticking in his armor.[144]

We continued our march through the other districts of *Cimatlan* and *Talatiopan*, where we were attacked by a numerous body of archers, by whom above twenty of our soldiers were wounded and two horses killed; but we very soon defeated them. These people were the most powerful archers I had yet seen, as they were able to drive their arrows *through two suits of well quilted cotton armour*.[145]

Putting it all together, the Smiths stayed very close to their source material. Studying the battle scenes below, placed side by side, you will see that the conquistadores and the Nephites (1) go through a pass, (2) are attacked by Indians or Lamanites, (3) with bow and arrows, and (4) remain protected by their armor. Also (5) no Nephites or Spanish are killed, but (6) some were wounded, (8) with arrows in their legs.

Figure 60. Cullen, *History of Mexico*, Plate 15, "Mexican Armour"

Kerr, Vol. IV, p. 242	Alma 21, p. 362
We soon arrived at a pass among lakes and marshes, where the Indians had thrown up a strong circular entrenchment of large trees and pallisades . . . where they gave us a very warm reception with a flight of darts and arrows,	and thus the Lamanites did attempt to destroy the Nephites . . . and more than a thousand of the Lamanites were slain . . . there was not a single soul of the Nephites which were slain.
by which they killed seven horses, and wounded Rangel and seven of our men.	There were about fifty which were wounded,
	which had been exposed to the arrows of the Lamanites through the pass; but they were shielded by their shields, and their breast-plates, and their head-plates,
On this occasion	insomuch that
I received a wound in my leg,	their wounds were upon their legs;
and had seven arrows sticking in my cotton armour.	many of which were very severe.

General Cortes was also wounded in the leg during the siege of Mexico City, which can be added to the Nephite source of "wounds were upon their legs."

Cortes used every effort to rally his men, but all in vain, and was *wounded in the leg* at the narrow pass by some of the enemy canoes.[146]

Based on research using *The Travels of Marco Polo*, Robert Kerr's version of Diaz's *Conquest of Mexico*, Charles Cullen's book, and the *Modern Traveller* volume on *Mexico*, we assembled this chart of weapons.

Weapon	Nephite or Jaredite	Lamanite	Tartar	Mexican & Other Indians	Cortes & Spanish Army
Axe/Hatchet	▨	▨		▨	▨
Armor	▨		▨	▨	▨

Weapon	Nephite or Jaredite	Lamanite	Tartar	Mexican & Other Indians	Cortes & Spanish Army
Bow and Arrow/ (Spanish crossbow)	■	■	■	■	■
Sword (steel, straight blade)	■				■
Clubs or Two-handed swords (wood/stone)		■		■	
Scimeter or Cimetar (steel, curved blade)	■		■		
Mace			■		
Darts	■			■	
Sling	■	■		■	
Lance/Javelin	■		■	■	■
"Buckler" (type of Spanish lance)	■				■
Horse	■		■		■
Chariot	■		■		
Elephant	■		■		

Ancient Forts

Twenty-five-year-old Captain Moroni knew trouble was brewing among the Lamanites across the land of Zarahemla. As the chosen leader of the Nephite army, he needed to prepare the soldiers for battle. Moroni was particularly adept at building Nephite cities and then fortifying them against Lamanite offensives:

> And now it came to pass that Moroni did not stop making preparations for war, or to defend themselves against the Lamanites; for he caused that his armies should commence in the commencement of the twentieth year of the reign of the Judges, that they should commence in digging up heaps of earth round about all the cities. (Alma 22: pp. 362–363 [50:1])

Pay attention to the details from chapter twenty-one of "The Book of Alma," and then we will investigate where the Smiths found their specifications for Nephite fortifications.

> . . . yea, he had been strengthening the armies of the Nephites, and erecting small forts, or places of resort; *throwing up banks of earth round about,* to enclose his armies, and also building walls of stone to encircle them about, round about their cities, and the borders of their lands; yea, all round about the land; (p. 358 [48:8])

> . . . and in their weakest fortifications, he did place the greater number of men; and *thus he did fortify and strengthen the land which was possessed by the Nephites.* (p. 358 [48:9])

> And behold, the city had been re-built, and Moroni had stationed an army by the borders of the city, *and they had cast up dirt round about, to shield them from the arrows and stones of the Lamanites;* for behold, they fought with stones, and with arrows. (p. 359 [49:2])

> And thus were *the Nephites prepared to destroy all such as should attempt to climb up to enter the fort by any other way, by casting over stones and arrows at them.* (p. 361 [49:19])

Moroni oversaw the building of circular stone walls, the mounding of earthen banks around the cities, and the arming of soldiers for defense. Later, after defeating the Lamanites in battle, the captain of the Nephite armies continued construction elsewhere:

> . . . by the orders of Moroni, caused that they should commence laboring in *digging a ditch round about the land or the city Bountiful;*

> and he caused that *they should build a breastwork of timbers upon the inner bank of the ditch; and they cast up dirt out of the ditch against the breastwork of timbers;* and thus they did cause the Lamanites to labor, until

they had encircled the city of Bountiful round about with *a strong wall of timbers and earth, to an exceeding height.* (Alma 24: pp. 374–375 [53:3–4])

Where did the authors of *The Book of Mormon* learn military strategy for their tale—the fortresses, walls of stone and timbers, and the ditches that would lend realism to a story about ancient Mesoamerica? From Marco Polo? Bernal Diaz's record of Cortes's conquest? Possibly they gained knowledge from seeing a copperplate of a walled fort built by ancient Indians in America. John Pinkerton's "Palace of the Inca's at Canar" was engraved in 1813 for the same set of geography books that the Smiths relied on for their fictitious record from gold plates.[147] (Figure 61)

Or perhaps just reading about the Indian fort with its walls, towers, and loopholes was enough:

Figure 61. Pinkerton, *Voyages and Travels*, Vol. 15, Plate 5, "Palace of the Inca's at Canar"

About two leagues north-east of the town of Atun-Canar, or great Canar, is a fortress or palace of the yncas. It is the most entire, the largest, and best built in all the kingdom. Close by its entrance runs a little river, and the back part of it terminates in a high and thick wall at the slope of a mountain. In the middle of it is a kind of oval tower, about two toises high from the ground within the fort, but without it rises six or eight above that of the hill. . . . In the sides towards the country are loop-holes; and in critical times it was made a court of guard. . . . It had only one entrance, which was in the side opposite to the tower, and facing the last angle on the right near the rivulet.[148]

The Spanish found numerous Indian fortifications in Mexico, all of which Cortes and his little army invaded. Some words used by Bernal Diaz to describe them are *barbican, pallisade* (sic), *pale,* and *ramparts.*

If the Smiths wanted to use Diaz as a model, they might be unfamiliar with the term *barbican,* an outward fortification; *palisade,* an enclosure made of wooden stakes used for defense; *pale,* a wooden stake or post used to make a fence; and *rampart,* a defensive wall used to defend a stronghold. They might have used a dictionary. These words and definitions are all found in the 1817 *Dictionary of the English Language* by Noah Webster. Or, another helpful reference in the early 1800s might have been *The Second American Edition of the British Encyclopedia, a Dictionary of Arts & Sciences,* which was printed in Philadelphia in 1818.[149] (Figure 62).

BARABCAN, or BARBICAN, an outer defence (sic) or fortification to a city or castle, used especially as a fence to the city, or walls; also, an aperture made in the walls of a fortress, to fire through upon the enemy. It is also used as a watchtower, to descry the approach of the enemy; and it sometimes denotes a fort at the entrance of a bridge, on the outlet of a city having a double wall with towers.

Comparing all these definitions plus the details of the Indian fortresses from Bernal Diaz's history book to *The Book of Mormon,* you'll find that the sourcebooks gave the Smiths plenty of material for their scriptures. One of these sources says:

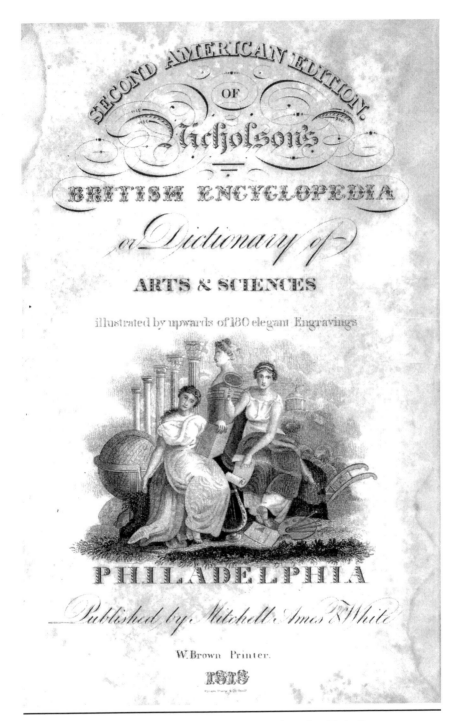

Figure 62. Nicholson's British Encyclopedia, Title Page

... we came in two days to a district inhabited by a nation called "Mazo-tecas," where we found a newly built town, *fortified by two circular enclo-sures of palisades, one of which was like a barbican,* having loop-holes to shoot through, *strengthened by ditches.*[150]

Cortes's army also passed fortifications on their way to Tlascala:

About two leagues from the last resting place, we came to a fortification built of stone and lime, excellently constructed for defence, and so well cemented that nothing but iron tools could make an impression on it ... which had been built by the Tlascalans to defend their territory against the incursions of their Mexican enemies. ...[151]

Immediately after victory [at the Battle of Otumba], we resumed our march for Tlascala. ... *We came to a rampart built in ancient times as a boundary between the state of Tlascala and the dominions of Mexico.*[152]

That fort or rampart seems to be illustrated in a plate that Charles Cullen called "Entrance of the Tlascalan Territories" (Figure 63).

The Spanish conqueror's men encountered many ditches, ramparts, and palisades in their ninety-three-day assault on Mexico City. Captain Diaz wrote:

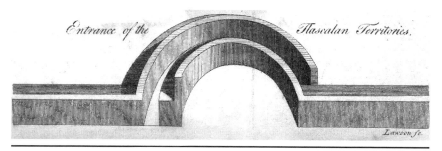

Figure 63. Cullen, *History of Mexico*, Plate 16, "Entrance of the Tlascalan Territories"

On our attack, the Mexicans broke down one of the bridges in the rear of their own barricades and parapets, leaving one narrow passage at a place where the water was very deep as a decoy, and even *dug trenches and pit-falls where the water was more shallow, placing pallisades in the deep water* to prevent the approach of our vessels, and constructing parapets on both sides of the breach.[153]

But the enemy continued their attacks daily, and even gained ground, *making new ramparts and ditches.*[154]

The Mormon scriptures use several stories from Bernal Diaz's descriptions for their Nephite forts. The tale of Captain Moroni's forts is in the right column of this table, with corresponding excerpts from Bernal Diaz regarding the nation of Mazotecas on the left.

A few elements of these stories related to the construction of forts may stand out to you: (1) *strengthened by ditches* becomes *digging up heaps of earth,* (2) two circular enclosures of palisades becomes (a) placing timbers "round the cities" and (b) "frame of pickets built upon the timbers," and (3) the Indians' circular palisades, "one of which was like a barbican, having loop-holes to shoot through," becomes Moroni's "towers to be erected that overlooked those works of pickets; and [Moroni] caused places of security to be built upon those towers."

R. Kerr, Vol. IV, Conquest of Mexico by Bernal Diaz, p. 260	The Book of Alma Chapter 22 pp. 362–363 [50:1–33]
district inhabited by a nation called the Mazotecas, where we found a newly built town,	[see below "throughout all the land that was possessed by the Nephites."]
[see below "strengthened by ditches"]	that they should commence in digging up heaps of earth round about all the cities, throughout all the land which was possessed by the Nephites;
fortified by two circular enclosures of pallisades,	and upon the top of these ridges of earth he caused that there should be timbers; yea, works of timbers built up

R. Kerr, Vol. IV, Conquest of Mexico *by Bernal Diaz,* p. 260	The Book of Alma Chapter 22 pp. 362–363 [50:1–33]
	to the height of a man, round about the cities.
	And he caused that upon those works of timbers, that there should be a frame of pickets built upon the timbers, round about; and they were strong and high;
one of which was like a barbican, having loop-holes to shoot through, and was strengthened by ditches.	and he caused towers to be erected that overlooked those works of pickets; and he caused places of security to be built upon those towers,
Another part of the town was inaccessible, being the summit of a perpendicular rock, on the top of which the natives had collected great quantities of stones for their defence:	that the stones and the arrows of the Lamanites could not hurt them. And they were prepared, that they could cast stones from the top thereof, according to their pleasure and their strength,
And a third quarter of the town was defended by an impassable morass . . . While we were expressing our	and slay him which should attempt to approach near the walls of the city.
astonishment at these circumstances,	Thus Moroni did prepare strongholds . . . (p. 363)
fifteen Indians came out of the morass in the most submissive manner, and told us that they had been forced to the construction of this fortress as their last resort, in an unsuccessful war with a neighboring nation.	[Moroni] did cause the Lamanites which had taken prisoners, that they should commence a labor in strengthening the fortifications round about the city Gid. (Alma 25: p. 381 [55:25])

As for building forts, Marco Polo has the last word.

Similarities of the Terrain Descriptions and Fortifications of the Province of Zorzania and City of Moroni

In one of his journeys, Marco Polo visited a province called Zorzania. Part of Zorzania was controlled by the Tartars, but another area was ruled by local princes because that region's strong fortresses successfully repelled the Tartars.[155] First, Marco Polo mentions "Melik," the king of Zorzania,[156] and the name becomes the Joseph Smiths' "Mulek," a city under siege. (Alma 22, p. 372 [52:15–16])

Polo's story is about Alexander the Great's famous "Gate of Iron" and other fortifications in the province of Zorzania. Notice in the comparison chart below that both Polo and Smith described the locations of the new city as being by the "east sea" or "on the east by the Caspian sea." Although these descriptions are far apart in terms of percentage points into the text (7 percent for Polo and 62 percent for *The Book of Mormon*), this is a good example of plagiarism used in different parts of the books. Try using this test: can you count how many times the Smiths copied from *Marco Polo*? Authors' note: brackets [ ] are inserted to show out-of-order phrases, but the parentheses (()) on the Polo side are copied exactly as they appear in the original text of Marsden's 1818 version.

The Travels of Marco Polo Book I, Ch. V, p. 52–57	The Book of Mormon The Book of Alma
(p. 56, n. 115)	(Alma 22: p. 364 [50:13])
The natives in general are of the opinion . . . that the	the Nephites
city of Derbent was built by Alexander the Great,	began the foundation of a city; and they called the name of the city Moroni; and it was
and that the long wall that reached to the Euxine (Greater sea), was built by his order . . .	
(p. 57, n. 116) Comania was bounded on the **east** by the **Caspian sea**;	by the East Sea;
on the west by the mountains that divide it from Circassia; on the north by the dominions of Russia; and	and it was
on the south by	on the south by
Georgia.	the line of the possessions of the Lamanites.

The Travels of Marco Polo Book I, Ch. V, p. 52–57	The Book of Mormon The Book of Alma
(p. 53)	(Alma 22: p. 363 [50:10])
Alexander caused	And he ... caused
a great wall to be constructed at the entrance of the Pass, and	them to erect
fortified it with towers,	fortifications,
in order to restrain those who dwelt beyond it	that they might secure their armies and their people
from giving him molestation.	from the hands of their enemies.
From its uncommon strength the Pass obtained the name of the Gate of Iron, and	
	(Alma 22: p. 363 [50:11])
Alexander is commonly said	And thus he
to have enclosed the Tartars between two mountains.	cut off all the strong holds of the Lamanites ... fortifying the line between the Nephites and the Laman-ites ... from the West Sea.
	(Alma 26: p. 383 [56:13–14])
[Note: *Manji* is Marco Polo's name for southern China (p. 536), and Joseph Smith used *Manti* for the name of the southern land of the Nephites].	And now these are the cities which the Lamanites have obtained possession ... The land of **Manti**, or the city of **Manti**, and the city of Zeezrom, and the city of
(p. 53, cont'd) It is not correct however to call the people Tartars, which in those days they were not, but a race named *Cumani* ...	Cumeni ...
	(p. 364 [50:15])
In this province there are	And they also began ... to build
many towns and castles;	many cities
the necessaries of life are in abun-dance; the country	on the north ... by the borders of the seashore.
produces a great quantity of silk, and a manufacture is carried on of silk interwoven with gold.	

The Travels of Marco Polo Book I, Ch. V, p. 52–57	The Book of Mormon The Book of Alma
	(Alma 27: p. 365 [50:34])
This is the province into which, when Alexander the Great	. . . there they **did head them**, by
attempted to advance northwards,	[see "land northward" below]
he was unable to penetrate, by reason of	
the narrowness	the narrow
and difficulty of a certain **pass,**	pass
which on one side is washed by the	which led
sea . . .	by the sea
[see "advance northwards" above]	into the **land northward;** yea,
(p. 52 . . .	
It is situated **between two seas,**	by the sea,
of which that on the northern	
(western) side	on the west,
is called the Greater sea (Euxine), and the other,	and
on the eastern side,	on the east.
is called the sea of *Abakû* (Caspian).	

The numbered keywords and phrases are:

	Marco Polo	Book of Mormon
1	The natives	the Nephites
2	city of Derbent was built	began the foundation of a city
3	east by the Caspian sea	by the East Sea
4	on the south by	on the south by
5	caused . . . wall to be constructed	he . . . caused them to erect
6	fortified	fortifications

7	in order to restrain	that they might secure
8	from giving him molestation.	from the hands of their enemies.
9	enclosed the Tartars	cut off all the strong holds
10	Cumani	Cumeni
11	many towns	many cities
12	advance northwards	land northward
13	narrowness . . . of a . . . pass	the narrow pass
14	by the sea	by the sea
15	between two seas	by the sea
16	on . . . western side	on the west
17	on eastern side	on the east

And don't forget Melik/Mulek and Manji/Manti, which makes a grand total of *nineteen* plagiarized lines in this story about fortifying the Nephite city of Moroni.

Save Us from the Cannibals

This final story of battle preparations of the Nephites comes from an experience that Marco Polo had when he was traveling by ship to Persia on his return to Venice. The ships had to dock at the island kingdom of Samara for five months, during which time Polo had defensive fortifications constructed to guard against natives who were cannibals. Polo ordered two thousand Tartar sailors and soldiers to dig a ditch around their port and reinforce it with timber and by other means.

Within chapters twenty-three and twenty-four (pages 374 to 377) in "The Book of Alma" are two Nephite commanders, "Teancum" and "Helaman." Helaman marched with his troops, and Teancum ordered his troops to fortify a position. After reading our Marco Polo summary above, can you guess how many troops Helaman had in his garrison and what kind of defenses Teancum built? After reading the next table, can there be any question that the Smiths placed Helaman and Teancum into Marco Polo's shoes?

Travels of Marco Polo Ch. XIII, p. 606 Of the third kingdom, named Samara.	The Book of Mormon The Book of Alma Chapters 23, 24
As it was necessary to continue for so long a time at this island,	(p. 376–77 [53:22])
Marco Polo established himself	. . . Helaman did
on shore,	
with a party of about	march at the head of his
two thousand men;	two thousand stripling soldiers,
[see "on shore" above]	to . . . the land on the south, by the West Sea.
and in order to guard against mischief from the savage natives, who seek for opportunities of seizing stragglers, putting them to death, and eating them,	
	(Alma 23, p. 374–75 [53:3–4]) . . .
he caused a	Teancum, by the orders of Moroni, caused that they should commence in laboring in
large and deep ditch to be dug	digging a ditch
around him, on the land	round about the land,
side, in such a manner that each of its extremities terminated in the port, where the shipping lay.	or the city Bountiful;
This ditch he strengthened by	and he caused that they should
erecting several blockhouses or redoubts, of wood,	build a breastwork of timbers
the country affording an abundant supply of that material; and being defended	upon the inner bank of the ditch . . . thus they did cause the Lamanites to labor, until they
[see above, "ditch to be dug around him"]	had encircled the city of Bountiful round about with

Travels of Marco Polo Ch. XIII, p. 606 *Of the third kingdom, named Samara.*	*The Book of Mormon* The Book of Alma Chapters 23, 24
by this kind of **fortification**, he kept the party in complete security, during the five months of their residence.	a **strong wall of timbers and earth**, to an exceeding height.

The ten phrases we tracked from the story are:

	Marco Polo	Joseph Smith
1	on shore	land . . . by the West Sea
2	two thousand men	two thousand . . . soldiers
3	caused a large and deep	caused that they should
4	ditch to be dug	digging a ditch
5	around him, on the land	round about the land
6	erecting blockhouses or redoubts	build a breastwork
7	of wood	of timbers
8	around him, on the land	encircled the city
9	ditch he strengthened	upon inner bank of ditch
10	fortification	strong wall of timbers and earth

Their forts are built, their steel swords and cimeters sharpened, and their quivers are full of arrows. The Nephites are wearing their defensive armour of thick clothing and mounting their horses and chariots. Prepare for battle!

Tecozauhtla

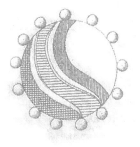

13

WARRIORS
AND WARFARE

The *Book of Mormon*'s cast of characters depicts the adventures of courageous heroes and power-hungry villains. With the rogue Lamanites on the attack, the Nephites were ready for war. All they needed to begin their battles were some good historical narratives on which these clashes could be based. For this, the Joseph Smiths took their plot and details from the nomadic Tartars in *The Travels of Marco Polo*[157] and Hernan Cortes's conquistadores in *History of the Discovery and Conquest of Mexico, Written in the Year 1568, by Captain Bernal Diaz Del Castillo, One of the Conquerors.*[158] The plagiarists also stripped editor James Duncan's *The Modern Traveller* series, specifically the volumes focusing on Arabia,[159] Mexico, and Guatemala.[160]

As you know, the Smiths set their tale in Mesoamerica and created the setting of Zarahemla. Now their story becomes a war epic, which makes sense only in light of the sourcebooks the father and son selected. What comes to mind when we think of the Tartars and the conquistadores? Brutal confrontations between dangerously armed, fierce warriors. The Mongolian armies faced the formidable adversaries of Asian kingdoms; the Spaniards wiped out a whole advanced civilization of Mexico's indigenous people.

Apparently lacking knowledge of war, weapons, and military strategy, the composers of *The Book of Mormon* leaned heavily on their reference books. The plagiarized material shows up in the scripture's chapters and even in historical accounts in the post-*Book of Mormon* scripture, *Doctrine and Covenants*.

Pinpointing the copying is not always easy at this point in *The Book of Mormon*. Now having completed a few hundred pages of their secret manuscript, the father and son were increasingly proficient at plagiarism. Yet at times, the Smiths copied line by line from Polo. Perhaps since they were ignorant about the ways of war, the duo stayed close to the sourcebooks regarding armaments and battles, as errors in those two areas would be easy to detect and disastrous for them.

Oftentimes the Smiths combined the characteristics of several men and battles from Marco Polo's and Captain Diaz's accounts as well as using history books published before 1830. They generally continued their stories with Spaniards to provide the content for the light-skinned Nephites, who lived by God's law, and with the Aztecs as the heathen Lamanites, cursed by God with dark skin.

Sometimes the Lamanites become Nephite allies, however, just as the Indian tribes who were enemies of the Aztecs aligned themselves with Cortes for the assault on Mexico City.

Let's revisit the description of the Lamanites. It is a good example of blending sources, this time with the Smiths' description of their savagery:

And I bear record that *the people of Nephi did seek diligently to restore the Lamanites unto the true faith in God.* But our labors were vain; their hatred was fixed, and they were led by their evil nature, that *they became wild, and ferocious, and a blood-thirsty people; full of idolatry, and filthiness; feeding upon beasts of prey, dwelling in tents, and wandering about in the wilderness,* with a short skin girded about their loins, and their heads shaven; and *their skill was in the bow, and the cimeter, and the ax.* And many of them did eat nothing save it was *raw meat;* and they were continually seeking to destroy us. (Enos 1: pp. 144–145 [1:20])

The Lamanites are also based on the Tartars.

The last sentence of the italicized material in the excerpt would not be an apt description of the Aztecs, a sophisticated people inhabiting a city so grand that it left the Spaniards breathless. No, here the Lamanites found their genesis in Polo's description of the nomadic, ferocious idolaters, the Tartars, right down to the detail of their eating raw meat.

This is no truer than in a story not in *The Book of Mormon* but in the later Mormon scripture containing Joseph Jr.'s revelations, the *Doctrine and Covenants*. The younger Joseph Smith claimed that this powerful verse came to him directly from the voice of God. Let's explore this text for any indication of a different source for the sun, moon, and an army with banners:

The Travels of Marco Polo Book II, Chapter I	*Doctrine and Covenants* Section 32 (pub. 1835)
(p. 262)	
Kublaï-kaan;	I, the Lord, am God,
the latter word implying in **our language lord of lords**	and have given these things unto you, my servant **Joseph Smith, jr.**
(p. 263)	
he [Nayan] privately **dispatched messengers to Kaidu** . . . although a nephew of the Grand *khan,*	**go forth and deliver my words to the children of men.**
was in **rebellion**	**stiffnecked generation**—mine anger is kindled
against him,	**against them.**
and **bore him determined ill will**	
	they shall know of a surety that these things are true: for from heaven will I declare it unto them
(p. 269)	
Kublaï took his station in a large wooden castle, borne on the backs of four elephants	and to none else will I grant this power, to receive this same testimony, among this generation, in this the beginning of the
on top of it was hoisted	**rising up, and coming forth**

The Travels of Marco Polo Book II, Chapter I	*Doctrine and Covenants* Section 32 (pub. 1835)
the imperial standard, adorned with representations of	of my church out of the wilderness—clear as
the sun	the moon, and fair as
and moon.	the sun,
His army,	and terrible as an army
which consisted of the thirty battalions of horse, each battalion containing ten thousand men, armed with bows, he disposed in	
[see below: "in his **banners**"]	with banners.
three grand divisions	And the testimony of **three** witnesses
(p. 270) Nayan, who had privately undergone the ceremony of Baptism, but never made **open profession of Christianity**,	will I send forth of my word.
thought proper, on this occasion to **bear the sign of the cross in his banners.**	[see above: "with banners"]

The connecting key words are:

	Marco Polo	Joseph Smith
1	lord of lords	Lord, am God
2	dispatched messengers	deliver up my words
3	rebellion	anger
4	sun	sun
5	moon	moon
6	His army	terrible army
7	three	three
8	open profession of Christianity	will I send forth my word,
9	in his banners	with banners.

The younger Joseph Smith copied Kublai Khan as if the khan were God and Marco Polo's words as if they were spoken by God in a revelation to Smith.

This brings us to the longest chapter in *The Book of Mormon* called the "Book of Alma, The Son of Alma," which itself has thirty chapters and is 185 pages long. The events related here supposedly occurred in the Nephite calendar of dates that, if the Nephites followed our modern calendar, would be roughly 91 BC to 53 BC. The writer, and keeper of the plates, was the son of the prophet Alma, whom we first encountered in "The Book of Mosiah" as the priest of King Noah, who spoke for the prophet Abinadi.

Comparison of Black and Naked Soldiers

As you may recall, a group in the ancient Americas that descended from Laman, the brother of Nephi, had rebelled against God. As a result, God turned their skin dark as a curse. Moroni and the Nephites were in conflict with Zerahemnah, leader of the Lamanites.

First we will show the phrases relating to naked soldiers, and second we will again use the text where the Lamanites were turned black by the curse of God. In *Marco Polo*, the medieval traveler describes the province of Maabar, "which is not an island, but a part of the continent of the greater India." In note 1256, William Marsden describes this territory as the province of Malabar. Certain armaments of the Tartars are taken from other parts of the book, as we explained in the previous chapter.

The Travels of Marco Polo p. 638 Of the Province of Maabar	The Book of Mormon Alma Ch. 20, p. 342 [43:20, 37]
The people go to battle with lances and shield	Now the army of Zerahemnah was not prepared with any such thing [war or battle with Nephites]. They had only
[p. 270, "lances, swords, and maces"	their swords, and their cimeters, their

The Travels of Marco Polo p. 638 Of the Province of Maabar	The Book of Mormon Alma Ch. 20, p. 342 [43:20, 37]
[p. 451, n. 878, "cimetars"]	
[p. 212, n. 202, "They are armed . . .	bows and their arrows,
with bows and arrows,	their stones and their slings;
a sabre"]	
but without clothing,	but they were naked,
and are a despicable and unwarlike race.	(see below, "loathsome . . . people")
(p. 631)	
The natives of this part of the country always go naked,	(see "they were naked" above)
excepting that they	save it were
cover those parts of the body which modesty dictates.	a skin which was girded about their loins
(see "lances and shields" above)	But they were not armed with breast-plates, nor shields

Whereas in Polo's story the natives "esteemed blackness the perfection of beauty," Smith claimed that this was a curse from God.

(Polo, p. 649)	(2 Nephi 4: p. 73 [5:21, 22])
	the Lord God did cause a
In this province the natives, although black,	skin of blackness
are not born of so deep a dye as they afterwards	
attain by artificial means;	to come upon them (Lamanites).
esteeming blackness the perfection of beauty.	they shall be loathsome unto thy people

Battles Fought between Nestardín and the King of Mien and between Moroni and Zerahemnah

This story from *Marco Polo* has useful historical accounts of fierce, brutal battles waged by the grand khan Kublaï. The unusual details provided the Smiths with authenticity for ancient battle scenes.

Beginning on page 441, Polo describes a "memorable battle" fought between the Grand Khan's army and the kingdom of Vochang in the year 1272. According to Polo, "the Grand khan sent an army into the countries of Vochang and Karazan for their protection and defence" against foreign aggressors. The king of Mien and Bangala, which were in India but bordered Vochang, learned that the Tartar army was advancing and decided to launch a pre-emptive attack. The king assembled a great army of sixty thousand men, including horses and foot soldiers and a "multitude of elephants . . . upon whose backs were placed battlements or castles, of wood, capable of containing to the number of twelve or sixteen in each."

The Tartar commander had only twelve thousand men in his army, but he used some woods as cover to protect his troops and flanked the king's army. Polo said that the Indian king's army could not "any longer sustain the conflict or to withstand the impetuosity of the Tartars" and therefore retreated in defeat.

In the Mormon version, this story is found in "The Book of Alma," beginning on page 343. In the Mormon battle, Moroni is the military leader of the Nephites who confronts Zerahemnah, the leader of the Lamanites, and the Lamanite army. The Lamanites intend to destroy the Nephites, reportedly to establish a Lamanite kingdom to rule over all the land.

To create this story, the Smiths combined parts of the battle and the two armies described in *Marco Polo*. This means that actions or descriptions of one or both armies in *Marco Polo* may be used to describe only one leader or army in the Mormon story. The Smiths' tale also took information from pages 262 to 271 in *Marco Polo*. This further demonstrates the growing sophistication of the plagiarism as the copying progressed through *Marco Polo*, using multiple stories of battles in *Marco Polo* to create a single battle in *The Book of Mormon*.

This battle is placed *at the same percent through the text in both books* when calculated as a percent carried to the fourth decimal point or more (thus the two stories correspond *exactly* to more than ten-thousandth of one percent or, more exactly, 0.0001 percent). The calculations are as follows:

Marco Polo: p. 441 ÷ 756 total pages = 0.58333,
                or 58.33% through the text.

Joseph Smith: p. 343 ÷ 588 total pages = 0.58333,
                or 58.33% through the text.

The battle in *The Travels of Marco Polo* begins at 58.33 percent and proceeds to 58.73 percent. In *The Book of Mormon*, it begins at the same percentage point and ends at 59.01 percent. The first scene has military leaders planning to protect their country against a foreign aggressor.

The Travels of Marco Polo Book II, Ch. XLII, pp. 441–444 "Of the manner in which the Grand khan effected the conquest of the kingdom of Mien and Bangala."	*The Book of Mormon* "The Book of Alma" Ch. 20, pp. 343–347 (p. 343 [43:29, 30, 35, 37, 38])
(p. 441) It happened that in the year 1272, the Grand *khan* sent an army into the countries of *Vochang* and *Karazan* for their protection and defense against any attack	And now as Moroni knew the intention of the Lamanites, that it was their intention to destroy their brethren, or to subject them and bring them into bondage,
that foreigners might attempt to make . . .	that they might
the King of *Mien* . . . heard that an army of Tartars had arrived . . . he took the resolution of advancing immediately to attack it, in order that by its destruction the Grand *khan* should be deterred from again attempting to station a force upon the borders of his dominions.	establish a kingdom unto themselves, over all the land; and he also knowing that it was the only desire of the Nephites to preserve their lands and their liberty . . . he thought it no sin that he should defend them by stratagem.

While the Tartars were camped, the king of Mien sneaked up on them with a large army. Once the Tartar commander learned about the advancing army, he was alarmed. One of Moroni's captains, Lehi, concealed the army from the Lamanites.

With these, and

a numerous army of horse and foot,	the army which was concealed on the south of the hill, who was led by a man named Lehi; and
he took the road to *Vochang,*	he led his army forth
where the Grand *khan's* army lay, and encamping at no great distance from it. . . . As soon as the approach of the king of *Mien* with so great a force, was known to *Nestardín* . . . he felt much alarmed . . .	

Regarding troop movements, the Tartars and Mien's troops descend into a plain, and the Lamanites poured into the valley.

	And it came to pass that as
but [the Tartars] descending into the plain of *Vochang,*	the Lamanites had passed the hill Riplah, and
took a position in which his flank was covered by a thick	
(p. 442)	
wood of large trees . . .	
Upon the king of *Mien's* learning that the Tartars had	
descended into the plain	came into the valley

In the battle, the Tartars "galled" Mien's troops and took the upper hand, mainly because of the Tartars' defensive armor. The Lamanites suffered the same fate as Mien's troops because of their own lack of armor.

(p. 443) But the Tartars . . . and the work of death commenced, on both sides; but

galled them the more exceedingly, it was more dreadful on the part of the Lamanites;

from their not being provided with such armour as was worn by the former. for their nakedness was exposed to the heavy blows of the Nephites, with their swords and their cimeters . . .

(p. 444) but the Tartars troops were finally victorious: a result that was materially to be attributed to the while on the other hand, there was now and then a man fell among the Nephites, by their swords, and the loss of blood;

troops of the king of *Mien* and *Bangala* not wearing armour as the Tartars did. they being shielded from the more vital parts of the body, or the more vital parts of the body being shielded from the strokes of the Lamanites, by their breast-plates, and their arm-shields, and their head-plates;

The Tartars and the Nephites were significantly outnumbered.

(p. 441) not having under his (*Nes-tardín*) orders more than twelve thousand men . . . (p. 345)

Now

whereas

the enemy had sixty thousand . . . the Lamanites were more numerous;

(p. 442) as well from the yea, by

superiority of their [Mien] numbers, being four to one. more than double the number of the Nephites.

Despite being outnumbered, the Tartars fought with their swords and maces, and the Nephites battled with swords and cimeters.

instead of being discouraged by the superior number of foes . . .

(p. 443) (p. 343)

the men grasped the heavy blows of the Nephites, with

282

their swords	their swords
and iron maces,	and their cimeters,
and violently encountered each other. Then in an instant were to be seen many horrible wounds,	which brought death almost at every stroke.

Arms and legs were severed, and the wounded fell to the ground, bleeding profusely.

	(p. 344)
limbs dismembered, and	they did smite off many of
	their arms
	(p. 343)
	there was now and then
multitudes falling	a man fell
to the ground, maimed and dying; with such	among the Nephites, by their swords, and the
effusion of blood	loss of blood
as was dreadful to behold.	

As the battle raged, the enemy troops began to give way or succumb to fear.

(p. 444) but perceiving at length that it was impossible any longer to sustain the conflict	thus the Nephites
or to withstand the impetuosity of the Tartars;	did carry on the work of death among the Lamanites.
	(pp. 343–344) the Lamanites became frightened, because of the
the greater part of his troops being either killed or wounded, and all the field covered with the carcasses of men and horses, whilst those who survived were beginning to give way;	great destruction among them,

As the battle wound down, the Lamanites and the king of Mien's men are pursued and killed in the retreat.

he also found himself	even until
compelled to take to flight	they began to flee . . .
with the wreck of his army;	
but of whom	(p. 344) And
numbers were afterwards	they were,
slain in pursuit.	pursued by Lehi and his men . . . Moroni and his men began to . . . slay them.

In the final stage, the victorious soldiers stop and reorganize. Nephites pursue the Lamanites, while the Tartars enter some woods to round up armed elephants and finish off the enemy.

(58.73%, p. 444)	(58.67%, p. 345 [44:1])
The Tartars, having collecting their force	they did stop, and
after the slaughter of the enemy,	
returned towards the wood	withdrew a pace from them.
into which the elephants had fled for shelter, in order to take possession of them,	
	(p. 347)
where they found that the men who had escaped from the overthrow were	Zerahemnah . . . did stir up the remainder of his soldiers to anger
employed in cutting down trees and barricading the passages, with the intent of defending themselves.	[44:17] therefore he [Moroni] commanded his people that they should fall upon them and
But their ramparts were soon demolished by the Tartars, who	
slew many of them.	slay them.

Recall that Marco Polo's Venetian dialect included many words beginning with the letter Z, which figures prominently in the text. Performing a "Z comparison" in the above battles shows that the Tartars came from the territory of "Zardandan." Joseph Smith used the Z for "Zerahemnah," the Lamanite leader who was from the land of the "Zoramites."

The next story uses a different battle from Marco Polo for another clash between Moroni and Zerahemnah.

Battles Fought between Kublaï Khan and Nayan and between Moroni and Zerahemnah

As we learned in the introduction to this chapter, the Tartar lord Nayan was a baptized Christian who displayed the cross on his banners. He was also the uncle of Kublaï Khan, although only a few years his senior. Nayan was executed by the Grand khan after the battle, possibly the last Christian Tartar lord serving under Kublaï Khan.

Now look for the ages and descriptions of the commanders and advice from astrologers or a prophet and notice that a part of each army was left behind, that forces arrived secretly, that lookouts were placed in every direction, and that each army was divided for the attack. The battle record begins with a description of military commanders who came to power when they were very young, in their twenties.

The Travels of Marco Polo Book II, Ch. I, Sect. I–II, pp. 262–271. "Of the admirable deeds of Kublaï-kaan, the emperor now reigning; of the battle he fought with Nayan, his uncle, and of the victory he obtained."	*The Book of Mormon* "The Book of Alma" Ch. 20 pp. 341–42 [43:17–28]
(pp. 262–263)	(p. 341)
the Grand *khan*, now reigning,	and Moroni took all the command,
who is styled *Kublaï-kaan*; the latter word implying in our language lord of lords	and the governments of their wars. And

The Travels of Marco Polo Book II, Ch. I, Sect. I–II, pp. 262–271. "Of the admirable deeds of Kublaï- kaan, the emperor now reigning; of the battle he fought with Nayan, his uncle, and of the victory he obtained."	*The Book of Mormon* "The Book of Alma" Ch. 20 pp. 341–42 [43:17–28]
he surpasses every sovereign that has heretofore been or that now is in the world . . . He [Kublaï-kaan] is the sixth Grand *khan*, and began his reign in the year 1256,	
being then twenty-seven years of age.	he was only twenty and five years old
Not only was he brave and daring in action but in	when
point of judgment and	he was appointed
military skill, he was considered to be the most able and	
successful commander	Chief Commander
that ever led the Tartars to battle.	over the armies of the Nephites.

The commanders consult astrologers (the Tartars) or prophets (the Nephites) regarding whether their side will win the battle in the land of Manji or Manti.

(p. 269) he (*Kublaï*)	(p. 342) Moroni, also, knowing of the prophecies of Alma,
called upon his astrologers	sent certain men unto him,
to ascertain by virtue of their art, and to declare in presence of the whole army,	desiring him that he should inquire of the Lord whither
to which side the victory would incline.	the armies of the Nephites should go, to defend themselves against the Lamanites.
They pronounced	the word of the Lord came unto Alma; and Alma informed the messengers of Moroni

	that the armies of the Lamanites were marching round about in the wilderness, that they might come
(see province of "Manji," where this battle was occurring, p. 264)	over into the land of Manti, that they might
that it would fall to the lot of *Kublaï.*	commence an attack upon the more weak part of the people. And those messengers went and delivered the message unto Moroni.

After hearing of their victories, each army is divided, and one group is left behind. The Tartars or Nephites find their enemies in Manji or Manti.

(p. 263) He [Kublaï-kaan] then gave orders for collecting, with utmost celerity,	Now Moroni,
the whole of the troops stationed within ten days march of the city of *Kambal.*	leaving part of his army in the land of Jershon.
These amounted to three hundred and sixty thousand horse. . . . Had he assembled the armies kept up for the constant protection of the different provinces of *Kataia,* it must necessarily have required thirty or forty days.	
(p. 264) It may be proper here to observe, whilst on the subject of the armies of the Grand *khan,* that	took the remainder part of his army and marched over into the
in every province of . . . *Manji*	land of Manti.

Next, the armies arrived secretly. The Tartars posted guards along the roads to watch for the enemy, and Moroni placed spies about the land to watch for the Lamanites. Nayan's army negligently failed to post scouts and was surprised by the Tartars.

(p. 268–269) the Grand *khan* proceeded towards the territories of Nayan, and by forced marches . . . reached it . . .	(pp. 342–343) Moroni caused that his army

So prudently, at the same time, was the expedition managed, that

neither that prince himself nor any of his dependents were aware of it;	should be secreted in the valley which was near the bank of the river Sidon . . .
all roads being guarded in such a manner that no persons who attempted to pass could escape from being made prisoners.	(p. 343) And Moroni placed spies round about, that he might know when the camp of the Lamanites should come.
they [Grand *khan's* army] ascended the hill with alacrity the next morning, and presented themselves before the army of *Nayan*, which they found negligently posted, without advanced parties or scouts. . . .	

Both Nayan and Moroni divide their army before the impending attack.

(p. 269)	(Alma 20: p. 343)
His army, which consisted of thirty battalions of horse, each battalion containing ten thousand men, armed with bows,	
he disposed in three grand divisions;	he divided his army,
and those which formed the left and right wings, he extended in such a manner as to out-flank the army of *Nayan*.	and brought a part over into the valley, and concealed them on the east, and on the south of the hill Riplah.

A large battle ensues, and the vanquished surrender. For the Tartars, it was a "slaughter." The Lamanites were "swept down."

(p. 270)	(Alma 20: p. 344)
and such was the slaughter, and	[The Nephites] began to slay [the
so large were the heaps of the carcasses of men, and more especially of horses, on the field,	Lamanites] . . . and did fall exceeding fast before the swords of the Nephites, and they began to be swept down . . .

that it became impossible for one party
to advance upon the other.

When Nayan realized he was surrounded, he tried to run and save himself. He didn't get far. When Zerahemnah realized that he was surrounded,
he surrendered.

(p. 270)	(Alma 20, p. 345–346)
At length, however,	therefore when
Nayan perceiving	Zerahemnah saw . . .
that he was	that they were
nearly surrounded,	encircled
attempted to save himself by flight, but	about by the Nephites, they were struck with terror . . .
	(p. 346) . . . Zerahemnah . . .
was presently made prisoner,	
and conducted	came forth
	and delivered up his sword and his cimeter, and his bow,
to the presence of *Kublaï*.	into the hands of Moroni.

After the surrender, the two stories diverge. The Joseph Smiths used
an opposite approach from the one in Marco Polo's story. While Nayan
was punished and then executed, Zerahemnah was scalped and ultimately
banished to the wilderness.

	(Alma 20, p. 346 [44:12, 20])
who gave orders for his being put to death.	one of Moroni's soldiers . . . smote Zerahemnah, that he took off his scalp . . .
This was carried into execution by enclosing him between two carpets, which were violently shaken until the spirit had	(p. 347) . . . they were suffered
departed from the body.	to depart into the wilderness.

After seeing their leaders fall, both defeated armies sign a peace treaty with the victors.

(Alma 20, p. 347 [44:20])

Those of (*Nayan's*) troops which survived the battle came to make their submission and	and after they [Zerahemnah and Lamanites] had
swear allegiance to *Kublaï*.	entered into a covenant with him [Moroni] of peace, they were suffered to depart into the wilderness.

Army Divisions

The Tartar military forces were divided into divisions of one hundred, one thousand, and ten thousand troops, and the commanding officers received gold or silver tablets determined by their rank. Here is a copy of the text from *The Travels of Marco Polo*, page 278, explaining the Tartar divisions and tablets (Figure 64).

If the ancient Mexicans were descendants of Tartars, as John Pinkerton theorized, then it would seem natural that their troop divisions and commands matched those of the Tartars, which they do. The Tlascalans were also noted as descendants of the original Aztec inhabitants, and they formed divisions of ten thousand soldiers as well, as related by Bernal Diaz:

> The army now opposed to us consisted of the troops or quotas of *five great chiefs, each consisting of 10,000 men. . . . Thus, 50,000 men were now collected against us* under the banner of Xicotencatl, which was a white bird like an ostrich with its wings spread out.[161]

Knowing this, *The Book of Mormon* authors, in the chapter called "The Book of Mormon" (the chapter in which the great battle at Camorah takes place), also used troop divisions of ten thousand men.

And it came to pass that my men were hewn down, yea, even my *ten thousand* who were with me. . . . And we also beheld the *ten thousand* of my people which were led by my son Moroni. And behold, the *ten thousand* of Gidgiddonah had fallen, and he also in the midst; and Lamah had fallen with his *ten thousand*; and Gilgal had fallen with his *ten thousand*; and Limhah had fallen with his *ten thousand*; and Joneum had fallen with his *ten thousand*; and Camenihah, and Moronihah, and Antionum, and Shiblom, and Shem, and Josh, had fallen with their *ten thousand each*. (Mormon 3, pp. 529–530 [6:10–15])

CHAPTER III.

Of the kind of rewards granted to those who conduct themselves well in fight, and of the golden tablets which they receive.

THE Grand *khan* appoints twelve of the most intelligent amongst his nobles, whose duty it is to make themselves acquainted with the conduct of the officers and men of his army, particularly upon expeditions and in battles, and to present their reports to his majesty,[515] who, upon being apprised of their respective merits, advances them in his service; raising those who commanded an hundred men, to the command of a thousand, and presenting many with vessels of silver, as well as the customary tablets or warrants of command and of government.[516] The tablets given to those commanding an hundred men are of silver, to those commanding a thousand, of gold or of silver gilt; and those who command ten thousand receive tablets of gold, bearing the head of a lion;[517] the former being of the weight of an hundred and twenty *saggi*,[518] and these with the lion's head, two hundred and twenty. At the top of the inscription on the tablet is a sentence to this effect: " By the power and might of the great God, " and through the grace which he vouchsafes to our empire, be the " name of the *Kaan* blessed; and let all such as disobey (what is " herein directed) suffer death and be utterly destroyed." The officers

Figure 64. Marsden, Marco Polo, 278

The Nephite troop divisions perfectly match those of the Tartar division commanders who receive a *golden tablet* for commanding ten thousand men and also match the division size of each division under a Tlascalan chief.

Council of War

Cortes began the invasion of the Mexican empire with three commanders. His little army of barely more than five hundred soldiers faced literally tens of thousands of Indians in a series of battles. Even when his forces grew to over a thousand Spaniards and with the addition of numerous divisions of Indian allies, he was greatly outnumbered by the Mexicans (Figure 65).

Figure 65. Cullen, *History of Mexico*, Plate 25, "Cortes and Officers Alvarado, Sandoval, and Olid."

Captain Moroni and General Cortes began a campaign to make a final assault on the Lamanites/Aztecs. They needed to clear the enemy from outlying areas before their main attack on the land of Zarahemla/Mexico.

To help readers with city names and directions, editor Robert Kerr included a map of Mexico and its surroundings, which we provide here again, for context (Figure 66).

The Spanish general sought advice from his officers. He called a war council:

> ... everything prepared for our *expedition against Mexico*, it was debated in our *council of war* in what place we should establish our head-quarters. . . . Cortes and others preferred Tezcuco, as best adapted for making incursions into the Mexican territory. . . .[162]

Moroni, likewise, held his own war council:

> Moroni and Teancum, and many of the Chief Captains held *a council of war*, what they should do to cause the Lamanites to come out against them to battle; or that they might by some means, flatter them out of their strongholds, that they might gain advantage over them, and take again the city of Mulek. (Alma 24: p. 372 [52:17–22])

The strategy of the Spanish council was to cut off the Mexicans to the east and south of Mexico City from Tezcuco to Chalco and all along the shores of the Salt Lake of Mexico. The Smiths used this same strategy for Moroni's forces against the Lamanites and included the same words: *drive, east,* and *borders of the seashore* for *borders of the lake.*

Conquest of Mexico Kerr, Vol. IV, p. 129	Book of Alma Alma 22: p. 363 [50:8–9]
All the country around Tlascala and to the **eastwards** being now reduced to subjection. Cortes went out . . . to **drive in the Mexicans** . . . the real cause of contention on the present	And it came to pass that when Moroni had **driven all the Lamanites out of the east wilderness**, which was north of the lands of their own possessions, he caused that the inhabitants which were

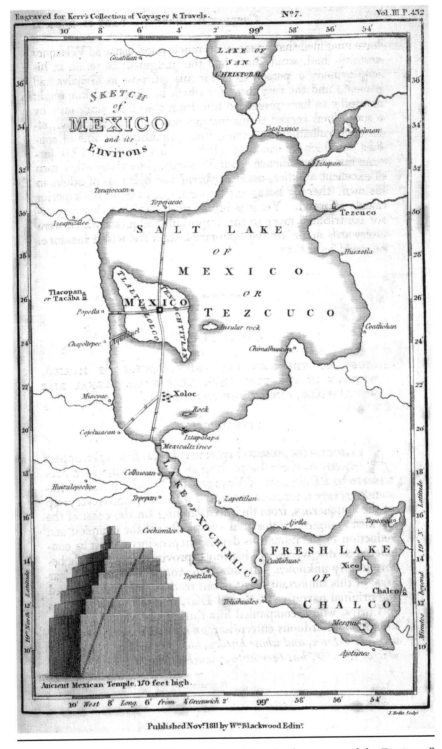

Published Nov.ʳ 1811 by Wᵐ Blackwood Edinᵗ

Figure 66. Kerr, *Voyages and Travels*, Vol. 3, "Sketch of Mexico and the Environs"

Conquest of Mexico Kerr, Vol. IV, p. 129	Book of Alma Alma 22: p. 363 [50:8–9]
occasion was concerning the crop of maize growing on the	in the land of Zarahemla, and in the land round about, should go forth into the east wilderness, even to the
borders of the lake. . . .	borders by the seashore, and possess the land.

The north, south, and west wilderness areas were also attacked and cleared of Lamanites/Mexicans by the commanders. If you refer to Robert Kerr's map, you will find Cortes's headquarters at Tezcuco along the northeast border of the Salt Lake, *Xochimilco* (or *Xoloc*) on the Salt Lake at the entrance to the southern causeway to Mexico City, and *Tacuba* near the entrance to the western causeway.

The object of our next march was against Xochimilco, a large city on the fresh water lake of Chalco, in which most of the houses are built.	
. . . and the third, under Sandoval, by the left, to the	And he also placed armies
south end of the lake." (p. 163)	on the south, in the borders of their possessions, and caused them to erect fortifications . . .
When we arrived at our quarters in Tacuba . . . (p. 159)	yea, and also on the west, fortifying the line between the Nephites and the Lamanites, between the land of Zarahemla and the land of Nephi; from the West Sea . . .
The division of Alvarado and De Oli were ordered to march from Tezcuco to the right, going round the	the Nephites possessing all the
northern side of the lake . . . p. 163)	land northward; yea,
The Tlascalan chiefs were very anxious to be employed . . . Cortes resolved to	even all the land which was northward of the land Bountiful, according

indulge them by an expedition against Xaltocan, a town situated on an island of a lake **to the northward** of the great lake of Mexico. (p. 143).

to their pleasure. (Alma 22: p. 363 [50:10–11])

The commanders fought a long series of tough battles. To the southwest, de Oli took Cuyocan (Cojohuacan), and Moroni pushed his foes all the way to the borders of the West Sea. Both armies were harassed by the enemy. Notice the use of even the same words in the battle descriptions: Captain Diaz wrote that the "enemy *harassed* us by continual assaults . . . on the *borders of the lake*," which became "they should *harass* the Nephites on the *borders by the East Sea*."

	Now, **the king** [Ammoron] . . . was endeavoring to
The **enemy harassed us** by continual assaults all the way from Xochimilco to Cuyocan, or Cojohuacan,	**harass the Nephites,** and to draw away a part of their forces to that part of the land,
	while he had commanded those which he had left to **possess the cities** which he had taken, that they should also **harass the Nephites on**
a **city** on the **borders of the lake,** near one of the causeways leading to Mexico . . . (p. 158)	the borders by the East Sea . . . Alma 24, p. 371 [52:11–13]

Now we can better understand the phrase *line between the Nephites and the Lamanites* in the earlier verse; it means a circular battle line that Cortes formed around the Lake of Mexico. With each Spanish victory, Cortes was tightening the noose around the Mexican Empire.

Creating Alliances

Cortes allied himself with the Tlascalans to such a degree that they wanted to send ten thousand of "their best warriors" to guard Cortes during the first peaceful march into Mexico City. Diaz recollected: ". . . but our general considered this number as too many for a visit of peace and would only accept 2,000, who were immediately made ready to attend us."[163] This allied force of two thousand Indian warriors played a crucial role in the Spanish conquest of Mexico and in *The Book of Mormon*.

Helaman, the son of Alma II, was another Nephite warrior-priest in Zarahemla. Helaman recruited "many sons" of the Lamanites from the "people of Ammon," who had come "unto the Lord" and joined him as Lamanite allies. Next "they entered into a covenant to fight for the liberty of the Nephites." After reading the table below, is it any surprise that the number of the converted, allied Lamanite contingent that fought for Helaman totals *two thousand*? The full verse is as follows:

> Now, behold, there were *two thousand* of those young men which entered into this covenant, and took their weapons of war *to defend their country* . . . and they would that Helaman should be their leader. . . . *Helaman did march at the head of his two thousand stripling soldiers.*" (Alma 24: p. 376 [53:18])

History of the Conquest of Mexico Kerr, Vol. IV	"The Book of Alma" Chapter 26
to prepare **2000** of their best warriors to accompany [Cortes] next day on his march to Mexico. (p. 27)	two thousand sons of those men . . . two thousand of these young men . . . these two thousand young men . . . and I did join my two thousand sons . . . p. 382)
2000 warriors of our allies the Tlascalans. (p. 119)	I did return with my two thousand. (p. 385)
	Helaman came upon their rear with his two thousand. (p. 386)

Bernal Diaz often wrote of "our little army [that] did not exceed four hundred and fifty men."[164] After the Lamanites joined Helaman, his troops also became "our little army" in the Nephites' struggle for freedom. (Alma 26: p. 383)

Will the Nephites survive the onslaught of the Lamanites? Will Captain Moroni play the hero once again and free the Nephites? Zerahemnah may be defeated, scalped, and banished for now, but Moroni is not basking in his victory. He knows the worst is yet to come.

⇒ 14 ⇐

CAPTAIN MORONI

The *Book of Mormon* contains a wonderful episode that comes from Mexico's nineteenth-century War of Independence from Spain. Here's how it goes: The prophet Alma sent his son Helaman throughout Zarahemla to establish churches in the regions occupied by the Nephites. Helaman did so, appointing priests and teachers for each one.

His actions led to a power struggle. A "strong man" named Amalickiah rebelled against Helaman and Alma. Amalickiah wanted to be king of the Nephites. He was "a man of many flattering words, that he led away the hearts of many people to do wickedly . . . to seek to destroy the church of God, and to destroy the foundation of liberty which God had granted unto them . . ." (Alma 21: p. 350)

When Moroni heard that Amalickiah had persuaded a great number of Nephites and their high priests to support his ascension to the throne, the captain was enraged. He tore off his coat and rent the material. On one length of the fabric he wrote, "In memory of our God, our religion, and freedom, and our peace, our wives, and our children." (Alma 21: p. 351) That piece of fabric he attached to a pole, and it was called the "title of liberty." Moroni used it as a banner, or battle standard, for the Nephites to rally around and unite against Amalickiah.

That's a dramatic moment in *The Book of Mormon*, but the Smiths took the idea from Mexican history. In the early 1800s, the Mexicans revolted twice against the Spanish Crown. The genesis of Captain Moroni's bold action is based on a stunning gesture in those rebellions. The story begins in "The Book of Mosiah," with the first Mexican rebellion led by revolutionary Miguel Hidalgo, and evolves in "The Book of Alma" with the final revolution led by General Agustín Cosme Damián de Iturbide.

Iturbide was a lieutenant in the royalist army in Mexico. He distinguished himself in battle against the rebel forces. Because of political upheaval in Spain, he changed his loyalty and assembled an improbable coalition of noblemen, insurgents, and the Church. When he abandoned the royalist contingent, he ripped the Crown's military insignia from his uniform jacket in a spectacular proclamation of his new allegiance.

A hero of the revolution, Iturbide wrote the Plan of Iguala, which declared freedom from Spain, established Catholicism as the national religion, and promised equality for all ethnic and social groups. The general marched into Mexico City in September 1821 and decisively ended the war against the Crown.

The story about Moroni's fight with Amalickiah's "king-men" and "dissenters" was copied from the one about the nobles and others in Mexico who had been loyalists to Spain and the Spanish-controlled Mexican government. Like Iturbide, Moroni fought against tyranny.

Let's look at material from James Duncan's *Modern Traveller* book on Mexico in the left column and verses from "The Book of Alma" in the right column. Iturbide has just renounced his loyalty to the Spanish government by tearing off his officer's insignia and announcing the twenty-four articles of the plan for the new republic.

"Mexico, Second Revolution" Duncan, *Modern Traveller*, pp. 133–134	"The Book of Alma" Alma: 21, p. 351 [46:12]
Yesterday I refused the title of lieutenant-general, which you would have conferred upon me; and now I renounce this distinction,	And it came to pass

"Mexico, Second Revolution" Duncan, *Modern Traveller,* pp. 133–134	"The Book of Alma" Alma: 21, p. 351 [46:12]
(tearing from his sleeves the bands of lace which distinguished a colonel in the Spanish service).	that he rent his coat; and he took a piece thereof, and wrote upon it,
The leading points of this plan (Iguala) are as follows:	
Article 1st maintains the	In memory of our God, our
Roman Catholic religion,	religion, and
to the entire exclusion (*intolerencia*) of any other.	
2d-Declares New Spain independent of Old Spain . . .	freedom, and our peace,
13th—Secures persons and property . . .	our wives, and our children;

Captain Moroni writes a message on his torn coat and places it on the end of a pole as a flag of freedom. The source of torn clothing on poles can be found in the previously cited *Modern Traveller* book on *Arabia,* which documents Johann Ludwig Burckhardt's tour of the Sinai in 1816.

> Proceeding southward . . . passed the rude tomb of a female saint called Arys Themman (the bridegroom of Themman), where the Arabs are in the habit of saying a short prayer, and suspending some *rags of clothing upon some poles* planted round the tomb.[165]

	Alma: 21, p. 351 [46:12]
and suspending some **rags of clothing upon some poles** planted round the tomb.	and he fastened it upon the end of a pole thereof.

Back in Mexico, the words used to name the Plan of Iguala are turned into the Nephite "Title of Liberty."

	And he fastened on his head-plate, and his breast-plate, and his
Iturbide proposed to the chiefs the scheme of government which bears the	shields, and girded on his armour about his loins; **and he took the pole, and which had on the end thereof his rent coat**, (and he called it the
title of the Plan of Iguala.[166]	title of liberty). (Alma: 21, p. 351)

Next Captain Moroni waves his flag in the air as a rallying point for the Nephites. There was another flag waving on a pole in the New World, and the information about that came from editor Robert Kerr's chapter about the Spanish explorer Juan de Grijalva:

> Beyond this they came to the mouth of another river, which they named Rio de las Banderas, or Flag-river, because the *Indians waved large white cloths on long poles*, like colours, as if inviting the Spaniards to land.[167]

| the Indians | And when Moroni had said these words, he went forth among the people, |
| **waved large white cloths on long poles**, like colours . . .[168] | **waving the rent of his garment** in the air, that all might see the writing which he had wrote upon the rent, |

Next, the Mexican rebel army took an oath to preserve their religion and the people's freedom. Moroni asks his people to enter into a covenant to accomplish the same things.

| On the ensuing day, the army **took an oath** to maintain the Plan of Iguala, | ("**enter into covenant**," below) |
| and on that occasion Iturbide addressed them in the following words: | and crying with a loud voice, saying: |

"Soldiers, you have this day sworn to preserve the Catholic, Apostolic, and Roman religion; to protect the union of Europeans and Americans; to

effect the independence of this empire; and on certain conditions to obey the King." (Duncan, *Mexico*, p. 133)

Behold, whosoever will maintain this title upon the land, let them come forth in the strength of the Lord, and enter into a covenant that they will

maintain their rights, and their religion, that the Lord God may bless them. (Alma: 21, p. 351 [46:19–20])

The speeches had profound effects. The Mexicans shouted, "*Vivas!*" and later "flocked to his standard," while the Nephites "came running together."

He was interrupted by shouts of vivas from the officers, who not only approved the plan, but insisted upon creating him lieutenant-general. (Duncan, *Mexico*, p. 133)

Guadelupe Victoria was accordingly declared commander-in-chief: the

people flocked to his standard, and the insurrection spread throughout the whole province. (Duncan, *Mexico*, p. 150)

And it came to pass that when Moroni had proclaimed these words, behold,

the people came running together, with their armours girded about their loins, rending their garments in token, or as a covenant, that they would not forsake the Lord their God . . . (Alma: 21, p. 351 [46:21])

The Plan of Iguala was sent to all provinces of Mexico, while the words of Captain Moroni went forth to all parts of the land. There were dissenters in both movements.

It was unanimously adopted, and was immediately transmitted to the viceroy, and to all the governors of provinces. (Duncan, *Mexico*, p. 133)

And now it came to pass that when Moroni had said these words, he went forth, and also sent forth in all the parts of the land where there were

dissensions, and gathered together all the people which were desirous to maintain their liberty, to stand against Amalickiah and those which had dissented, which were called Amalicki-ahites. (Alma: 21, p. 352, [46:28])

... on the part of the royalists, **there was a show of resistance in some of the provinces.** (Duncan, *Mexico*, p. 134)

And now it came to pass that when Moroni had said these words, he went forth, and also sent forth **in all the parts of the land where there were dissentions,** and gathered together all the people which were desirous to maintain their liberty, to stand against Amalickiah, **and those which had dissented,** which were called Amalickiahites. (Alma: 21, p. 352)

The people of each land joined with their leaders and outnumbered those who opposed the plans.

But the public opinion, now no longer restrained by ecclesiastical influence, manifested itself so powerfully as to affect the revolution in every part of the empire, without bloodshed, and almost without a struggle. (Duncan, *Mexico*, p. 134)

And it came to pass that when **Amalickiah saw that the people of Moroni were more numerous than the Amalickiahites;** and he also saw that his people were doubtful concerning the justice of the cause in which they had undertaken. (Alma: 21, p. 352)

The armies made key troop movements to cut off enemies or gain control of an area.

From Iguala, **Iturbide crossed over to the Baxio** ... Among others, Guadalupe Victoria, who had resisted the royalists to the last ... joined him at San Juan del Rio. The army of the Three Guarantees marched upon Querataro, which, from its position, may be considered as the military key of the interior provinces, and gained immediate possession of the place. (Duncan, *Mexico*, p. 134)

... therefore Moroni thought it was expedient **that he should take his armies,** which had gathered themselves together, and armed themselves, and entered into a covenant to keep the peace:—And it came to pass that he took his army, **and marched out into the wilderness, to cut off the course of Amalickiah in the wilderness.** (Alma: 21, p. 353 [46:31])

To choose a leader, a group of the provincial leaders of the Mexican revolution "appointed" Iturbide as their generalissimo. For the land of Zarahemla, a group of chief judges "appointed" Moroni as chief commander of the army.

Conformably to the treaty of Cordova, a junta of thirty-six members was appointed, and by them a regency, consisting of five persons, was chosen, of which Iturbide was made president. He was at the same time appointed admiral and generalissimo of the navy and army. (Duncan, *Mexico*, p. 136)	Now Moroni being a man which was appointed by the Chief Judges and the voice of the people, therefore he had power according to his will, with the armies of the Nephites, to establish and to exercise authority over them. (Alma: 21, p. 353 [46:33–34])

How many accounts of revolutions include deaths from frequent fevers?

At this moment, O'Donoju caught the yellow fever, and died, to the great sorrow of all parties. (Duncan, *Mexico*, p. 136)	And there were some who died with fevers, which at some seasons of the year, was very frequent in the land. (Alma: 21, p. 353 [46:40])

Some of the dissenters, including royalists and Creoles, were not satisfied with the appointment of a new monarch, but for the most part they did not want to confront the new army under Iturbide. Some of the Lamanites were in favor of the king, but appointed a new sovereign so as to avoid confronting the Nephites. The Smiths changed the account of "public opinion . . . manifested itself so powerfully" into "fixed in their minds with a determined resolution."

The Creoles were dissatisfied with its pledging them to receive a prince of the house of Bourbon as their monarch; and on the part of the royalists, there was a show of resistance in some of the provinces. But the public opinion, now no longer restrained by ecclesiastical influence,	And they had appointed a man to be a king and a leader over them,
manifested itself so powerfully as to effect revolution in every part of the empire, without bloodshed, almost without struggle. (Duncan, *Mexico*, p. 134)	being fixed in their minds with a determined resolution that they would not be subjected to go against the Nephites. (Alma 21: p. 354 [47:6])

The newly commissioned governor O'Donoju arrived in New Spain with no troops or even bodyguards. He had no choice but to fully recognize the Plan of Iguala. It stipulated the recognition of New Spain as a sovereign and independent nation under the title the Mexican Empire. As the new government's representatives, commissioners should be sent to Spain to offer the crown to Ferdinand VII. The European dissenters were "compelled to submit" to the new independent government. In Zarahemla, dissenters against Captain Moroni were likewise "compelled" to hoist Moroni's Title of Liberty. (Below, *Cortes* is what they called their parliament.)

The Europeans were startled by the establishment of a Cortes, and the avowal of an intention to control the monarch . . . and, as the clergy were satisfied,

they were compelled to submit.

(Duncan, *Mexico*, p. 132–133)

And the remainder of those dissenters, rather than be smote down to the earth by the sword, yielded to the standard of liberty, and

were compelled to hoist the title of liberty upon their towers,

and in their cities, and to take up arms in defence of their country. (Alma 23, pp. 368–369 [51:20])

Now that you have seen the stunning correlations between *The Modern Traveller* and "The Book of Alma," let's return to Captain Moroni and the reason why he traversed Zarahemla waving a pole with the "rent of his garment in the air," exhorting the people to rise up against the king. Think about this for a moment: In 70 BC, in Central America, we supposedly have a soldier fighting for "liberty" from the king and the nobles who support a monarchy. The nobles are attempting to change the laws to allow a king to rule; the free people want to retain the law, to support a free government and their liberty.

And it came to pass that those who were desirous that Pahoran should be dethroned from the judgment seat, were called king-men, for they were desirous that the law should be altered in a manner to overthrow the free government, and to establish a king in the land . . . the freemen had sworn or covenanted to maintain their rights, and the privileges of their religion, by a free government. (Alma 23: p. 367 [51:6])

... king-men ... would not take up arms to defend their country. (Alma 23: p. 368 [51:13])

... remainder of those dissenters ... yielded to the standard of liberty ... and to take up arms in defence of their country. (Alma 23: pp. 368–369[51:20])

Do these political embroilments sound as if they involved ancient Mesoamerican Indians, or do they more logically represent a modern society, with the Mexicans in New Spain taking action against King Ferdinand? Or the American colonists taking action against King George III?

The Joseph Smiths wrote that the fighting between the Nephites and Lamanites was "one complete revolution." (Mormon 1: p. 520 [2:8]). Strange: the word *revolution* is out of place at this juncture in the Nephite struggle and would be incorrect anywhere else in the chapter. The Nephites did not engage in an *overthrow* as did the Mexicans. Rather, theirs was a war for survival. The Lamanites were intent upon exterminating the Nephites. Why, then, write *revolution* into the text? Were the plagiarists getting sloppy?

James Duncan wrote a footnote that appears on page 105 of his 1825 *Modern Traveller* for Mexico that discusses the first and second Mexican revolutions. His sourcebook was titled *Notes on Mexico, Made in the Autumn of 1822*, written by "A Citizen of the United States." It was published in Philadelphia in 1824. Here is a copy of that book's cover page (Figure 67).

The "citizen" was Joel Roberts Poinsett, a United States congressman. Poinsett visited Mexico in 1822 as a special envoy for U.S. President James Monroe. He reported on the first Mexican revolution, which began in 1810. *Modern Traveller* begins its summary on page 100, titled "History of the First Revolutionary War." The instigator of the initial revolt, Miguel Hidalgo y Costilla, was the Catholic priest in the city of Dolores. He rang his church bells on September 16, 1810, and when the local Indians responded, Hidalgo ordered the arrest of the native Spaniards in the village. Father Hidalgo

NOTES ON MEXICO,

MADE IN THE AUTUMN OF 1822.

ACCOMPANIED BY

AN HISTORICAL SKETCH OF THE REVOLUTION,

AND

TRANSLATIONS

OF

OFFICIAL REPORTS ON THE PRESENT STATE OF THAT COUNTRY.

WITH A MAP.

BY A CITIZEN OF THE UNITED STATES.

———

PHILADELPHIA:

H. C. CAREY AND I. LEA, CHESNUT STREET.

••••••••••••••

1824.

Figure 67. Poinsett, *Notes on Mexico*, Title Page

became generalissimo of the rebellion. His army, which was described in Poinsett's report as "a heterogeneous mob without order or discipline," consisted of twenty thousand men.[169]

Pursuing Hidalgo's forces was Don Felix Maria Calleja, captain of six thousand royalist troops, who punished the rebels with excessive brutality. Eventually Hidalgo was apprehended and executed.

This history lesson is important because it became the foundation for the last stand of the Nephites against the Lamanites. The final Nephite battle was at Camorah, the same hill "Ramah" in New York where the Jaredites fought each other to extermination. In the *Modern Traveller*, the name of the battle site where the warrior-priest's forces and the royalist army fought was called *Zamora*.

In their fiction, the Smiths replaced Hidalgo with the warrior Mormon; Hidalgo's army of rebel Indians with the Nephites; and the royal Spanish troops and loyalists to the Crown with the Lamanites.

Let's step back for a moment and think about what was going on at Joseph and Lucy Smith's kitchen table. Reference books, maps, printed engravings, and the pages of *The Book of Mormon* manuscript were all scattered about. We can say without hesitation that at this point in their secret manuscript the Smiths had become quite sophisticated in their plagiarism. Could anyone have imagined mixing the ancient *and* modern history of Mexico in *The Book of Mormon*? With only what you know so far, is it so hard to believe that this secret remained buried for over 180 years?

In the following charts we compare the stories about two wars of extinction. On the left is the tragic fate of Hidalgo and his colonist rebels copied from *The Modern Traveller, Mexico and Guatemala*, Volume I, 1825. On the right is the last struggle of the Nephites. The verses are organized in proper sequence from *The Book of Mormon*'s chapter titled "The Book of Mormon," published in 1830. It begins with the opposing forces gathering their armies for war.

Hidalgo's army (if such a name may be applied to a heterogeneous mob without order or discipline), **now**	. . . the Nephites had gathered together a great number of men, even to exceed the

consisted of 20,000 men.(Duncan, *Mexico*, p. 103)

number of thirty thousand. (Mormon 1: p. 519 [1:11]) . . . that in the same year, there began to be a war again between the Nephites and the Lamanites. (Mormon 1: p. 520)

Hidalgo's army of thirty thousand went on the march, and they killed many of the royalists and loyalists. In Zarahemla, the Nephites "did slay" many Lamanites.

In every place they **passed** through, **all the European Span- iards fell into their hands, and many Creoles, were massacred**. (Duncan, *Mexico*, p. 103)

And it came to **pass** that they did have in this same year a number of battles, in the **which the Nephites did beat the Lamanites, and did slay many of them**. (Mormon 1: p. 519)

Much is written in *The Book of Mormon* about a band of robbers led by "Gadianton." Kendal Sheets, the co-author of this book, thought it was peculiar that the Smiths wrote such a departure from the main storyline of Lamanites on the warpath. Then he found a footnote by John Duncan in the story of Hidalgo about an Indian term for *robber*. There is a connection that goes back to the days when the Spaniards terrorized the Indians with their horses. *Gachupins*, which means "robber," becomes the "Gadianton robbers" of *The Book of Mormon*.

(Duncan, *Mexico*, pp. 102–103)

The war-cry of [Hidalgo's] followers was, "Destruction to the

Gachupins,"

a word of contempt, said to be as old as the days of Cortes;* . . . *The Spaniards say that it means "a man with two heads," and that it originated in the exclamation of the Indians on first dis- covering that the horse was a distinct animal from his rider. The story is that one of Cortes's officers being slain,

(Mormon 1: p. 520)

And these

Gadianton

they expressed their surprise on a close examination of the phenomenon, by exclaiming Catchupin. The Indians, however, deny the truth of the tale, and

say the word means **robber**.

robbers, which were among the Lamanites, did infest the land . . .

Returning to the story of the two wars, we read that a leader was appointed for each army. For the independents, a priest was selected—a man who was said to be incompetent. For the Nephites, a young man was selected who questioned his own maturity. The battles began, but ended quickly. In a demonstration of fear, both the independents and the Nephites hastily retreated.

(Duncan, *Mexico*, p. 102)	(Mormon 1: p. 520)
Unhappily, the first individual who raised the standard of revolt was a man wholly incompetent to direct the popular movement. He was a priest, named Hidalgo.	And notwithstanding I being young, was large in stature, therefore the people of Nephi appointed me that I should be their leader, or leader of their armies.
Hidalgo was proclaimed generalissimo of the Mexican armies. (p. 105)	I did go forth at the head of an army of the Nephites, against the Lamanites. (p. 520)
After some **skirmishes** . . . the independents . . . shewed themselves on the heights of Santa Fe. The **royalists, not more than 2000 men**, were drawn up to defend the city, when,	the Lamanites did come upon us with exceeding great power,
to the astonishment of every one,	insomuch that they did frighten my armies; therefore
Hidalgo withdrew his troops, taking the route to Guanaxuato. (p. 105)	**they would not fight**, and they began to
This **retreat** was attended with some confusion. (Duncan, p. 106)	**retreat** towards the north countries.

Because of the growing lawlessness in Mexico, bands of guerillas began preying on the helpless. This added more resources for the notion of "robbers" in Zarahemla.

(Duncan, pp. 111–112)

. . . the open country was **desolated by small bands of guerillas,** who, if they owned (sic), obeyed no superiors, who lived on the **plunder of the country,** and, without the least compunction, massacred every European that fell in their way.

(Mormon 1: p. 520 [2:8])

And we marched forth, and came to the land of Joshua, which was in the borders west, by the seashore. But behold, **the land was filled with robbers and with Lamanites** . . .

In these bloody wars, both sides committed atrocities.

(Duncan, p. 111)

During these military transactions, the work of havoc never ceased. No quarter was given by either side.*

. . . the disgraceful and **barbarous mode of warfare** adopted in Mexico, had its origin solely in the

outrageous decrees of the **Spanish government** . . . the outrages and massacres **committed by Hidalgo's Indians in** the first rising, cannot, however, have the benefit of this apology.

(Mormon 1: p. 520 [2:8])

therefore **there was blood and carnage spread throughout all the face of the land,**

both on the part of the Nephites, and also on the part of the Lamanites.

In the next verse, we finally locate the origin of the Smiths' word *revolution* as the type of campaign being fought. It came from the "revolt" that spread over the "whole country," which became "all the face of the land" in *The Book of Mormon.*

(Duncan, p. 104)

The revolt had by this time spread with electric rapidity,

over the whole country north of Queretaro.

(Mormon 1: p. 520 [2:8])

and it was one complete **revolution**

throughout all the face of the land.

As with their use of *The Travels of Marco Polo*, numbers continue to play an important role for the storytellers. Note the use of 40,000 for 44,000/42,000 and 30,000 for 30,000.

(Duncan, p. 108)

The command of the **army** left by Hidalgo was assumed by Rayon, a lawyer, who soon found himself at the head of

40,000 men.

(Mormon 1: p. 520–521 [2:9])

And now the Lamanites had a king, and his name was Aaron; and he came against us with an **army of**

forty and four thousand. And behold, I withstood him, with **forty and two thousand.**

(Mormon 1: p. 522 [2:25])

Hidalgo's army, though he had lost at least

30,000 men

in killed, prisoners, and deserters, was still nearly

80,000 strong. (Duncan, p. 107)

And it came to pass that we did contend with an **army of**

thirty thousand,

against an army of

fifty thousand.

The tide was turning against the insurgents, and they were forced to retreat. The Nephites, too, felt the sting of their losses and were driven back by the Lamanites.

Don Felix Maria Calleja . . . at the **head** of 6000 men, now pursued Hidalgo so closely,

. . . the armies of the Nephites were driven back again to the land of Desolation. And while they were yet weary, a fresh army of the Lamanites did come upon them; and they had a sore battle, insomuch that the

as to bring an action at **Aculco**

Lamanites did take possession of the city Desolation,

the insurgents lost 10,000 men, of whom 5000 were deliberately put to the sword (p. 106)

and did slay many of the Nephites, and did take many prisoners;

Hidalgo retreated . . . was compelled to retire with the remains of his troops upon Hidalgo. (p. 106–107)

and the remainder did flee and join the inhabitants of the city Teancum. (Mormon 2: p. 525 [4:2–3])

The Spanish commander entered an undefended city and took prisoners of men, women, and children and "butchered" them by cutting their throats. The Lamanites also entered a city and took Nephite women and children as prisoners, only to sacrifice them to their idols. Towns were razed or burned by the enemies.

Calleja now entered Guanaxuato as a conqueror, and he determined to

the Lamanites did take possession of the city Desolation . . . and they did also march forward against the city of Teancum, and did

"purge the city of its rebellious population."

drive the inhabitants forth out of her, and did take many prisoners of

Men, women, and children, were driven, by his orders, into the great square, where, to the number of several thousands, they were

women and of children, and

butchered in the most barbaric

did offer them up as

manner . . . and therefore their throats were cut. (p. 107)

sacrifices unto their idol gods.

This was only the commencement of a series of atrocious barbarities, committed by Calleja and his subalterns, in all the towns and villages of the Baxio. p. 107

And when they had come the second time, the Nephites were driven and slaughtered with an exceeding great slaughter; their women and their children were again sacrificed unto idols. (Mormon 2: p. 526 [4:21])

By a "solemn decree," the property of the inhabitants of this town was confiscated, and the town itself

whatsoever lands we had passed by, and the inhabitants thereof were not gathered in,

razed to the ground. (Duncan, p. 108)

were destroyed by the Lamanites, and their

The royal troops, on their part, wherever they passed, marked their track by thousands of Indians hung on the trees by the sides of the

road, and by the smoking ruins of the plantations they had burned. (Duncan, p. 112)

towns, and villages, and cities were burned with fire. (Mormon 2: p. 527 [5:5])

Do you remember one of the first examples of copying we showed for Camorah/Ramah coming from Comari/Rama? The next paragraphs add another dimension to those words. By the end of their manuscript, the father-son writing team from Palmyra, New York, had become adept at their plagiarism.

In the meantime, the royalists, under General Cruz, defeated the independents at

we might gather together our people unto the land of

Zamora.

Camorah,

The heavy guns from the works at San Blas had been conveyed to Guadalaxara, and lines were thrown up which at least bore the appearance of fortifications.

by a hill which was called Camorah, and there we would give them battle ... the king of the Lamanites did grant unto me ...

He drew up his army in an

... we did march forth to the land of Camorah ... round about the hill Camorah ... and here we had hope to gain

advantageous position

advantage over the Lamanites.

at the Puente [bridge] de Calderon, eleven leagues from the city, and here resolved to wait the attack of Calleja. (Duncan, *Mexico*, p. 107)

(Mormon 3: p. 529 [6:4])

After the defeat of the rebels, Hidalgo escapes along with the chief officers. Mormon also escapes, along with his son Moroni and twenty-two other Nephites.

An obstinate battle was fought on the 17th of January, 1811,

And when

which ended in the total defeat and dispersion of the independents.

they had gone through and hewn down all my people

Hidalgo, with some of his chief officers,

save it were twenty and four of us (among whom was my son Moroni,) and we having survived the dead of our people ... and a few which had

escaped, and took the road for the internal provinces. (Duncan, pp. 107–108)	escaped into the south countries . . . (Mormon 3: pp. 529–530)

Some warriors defected to the enemy just before the retreating independents/Nephites were slaughtered for "seven leagues" or over the "whole face of the earth":

Thus, hemmed in on all sides,	. . . and
[Hidalgo] was betrayed by Bustamante, one of his own officers, and made prisoner with all his staff. (p. 108)	a few which had dissented over unto the Lamanites
They were closely pressed and harassed in their retreat by Calleja, who says . . .	
"an extent of seven leagues was covered with the dead bodies of the enemy."	and their flesh, and bones, and blood lay upon the whole face of the earth.
(Duncan, p. 110)	(Mormon 4: p. 532)
[Hidalgo] was closely followed by Calleja, and by a division of Spanish troops	the Nephites . . . were hunted by the Lamanites,

In the final retreat, there was no quarter given to the rebel independents. All were executed:

Fifty of his officers were executed on the field of battle. Hidalgo and Allende, with eight or ten others, were removed to Chihahua, where, after the form of a trial, Allende was shot on the 10th of June; Hidalgo, having previously been deprived of his priest's orders, on the 27th of July.[170]

The Nephites were exterminated just as ignominiously (because it was a copy of Hidalgo's fateful retreat). The Lamanites killed them all, including their leader, Mormon.

. . . until they were *all destroyed*; and my father also was killed with them. (Mormon 4: p. 532 [8:2–3])

Although the battle at Camorah was the end of the Nephites, it is far from the end of our story. We will visit Zarahemla again, when it was the pinnacle of the Nephite civilization. All the prophets, beginning with Lehi, had predicted one singular event that would change human history: the coming of Jesus Christ.

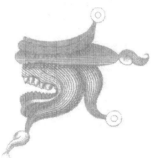

Atenco

✺ 15 ✺

JESUS VISITS
THE NEPHITES

O ur next discussion scrutinizes the prophecies and preaching that
span many years in *The Book of Mormon*. Almost six hundred years
have passed since Lehi and his family departed from Jerusalem. Up to this
point in their story, Joseph Smith Sr. and Joseph Smith Jr. drew their material primarily from pre-1830 history texts and memoirs. While they continued to do so, they also began to integrate whole sections of the King James
translation of the Bible because *The Book of Mormon*'s plot turns to the life
and death of Jesus Christ.

For our discussion in "Jesus Visits the Nephites," all Old and New
Testament quotes come from a text that would have been available to
the plagiarists: The Holy Bible by the Special Command of King James I,
of England. One version was published in Walpole, New Hampshire, by
Anson Whipple in 1815[171] (Figure 68).

In the New Testament, John the Baptist anticipated the coming of a
messianic figure. In *The Book of Mormon*, John the Baptist and Samuel the
Lamanite are the forerunners.

In an earlier chapter we discussed the Smiths' tactic of referencing
people, places, and events from the Old Testament to lend credibility to

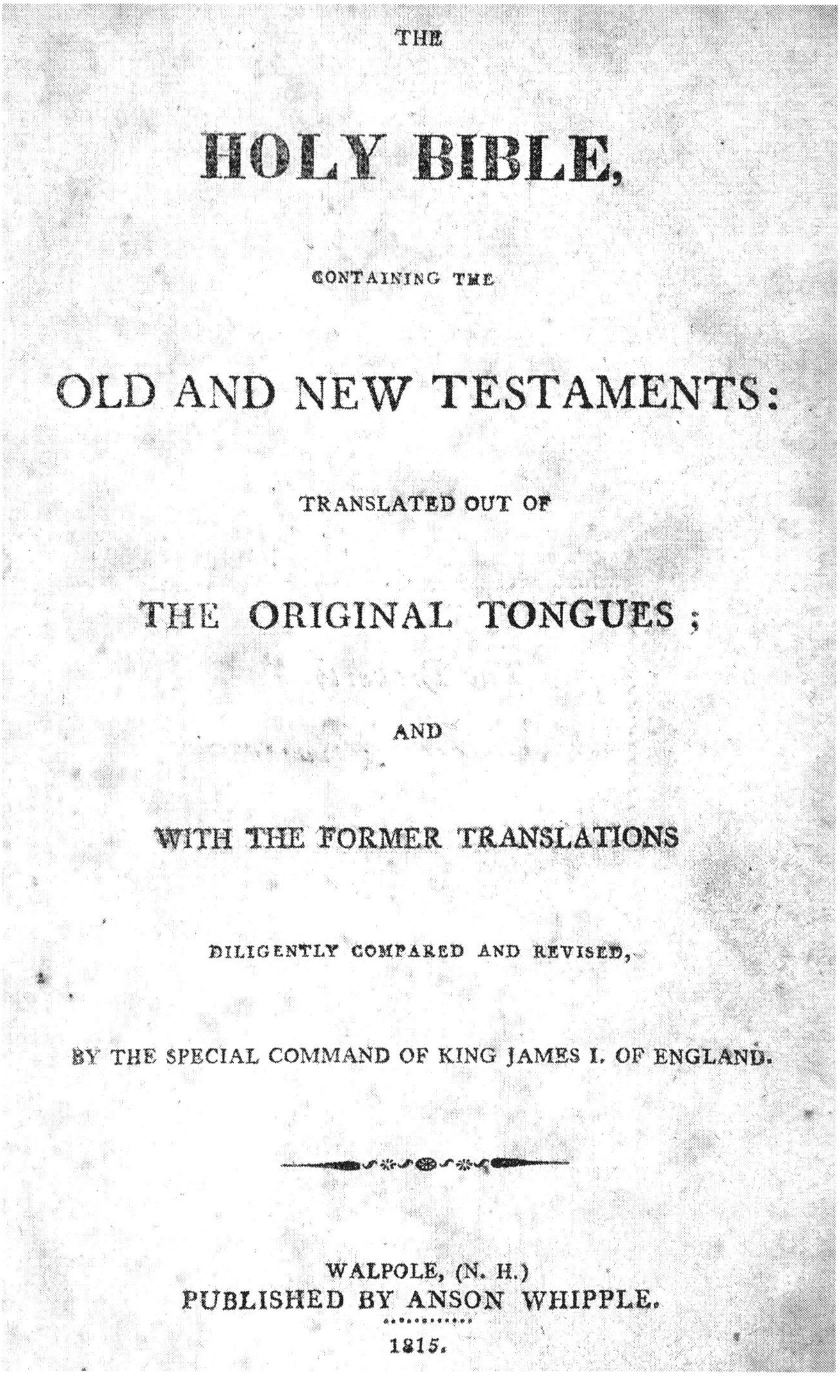

THE

HOLY BIBLE,

CONTAINING THE

OLD AND NEW TESTAMENTS:

TRANSLATED OUT OF

THE ORIGINAL TONGUES ;

AND

WITH THE FORMER TRANSLATIONS

DILIGENTLY COMPARED AND REVISED,

BY THE SPECIAL COMMAND OF KING JAMES I. OF ENGLAND.

WALPOLE, (N. H.)
PUBLISHED BY ANSON WHIPPLE.

1815.

Figure 68. Whipple, *The Holy Bible*, Title Page

their newly penned *Book of Mormon*. They frequently intermingled biblical events with their own composition. As an example of the Smiths' strategy, John the Baptist is mentioned in *The Book of Mormon*, and then he serves as the model for the Lamanite holy man.

Obviously the plagiarists needed to implement their ploy in *The Book of Mormon*'s opening pages in order to entice prospective followers to continue reading their 1830 scripture. In "The First Book of Nephi," which is the first chapter in *The Book of Mormon*, you'll find references to John the Baptist, who will not be born for another six hundred years. Lehi has a vision that foretells John's appearance and describes his mission—preparing the world for the coming of Jesus Christ—and his baptism of the Messiah. In essence, Lehi becomes the forerunner of the forerunner.

Beginning with chapter three, page twenty-two [10:6–10], Lehi's son Nephi describes one of his father's revelations:

Wherefore, all mankind was in a lost and in a fallen state; and ever would be, save they should rely on this Redeemer.

And he spake also, concerning a *prophet*, which should come before the Messiah, to *prepare the way of the Lord;*

. . . yea, even he should go forth and *cry in the wilderness*, Prepare ye the way of the Lord, and *make his paths straight*; for there standeth one among you whom ye know not; and *he is mightier than I, whose shoe's latchet I am not worthy to unloose.* And much spake my father concerning this thing.

Now let's look at what a rearrangement of the Anson Whipple King James New Testament quotes have to say about this prophet:

But, What went ye out for to see? *A prophet?* Yea, I say unto you, and more than a prophet. For this is he, of whom it is written, Behold, I send my messenger before thy face, which *shall prepare thy way before thee.* (Matthew 11:9)

He said, I am the voice of one *crying in the wilderness, Make straight the way of the Lord,* as saith the prophet Esaias. (John 1:12) And preached, saying, There cometh *one mightier than I* after me. (Mark 1:7) . . . *whose shoe's latchet I am not worthy to unloose.* (John 1:27)

Nephi went on to describe the revelation with details of where the prophet should perform the religious rite of baptism:

And my father saith that he should baptise in *Bethabara, beyond Jordan;* and he also spake, that he should baptise with water; yea, even that he should baptise the Messiah with water. And after he had baptised the Messiah with water, he should behold and bear record, that he had baptised *the Lamb of God, which should take away the sins of the world.* (1 Nephi 3: p. 22 [10:9])

Nephi mentions a location and title of Jesus that happens to be exactly like the King James version of the Book of John (one of Jesus' disciples, not John the Baptist):

These things were done in *Bethabara beyond Jordan,* where John was *baptizing.* The next day John seeth Jesus coming unto him, and saith, Behold *the Lamb of God, which taketh away the sin of the world!* (John 1:28–29)

Young Nephi also has a vision in "The First Book of Nephi," chapter three, on page twenty-five [11:27]:

And I looked and beheld the Redeemer of the world, of which my father had spoken; and I also beheld the prophet, which should prepare the way before him. And the Lamb of God went forth, *and was baptised* of him; and after that he was baptised, I beheld *the Heavens open, and the Holy Ghost come down out of Heaven and abode upon him in the form of a dove.*

Nephi's version of the vision borrows a well-known verse of Christian scripture that describes the initiation of Jesus' ministry:

And Jesus, *when he was baptized,* went up straightway out of the water: and, lo, *the heavens were opened unto him, and he saw the Spirit of God descending like a dove,* and lighting upon him. (Matthew 3:16)

John the Baptist earns yet another mention in *The Book of Mormon*'s next chapter, "The Second Book of Nephi."

Wherefore, I would that ye should remember that I have spoken unto you, concerning that Prophet which the Lord showed unto me, that should baptize the Lamb of God, which should take away the sins of the world. (2 Nephi 13: p. 118 [31:4])

We can clearly see what the Smiths tried to accomplish: they used John the Baptist to establish the veracity of *The Book of Mormon.* Later in that tome they again make use of him, along with the circumstances surrounding his life, as the basis for their own fabrication, Samuel the Lamanite.

Let's review the Smiths' plotline: Disharmony prevails in Zarahemla. The wickedness of the people provides a ripe setting for a holy man's admonishments and divine retribution. Nephite dissenters abandon their tribe to join the dark-skinned, cursed Lamanites and a ferocious band of robbers called the Gadiantons. War erupts, pitting brother against brother. The defectors commit murder among their own tribe of Jews and plunder their land:

But behold, satan did stir up the hearts of the more part of the Nephites, insomuch that they did unite with those bands of robbers, and did enter into their covenants, and their oaths, that they would protect and preserve one another, in whatsoever difficult circumstances they should be placed in, that they should not suffer for their murders, and their plunderings, and their stealings.

And it came to pass that they did have their signs, yea, their secret signs, and their secret words; and this that they might distinguish a brother who had entered into the covenant, that whatsoever wickedness his brother should do, he should not be injured by his brother, nor by those who did belong to his band, who had taken this covenant; and thus they might murder, and plunder, and steal, and commit whoredoms, and all manner of wickedness, contrary to the laws of their country, and also the laws of their God. (Helaman 2: p. 424 [6:21–6:23]).

And from "The Book of Helaman," chapter two, page 425:

And now behold, he had got great hold upon the hearts of the Nephites; yea, insomuch that they had become exceeding wicked; yea, the more part of them had turned out of the way of righteousness, and did trample under their feet the commandments of God, and did turn unto their own ways, and did build up unto themselves idols of their gold and their silver.

Now we're going to talk for a moment about a man who shows the way in "The Book of Helaman." His name is Nephi, and he precedes Samuel. Nephi, son of Helaman, was considered to be a prophet by some Nephites. He was:

. . . thus pondering, being much cast down because of the wickedness of the people of the Nephites, their secret works of darkness, and their murderings, and their plunderings, and all manner of iniquities. (Helaman 3: p. 434 [10:3]).

Nephi told them:

. . . yea, wo be unto you because of that great abomination which hath come among you; and ye have united yourselves unto it, yea, to that secret band which was established by Gadianton. (Helaman 3: p. 428 [7:25])

God empowers Nephi to bring destruction to the Nephites, and a terrible drought sears the land. When the starving people repent, rain falls and crops grow. During this time the Gadiantons are driven from Zarahemla. Nephi says:

O Lord, behold this people repenteth; and they have swept away the band of Gadianton from amongst them, insomuch that they have become extinct, and they have concealed their secret plans in the earth. (Helaman 4: p. 437 [11:10])

As is habitually the case with the Smiths' writing, the penitents fall back into their old, sinful ways. Nephite dissenters join the evil Lamanites, and the Gadiantons rise again. Helaman 4, pages 439–440 says:

O how foolish, and how vain, and how evil, and devilish, and how quick to do iniquity, and how slow to do good, are the children of men; yea, how quick to hearken unto the words of the evil one, and to set their hearts upon the vain things of the world.

God wants the sinners in this blasphemous society to repent and be ready to receive Jesus Christ, who is prophesied to be born in fewer than ten years. This echoes events in the Bible, when God wanted the Israelites to prepare for the birth of Jesus.

In the New Testament, God sent John the Baptist to urge the Israelites to repent before Jesus comes to them. In *The Book of Mormon*, God sends the Lamanite prophet Samuel to warn the Nephites of God's impending wrath, to preach repentance, and to foretell the coming of Jesus Christ to the land of Zarahemla.

Both John the Baptist and Samuel the Lamanite were first-century Jewish prophets and public preachers. Both were forerunners with a message of warning. We can call them the bearers of bad news (God's imminent, catastrophic judgment) and good news (the coming of Jesus Christ).

Both John and Samuel described the Lord's anger as righteous—a response to the people's sins—and both men demanded repentance. They recognized Jesus as the Messiah.

John the Baptist was an outsider, an ascetic. He preached in the wilderness and wore a loincloth and camel-hair clothing. He ate locusts and wild honey. Samuel, too, was an outcast. In "The Book of Helaman," he was a Lamanite, come to minister to the Nephites. John and Samuel also used the same methods when exhorting the masses. They did not flatter the listeners. Instead the prophets berated them for their wickedness.

The Nephites did not allow Samuel to enter the city of Zarahemla. Undeterred, he climbed a city wall and offered his sermon from the heights.

And it came to pass that they [the Nephites] would not suffer that he [Samuel the Lamanite] should enter into the city; therefore he went and *got upon the wall* thereof, and stretched forth his hand and *cried with a loud voice, and prophesied unto the people.* (Helaman 5: p. 441 [13:4])

When Samuel climbed atop the wall at Zarahemla, the Smiths had turned their attention from the Bible to Captain Bernal Diaz's account of Hernan Cortes's subjugation of the Aztecs. Samuel's actions are reminiscent of an episode from the conquistador's journal, published in Robert Kerr's collection.[172] In it, Montezuma, the Aztec emperor, ascended a roof terrace and, at the behest of the Spaniards, addressed an angry mob of Indians. (You will recall from the previous chapter that Zarahemla is based on Mexico City, the location of Montezuma's court.)

According to Captain Diaz, Montezuma's followers were in revolt against the Spaniards, who had wrested control of the empire, looted it, and made Montezuma their prisoner. Left without an emperor, the Indians had to appoint a new ruler.

Diaz's commander, Hernan Cortes, needed to end the Indians' revolt so he and his army could escape from Mexico City. He ordered a tearful Montezuma to address his people from the rooftop. According to the captain:

[Montezuma] *made his appearance at the railing of a terraced roof,* attended by many of our soldiers, and made a very affectionate *address to the people below,* earnestly entreating a cessation of hostilities, that we might evacuate Mexico.[173]

Aztec noblemen approached Montezuma, asked for forgiveness, and prophesied that the Spaniards would be "utterly destroyed."

As soon as Montezuma was perceived, the chiefs and nobles made their troops to desist from the attack, and commanded silence. Then four of the principal nobles came forwards, so near as to be able to hold conversation with Montezuma whom they addressed, lamenting the misfortunes which had befallen him and his family. They told him that they had raised Cuitlahuatzin to the throne; that the war would soon be ended, as they had *promised to their gods* never to desist till they had *utterly destroyed the Spaniards;* that they offered up continual prayers for the safety of Montezuma their beloved sovereign, whom they would venerate and obey as formerly, as soon as they had rescued him from our hands, and *hoped he would pardon all they had done for the defense of their religion and independence, and their present disobedience.* (Kerr, Vol. IV, pp. 109)

How does this scene play out in *The Book of Mormon?* The Aztec noblemen's promise to "utterly" destroy the Spaniards becomes Samuel's, and thereby God's, prophecy of the "utter destruction" of the Nephites:

. . . yea, *heavy destruction* awaiteth this people, and it surely cometh unto this people . . . I will visit them in my fierce anger, and there shall be those of the fourth generation, which shall live, of your enemies, to behold your *utter destruction. . . .* (Helaman 5: pp. 441–442 [13:6, 10])

The nobles' entreaty for pardon from Montezuma becomes the Nephites' plea for forgiveness. First Diaz and then the Smiths:

Then four of the principal nobles came forwards . . . hoped *he would pardon all they had done* for the defense of their religion and independence, and their present disobedience.

And as many believed on his words, *went forth and sought for Nephi;* and when they had come forth and found him, they *confessed unto him their sins* and denied not, desiring that they might be baptized unto the Lord. (Helaman 5: pp. 449 [16:1])

John the Baptist received the same results. The people sought him out, confessed, and were baptized:

Then *went out to him* Jerusalem, and all Judaea, and all the region about Jordan, And were *baptized* of him in Jordan, *confessing* their sins. (Matthew 3:5–6)

Both Indian and Lamanite speakers on the roof/wall become the victims of identical attacks. The mobs below cast stones and launch arrows at Montezuma and Samuel. The Aztec chief is protected by Spanish soldiers; Samuel's protection is divine. But Montezuma is struck and later dies of his wounds.

Just as they concluded with this address, a *shower of arrows* fell about the place where Montezuma stood; and though *the Spaniards had hitherto protected him by interposing their shields*, they did not expect any assault while he was speaking to his subjects, and had therefore uncovered him for an instant; in that unguarded state, *three stones hit him on the head, arm, and the leg*, wounding him severely. (Kerr, Vol. IV, pp. 109)

Samuel remains unscathed:

But as many as there were which did not believe in the words of Samuel were angry with him; and they *cast stones at him upon the wall, and also many arrows* at him, as he stood upon the wall; but the *spirit of the Lord was with him*, insomuch that *they could not hit him* with their stones, neither with their arrows. (Helaman 5: p. 449 [16:2])

What predictions has Samuel made from the city walls? He prophesies wonders and issues warnings (see first extract above). First, a new star and three days without darkness will announce the birth of Jesus Christ, he says, and he tells them about Christ's inevitable death, which was taken from the Bible's Book of Mark, 8:31 (second extract above).

Lord Jesus Christ, which surely shall come into the world, and *shall suffer many things, and shall be slain* for his people. (Helaman 5: p. 442 [13:6])

And he began to teach them, that the *Son of Man must suffer many things,* and be rejected of the elders, and of the chief priests, and scribes, *and be killed,* and after three days rise again.

Samuel the Lamanite speaks prophetic words as if they are from God, warning the cities of the Nephites of their impending destruction, unless they repent, saying "wo unto this great city,"

... but *wo unto him that repenteth not; yea, wo unto this great city of Zara-hemla;* ... But *blessed are they who will repent,* for them will I spare. But behold if it were not for the righteous which are in this great city, *behold I would cause that fire should come down out of heaven, and destroy it.* ... yea, *wo be unto this great city,* because of the wickedness and abomina-tions which is in her: yea, and *wo be unto the city of Gideon,* for the wick-edness and abominations which is in her; yea, and *wo be unto all the cities which are into the land* round about, which is possessed by the Nephites. (Helaman 5: p. 442)

Jesus, during a sermon in the Book of Matthew, criticized the people of the cities he had visited with "*woe unto thee.*"

Then he began to *upbraid the cities* wherein most of his mighty works were done, *because they repented not: Woe unto thee, Chorazin! woe unto thee, Bethsaida!* ... And thou, Capernaum, which art exalted unto heaven, shall be brought down to hell; for if the mighty works, which have been done in thee, had been done in Sodom, it would have remained until this day. (Matthew 11:20–23)

Here is one intelligent rewrite: Jesus says that Sodom would have remained, but Samuel the Lamanite says that God would cause fire to come out of heaven and destroy Zarahemla. In the Old Testament, fire from heaven destroyed the city of Sodom.

Samuel, speaking for God, chastises the Nephites as a "perverse generation."

> O ye wicked and ye perverse generation; ye hardened and ye stiffnecked people, how long will ye suppose that the Lord will suffer you; yea, how long will ye suffer yourselves to be lead by foolish and blind guides. (Helaman 5: p. 444 [13:29])

Just as Jesus admonished the Jews:

> And Jesus answered, and said, O faithless and perverse generation, How long shall I be with you? How long shall I suffer you? (Matthew 17:17)

Samuel warns of the consequences of the Nephites' eternal damnation if they don't repent.

> But behold, the resurrection of Christ redeemeth mankind, yea, even all mankind, and bringeth them back into the presence of the Lord; yea, and it bringeth to pass the condition of repentance, that whosoever repenteth, the same is not hewn down and cast into the fire. (Helaman 5: p. 446 [14:17–18])

But this sermon wasn't uttered by God through a Lamanite; it comes straight out of the Gospel of Luke, where Jesus warns everyone about the end of the world:

> And now also the axe is laid unto the root of the trees: every tree therefore which bringeth not forth good fruit is hewn down, and cast into the fire. (Luke 3:9)

The Smiths copied parts of the New Testament's Jesus speaking about his own death and resurrection and recast it as a sermon from Samuel the Lamanite to foretell impending doom across Zarahemla during Christ's death and resurrection. In "The Book of Helaman," chapter four, pages 446–447 [14:20–27], Samuel says:

> But behold, as I said unto you concerning another sign, a sign of his death: behold, in that day that he shall suffer death, *the sun shall be darkened and refuse to give his light unto you; and also the moon, and the stars;* and there shall be no light upon the face of this land.

In the original version in the Gospel of Matthew, Jesus said:

> Immediately after the tribulation of those days *shall the sun be darkened, and the moon shall not give her light, and the stars shall fall from heaven,* and the powers of the heavens shall be shaken: And then shall appear the sign of the Son of Man in heaven. (Matthew 24:29–30)

The prophet Nephi continues the prophecy of the signs, saying:

> . . . even from the time that he shall suffer death, for the *space of three days,* to the time that *he shall rise again* from the dead. (Helaman 5: p. 446 [14:20])

We find this a few chapters later in Matthew:

> Saying Sir, we remember that deceiver said, while he was yet alive, *After three days I will rise again.* (Matthew 27:63)

What follows is a portion of Nephi's writing that describes the death of Jesus:

> . . . yea, at the time that he shall yield up the ghost there shall be *thunderings and lightnings* for the space of many hours, and the earth shall shake and tremble; and the rocks which is upon the face of this earth.

> . . . yea, they shall be rent in twain. . . .

And behold, there shall be great tempests, *and there shall be many moun-*
tains laid low, like unto a valley, and there shall be many places, which are
now called valleys, which shall become mountains, whose height thereof is
great. (Helaman 5: pp. 446–447 [14:21–23])

This text was mostly taken from the biblical scripture in the Gospel
of Luke, chapter three, verses three to five, which speaks about John the
Baptist:

And he came into all the country about Jordan, preaching the baptism
of repentance of the remission of sins. . . . The voice of one crying in
the wilderness, Prepare ye the way of the Lord, make his paths straight.
Every valley shall be filled, and every mountain and hill shall be brought
low; and the crooked shall be made straight, and the rough ways shall be
made smooth.

Nephi continues this ominous and magical prophecy of cities destroyed
and saints rising from the grave:

And many highways shall be broken up, and many cities shall become
desolate, and *many graves shall be opened, and shall yield up many of their*
dead; and many saints shall appear unto many.

. . . and that *darkness should cover the face of the whole earth,* for the space
of three days. (Helaman 5: pp. 446–447 [14:25–27])

This looks strikingly similar to this Bible verse from Matthew Chapter 27, which describes what happened after Jesus died (if you recall the
language of Nephi's prophecy above about earthquakes and the rocks, the
declaration *yea, they shall be rent in twain* also comes from here):

Now from the sixth hour there was *darkness over all the land* unto the
ninth hour . . . 50 Jesus, when he had cried again with a loud voice, yielded
up the ghost. 51 And, behold the veil of the temple was *rent in twain* from

the top to the bottom; and the *earth did quake, and the rocks rent;* 52 *And the graves were opened; and many bodies of the saints which slept arose,* 53 *And came out of the graves after his resurrection, and went into the holy city, and appeared unto many.* (Matthew 27:45)

Samuel continues in this quote from "The Book of Helaman" to give the Nephites dire warnings of impending doom:

And now my beloved brethren, behold, I declare unto you that except ye shall repent, *your houses shall be left unto you desolate;* yea, except ye repent, your *women shall have great cause to mourn in the day that they shall give suck; for ye shall attempt to flee, and there shall be no place for refuge; yea, and wo unto them which are with child,* for they shall be heavy and cannot flee; therefore they shall be trodden down. (Helaman 5: p. 447 [15:1–2])

This turns out to be merely a paraphrase of Jesus' speaking to his disciples:

Then let them which be in Judea flee into the mountains: Let him *which is on the housetop not come down to take any thing out of his house. . . .* Neither let him which is in the field return back to take his clothes. And *wo unto them that are with child, and to them that give suck in those days!* . . . for then shall be great tribulation, such as was not since the beginning of the world to this time, no, nor ever shall be. (Matthew 24:16–21)

Jesus' disciples revered his words. The Nephites, however, would have none of it. The mob pursues Samuel, shoots arrows and hurls stones at him, and chases him out of the city. He flees Zarahemla and is never heard from again. "The Book of Helaman" ends, and a new chapter begins.

John the Baptist is recognized as the last of the Old Testament prophets and as the bridge to the New Testament. Similarly, Samuel is the last prophet of Helaman and the bridge to *The Book of Mormon*'s next chapter, titled "The Third Book of Nephi, the Son of Nephi, Which was the Son of

Helaman." It begins on page 452. (In the modern version published by the Salt Lake City Latter-day Saints, the title was changed to ". . . Who was the Son of Helaman.")

The Nephite year is 91, which is six hundred years when calculated after the time Lehi departed Jerusalem. Helaman's son Nephi leaves Zarahemla to preach and baptize sinners across the land. Now *his* son, *also* called Nephi, is in charge of the Nephites' brass plates and other records. God is going to use this Nephi to astonish the unbelievers with fulfillment of Samuel's prophecies. We can consider him to be an "in-between prophet," filling the gap between Samuel and Jesus.

In "The Third Book of Nephi," which comes after "The Book of Helaman," Samuel's predictions begin to come true. The sun sets, but the night remains as bright as midday. People gather, realizing that the Son of God must shortly appear. Next, a new star appears in the sky. Believing in the coming of Jesus Christ, the people repent and are baptized. Having learned of his birth, the Nephites reset their calendar to start with that event.

For the next section of *The Book of Mormon*, Joseph Smith Sr. and his namesake son turn again to the King James translation of the New Testament. At first we find almost identical phrases, but soon whole pages in *The Book of Mormon* spring from the Christian Bible, only now the immediately recognizable sermons take place in Mesoamerica rather than in Jerusalem.

For example, in Third Nephi 5, page 480 (12:17–18) Nephi preaches:

Think not that I am come to destroy the law or the prophets. I am not come to destroy but to fulfil:

For verily I say unto you, one jot nor one tittle hath not passed away from the law, but in me it hath all been fulfilled.

This paraphrases Matthew, chapter five, verses seventeen and eighteen, in the New Testament:

Think not that I am come to destroy the law, or the prophets: I am not come to destroy, but to fulfill. For verily I say unto you, Till heaven and earth pass, one jot or one tittle shall in no wise pass from the law, till all be fulfilled.

You may have noticed that the Smiths changed certain punctuation marks—a period to a colon, a semicolon to a period. The Smiths added a phrase here and there, such as "Till heaven and earth pass" or modified a few words. "[H]ath not passed away from the law" becomes "in no wise pass from the law," and so on.

The plagiarism unabashedly continues. After the resurrection, Jesus preaches to the Nephites in ancient Mexico. The Mormons' Jesus ministers in much the same way as the New Testament's Jesus. He says he is the light of the world; he gives the Sermon on the Mount and the parable of the fruit tree; he teaches repentance and preaches baptism. The Smiths lifted words, phrases, and pages right out of the Bible, in proper King James English, and dropped them into *The Book of Mormon*, as if Jesus were repeating himself almost verbatim or cued by a script of past sermons for the benefit of the Nephites and Lamanites.

But a huge logistical problem arises from the Smiths' subterfuge. Consider the gold plates Junior supposedly unearthed in New York State. These tablets were inscribed with Jesus' words in "reformed Egyptian" by the prophet Nephi. Pretend, if you will, that Nephi did indeed translate Jesus' sermons from Hebrew at the time Jesus uttered them in ancient Mexico in 34 AD, writing in "reformed Egyptian," a language never heard of before it is mentioned in *The Book of Mormon*. Reformed Egyptian supposedly has no alphabet. It is only hieroglyphic symbols that could mean anything from a single letter to an entire phrase in some ancient, derived Egyptian language but has no meaning in Hebrew or English. How, then, could the plates have been translated in New York in 1828 into *Old King's English from Britain of the 1600s* in such a way that they came out sounding and ordered in sequence exactly like the *King James Bible*? How could Nephi have been privy to the King James translation and use it verbatim while engraving the plates that Joseph Smith Jr. would "discover" centuries later? We can wonder also at Nephi's skill as an engraver: He must have been very adept at transcribing the spoken word from Hebrew into Egyptian onto a plate so as not to have missed any of Jesus' words and phrases.

But how does the timing of this work out? Would Nephi have written down Jesus' words centuries after he uttered them? Then we'd have to question which came first—King James or *The Book of Mormon*. If King James came first, then it obviously had been plagiarized, because the verbiage is almost identical to *The Book of Mormon*. If *The Book of Mormon* came first, then the Bible was the work of plagiarists, because the verbiage in the Bible is almost identical to *The Book of Mormon*. Because one echoes the other, someone was a plagiarist, or else the two composers worked together, writing the Bible and the plates at the same time.

Let's think about the timing in more detail. If we assume that Nephi engraved the plates soon after Jesus spoke the words, that would have been prior to the New Testament writing. King James was published in the 1600s—sixteen centuries after Nephi, son of Helaman, engraved his plates. Also, King James was in Europe, and Nephi was in the American wilderness in a different time period. The whole scenario is ridiculous. Quite simply, the whole thing is impossible. "The Third Book of Nephi" could not have been translated from tablets. It came straight from a Christian Bible published in 1815.

☙

Back in Zarahemla, eventually the robbers are defeated, cities rebuilt, and roads laid from city to city. The people, now prosperous, turn away from God, as is the Smiths' well-established—and perhaps overused—plotline. Again the tribes must repent. They need a messiah, and so a resurrected Jesus comes to visit the Nephites.

How could the Smiths have conceived such a far-fetched notion? Remember, these men were plagiarists; the idea must have come from *somewhere*. Might they have read stories about Jesus Christ's preaching to the ancient Indians? *Someone's* account must have inspired them to write about Jesus' visiting Zarahemla. The Smiths' repeated references to Mexican history may guide us to several possibilities.

First let's return to James Duncan's *Modern Traveller* volume on Mexico—the same book from which the Smiths drew the robbers and Captain

Moroni's Title of Liberty. The book includes excerpts from Diaz's record of the conquest of Mexico. When the Aztecs first laid eyes on the Spaniards, they believed the conquistadores were gods whose arrival had been prophesied. In the opening section that paraphrases Bernal Diaz's story, the author writes:

> [Cortes] urged Montezuma to acknowledge himself as a vassal to the crown of Castile. . . . [Montezuma] called together the chief men of his empire, and . . . reminded them of the traditions and prophecies which led them to expect the arrival of a people sprung from the same stock with themselves, in order to take possession of the supreme power; he declared his belief that the Spaniards were this promised race.[174]

The Spanish conquerors and Catholic priests learned of this idea and used it to their advantage. Let's return now to Robert Kerr's series for the following account of Cortes's adventures. When the Aztec emissaries asked Cortes if he and his army were the men from the prophecy, Cortes replied, "that he and all his brethren . . . certainly were those men to whom the Mexican prophecies related."[175]

Editor Robert Kerr also wrote about this prophecy in his own footnote five on the same page forty:

> . . . there was an ancient tradition current among the Mexicans, that Quetzalcoatl, their god of the air, had disappeared long ago, promising to return after a certain period, and to govern them in peace and happiness; and on the first appearance of the Spaniards on their coast, observing certain marks of resemblance between them and their mythological notions of this god, they believed their god of the air had returned, and was about to resume the government.

So the Mexicans believed, at least in their first encounters, that the Spanish commander was the returning Quetzalcoatl, the "god of the air."

Could this have sparked the Smiths' imagination? Does this somehow relate to Jesus' preaching Christianity to the Nephites? Kerr addressed this idea, too, on page 199. He followed the text of explorer Alexander von Humboldt, who wrote:

It is remarkable, that the legends of Mexico, Peru, and Brazil, all unite in ascribing the civilisation of the country to a foreigner. As the Indians of the southern peninsula ascribed the first cultivation of the madioc to their Payé Zome, so the Mexican Indians adore a mysterious personage under the name of Quetzalcoatl, who is said to have landed at the head of a band of strangers from the north. . . . Their leader was a white man, florid, and with a large beard. . . . *The Mexican clergy are disposed to identify this person with the apostle St. Thomas;* and many coincidences in the cosmogony and traditions of the Aztecs, together with the universal belief that white men, with long beards and sanctity of manners, had changed their religion and political system, *favour the hypothesis that, at some remote epoch, Christianity had been preached in the new continent.*

From this the Smiths would have learned that the Catholic priests believed Christianity had been brought to the ancient Indians and that the good fathers thought St. Thomas the apostle had visited ancient America.

In the book *The Conquest of Peru, Mexico . . . In the Thirteenth Century by Mongols, Accompanied with Elephants*, published in London in 1827, author John Ranking's footnote on page 327 explained that Quetzalcoatl arrived with the Toltecs.[176]

According to the Indians' mythology, Quetzalcoatl was believed to be the creator of the universe and of humankind. The divinity of all the nations in ancient Mexico, he could take on human form and live in the water and the air and on land. In the myth, the creator-god came to earth as King Quetzalcoatl.

He wore cotton garments, white, narrow, long, and over that, a mantle set with certain red crosses. . . . Quetzalcoatl was the high priest of Tula. . . . he went to the eastern coast, where he disappeared, after declaring to the Cholulans that he would return in a short time to govern them again and renew their happiness.

On page 329 Ranking cited other authors when he asserted: "This appears to prove with a certainty, that the Mexicans expected children of the sun (the Mongols) and that Cortes had assumed that character," and that "Quetzalcoatl was St. Thomas."

The Smiths' plan could very well have been designed to build on the accepted legend of an Indian god whom many thought to be a white Jewish man with a beard (St. Thomas) from the east (i.e., from Jerusalem). This man ostensibly settled in or near Mexico City and other cities to preach Christianity to the Aztecs and other tribes. The Smiths altered this to Jesus Christ, a Jew traditionally conceptualized as having a beard, preaching Christianity to the Nephites in the city of Bountiful, just north of Zarahemla, and other cities in that region.

As reported in *The Book of Mormon*, Jesus had been crucified in Jerusalem and had arisen from his grave and returned to heaven. He is about to visit the land of Zarahemla from heaven, but first God's judgment descends on the people, and its form is as Samuel foretold. A terrible storm strikes Zarahemla (3 Nephi: 4, pp. 470–471 [8:9–18]):

> And it came to pass in the thirty and fourth year, in the first month, in the fourth day of the month, there arose a great storm, such an one as never had been known in all the land. . . . the city of Zarahemla did take fire; and the city of Moroni did sink into the depths of the sea, and the inhabitants thereof were drowned; and the earth was carried up upon the city of Moronihah, that in the place of the city there became a great mountain; and there was a great and terrible destruction in the land southward.

> But behold, there was a more great and terrible destruction in the land northward: for behold, the whole face of the land was changed, because of the tempest, and the whirlwinds, and the thunderings, and the lightnings, and the exceedingly great quaking of the whole earth.

> . . . and there were some who were carried away in the whirlwind; and whither they went, no man knoweth, save they know that they were carried away.

And behold, the rocks were rent in twain; yea, they were broken up upon the face of the whole earth, insomuch that they were found in broken fragments, and in seams, and in cracks, upon all the face of the land.

Is this a product of the Smiths' imagination? Again we have to suspect their plot took shape from other sources. Let's refer to *The Travels of Marco Polo*,[177] page 621, which could have inspired the story of this catastrophic event:

[The island of Zeilan] is in circuit two thousand four hundred miles, but in ancient times it was still larger, its circumference then measuring full three thousand six hundred miles, according to what we find in maps possessed by the navigators of these seas. *But the northern gales which blow with such prodigious violence, have in a manner corroded the mountains, so that they have in some parts fallen and sunk in the sea,* and the island, from that cause, no longer retains its original size.

What is remarkable is how well the percentages of these two excerpts match in *The Book of Mormon* and *The Travels of Marco Polo*. Third Nephi, Chapter IV, begins on page 470 and continues through page 476. The percent of the way through the text is from 79.93 to 80.95 percent (pages 470 to 476 divided by 588 pages). That calculation tells us that the material is 80 to 81 percent through *The Book of Mormon*.

Let's apply this calculation to Marsden's *Polo*. We find ourselves on pages 604 to 612 (page 756 times .80 to .81). A mere nine pages later, on page 621, is the extracted paragraph about the island of Zeilan. The Nephites had cities sinking in the sea—"that great city of Moroni, have I caused to be *sunk in the depths of the sea*"—and Marco Polo described an island sliding into the ocean. The Smith story is at 80 to 81 percent into the text, and the Polo story is at 82 percent. (Keep in mind that although we are beginning with *The Book of Mormon* and then searching its possible sourcebooks, the Smiths obviously would have done the opposite; they would have read a reference book for plot ideas, then inserted them into their writing project.)

Look at the matching of keywords, one story to the other:

82% *The Travels of Marco Polo* Book III, Chapter XIX Pages 621–623	80–81% *The Book of Mormon,* "The Book of Nephi, The Son of Nephi, Which was the Son of Helaman" Ch. IV, pp. 470–76 [3 Nephi Ch. 8]
have in a manner corroded the mountains . . . have in some parts fallen and	that great city Moroni have I caused to be
sunk in the sea,	sunk in the . . . sea (472)
and the island, from that cause, no longer retains its original size.	many great and notable cities were sunk
	the city . . . did sink into the depths of the sea (p. 471)
	all these [cities] have I caused to be sunk
the mountains	a great mountain
steering a course to the	a great and terrible destruction in the land
southward of west	southward. (471)
the northern gales	whirlwinds . . . tempests (471)
which blow with prodigious violence	there were some which were carried away in the whirlwind (471)
measuring full	did last for about . . .
three thousand . . . miles	three hours(471)
	there was a more great and terrible destruction in the land
northern gales	northward (471)
	Behold I am Jesus Christ, the Son of God. (473 . . . the prophet Zenos . . . 475)

The Smiths recorded the "quaking of the earth" during the storm on page 471. They also wrote "and the earth was carried up upon the city of Moronihah, that in the place of the city thereof, there became a great mountain." We might ask, How could Joseph Smith Jr. know about earthquakes and cities being covered with the earth during an earthquake in ancient America? Surely there were no earthquakes in his hometown in New York. One obvious source is the writings of James Duncan in the *Traveller* series about Mexico and Guatimala. Duncan wrote:

> Earthquakes are by no means rare on the coast of the Pacific, and in the neighborhood of the capital, but they have never been known to produce such desolating effects as have been witnessed in the cities of Lima, Riobamba, Guatimala*, and Cumana. Nevertheless, on the 14th of September, 1759, the plains of Jorullo, on the shores of the Pacific, formed the scene of one of the most tremendous catastrophes that the surface of the globe has ever exhibited. In one single night, there issued from the earth a volcano 1494 feet in elevation, surrounded by more than 2000 apertures, which continue to emit smoke to the present day. (*Guatimala was for a long time kept in a state of constant alarm by the vicinity of two mountains, one of which vomited fire, and the other water, till at length the city was swallowed up by a tremendous explosion.)[178]

This footnote could have even inspired the incidence of God's vengeance against the Nephites where Jesus said, ". . . city of Jerusalem and the inhabitants thereof, and waters have I caused to come up in the stead thereof." (Helaman 4:, p. 472)

Explosions from volcanoes, earthquakes, and even describing a unique catastrophe where cities were destroyed and "swallowed up" by water and lava were all part of the history of Central America that the Smiths learned about, and incorporated, into *The Book of Mormon*.

After divine justice has been meted out and the indicators of Jesus' crucifixion seen, the Messiah is risen. For all the plagiarism of the Bible, the Smiths added some new material: they have Jesus speak from heaven to the Nephites. On page 472 of *The Book of Mormon*, his voice from heaven is heard throughout Zarahemla and the surrounding area. In his first words to the Nephites before he returns to see them, Jesus reviews the disaster of the city sunk into the sea:

Behold, that great city Zarahemla have I burned with fire, and the inhabitants thereof. And behold, that great city Moroni *have I caused to be sunk in the depths of the sea,* and the inhabitants thereof to be drowned. (3 Nephi 4: p. 472 [9:2–4])

The mysterious voice continues until the bottom of page 473:

Behold I am Jesus Christ, the Son of God. I created the Heavens and the earth, and all things that in them is. I was with the Father from the beginning. I am in the Father, and the Father in me; and in me hath the Father glorified his name. I came unto my own, and my own received me not. And the scriptures, concerning my coming, are fulfilled. As many as have received me, to them have I given to become the Sons of God; and even so will I to as many as shall believe in my name: for behold, by me redemption cometh, and in me is the law of Moses fulfilled. I am the light and the life of the world.

This sermon by the Mormon Jesus is a hodgepodge of paraphrased Christian Bible verses. Let's deconstruct it and attribute the material to its rightful sources:

Behold I am Jesus Christ, the Son of God.

And Simon Peter answered and said, "Thou art the Christ, the Son of the living God." (Matthew 16:16)

I am the Son of God. (John 10:36)

⚬⚬⚬

I created the Heavens and the earth, and all things that in them is.

In the beginning, God created the heaven and the earth. (Genesis 1:1)

⚬⚬⚬

I was with the Father from the beginning. I am in the Father, and the Father in me;

I am in the Father and the Father is in me. (John 14:11)

In the beginning was the Word, and the Word was with God, and the Word was God. The same was in the beginning with God. All things were made by him. (John 1:1–3)

❦

. . . and in me hath the Father glorified his name.

Father, glorify thy name. (John 12:27–28)

❦

I came unto my own, and my own received me not.

He came unto his own, and his own received him not. (John 1:11)

❦

And the scriptures, concerning my coming, are fulfilled.

And he began to say unto them, This day is this scripture fulfilled in your ears. (Luke 4:21)

❦

As many as have received me, to them have I given to become the Sons of God;

For as many as are led by the Spirit of God, they are the sons of God. (Romans 8:14)

❦

... and even so will I to as many as shall believe in my name: for behold, by me redemption cometh,

... *ye are in Christ Jesus, who of God is made unto us ... redemption.* (1 Corinthians 1:30)

⌘

... and in me is the law of Moses fulfilled.

... *all things must be fulfilled which were written in the law of Moses ... concerning me.* (Luke 24:44)

⌘

I am the light and the life of the world.

I am the light of the world. (John 9:5)

Not all of the Smiths' words from Jesus were copied from the sermons of Jesus Christ. Some of them come from New Testament chapters called "Romans" and "Corinthians," which were the apostle Paul's letters to church members. One comes from the very beginning of the Old Testament, in "The Book of Genesis." This sort of paraphrasing and biblical patchwork continues for another page (474) until the prophet Nephi begins writing again.

For the next thirty-eight pages, the Smiths' preaching of Jesus and comments about him include a blend of New Testament paraphrases and quotes interspersed with *The Travels of Marco Polo.*

The story of Jesus physically coming down from heaven to Zarahemla begins with another mysterious voice:

And now it came to pass that there were a great multitude gathered together, of the people of Nephi, round about the temple which was in the land Bountiful ... *they heard a voice, as if it came out of Heaven ...*

Behold, *my beloved Son, in whom I am well pleased,* in whom I have glorified my name, hear ye him." (3 Nephi 5, p. 476 [11:7])

In the New Testament, Matthew 3:17, God speaks to the disciples. "And lo, a *voice from heaven,* saying, This is *my beloved Son, in whom I am well pleased.*"

The Nephites witness another miracle. Jesus comes down to them at the temple in Bountiful (the city in Zarahemla, not the place in Arabia). On pages 476 and 477 in *The Book of Mormon* we find:

And it came to pass as they understood, they cast their eyes up again towards Heaven, and behold, they saw a man descending out of Heaven; and he was clothed in a white robe, and he came down and stood in the midst of them, and the eyes of the whole multitude were turned upon him . . . for they thought it was an angel that had appeared unto them.

. . . he stretched forth his hand, and spake unto the people, saying: Behold I am Jesus Christ, of which the prophets testified that should come into the world; and behold I am the light and the life of the world, and I have drank out of that bitter cup which the Father hath given me, and have glorified the Father in taking upon me the sins of the world, in the which I have suffered the will of the Father in all things, from the beginning.

And it came to pass that when Jesus had spake these words, the whole multitude fell to the earth, for they remembered that it had been prophesied among them that Christ should shew himself unto them after his ascension into Heaven. (3 Nephi 5: pp. 476–477 [11:8–12])

Just how far were the Smiths willing to go with writing false stories about Jesus? Does this show disdain or disrespect for Christianity?

After they had Him descend from Heaven to the land of Zarahemla, the Smiths used material from Jesus' preaching in the New Testament's Book of Matthew and transformed it into sermons to the Nephites. Below you will find a few examples. The Smiths, as you shall see, made revisions so minor that only close scrutiny exposes them. Look for changes in punctuation, words added here and there, and a few phrases left out from the Smiths' copying. The Smiths' slight revisions are highlighted for ease of comparison. There are many examples of this, but we have room to show only a few. Below, the plagiarists took Jesus' Sermon on the Mount from chapter five in the Gospel of Matthew and slipped it into Third Nephi, chapter five. (This same technique continues through chapters six and seven of Matthew.)

The Gospel According To Saint Matthew Chapter V (1815) Verses 3–48, Pages 741–742	"The Book of Nephi the Son of Nephi, which Was the Son of Helaman" Chapter V 81.46%–82.48%, Pages 479–485
	Line 34, Page 479: Yea,
3 Blessed are the poor in spirit:	blessed are the poor in spirit, which cometh unto me,
for theirs is the kingdom of heaven.	for theirs is the kingdom of Heaven.
	Line 36: And again,
4 Blessed are they that mourn: for they shall be comforted.	blessed are all they that mourn, for they shall be comforted;
	37 and
5 Blessed are the meek: for they shall inherit the earth.	blessed are the meek, for they shall inherit the earth.
	38 And
6 Blessed are they which do hunger and thirst after righteousness:	blessed are all they which do hunger and thirst after righteousness,
for they shall be filled.	for they shall be filled with the Holy Ghost.
	40 And
7 Blessed are the merciful: for they shall obtain mercy.	blessed are the merciful, for they shall obtain mercy.
	41 And
8 Blessed are the pure in heart: for they shall see God.	blessed are all the pure in heart, for they shall see God.
	42 And

The Gospel According To Saint Matthew Chapter V (1815) Verses 3–48, Pages 741–742	"The Book of Nephi the Son of Nephi, which Was the Son of Helaman" Chapter V 81.46%–82.48%, Pages 479–485
9 Blessed are the peacemakers: for they shall be called the children of God.	And blessed are all the peace-makers, for they shall be called the children of God.
	Line 1, Page 480: And
10 Blessed are they which are perse-cuted for righteousness' sake:	blessed are all they which are perse-cuted for my namesake,
for theirs is the kingdom of heaven.	for theirs is the kingdom of Heaven.

Jesus' commands to the Jews in Jerusalem are nearly duplicated in the preaching to the Nephites. See if you can find the differences between the King James translation of the New Testament on the left and Nephi's tran-scriptions of hieroglyphics onto the tablets on the right:

39 But I say unto you, That ye resist not evil: but whosoever shall smite thee on thy right cheek, turn to him the other also.	24 But I say unto you, That ye shall not resist evil: but whosoever shall smite thee on thy right cheek, turn to him the other also. (p. 481)

Nor does the traditional "Lord's Prayer" escape prominence in *The Book of Mormon*, although for reasons unknown the Nephite version is two verses shorter than that of the New Testament's:

The Gospel According To Saint Matthew Chapter VI Verses 9–34, Pages 742–743	"The Third Book of Nephi" p. 482, 81.97%, lines 19–41.
9 After this manner therefore pray ye:	19 After this manner therefore pray ye:
Our Father which art	Our Father which art
in heaven,	in heaven,
Hallowed be thy name.	Hallowed be thy name.
10 Thy kingdom come.	

The Gospel According To Saint Matthew Chapter VI Verses 9–34, Pages 742–743	"The Third Book of Nephi" p. 482, 81.97%, lines 19–41.
Thy will be done in earth, as it is in heaven.	Thy will be done in earth as it is in heaven.
11 Give us this day our daily bread.	
12 And forgive us our debts, as we forgive our debtors.	22 And forgive us our debts, as we forgive our debtors.
13 And lead us not into temptation, but deliver us from evil:	23 And lead us not into temptation, but deliver us from evil.
for thine is the kingdom, and the power, and the glory, for ever. Amen.	24 For thine is the kingdom, and the power, and the glory, for ever. Amen.

When we totaled the count of Old and New Testament Bible verses used for just "The Book of Helaman," we found at least 182 verses copied. The Smiths' favorite pattern was stealing a verse from Matthew, Mark, or Luke and then following that verse with a quote from the chapter of John. This table gives a brief list of how many King James Bible verses the Smiths copied into "The Book of Helaman." While they relied mostly on Matthew, they also cherry-picked text from Exodus, Deuteronomy, Samuel, Job, and the Psalms:

Old Testament Chapter	Number of Verses	New Testament Chapter	Number of Verses
Exodus	1	Matthew	62
Deuteronomy	4	Mark	6
Joshua	1	Luke	18
I Samuel	4	John	23
Job	2	Acts	16
Psalms	7	Romans	3
Isaiah	2	1 Corinthians	1
Jeremiah	1	2 Corinthians	4

Old Testament Chapter	Number of Verses	New Testament Chapter	Number of Verses
Zechariah	1	Galatians	1
		Ephesians	1
		Philippians	1
		I Thessalonians	3
		1 Timothy	3
		Hebrews	5
		James	2
		1 John	2
		Revelation	9

Let's review the Smiths' writing about the Mormon counterparts of Jesus and John the Baptist as percentages into the text and the source of the writings to see if more patterns emerge.

Book Source	Subject	Book of Mormon Pages
Duncan, *Mod. Trav. Mexico*	Gadianton's robbers copied from Gachupins and bandits in Mexican revolution	423–426
Robert Kerr	Samuel the Lamanite copied from Montezuma in Conquest of Mexico	441–442
King James Bible	Samuel the Lamanite copied from Bible	442–448
Robert Kerr	Samuel the Lamanite copied from Montezuma in Conquest of Mexico	449
King James Bible	Nephi, son of Helaman, preaches, copied from Bible	452–455
Mod. Trav. Mexico	Fight against Gadianton robbers copied and embellished from *Modern Traveller, Mexico*	456–463
Travels of Marco Polo	Marco Polo copied for city of Moroni sinking into the sea, Jesus speaking	470–475
King James Bible	Jesus speaking, copied from Bible	473–476

Book Source	Subject	Book of Mormon Pages
Mod. Trav. Mexico & King James Bible	The Smiths' story of Jesus' arrival to the Nephites (idea of Queztalcoatl, god of the air)	476–477
King James Bible	Duplication of the Bible for Jesus' instructions to the Nephites	477–493
Travels of Marco Polo	Plagiarizing Marco Polo as the words of Jesus Christ	493–504
King James Bible	Duplication of the Bible for Jesus' instructions to the Nephites	505–510
Travels of Marco Polo	Plagiarizing Marco Polo as the words of Jesus Christ	511
King James Bible	Duplication of the Bible from chapter of Acts of the Apostles	514–515
	Total pages in *The Book of Mormon*	423–515

Can you see the Smiths' repetitive process? The story bounces around a variety of sources: a historic geography book; the King James Bible; Robert Kerr; Bible; James Duncan of *Modern Traveller*; *Marco Polo*; Bible; *Traveller*; Bible; *Polo*; Bible; and so on. Anyone looking for a single book from which the Smiths could have copied will be disappointed.

How do we conclude a chapter such as this? An American family in the 1800s willfully created false scripture and copied the sermons of Jesus Christ. Their deceit fabricated a religion that now has millions of followers. Perhaps an apt ending can be taken from "The Third Book of Nephi," chapter six. In it is blatant plagiarism of Jesus Christ's words in the Christian Bible for an imagined Jesus' teaching to the Nephites in *The Book of Mormon*. It says,

> Beware of false prophets, which come to you in sheep's clothing, but inwardly they are ravening wolves. Ye shall know them by their fruits.[179]

Tlachco

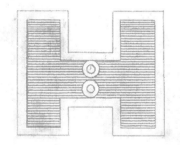

✳ 16 ✦

MONGOLS ON
ELEPHANTS INVADE
"THE BOOK OF ETHER"

An important year for Mormons was 1827. Their prophet, Joseph Smith Jr., claimed he had dug up a stone box containing the fabled gold plates from the hill called Camorah in Upstate New York; the angel Moroni had warned him not to show the plates to anyone; and while Junior was transporting them to the family farm, he had to stop and hide them inside a hollow log. Not until 1828 did he start translating their hieroglyphics, using his seer stone placed in his hat while Martin Harris sat on the other side of a curtain, taking Smith's dictation.

We can't disprove the existence of an assumed but unknown and secret 1827 manuscript the Smiths made for *The Book of Mormon*, but we can make some educated assumptions based on the actions of Joseph Smith Jr. The original manuscript was certainly completed by 1827, because the Smith father and son would have had to finish their book before reporting that Junior had found the gold plates and brought them home.

If that is the case, then why would they have waited a year before starting the translation? We propose that something occurred in 1827 to delay the translation and publication of *The Book of Mormon*. In 1827 British author John Ranking published his second book, and the Smiths wanted to add parts of it to their manuscript. Ranking's work has a map (Figure 69)

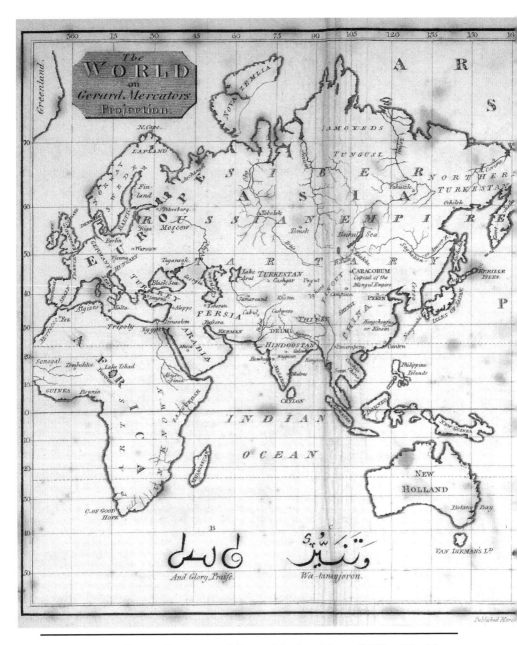

Figure 69. Ranking, *Conquest of Peru, Mexico*, Map of "The World on
Gerard Mercator's Projection"

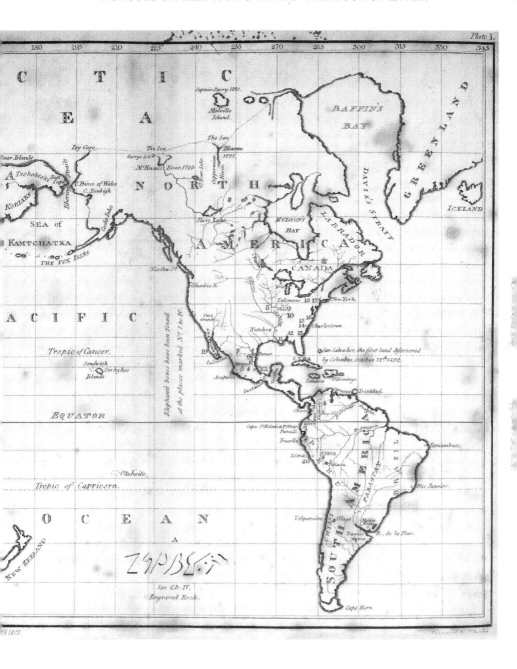

and a long title on the cover page below, which we will shorten for our needs to *Conquest of Peru and Mexico*[180] (Figure 70).

Ranking was the first author to attempt to connect all the material about Marco Polo, hieroglyphics, religion, civilizations, and the Tartars to the Indians, cities, and kingdoms of North America.

∽∞∞∿

He compiled all the writings he could obtain from William Marsden's 1818 *Travels of Marco Polo* and from the *Modern Travellers* series of volumes. He used the writings of many historians and travelers (such as Pinkerton) as his reference books, all of which he listed in his bibliography.

Ranking was looking for evidence for theories about the origin of the ancient Incas and Aztecs. He, among others, believed that the advanced civilizations of ancient American cities and kingdoms came from eastern Asia in a remote time and that the Aztecs and Incas were actually Tartars—also known as Mongols—who arrived in the Americas in the thirteenth century.

> Thus we find everywhere in America, proofs, traditions, and conjectures that the *natives are descended from the rude Asiatics, north of the latitude of China*; until the conquest of Peru and Mexico, at which period China was governed by those rude Tartars, who had attained to a knowledge of several of the arts and handicraft trades of the Celestial Empire, but not to the literature.

> *The probability of this being the true solution of this interesting question is supported by many authorities, Robertson, Humboldt, Pennant, Carver, Barton. Added to this, any one who casts his eye on the Map of the World, will at once allow the geographical question to favour this theory.*

> To attempt to ascertain the epoch when accidents or emigrations *first* supplied America with eastern Asiatics, would be a vain task. Any one who is desirous to inquire into this point, will have no remains of the works of man, no progress in civilization, no numbers of population, or any other fact as far as is now known, to warrant the conclusion of a very ancient population.[181]

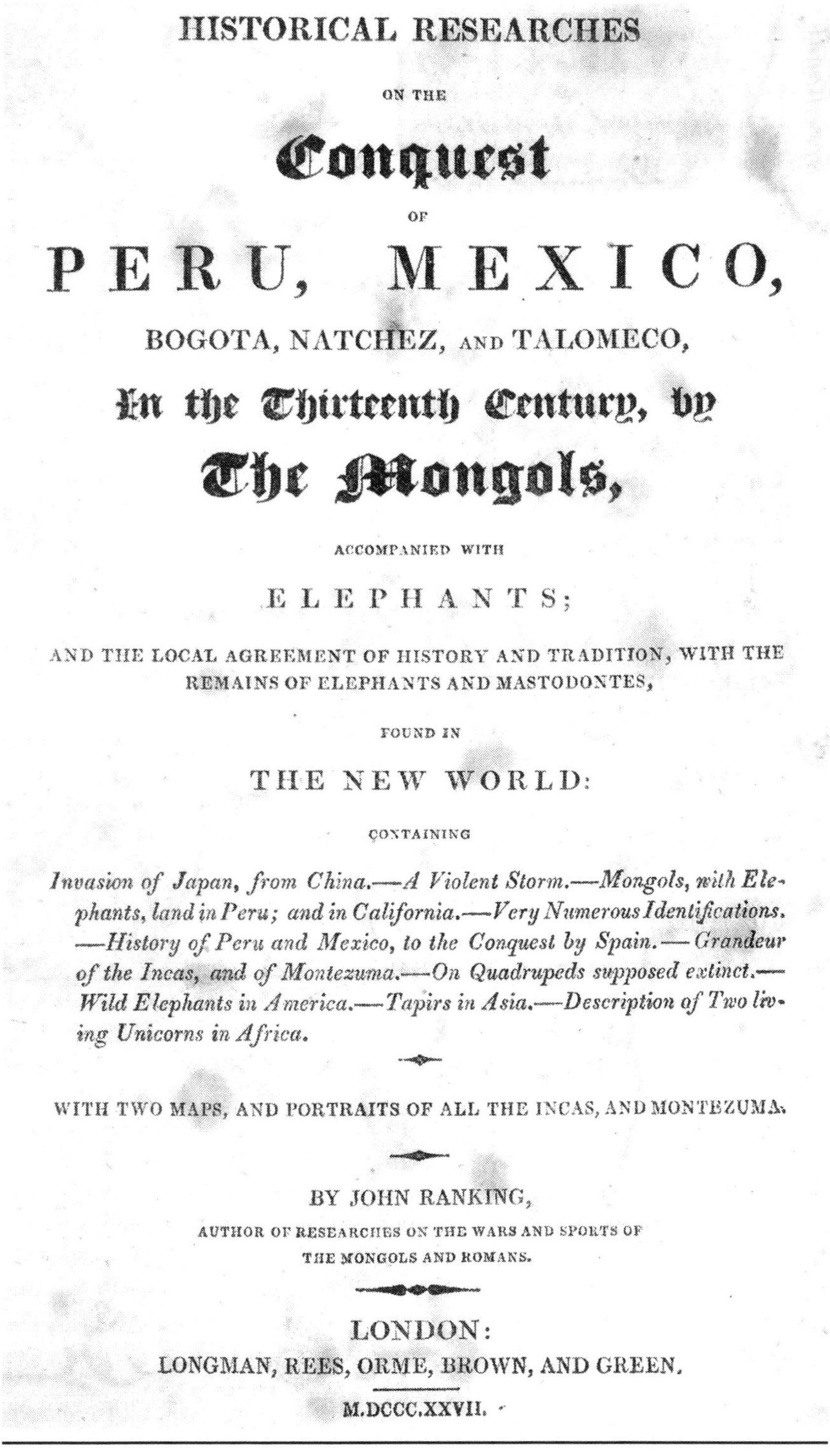

HISTORICAL RESEARCHES

ON THE

Conquest

OF

PERU, MEXICO,

BOGOTA, NATCHEZ, AND TALOMECO,

In the Thirteenth Century, by

The Mongols,

ACCOMPANIED WITH

ELEPHANTS;

AND THE LOCAL AGREEMENT OF HISTORY AND TRADITION, WITH THE
REMAINS OF ELEPHANTS AND MASTODONTES,

FOUND IN

THE NEW WORLD:

CONTAINING

Invasion of Japan, from China.—A Violent Storm.—Mongols, with Elephants, land in Peru; and in California.—Very Numerous Identifications. —History of Peru and Mexico, to the Conquest by Spain. — Grandeur of the Incas, and of Montezuma.—On Quadrupeds supposed extinct.— Wild Elephants in America.—Tapirs in Asia.—Description of Two living Unicorns in Africa.

WITH TWO MAPS, AND PORTRAITS OF ALL THE INCAS, AND MONTEZUMA.

BY JOHN RANKING,

AUTHOR OF RESEARCHES ON THE WARS AND SPORTS OF
THE MONGOLS AND ROMANS.

LONDON:

LONGMAN, REES, ORME, BROWN, AND GREEN.

M.DCCC.XXVII.

Figure 70. Ranking, *Conquest of Peru, Mexico*, Title Page

This material would have been so irresistible to the Smiths that they decided to devote additional time to incorporate it into *The Book of Mormon* by creating a new chapter.

Ranking stated that the Tartars brought elephants to America, citing Indian legends, and compared the cultures and languages and excavated bones of elephants as his proof. Here is a comparison of the last Inca emperors with Tartar rulers (Figure 71).

This theory fit perfectly into what was going on behind the curtains at the Smith household. The Smiths built on Ranking's assertion. If American Indians were indeed descendants of Kublai Khan's Tartars who could write on gold tablets, then the Smiths could use Marco Polo's Tartar stories to create *The Book of Mormon*'s tales. They would set Polo's accounts in ancient America and include gold plates. It would be a natural fit.

After reading Ranking's book, they would have recognized the material's huge potential. To make use of it, they would simply add a new book to their Mormon epic. They invented a Hebrew tribe, the Jaredites, and said they came to the Promised Land from the Tower of Babel centuries before Lehi and his clan arrived.[182]

The reasons for a different group of Hebrews and a new chapter near the end of *The Book of Mormon* are mainly twofold. First, Ranking had theorized that Tartars were blown across the Pacific Ocean by monsoon and trade winds in the thirteenth century. They made the voyage in Chinese *barques*—small craft powered by sails and oars. In the Mormon version, the Jaredites—unlike Lehi, who sailed on a ship—traveled in small, light, tight *barges* (a word close enough to *barque* to satisfy the plagiarists). The Jaredites landed on the coast of America, used elephants and horses, and built cities and empires.

Second, the Smiths knew from Ranking's research that in 1827 the known history of the Indians in America dated back only to the sixth century (500 AD):

The Toltecs being, as they say, banished from their own country, Huehuetlapallan, supposed to be in the kingdom of Tollan . . . began their journey [from the most eastern parts of Asia], AD 544.[183]

Figure 71. Ranking, *Conquest of Peru, Mexico*, Plate 4, Comparison of Incas and Mongols

If nothing in history books predated the sixth century, then no one could argue that the new chapter in their *Book of Mormon* was a fraud. There was nothing to compare it with; the other published books about the Indians in North and South America didn't make such solid statements about the dates for known Indian history.

Having a specific timeframe to work within, the Smiths made sure the dates of the Nephites' history ended at a time earlier than 500 BC. They aligned the Jaredites with a specific event in history that Ranking said the Indians must have known about: the Tower of Babel.

"The Book of Ether," then, was composed after the rest of *The Book of Mormon* was completed. Think of "The Book of Ether" as a 2,000-year-old prequel to "The First Book of Nephi." The Smiths inserted it after the chapter called "The Book of Mormon" and before the final chapter of *The Book of Mormon*, which is titled "The Book of Moroni."

The storyline generally rehashes the story of Lehi and his people: An ancient Hebrew group led by God leaves the Holy Land, crosses the ocean, and arrives in the Promised Land, where they create great cities and empires in Mesoamerica and eventually fight among themselves to the death.

The Jaredites, too, wrote their history on metal plates. Their record was preserved on twenty-four gold plates by a prophet named Ether. Those plates were later discovered near Zarahemla by the Nephite king Limhi and incorporated into the Nephite record.

A detailed map of Anahuac, showing the empire of Mexico, would have helped the Smiths visualize the kingdoms of ancient America, which would help organize their new setting and tales (Figure 72).

Ranking's research provided one answer for a universal question in the early 1800s: where did the native inhabitants of North and South America come from?

From Ranking's book the Smiths would have learned this:

> [Ranking] now ventures confidently to affirm that Peru, Mexico, and other countries in America, were conquered by the Mongols, accompanied with *elephants*, in the thirteenth century.[184]

When these Mongols arrived, America, we shall see, was in the rudest condition. Suddenly, two empires are founded with pomp, ceremonies, and grandeur, of Asiatic sovereigns: architecture, that rivaled the stupendous works of the Romans; elegance in the arts of goldsmiths, surpassing the most delicate works of the Europeans; order, justice, and subordination: all of whose laws, military and civil, institutions, religion, and customs, are so faithful in every respect to those of Genghis Khan's family, that their descent cannot for a moment be doubted. . . . All the ancient entrenchments and inscriptions discovered in America, as far as Narranganset Bay near Boston, are, there is every probability, of Mongol origin.[185]

The opinion of the writer [Ranking] is, that Mango Capac, the first Inca of Peru, was a son of the Grand Khan Kublai, and that Montezuma's ancestor was a Mongol grandee from Tangut, very possibly Assam.[186]

The Mexicans arrived at Tula in 1196. In their journey from Chicomoztoc they divided into two factions: one retained the name of Tlatelolcas, the other Tenochcas, or Mexicans. . . . They founded a town, AD 1325, which, from humble beginnings, grew to be the most considerable city in the new world.[187]

The Smiths would have learned that the Aztecs' "mode of hieroglyphic painting has been practised in the vale of Anahuac since the seventh century" and that "We are ignorant whether this system was invented in the new continent, or whether it was owing to the emigration of some Tartar tribe."[188]

Now the Smiths were armed with even greater knowledge of the Tartars' becoming Incas and Aztecs. This was beyond anything asserted by John Pinkerton or the authors of other history books in the Smith library. Now the plagiarists were ready to write a story of a Hebrew people who existed well before Lehi: the Jaredites, who discovered the Promised Land, built advanced cities and empires, and had elephants.

The Jaredite Story

The tale begins with the Lord talking to the brother of a man named Jared and then guiding the brother and his people from the Tower of Babel

Figure 72. Ranking, Conquest of Peru, Mexico, Map of "Anahuac in the
Year 1521. Containing the Empire of Mexico, the Kingdoms of Acolluacan
Michuacan &c. The Republics of Tlascalla & Huaxtecapan"

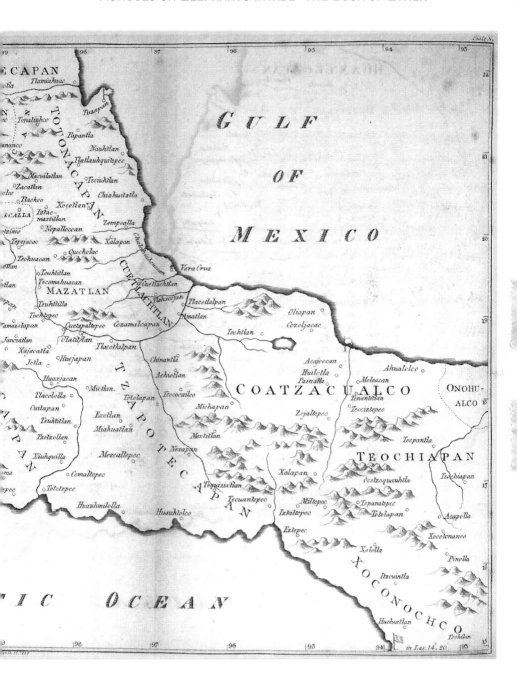

through the wilderness of the Arab peninsula to the American continents. The group started at the Tower of Babel in Mesopotamia rather than in Jerusalem, as did Lehi.

Ranking added a footnote on page 377 copied from Clavigero's history of Mexico, stating that the Toltecs no doubt knew of Babel. We also learned this in the previous chapter about the land of Zarahemla and the Aztec calendar.

After the confounding of languages at the Tower of Babel, the brother of Jared appealed to God for guidance. The Lord told him to "Go to and gather together thy flocks, both male and female, of every kind; and also of the seed of the earth of every kind." (Ether 1, p. 540 [1:41]) God told him to build barges and cross "many waters."

This is reminiscent of the Noah's ark scenario because God promises to protect the group from "the floods have I sent forth," although this refers to the turbulence of the ocean voyage.

Jared, his brother, and their families and friends "went down into the valley . . . with their flocks, which they had gathered together, male and female, of every kind." They caught birds and fish and put the fish into a giant vessel. They brought the "deseret," which was their name for a honey-bee, and kept "swarms" of them inside the barges.

The story of the honeybee appears at about ninety-one percent of the way through the Mormon scripture, which is almost the exact through-the-text location of a story in *Marco Polo* about sailing to a kingdom in Arabia called "Guzzerat." *Guzzerat* may not sound exactly like *Deseret*, but based on the surrounding text about preparing animals and seeds for a ship *to Arabia* in *Marco Polo* and *from Arabia* in "The Book of Ether," we are confident that it was at least an inspiration for the name of Jaredite honeybees:

Table 1: First Part of Stories
guzzerat/deseret, north/northward,
vessels/vessel, arabia/arabian, birds/fowls, etc.

Marco Polo (p. 690, 91.27–91.40%)	Joseph Smith (p. 590, 91.84%)
	And it came to pass that Jared, and his brother, and their

Table 1: First Part of Stories
guzzerat/deseret, north/northward,
vessels/vessel, arabia/arabian, birds/fowls, etc.

Marco Polo (p. 690, 91.27–91.40%)	Joseph Smith (p. 590, 91.84%)
The kingdom of **Guzzerat** . . . The	families, and also the friends of Jared and his brother, and their families, went down into the
north-star appears from hence to have six fathoms of altitude.	valley which was **northward,** (and the name of the valley was
This country affords harbour to pirates of the most desperate character. Here there is a	
(See "north-star" above)	Nimrod, being called after the
great abundance	mighty hunter,) with
buffaloes, wild oxen, rhinoceroses, and other beasts are dressed here; and	their flocks, which they had gathered together, male and
	female, of every kind. And they did also lay snares and
(see "**birds**" below)	catch fouls of the air; and . . .
vessels are loaded	prepare a **vessel,**
	in the
with them, bound to different parts of **Arabia.**	which they did **carry with them** the
Coverlets for beds are made of red and blue leather. . . .	fish of the waters; and they did
Upon these the Mahometans are accustomed to repose. Cushions also, ornamented with gold wire,	also carry with them
(The kingdom of **Guzzerat**)	**deseret,** which by interpretation,
in the form of **birds**	is a honey bee;
and beasts, are manufacture of this place.	and thus they did carry with them swarms of bees, and all manner of
Here there is great abundance of	that which was upon the face of the

Table 1: First Part of Stories
guzzerat/deseret, north/northward,
vessels/vessel, arabia/arabian, birds/fowls, etc.

Marco Polo (p. 690, 91.27–91.40%)	Joseph Smith (p. 590, 91.84%)
ginger, pepper, and indigo. Cotton is produced.	land, seeds of every kind.

The barges in which the Jaredites travelled were different from any other ship in *The Book of Mormon*, which piqued our interest in them.

> And the Lord said, Go to work and build, after the manner of barges which ye have hitherto built according to the instructions of the Lord. (Ether 1, p. 542 [2:16])

The marvelous Marco Polo (and William Marsden in footnotes) describes some Chinese barges on a lake in *The Travels of Marco Polo* from pages 508 to 544. In chapter LXVIII, Polo described the "noble and magnificent city of Kin-sai," which had two central islands in a large lake with "pleasure-vessels or *barges*" to float people around the body of water. Polo made detailed notes about the "vessels or barges" of Kin-sai, and these became the "vessels or barges" in "The Book of Ether":

"Vessels" or "barges"—Marco Polo
"Vessels" or "barges"— "The Book of Ether"

The Travels of Marco Polo p. 525 (69.44%)	*The Book of Mormon* Ether, pp. 542–543, 548–549 (92.18% and 93.20%)
In addition to this, there are upon the lake a great number of pleasure-vessels or barges	(p. 542) And the Lord said, Go to work and build, after the manner of barges which ye have hitherto built . . . and built barges . . . according to the instructions of the Lord. And they were small, and they were light upon the water . . . even that they

"Vessels" or "barges"—Marco Polo
"Vessels" or "barges"—"The Book of Ether"

The Travels of Marco Polo p. 525 (69.44%)	The Book of Mormon Ether, pp. 542–543, 548–549 (92.18% and 93.20%)
	would hold water **like unto a dish; and the**
. . . . . . **with a wide and flat flooring.**	bottom thereof was tight like unto a dish; and the sides thereof was tight like unto a dish; and the ends thereof were peaked; and the
The cabins have a **flat roof or upper deck,**	top thereof was tight like unto a dish; and the
. . . being from fifteen to twenty paces **in length,**	length thereof was the length of a tree;
with a wide and flat flooring,	and the door thereof, when it was shut, was
and are **not** liable to heel to either side in passing through the water.	tight like unto a dish.
	the brother of Jared cried unto the Lord, saying: O Lord, I have
(see above, "pleasure-**vessels or**	performed the work which thou hast commanded me, and I have made the
barges")	**barges** according as thou has directed me.
	(p. 543) What will ye that I should do that ye may have light in your
(see above, "pleasure-**vessels**")	**vessels?**
There are **windows** on each side, which may either be kept shut, or opened to given an opportunity to the company, as they sit at table.	For behold ye cannot have **windows,** for they will be dashed into pieces.
Such persons . . . either in the company of their women or that of their male companions, engage one of these barges, which are always kept in the nicest order, with proper seats and	(p. 548) they had prepared all manner of food, that thereby they might subsist upon the water

"Vessels" or "barges"—Marco Polo
"Vessels" or "barges"—"The Book of Ether"

The Travels of Marco Polo p. 525 (69.44%)	The Book of Mormon Ether, pp. 542–543, 548–549 (92.18% and 93.20%)
tables, together with every other kind of furniture necessary for giving an entertainment.	
calculated for holding ten, fifteen, to twenty persons.	. . . they got aboard of their
(see above, "pleasure-vessels or barges")	vessels or barges.

In a coincidence that might have amazed even the Smith household, Ranking tells us that Mongolian boats carrying strangers are also part of Incan legends. The Incas believed that in ancient times, giants came to the western shores of the continent by sea in a kind of rush boat "made like large barks." A citation by Ranking repeats a French version: *"bateaux de jonc, faits comme de grands barques."* (Ranking, p. 52) He thought they were Chinese-style "junks" and that the Tartars could have used some version of them to carry elephants and troops for the attack on Japan.

Taking another look at the Jaredite vessels, let's compare the barges in Ether with Ranking's research:

John Ranking Conquest of Peru, Mexico	"The Book of Ether" (Ether 1, p. 542)
The writer regrets that he has forgotten in what history he has read a description of	And the Lord said, Go to work and build, after
the manner in which large vessels were constructed	the manner of barges which ye have hitherto built
in these parts of the world, for the safe and easy mode of shipping and conveying elephants. (p. 46)	according to the instructions of the Lord.
Junk is said in Todd's Dictionary to be, probably, an Indian word, applied to large and **small ships**. (p. 46)	**And they were small,** and they were light upon the water, even like unto the lightness of a fowl upon the water;

John Ranking *Conquest of Peru, Mexico*	"The Book of Ether" (Ether 1, p. 542)
It appears to have been in consideration of the storms, that the ships	and they
were built in such a manner, (p. 49)	were built after a manner
. . . that they could with difficulty be sunk by leaks . . . (p. 49)	that they were exceeding tight, even that they would hold water like unto a dish;
for the safe and easy mode of shipping and conveying elephants:	and the bottom thereof was tight like unto a dish; and the
the side was made to open, so that the beasts walked in upon an even platform. (p. 46)	sides thereof was tight like unto a dish . . . and the door thereof, when it was shut, was tight like a dish.

Something else was unusual in the construction of the Jaredite barges: they had no windows. In a description of landlocked Tartar houses, on page 247, Ranking wrote:

> . . . to keep out the wind, they *do not build windows* to their houses, *but leave an opening at the tops of the rooms* . . .

This provided a good design for the Jaredite barges:

> O Lord, in them there is no light, whither shall we steer. And also we shall perish, for in them we cannot breathe, save it is the air which is in them; therefore we shall perish. And the Lord said to the brother of Jared, Behold, *thou shalt make a hole in the top thereof,* and also in the bottom thereof; and when thou shalt suffer for air, thou shalt unstop the hole thereof, and receive air. (Ether 1: p. 542 [2:20])

> For behold *ye cannot have windows,* for they will be dashed into pieces. (Ether 1: p. 543 [2:23])

The brother of Jared then asked God, "Behold, O Lord, wilt thou suffer that we shall cross this great water in darkness?" This is a practical question since they cannot have windows and cannot carry fire. God sent the brother up to the mountains. First he went up to "the mount Shelem . . . and did moulten out of a rock sixteen small stones; and they were white and clear, even as transparent glass." (Ether 1: p. 543) He prayed to the Lord to touch the stones, "that they may shine forth in darkness." The Lord touched the stones one by one, and the brother of Jared "saw the finger of the Lord; and it was as the finger of a man, like unto flesh and blood." (Ether 1: p. 544 [3:6])

The Lord gave the brother of Jared two special stones called "interpreters." These are the same stones that Joseph Smith Jr. called "Urim" and "Thummin" and claimed to have found in the stone box with the gold plates.

In chapter three, we continue with Jared and his faithful but nameless brother. Jared's brother comes down from the mount, Shelem, and puts one stone in each end of each barge, and God caused them to shine in the darkness.

John Ranking did not write about glowing stones. The Smiths must have consulted another book, so let's start with the 1818 *Marco Polo*. The glowing stones are at ninety-two to ninety-three percent of the way through the Mormon text. Turning to ninety-three percent through Marsden's *Travels of Marco Polo*, we found nothing about stones, but we found other comparisons between *Polo* and Ether. There is a story with some numbers to compare—eight with eight, and sixteen with sixteen—and possibly a strange use of the word *moulten*:

The Book of Mormon, 93.35% (Ether 1: p. 543 [3:1]):
And it came to pass that the brother of Jared, (now the number of vessels that had been prepared, was *eight*) went forth unto the mount, which they called the mount Shelem, because of its exceeding height, and did *moulten out of a rock sixteen* small stones. . . . He did carry them . . . upon the top of the mount.

The Travels of Marco Polo, 93.52%, p. 707:
The people of the island (Magastar) report . . . an extraordinary kind of bird, which they call a rukh . . . when the wings are spread they measure *sixteen* paces in extent, from point to point; and that the feathers are *eight* paces in length, and thick in proportion.

Throughout this province there is found a sort of black stone, which they dig out of the mountains where it runs in veins. When lighted, it burns like charcoal, and retains the fire much better than wood; insomuch that it may be preserved during the night, and in the morning be found still burning. These stones do not flame, excepting a little when first lighted, but during their ignition give out a considerable heat. It is true there is no scarcity of wood in the country, but the multitude of inhabitants is so immense, and their stoves and baths, which they are continually heating, so numerous, that the quantity could not supply the demand; for there is no person who does not

Figure 73. Marsden, *Marco Polo*, 373

The numbers *eight* and *sixteen* match in that paragraph, but what about the magic stones? At forty-nine percent through the text, where Polo's story begins in the province of Kataia, it reads (Figure 73).

We're presenting a shortened version of the Jaredite story for you to compare, because the whole story spans five pages of the chapter:

The Travels of Marco Polo Book II, Ch. XXIII Page 373, 49.34%	*The Book of Mormon* "The Book of Ether" Ch. III p. 543–548, 93.20–93.95%
Throughout this province there is found a sort of black stone, which they dig	went forth up into the mount . . . and did moulten out of a rock sixteen stones . . .
	. . . behold, the Lord stretched forth his hand and touched the stones, one by one, with his finger . . .
	after that the Lord had prepared the stones which the brother of Jared had carried up into the mount, the brother of Jared came down
out of the mountains where it runs in veins.	out of the mount,

The Travels of Marco Polo Book II, Ch. XXIII Page 373, 49.34%	The Book of Mormon "The Book of Ether" Ch. III p. 543–548, 93.20–93.95%
	and he did put forth the stones into the vessels which were prepared, one in each end thereof; and behold, they
When lighted, it burns like charcoal, and retains the fire much better than wood; insomuch that it may be	did give light unto the vessels, thereof. And thus the Lord caused
preserved during the night,	stones to shine in darkness,
and in the morning be found still burning.	
These stones do not flame, excepting a little when first	
lighted, but during their ignition give out a considerable heat. It is true there is no scarcity of wood in the country, but the	to give light
multitude of inhabitants is so immense.	unto men, women, and children, that they might not cross the great waters in darkness.

In the end, the Jaredites' shining stones were neither "moulten" out of a mountain nor touched by the finger of God. Their stones were Polo's *coal*, which burned all night in the province of Kataia.

Blown to the Land of Promise

In 1275 AD, Kublai Khan's general Moocow led a naval invasion of Japan that ended in a rare, devastating defeat of the Tartars. Upon their reaching the Japanese coast, a tempest "began to blow with great force, and the ships of the Tartars, which lay near the shore of the island, were driven foul of each other." (Ranking, p. 38)

Most of the ships sank. Ranking's theory was that some Tartar vessels were caught up in westerly monsoon winds, which blew them across the Pacific all the way to the American shoreline:

In the China seas the north-east or winter monsoon, commences about the month of October or November, and lasts till about February or March: the south-west monsoon sets in about April or May, and blows till August or September.[189]

. . . the probability is, that the ruins of Tiahuanaco and Vinaque, are remains of some buildings of Tartars, Japanese, or Chinese, *who had been blown across the Pacific in remoter times.*[190]

Jared's barges also were blown to the American shores. Coincidence? We believe Ranking's paragraph provided a plot element for *The Book of Mormon.* The Smiths would have known about the monsoon and trade winds from China for "The Book of Ether" from Ranking's *Mongol* book:

The shifting of the Monsoons is not all at once; and in some places the time of change is attended with calms, in others with variable winds; and particularly those of China, at ceasing to be westerly, *are very subject to be tempestuous; and such in their violence, that they seem to be of the nature of the West India hurricanes.* These tempests, the seamen call, the breaking up of the monsoons. They blow half the year one way, and the other half year on the opposite points.[191]

And now, from the "The Book of Ether":

. . . they got aboard of their vessels or barges, and set forth into the sea. The Lord God caused that there should be a *furious wind blow upon the face of the waters, towards the promised land;* and thus *they were tossed upon the waves of the sea before the wind.* (Ether 3: p. 548 [6:5])

The Jaredites were blown around for a specific number of days: "And thus they were driven forth, three hundred and forty and four days upon the water."

Why did the Smiths choose this particular number for the duration of the voyage? They seemed so specific about a voyage of just under a year. Perhaps this story sheds light on their rationale:

> In 1542, three Portuguese made an escape from Siam . . . to Liamp, in Lat. 30°, in a junk but there fell such a storm upon their stern, that in a few days they were blown to within sight of Japan. *"The whole voyage from Manilla to Acapulco, including detention at the latter place, till the arrival of the Galleon back at Manilla, takes up about eleven months."*[192]

The Portuguese were blown from China to Japan in a barque, then to Mexico, and then sailed back to the Philippines again in eleven months. Even though their return voyage had them sailing away from America, let's do the math for the whole journey: 11 months times 30 days/month equals 330 days (or 31 days/month equals 341 days). Either way the months are counted, the days total very close to the Jaredites' voyage of 344 days.

The Smiths also made a precise percentage selection directly from *Marco Polo*. From Ether we read about how strong the vessels/barges were:

> And thus they were driven forth; and no monster of the sea could break them, neither *whale that could mar them*. (Ether 3: p. 549 [6:10])

The Ether quote starts at 92.35 percent into the text. At 92.72 percent into Marsden's *Marco Polo* we find a quote about ships striking whales:

> . . . they *strike into the whales*. . . . There [*Magastar*] is also much amber-gris from the *whales* . . . tide throws it on the coast . . . of the *sea abounding with whales*.

Arriving at the Land of Promise

In Ether, when Jared's group arrives in the Promised Land, they wanted a monarch. They held a type of election for their first king from among the sons of Jared:

But Jared said unto his brother, Suffer them that they may have a king; and therefore he said unto them, *Choose ye out from among our sons a king, even whom ye will.* (Ether 3: p. 550 [6:24])

The Aztecs also held a form of election for the emperor:

The Mexican government was at first aristocratical, under, for their better security, *they formed it into a monarchy; and the election, by common consent,* fell on the most famous and prudent person among them; *he was son* of Opochitli, a very noble Aztec, and a princess of Colhuacan. (Ranking, p. 301) Montezuma, or Motezuma (the Archer of Heaven), *was elected* with general applause.[193]

Strangers with Elephants

The next part of the story is impossible to believe. In Ether, chapter four, under the reign of King Emer, the Jaredites became rich:

. . . all manner of cattle, of oxen, and cows, and of sheep, and of swine, and of goats, and also many other kind of animals, which were useful for the food of man; and they also had horses, and asses, and *there were elephants, and cureloms, and cumoms; all which were useful unto man, and more especially the elephants, and cureloms, and cumoms.* (Ether 4: p. 556)

Of all the animals that the Jaredites could have used or eaten, the plagiarists wrote that the Jaredites used *elephants.* Hebrews riding around America on elephants circa 2400 BC? What were they thinking? Where could they have found such an idea? Apparently from Mr. Ranking, who provided some research on this topic. Ranking believed that Peru and Mexico were conquered in the thirteenth century by Mongols *with their elephants* doing battle as they had in Kublai Khan's wars of conquest. He stated: "*Wild elephants are found near Bogotá, the probable descendants of those which accompanied the expedition;* for had these animals been indigenous in America, they could not fail to exist there in very great numbers."

(Ranking, p. 23) On page 396 he wrote, "It is now certain that *wild elephants* are in existence in New Granada."

Indian legends about giants, Ranking wrote, were based on the Mongols' riding elephants when they came ashore in Peru and set about decimating the entire country, as Tartars tend to do.[194] And in a footnote on pages 254 and 255, Ranking asserts:

> To all these reasons for concluding that the Bogotans were a part of the shipwrecked fleet, *wild elephants* now exist at Choco, and the plain between Suaca and Santa Fe de Bogota is called the Field of Giants. (Humbolt, Vol. ii, p. 21), a name probably derived from a tradition regarding a contest with men and *elephants,* as in Peru and Mexico.

After reading this, the Smiths would feel safe to copy elephants into a plagiarized ancient history of the Indians. Unfortunately for the father and son, Ranking's theory was wrong about the elephants. His mistake became a glaring blunder in *The Book of Mormon.* Neither Ranking nor the Smiths knew that domesticated elephants never existed in ancient America. While Ranking assumed that the legends must have meant there were elephants past and present, he had no scientific proof. We know today that the last wild American "elephants" became extinct thousands of years before the Tower of Babel incident.

Ivan T. Sanderson, author of "Elephants" in the *Encyclopedia Americana, International Edition*[195] wrote the following:

> The Elephantidae family includes both the present-day elephants (Elephas and Loxodonta) and the now extinct mammoths (Mammuthus). *Some mastodons and mammoths survived in North America until about 8,000 years ago.*

Louis A. Brennan's *Beginners Guide to Archaeology*[196] discusses Ice Age animals in America:

Ten thousand years ago what happened was that the Pleistocene mega-fauna, the large beasts, became extinct. These included several subspecies of mammoth, the mastodon, the American horse, the camel, giant bison (Bison antiquus, Bison occidentalis, Bison taylori), giant sloths, giant armadillos, giant rodents (the capybara), the giant dire wolf, the saber-tooth cat, the giant jaguar or American lion, and the short faced bear. Some of these species had disappeared some few thousands of years before 10,000 B.P.; some lingered a millennium or two afterwards. *But 10,000 B.P. was clearly the end of an era . . . elephants were actually prehistoric mammoths and not our modern version of elephants.*

A quote from the Latter-day Saints' early newspaper shows just how arrogant yet uninformed they were on this topic. Smith Jr. was the editor of this paper:

Surely "facts are stubborn things." It will be as it ever has been, the world will prove Joseph Smith a true prophet by circumstantial evidence, in experiments, as they did Moses and Elijah. (*Times and Seasons* 3:922)

Cureloms and Cumoms

There are two strange animals in *The Book of Mormon*: "cureloms" and "cumoms." Joseph Smith Jr. himself claimed that he did not know what these animals were. The best name comparison we found as a basis for cureloms and cumoms was on page 552 in Marsden's note 1093, which shows the name for a yellow dye called "curcuma longa." Could this have given Smith the idea for the names of these bizarre creatures?

From Marsden: "curcuma longa"
To Smith: "cureloms" and "cumoms"

Whether or not the yellow dye is the origin of the names, the more interesting question is what *were* these strange Jaredite animals? We began the investigation with their quote from "The Book of Ether," which is in the same sentence with the elephants:

and they also had . . . elephants, and *cureloms, and cumoms;* all of which were useful unto man, and more especially the elephants, and *cureloms, and cumoms.* (Ether 4: p. 556 [9:19])

Apparently these mystery animals are beasts of burden; they are listed in the same sentence with beasts of burden such as horses, asses, and elephants, and they are described as "useful unto man," meaning they must have been trained to work. What else do we know about them? Their name is given with the only mention of elephants in *The Book of Mormon* and on the same page as "cattle, oxen, and cows."

They are unidentifiable to Prophet Smith himself, so they are either unknown or have an unknown name. What could they be?

We found connections on pages 224 to 234 of the 1818 *Marco Polo,* where the medieval traveler remarks on a curious beast of burden with an *unknown name* that he saw in the kingdom of Erginul, in present-day China:

Book I, Chapter LI
Of the kingdom of Erginul adjoining to that of Kampion, and of the city of Singui of *a species of oxen covered with extremely fine hair;* of the form of the animal that yields the musk, and the mode of taking it; and of the customs of the inhabitants of that country and the beauty of the women.

Marco Polo called it "a species of oxen" but knew it was not an ox. Below is one of Marsden's footnotes together with "The Book of Ether" verse:

The Travels of Marco Polo p. 228, note 438	*The Book of Mormon* Ether 4: p. 556 [9:19]
They (the *yaks,* Turner adds) are very valuable property.	

The Travels of Marco Polo p. 228, note 438	The Book of Mormon Ether 4: p. 556 [9:19]
they are never employed in agriculture . . . but are	and cureloms and cumoms; all of which were
extremely	
useful as beasts of burden;	useful unto man,

Polo compares them in size to elephants, and as we noted above, there is the singular listing of elephants together with the cureloms and cumoms:

The Travels of Marco Polo (p. 224)	The Book of Mormon (p. 556)
Here are found many	. . . and there were
wild cattle that in point of size may be compared to elephants.	elephants, and cureloms, and cumoms . . .

Polo called these animals "wild cattle" or "species of oxen" but nothing more. He was so captivated by them, he carried a hide to Venice, where it was "esteemed by all who saw it." William Marsden inserts the correct name of the species as "bos."[197] It is particularly described by Turner, as well in his *Embassy to Tibet, as in the Asiatic Researches*, by the name of the yak or Tartary or bushy-tailed bull of Tibet.[198]

Cities

Could buildings, palaces, thrones, and "many cities" exist in 2,000 BC in the Americas? Once the Jaredites began populating the country, they built cities:

> And it came to pass that Coriantum did walk in the steps of his father, and did *build many mighty cities*, and did administer that which was good unto his people, in all his days. (Ether 4: p. 557 [9:23])

As we learned in the same-titled chapter, the most famous city of the Nephites was Zarahemla, which was patterned after Mexico City. Mr. Ranking adds to that history:

In the year 1324, the Mexican people first arrived at the place of the city. . . .
They made themselves a strong city, defended with banks and walls, *about
the waters,* and among the sedges.[199]

Recall that according to the Nephite record, Zarahemla was not originally built by the Nephites. It was ostensibly founded in the Jaredite days
by a ruler named Lib.

And they built *a great city by the narrow neck of land, by the place where
the sea divides the land.* (Ether 4: p. 560 [10:20])

The earlier city of the Jaredites didn't have a name, but it was located on
the same site that centuries later became the Nephites' city of Zarahemla.
That story parallels the history in Ranking's book: the Toltecs, who were
ancestors of the Aztecs, emigrated from Asia and arrived at a location near
what would centuries later become the Aztecs' city of Mexico:

The history of the country named Anahuac is not known earlier than
the arrival of the Toltecs, in the sixth century. When the Spaniards first
debarked at Vera Cruz, the Mexican state had existed a hundred and
ninety-seven years. (Ranking, p. 265) They are supposed to have come
from the more northern parts of America, or rather from the most eastern parts of Asia, to the western shores of America. . . . The Toltecs . . .
began their journey in 544 AD. They travelled southward for a hundred
and four years, till they arrived at Tolantizinco, *about fifty miles east of the
spot where, many centuries after, was founded the famous city of Mexico.*[200]

We can compare additional counterfeit history of the Jaredite throne to
the true history of the Incas. The Jaredite ruler Riplakish abused his power
by levying crushing taxes, constructing "spacious buildings," and indulging
in lascivious behavior:

Riplakish did not do that which was right in the sight of the Lord, *for
he did have many wives and concubines,* and did lay that upon men's

shoulders which was grievous to be borne; yea, he did tax them with heavy taxes; and with the taxes he did build many spacious buildings. (Ether 4: p. 558 [10:5])

This was also part of the Incan history noted in Ranking:

The Incas were to have but one lawful wife . . . but they *were permitted to keep many concubines.* (Ranking, p. 64)

Whoever didn't work was punished:

and *whoso refused to labor,* he did cause to be put to death. (Ether 4: p. 558 [10:6])

Extreme punishment was consistent with the Incas:

Mango instituted Decurians . . . they were censors, patrons, and judges in small controversies. *Idleness was punished with stripes.* Each colony had a supreme judge. Every man had one lawful wife, with the liberty of keeping other women. Theft, murders, disobedience to officers, and adultery were punished chiefly with death.[201]

Incas and Armaments

In "The Book of Ether," the Jaredites wield the same weapons as the Nephites, which are the weapons of the Tartars. The Smiths felt they were safe using that information because Ranking said the Aztecs used the same Tartar weapons. This also explains why the Nephites carried "cimetars"; if Ranking said the Aztecs had the same arms as Tartars, then the Smiths wrote the Tartar weapons into the Nephite story.

The Incas and Aztecs had similar arms—wooden swords. The Jaredites had steel swords. The Jaredites would "moulten" the ore out of a hill. (The correct spelling is *molten,* and it means "melted.") *The Book of Mormon* says:

... he [Shule] came to the hill Ephraim, and he did moulten out of the hill, and made swords out of steel for those which he had drew away with him; and after that he had armed them with swords. (Ether 3, p. 551 [7:9])

But in describing Mexico, Ranking makes no mention of steel swords:

The king had some armories containing all the munitions of war, bows and arrows, slings, lances, darts, clubs, swords, bucklers, and gallant targets, more trim than strong. . . . the swords are of wood and the edge is of flint.[202]

So where did the Smiths get the idea of arming the ancients with swords of steel? Remember our question in the armaments chapter: why did the Smiths take the steel swords of the Tartars and give them to the Nephites? Perhaps the footnote on Ranking's next page (page 351) prompted the Smiths to think that Mongol invaders could have brought their steel swords—or at least the know-how to make them—to America. What Ranking said in the footnote couldn't be any clearer than this:

The arms are exactly the same as those used by the Mongols; and most of the rest of the arts and customs are so faithfully copied from the manners of the Monguls and the Grand Khans in Kublai's time, that it is only necessary to refer the reader to Marco Polo, and Sir John Maundevile to be convinced that it is quite impossible the similitude should have arisen thus suddenly and from chance.

Wars and Religion

According to *The Book of Mormon*, the Lord helped Jared and his clan build barges, gather animals, light the barges at night with magical stones, and cross the ocean to the Promised Land. Once they populated the new land, the Jaredites often forgot about God and were nearly always engaged in a power struggle to control the kingdom:

> ... the brother of Lib did come against Coriantumr in the stead thereof, and the battle became exceeding sore. ... Shiz ... did *overthrow many cities,* and he did slay both women and children. (Ether 6: p. 568 [14:17])

The Incas and Aztecs were usually at war with one tribe or another, so such stories about Jaredites align with the real history:

> Lloque Ypanqui ... was the first who made use of arms against the natives. He *added to the empire the provinces* ... and adorned those conquests with public buildings, canals, high roads, a temple of the Sun, and a house of consecrated virgins. (Ranking, p. 67)

Often were the Jaredites in rebellion or overthrowing a kingdom. For example:

> And it came to pass that Kim did not reign in righteousness, wherefore he was not favored of the Lord. And *his brother did rise up in rebellion against him, in which he did bring him into captivity.* (Ether 4: p. 559 [13:23])

This is a paraphrase of the rebellion against the Inca Huasca by his brother Atahualpa:

> Atahualpa, relying on the skill and experience of his general and soldiers, remained on the frontier of his kingdom. ... *The two parties fought desperately* all day. ... *The emperor was seized.* ... The curacas and officers voluntarily submitted, or were captured with the emperor.[203]

In the Mormon scripture, Ether the prophet did not write much about religion. That content was inserted by Moroni, the narrator of the chapter about re-engraving the Ether chapter onto the gold plates of Camorah.

While he is engraving the plates, Moroni hears from the Lord: "Fools mock, but they shall mourn; and my grace is sufficient for the meek. ... I will shew unto them that faith, hope, and charity, bringeth unto me the fountain of all righteousness." Moroni answers on page 565:

And I, Moroni, having heard these words, was comforted, and said, O Lord, thy righteous will be done, for I know that thou workest unto the children of men according to their faith: for the brother of Jared said unto the mountain Zerin, Remove, and it was removed.

The Travels of Marco Polo is the source for this extract. Common to both stories is the portrayal of a prophet praying to the Lord and then speaking to a mountain as a demonstration of God's power, which inspired nonbelievers to convert and believers to grow in their faith. We will help to narrate this story of the mountains moving. As Moroni said, we "would speak somewhat concerning these things." (Ether 5: p. 563 [12:6])

The Travels of Marco Polo *Concerning the Capture and Death of* *the Khalif of Baldach (Baghdad), and* *the Miraculous Removal of a Mountain.* Page 69	*The Book of Mormon* "The Book of Ether," Chapter V Page 565 [12:29–31]

Opening words and seeking the Creator/Lord's support:

Here the pious (shoemaker),

kneeling before the cross and lifting up his hands to heaven,

And I, Moroni, having heard these words, was comforted, and said,

humbly besought his Creator that he would compassionately look down upon earth, and for the glory and excellence of his name, as well as for the support and

O Lord, thy righteous will be done,

Knowing that God helps his people/children of men and manifests his power/works according to faith:

confirmation of the Christian faith, would lend assistance to his people in the accomplishment of the task imposed upon them, and thus manifest his power to the revilers of his law.

for I know that thou workest unto the children of men according to their faith:

A prophet commands the mountain to move.

Having concluded his prayer, he cried with a loud voice: "In the name of the Father, Son, and Holy Ghost,	for the brother of Jared
I command thee, O mountain, to remove thyself!"	said unto the mountain Zerin, Remove, and

And in both stories:

. . . the mountain moved,	it was removed.

This event was so amazing that a terrified khalif became a Christian, and in *The Book of Mormon*, the Nephite disciples had faith.

and the earth at the same time trembled in a wonderful and alarming manner. The khalif and all those by whom he was surrounded, were struck with terror, and remained in a state of stupefaction. Many of the latter became Christians, and even the khalif secretly embraced Christianity.	for thus didst thou manifest thyself unto thy disciples. For after that they had faith, and did speak in thy name.

Extermination of the Jaredites

Most of the existing Incan nobles were slaughtered by Pizarro's Spanish army in 1531. Before Pizarro's invasion of Peru, however, the Incas did a fine job of killing one another. Because of the infighting among the nobles, the last Inca, Atahualpa, had terminated nearly every other noble bloodline.

The Smiths integrated this concept into their Jaredites plotline. Instead of two separate factions fighting each other and one side winning—such as the Lamanites' defeating the Nephites centuries later—we have Jaredite infighting to the point of extinction. No one survived except Ether, the prophet, to record their history on the plates.

The scene of the Jaredites' final battle was the same hill where the Nephites fell to the Lamanites: Camorah, near Palmyra, New York. In "The Book of Ether," the hill is named Ramah:

> And it came to pass that the army of Coriantumr did pitch their tents by the hill Ramah; and it was that same hill where my father Mormon did hide up the records unto the Lord, which were sacred. (Ether 6: p. 571 [15:11])

If you recall, "Rama," without the final *h*, was the leader of the monkey troops that we learned about in *Marco Polo*, and we showed how *Rama* and *Comari* appeared only one page apart in the medieval traveler's book.

Rama also shows up in John Ranking's research. A few pages after an explanation of Kublai Khan's "golden tablets" is a footnote on page 183 under the section titled "Raymi, or Solemn Festival of the Sun." This festival was led by the Inca as the high priest and eldest son of their God, the Sun:

> It is a curious circumstance that *Rama*, the Hindoo god, is one of the children of the Sun.—Sir W. Jones, i. 298. "His wife's name is Sita, and it is very remarkable that the Peruvians, whose Incas boasted the same descent, stile their great festival *Ramasitoa*."

The Incan and Jaredite tragedies are related, as you will see from their descriptions. The last legitimate ruler, Huasca Inca, and his brother Atahualpa lived in friendship for some time, but Atahualpa eventually forbade Huasca from passing through Atahualpa's dominions of the kingdom of Quito, north of Cuzco. Huasca became jealous and feared that Atahualpa's separation of territory could threaten his throne. (In truth, the nefarious Atahualpa had a strategy to gain the throne for himself.)

The ruler sent a messenger with royal orders to his brother: Atahualpa was to return to Cuzco to pay homage to Huasca Inca.

> Orders were sent out to the provinces of Quito to prepare for *this expedition;* and *secret communications* were made to the officers, to select the best soldiers, and to arm them secretly. (Ranking, p. 116–118)

Those "secret communications" from Atahualpa to his generals before the rebellion seem suspiciously similar to the "secret combinations" against the Jaredite king Moron before a rebellion:

> And it came to pass that there arose *a rebellion among the people*, because of that *secret combination* which was built up to get power and gain; and there arose a mighty man among them in iniquity, and gave battle unto Moron, in which he did overthrow half of the kingdom; and he did maintain the half of the kingdom for many years. (Ether 4: p. 562 [11:15])

Atahualpa ordered thirty thousand troops under command of the general of Quito to march, disguised as nobles, to Cuzco. The alarm was sounded to Huasca by governors in provinces who were shocked by the sizeable army from Atahualpa heading toward Cuzco.

Huasca dispatched couriers in all directions to summon the curacas and officers of the provinces to come immediately to Cuzco with all the troops they could muster. The superior valor and experience of Atahualpa's troops gave him the victory, and Huasca fled the capital.[204]

In the Jaredite kingdom, the buildup to the final battle begins in chapter six. King Moron has a son, Coriantor, who is the father of the prophet Ether. Ether lives in the days when Coriantumr became king. A great war breaks out among the Jaredite factions. Many men gather to fight and kill Coriantumr and to destroy his army, and Ether warns Coriantumr that if he does not repent, he will die. His words have no effect. Coriantumr continues his conquests, and a rebellion led by Shiz takes shape. The people join one of the two factions, Coriantumr's or Shiz's:

> ... yea, a cry went forth throughout the land: Who can stand before the army of Shiz? Behold, he sweepeth the earth before him! And it came to pass that the people began to flock together in armies, throughout all the face of the land. And they were divided, and a part of them fled to the army of Shiz, and a part of them fled to the army of Coriantumr. (Ether 6: p. 570 [14:19–20])

At this point in the Jaredite struggle, the Smiths chose plot elements from different parts of the Ranking text. The battles of the Jaredites come from Atahualpa's victory, his execution of nobles, Pizarro's slaughter of the Peruvians, and even the Aztecs struggle against Cortes.

The armies move near a river/seashore, fight for a whole day/three days, and some of the defeated flee:

> Shiz did pursue Coriantumr eastward, even to the *borders by the seashore,* and there he *gave battle unto Shiz for the space of three days;* and so terrible was the destruction among the armies of Shiz, that the people began to be frightened, and *began to flee* before the armies of Coriantumr. (Ether 6: p. 570 [14:27])

Back in Peru, the final battles between the two sides commenced:

> The general of the army of Quito was acquainted with the unprepared condition of Cuzco, and pushed on with twenty thousand troops *to the river Apurimac.* They crossed without any opposition; and now declared openly against the Inca.[205]

> The commander of the army of Quito instantly moved forward; and in the plain, which is two or three leagues from Cuzco, on the west side, the two parties, without any parley or explanation, *fought desperately for a whole day;* and numbers were slain on each side. The superior valour and experience of the troops of Atahualpa, gave them the victory, and *Huasca fled.* . . . His troops were resolved not to survive their unfortunate sovereign; and the whole of them fell either by the sword of the enemy, or by their own hands.[206]

"The Book of Ether" claims that *millions* of people died—a number that seems far-fetched for ancient America, especially in what we know as Upstate New York:

> . . . when Coriantumr had recovered of his wounds, he . . . saw that there had been slain by the sword already nearly two millions of his people, and he began to sorrow in his heart (Ether 6: p. 571 [15:2])

The Smiths would have felt confident enough to use this number, however, because John Ranking wrote:

The population of the New World was estimated by some at four millions, by Riccioli at three hundred millions. Pinkerton . . . thinks fifteen nearest the truth.[207]

Although the population of the new world was then estimated to consist of about forty millions, Las Casas charges his countrymen with having massacred more than that number. . . . De Las Casas . . . enumerates millions massacred in Honduras, Venezuala, Peru, Mexico, Hispaniola, 600,000 in Jamaica, &c.[208]

Ether introduces the slaughter of wives and children, probably because this was a practice among the Incas. First, from "The Book of Ether":

. . . yea, there had been slain two millions of *mighty men, and also their wives and their children.* (Ether 6: p. 571 [15:2])

And now Ranking's reference to Atahualpa's eliminating all the other royal lines that could challenge him:

. . . his ambition urged him to form the dreadful resolution to *extirpate all the descendants of Mango Capac,* including even those that were not legitimate, *that no one should be left in existence who could dispute his title or follow his own example.*[209]

Atahualpa used the pretext of restoring the emperor to invite the princes of blood, the governors, and officers of the provinces to Cuzco. All those who arrived were beheaded, hanged, or drowned. He massacred all Hualpa's relations, nobles under his charge, by mercilessly butchering them with hatchets and clubs.[210]

This atrocious Atahualpa was not yet satisfied with the numerous victims already sacrificed to his ambition, but *he became jealous of the female*

branches, who were every where sought out, down to the age of infancy,
and were put to torture and death, by every invention of cruelty, at *Yahuar-*
pampa, or the Field of Blood, (so called from a former event), until, in
the space of two years and a half, *few of that very numerous race remained*
alive, and none above the age of eleven years.[211]

This quote from Ether captures that last scene of carnage:

Now the brother of Lib was called Shiz . . . pursued after Coriantumr, and
he did overthrow many cities, and he did *slay both women and children,*
and he did burn the cities thereof. (Ether 6: p. 569 [14:17])

The two armies of Shiz and Coriantumr gathered the remaining people
and armed all the men, women, and children to fight:

. . . the army of Coriantumr did pitch their tents by the hill Ramah; and it
was the same hill where my father Mormon did hide up the records unto
the Lord . . . and the people which were for Coriantumr, were gathered
together to the army of Coriantumr; and the people which were for Shiz,
were gathered together to the army of Shiz . . . when they were all gathered together, every one to the army which he would, with their wives,
and their children; both men, women and children being armed with
weapons of war . . . they did march forth one against another, to battle;
and *they fought all that day, and conquered not.* (Ether 6: p. 571–572 [15:15])

The demise of the Incas was similarly dramatic. Pizarro arrived at
Tubez in 1526 for the first encounter with the Peruvians. He returned in 1531
as a conquistador. Atahualpa had recently imprisoned Huasca, and Pizarro
wanted an audience with the usurper. A Catholic priest held a crucifix in
front of Atahualpa and explained the doctrines of Christianity and why he
should convert. Atahualpa misunderstood the conversation and threw a
Bible onto the ground with disdain.

The priest called Pizarro and his troops to arms. Cannons and muskets
fired, cavalry charged, and infantry rushed in, sword in hand. *"The carnage*
did not cease till close of the day."

The Peruvians, confounded and distraught, did not resist, and four thousand died. Not a single Spaniard was wounded. Atahualpa was taken prisoner and forced to execute the former Inca, his brother Huasca.

Back at the Ramah battlefield, the war raged on. Now that the Smiths had read about the utter extinction of a race, they fit it into their book.

> And they were all gathered together . . . with their wives and their children being armed with weapons of war, having shields, and breastplates, and head-plates. (Ether 6: p. 572 [15:5]) They contended in their might with their swords and their shields all day. (Ether 6: p. 573 [15:24])

They fought all day and into the night for many days, until Coriantumr's army was reduced to fifty-two people and Shiz's to sixty-nine. The next day their numbers were cut to twenty-seven and thirty-two, respectively. *The day after that, they all killed one another:*

> . . . they had all fallen by the sword, save it were Coriantumr and Shiz, behold, Shiz had fainted with loss of blood. . . . Coriantumr . . . smote off the head of Shiz. . . . Coriantumr fell to the earth, and became as if he had no life. (Ether 6: p. 573 [15:29–32]).

Atahualpa was strangled at the stake in 1533. One of the few nobles left alive, a man named Mango Capac (who was also brother to Huasca and Atahualpa) was acknowledged by the people as their new ruler. He regrouped the Peruvians, and a final battle began. Mango Capac attacked Pizarro at Cuzco with an "immense number of his subjects, and by his heroic efforts endangering the Spanish power." But victory was not to be theirs. Mango retired to the mountains and died. (Ranking, p. 131) Pizarro appointed Sayri Tupac, the last prince, who surrendered his sovereignty to Phillip II.[212]

This was the end of the empire of the Peruvian monarchs and the end of the Jaredites, as well.

Tollantzinco

✴ 17 ✴

THE FABLED CHURCH

In researching this chapter, the authors uncovered another scandal. Instead of producing gold plates engraved with the history of the pure, ancient church of the Nephites, the Smith father-son team fabricated all of it by adapting the story of Spain's conquest of Mexico. To contrive the Nephite church, its prophets, and its counterfeit scripture, they plundered the text of Cortes's sermons and the story of his and his successor's efforts to spread Christianity in the New World.

To create a thrilling story with ferocious antagonists, the Smiths invented the Lamanites, whose wicked religious customs, including idolatry and human sacrifice, mirrored those of the Aztecs. Nephite prophets preached salvation to the Lamanites and baptized many of them. In Zarahemla, prophets also preached to fallen Nephites and built holy temples.

Temples and Synagogues, Jews and Christians

The Nephites built "temples," "synagogues," and other places of worship. Recall that Nephi's first task when he escaped to the wilderness in the Promised Land was constructing a building like the "temple of Solomon."

Many Nephite prophets traveled to temples in and around Zarahemla to preach the word of God:

> And Alma and Amulek went forth preaching repentance unto the people in their tempels [sic], and in their sanctuaries, and also in their synagogues, which was built after the manner of the Jews. (Alma 11: p. 268 [16:13])

> ... Aaron and his brethren went forth from city to city, and from one house of worship to another, establishing churches. (Alma 14: p. 289 [23:4])

> And the people which were in the land northward, did dwell in tents, and in houses of cement, and they did suffer whatsoever tree should spring up upon the face of the land, that it should grow up, that in time they might have timber to build their houses, yea, their cities, and their temples, and their synagogues, and their sanctuaries, and all manner of their buildings. (Hel. 2: p. 412 [3:9])

> Now when they had come into the land, behold, to their astonishment they found that the Zoramites had built synagogues, and that they did gather themselves together on one day of the week, which day they did call the day of the Lord; and they did worship after a manner which Alma and his brethren had never beheld ... (Alma 16 p. 311 [31:12])

No explanation is given as to why Alma was surprised that Judaism was practiced by Zoramites. All the people in Zarahemla were Jews, so it would seem natural that some would maintain traditional rituals.

In the historical records of ancient America were many examples of temples that would have been available to the Smiths for examination. Captain Diaz recorded that General Cortes visited various temples in and around the vale of Mexico. Some he destroyed, and some he converted into Catholic shrines. One ancient temple, possibly from Tlascala, looked like this (Figure 74).

During their initial meeting when they were on cordial terms, Cortes gently suggested that Montezuma convert the great temple in Mexico City into a Catholic church. Montezuma rejected the idea, but he eagerly agreed to build Cortes a chapel in his palace courtyard:

> As Montezuma was entirely adverse to the proposal of Cortes for convert-
> ing the great temple of Mexico into a Christian church, he was exceedingly
> desirous to *have a chapel and altar in our quarters*, and made application
> to Montezuma for this purpose. . . . This request was immediately com-
> plied with. . . . *it was completed in three days*. In this *new chapel* mass was
> celebrated every day, though we lamented the want of wine for the holy
> eucharist. (Kerr, Vol. IV, p. 52)

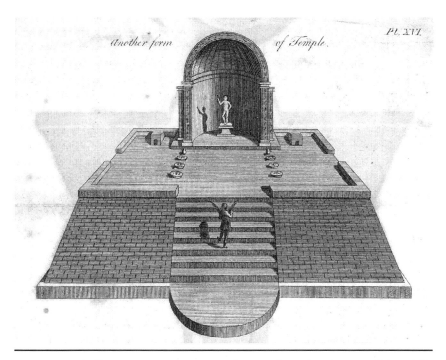

Figure 74. Cullen, *History of Mexico*, Plate 16, "Another Form of Temple"

As early as 1806, in Philadelphia, Charles Cullen published a detailed plate of the temple of Mexico[213] (Figure 75).

Beyond building materials such as cement and gold, the Smiths never provided much detail of the construction of buildings or temples. In the books contemporary with their writing, however, many details were available. From James Duncan's *Modern Traveller*, one would learn:

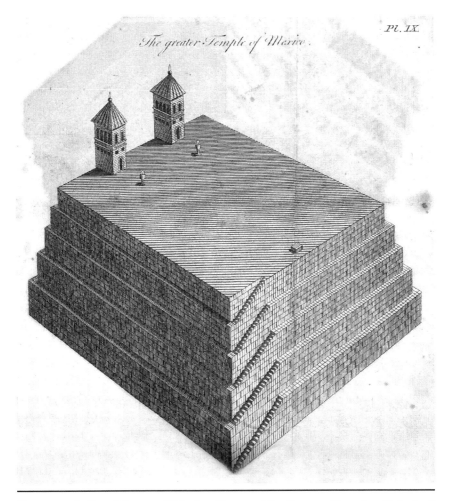

Figure 75. Cullen, *History of Mexico*, Plate 19, The Greater Temple of Mexico"

The *Teocalli*, or great temple of Mexitli, was a truncated pyramid 120 feet high, and 318 feet square at its base, situated in the midst of a vast enclosure of walls, and consisting of five stories, like some of the pyramids of Saccara. When seen from a distance, it appeared an enormous cube, with small alters, covered with wooden cupolas, on the top. The point where these cupolas terminated, was 177 feet above the pavement of the enclosure. The material of which the pyramid was built, is supposed to have been clay, faced with a porous stone resembling pumice-stone, hard and smooth, but easily destructible.[214]

De Solis provided a more chilling description. He wrote that the walls were wrought with twisting serpents "which gave a horror to the portico." Trees grew on the top level, where "from one tree to another, passed several bars run through the heads of men who had been sacrificed, of whose number (which cannot be repeated without horror) the priests of the temple took exact account, placing others in the room of those which had been wasted by time."[215]

Robert Kerr provided another example of a Mexican temple on his map of Mexico (Figure 76).

Other temples were built on pyramids more resembling the Egyptians' or Babylonians'. This plate shows the Pyramid of Cholula (Figure 77).

This plate is of the "Pyramid of the Sun"[216] (Figure 78).

Wicked Traditions of the Lamanites

In *The Book of Mormon* chapter titled "The Book of Enos," we learn just how far Lehi's descendants had fallen from the true religion not so long after settling in their land of promise. Nephi (the original one, who sailed with his father, Lehi) was dead. Nephi's faithful brother, Jacob, passed the brass plates to his son Enos. The Nephites labored in vain to save the Lamanites:

> And I bear record that the people of Nephi did diligently seek to restore the Lamanites unto the *true faith in God*. (Enos 1: p. 144)

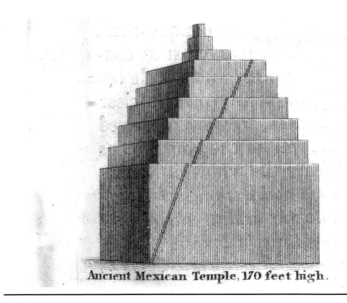

Figure 76. Kerr, *Voyages and Travels*, Vol. 3, Excerpt from "Sketch of Mexico and the Environs"

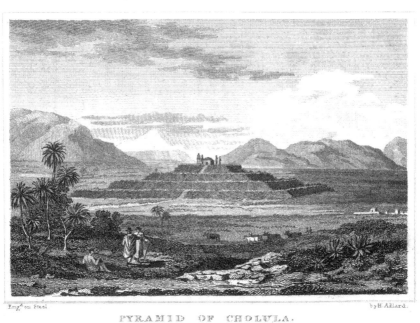

Figure 77. Duncan, *Modern Traveller, Mexico,* "Pyramid of Cholula"

Figure 78. Bullock, *Six Months in Mexico*, "Pyramid of the Sun or of San De Teothuacan"

Prophets painted a bleak picture of their former brethren:

> But our labors were in vain; their hatred was fixed, and they were led
> by their evil nature, that they became wild, and ferocious, and a blood-
> thirsty people; fully of idolatry, and filthiness; feading [sic] upon beasts
> of prey dwelling in tents, and wandering about the wilderness . . . (Enos
> 1: pp. 144–145)

A few chapters later, in "The Book of Alma," the prophet Alma converted the Lamanite king, and we read that "his people might be convinced concerning the wicked traditions of their fathers." (Alma 14: p. 289)
Prophets Nephi III and Lehi later preached to the Lamanites in Zarahemla,
who "were convinced of the wickedness of the traditions of their fathers."
(Helaman 2: p. 419)

During the Nephites' final battles, "[the Lamanites] did also march for-ward . . . and did take many prisoners of women and of children, and did offer them up as sacrifices unto their idol gods . . . the Nephites being angry because the Lamanites had sacrificed their woman and their children." (Mormon 2: pp. 525–526 [4:14]) A few battles later in the land of Desola-tion, ". . . the Nephites were driven and slaughtered with an exceeding great slaughter; their *women and their children* were again sacrificed unto idols." (Mormon 2: p. 526 [4:21])

What were the "wicked traditions"? In the source story, Bernal Diaz wrote, "In the first place, we purged the land of many *wicked customs*, and in particular from human sacrifices." (Kerr, Vol. IV, p. 320) From Captain Diaz, the Smiths would have learned about the ancient practice of sacrific-ing prisoners of war along with *women and children* from those abominable rituals of the Aztecs and others throughout the vale of Mexico. Captain Diaz continued (Figure 79),

Figure 79. Cullen, *History of Mexico*, Plate 11, "A Common Sacrifice"

... it appears that above 2500 human victims were sacrificed yearly in Mexico and some adjacent towns on the lake. . . . They fed on human flesh, as we do beef, having wooden cages in every town, in which men, *women, and children*, were kept and fed for that purpose, to which all the prisoners taken in war were destined. (Kerr, Vol. III, p. 320–321)

In the temples he found several bodies of men and boys recently sacrificed, and the stone knives yet smoking with which the horrible ceremony had been performed. The limbs had been severed from the bodies, and taken away to be eaten, as our people were informed. Our soldiers were exceedingly shocked at these abominable scenes; but such were everywhere in our after-progress through this country. (Kerr, Vol. III, p. 486)

Their manner of sacrifice was said to be as follows: They open the breasts of the living victim with large stone knives, offering his heart and blood to their gods; they feast on the head and limbs, giving the bodies to be devoured by the wild beasts, and hanging up the skulls in the temples as trophies of their misguided piety. (Kerr, Vol. IV, p. 45)

Although they did not perform sacrifices, the Nephites had their share of wicked priests. Alma was formerly a follower of priest Amulon, who served the fallen Nephite King Noah. Lamanites probably had their own priests to perform the sacrifices, but details are not provided in the text. Diaz described the ancient priests as (Figure 80):

The priests came likewise to meet us, in long loose white garments, having their long hair all clotted with blood proceeding from recent cuts in the ears, and having remarkably long nails on their fingers; they carried pots of incense, which they fumigated at us. (Kerr, Vol. IV, *Conquest of Mexico*, p. 18)

Could Jews with progenitors from the Holy Land really stray so far from their traditional doctrine? Joseph Smith would have you think so.

Figure 80. Cullen, *History of Mexico*, Plate 10, "Mexican Priest"

Saving the Lamanites

Regarding his intentions of exploring the New World, Hernan Cortes informed the Tlascalans,

> ... that our only object in coming among them, was to manifest the truths of our holy religion, and to put an end to human sacrifices, by command from God and our emperor. (Kerr, Vol. IV, p. 14)

When Xincotencatl (a Tlascalan chief) presented his own daughter to Cortes, the general replied,

> ... we must first obey the commands of our God, and the orders of our sovereign by abolishing human sacrifices and other abominations, and *by teaching them the true faith in the adoration of one only God.* He then shewed them a beautiful image of the *holy Mary, the queen of heaven, the mother of our Lord by the power of the Holy Ghost* ... that if they wished to become our bretheren, that they must renounce their idolatry, and worship our God ... whereas by persisting in the worship of their idols, which were representations of the devils, they would consign themselves to hell, where they would be plunged eternally into flames of fire. (Kerr, Vol. IV, pp. 19–20)

In his memoirs, Captain Diaz believed that the conquistadores deserved the credit for the conversion of Mexicans to Christianity. He wrote:

> It is now proper that I should make some observations on the good effects produced by our exertions and illustrious conquests, to the service of God and our king, in which many of our companions lost their lives, being sacrificed to the gods or idols of the Mexicans, Huitzilopochtli and Tezcatlipoca.
>
> By the will of God, and the sacred christianity of the emperor Don Carlos of glorious memory, and our present most fortunate sovereign the invincible Don Philip, all the natives of this great country have been

baptised to the salvation of their souls, formerly sunk and lost in the bottomless pit. We have many fathers of the different orders, who go about preaching and baptizing, by which means the knowledge of the holy Evangile is firmly planted in the hearts of the natives. (Kerr, Vol. IV, pp. 320–321)

For the Joseph Smiths, a sermon of Hernan Cortes to Montezuma was chosen as the sermon from the Nephite prophet Abinadi to King Noah. Under King Noah, the Nephites backslid from the faith. The prophet Abinadi was sent to preach for their repentance. Recall that Abinadi was executed by fire, a story that was percentage-copied from *The Travels of Marco Polo*. Abinadi preached that:

I would that ye should understand that God himself shall come down among the children of men, and shall redeem his people; and because he dwelleth in flesh, he shall be called the Son of God . . . because he was conceived by the power of God; and the Son, because of the flesh; thus becoming Father and Son: and they are one God, yea, the very Eternal Father of Heaven and of Earth . . . even so he shall be led, crucified, and slain . . .

. . . God breaketh the bands of death; having gained victory over death; giving the Son power to make intercession for the children of men; having ascended into heaven . . . (Mosiah 8: p. 186) having broken the bands of death, taken upon himself their iniquity and their transgressions; having redeemed them, and satisfied the demands of justice . . . were it not for this, that all mankind must have perished. (Mosiah 8: p. 187)

The time shall come when all shall see the salvation of the Lord . . . then shall wicked be cast out . . . and the devil hath power over them; yea, even that old serpent that did beguile our first parents, which was the cause of their fall; which was the cause of all mankind becoming carnal, sensual, devlish, knowing evil from good, subjecting themselves to the devil. Thus all mankind were lost; and behold, they would have been endlessly lost, were it not that God redeemed his people from their lost and fallen state. (Mosiah 8: pp. 188–189)

Portions of the original sermon that Cortez gave to Montezuma is placed on the left of the comparison table below, with matching portions of the sermon from Abinadi in the "Book of Mosiah" on the right.

History of the Discovery and Conquest of Mexico, Written in the Year 1568, by Captain Bernal Diaz Del Castillo, One of the Conquerors[217]	*The Book of Mormon* Mosiah 8: pp. 186–189
That he came to him in the name and for the service of the only true	
God, who was adored by the	he shall be called the
Christians, the **Lord Christ Jesus,** who had died to save us and all men.	**Son of God**
He endeavoured to explain the mystery of the cross, as an emblem	even so he shall be . . .
of the **crucifixion,**	crucified
by which **mankind had been redeemed.**	**having redeemed them** . . .
	God himself shall come down among the children of men, and shall **redeem his people** . . .
He recounted the sufferings and **death** of **our Lord and Saviour,**	even so **he shall be** led, **crucified,** and slain.
who had **risen** on the third day and	God **breaketh the bands of death;** having gained victory over death;
ascended to heaven,	**ascended into heaven**
where he now reigns, the **creator of the heavens, and the earth,** and the sea, and all that they contain.	the very **Eternal Father of Heaven and of Earth**
He asserted, that those idols which the natives held as gods, were	and the
devils which dared not to remain wherever the holy cross was planted.	**devil** hath power over them
That as **all mankind were** brothers,	Thus **all mankind were** lost . . .
	yea, even that old serpent that did beguile

History of the Discovery and Conquest of Mexico, Written in the Year 1568, by Captain Bernal Diaz Del Castillo, One of the Conquerors[217]	*The Book of Mormon* Mosiah 8: pp. 186–189
the offspring of the first pair,	our first parents
our glorious emperor lamented the	Thus all mankind
loss of their souls, which would be brought by the idols	were lost
into	and behold, they would have been
everlasting flames,	endlessly lost,
and had sent us to apply a sure remedy, by abolishing the worship of idols, the bloody and inhuman sacrifices of their fellow men, and their other odious customs so contrary to the law of God.	were it not that God redeemed his people from their lost and fallen state.

Patterns of Faith

General Cortes, and the priests who came after him, went from city to city preaching and converting the natives. Years after their conquest, Captain Diaz noted that:

> . . . this nobleman was informed of the heroic deeds of the conquerors of Mexico, and the great things they had performed for the *extension of the holy faith*, by the *conversion and baptism of such myriads of Indians*. (Kerr, Vol. IV, p. 234)

Likewise, in the land of Zarahemla, Nephite prophets brought their message to the Lamanites, who were similarly converted to the Christian faith:

> Aaron and his brethren went forth from city to city. . . . And *thousands were brought to the knowledge of the Lord, yea, thousands were brought to believe* in the traditions of the Nephites . . . (Alma 14: pp. 289–290)

The writings from Bernal Diaz reveal a pattern unique to the proselytization of the Mexican and other Indians. After confessing Christianity, the Indian women were both baptized and given a new Spanish-Christian name. The Smiths copied these same patterns to create the stories of Lamanite conversions. First, the Spanish version:

> Cortes summoned all the chiefs and priests of the Indians, to whom he made a long harangue . . . *to embrace the only true faith.* . . . He was followed by the reverend fathers, who exhorted them to become proselytes to the holy Catholic religion. . . . (Kerr, Vol. IV, p. 270)
>
> By the will of God . . . *all the natives of this great country have been baptised to the salvation of their souls,* formerly sunk and lost in the bottomless pit. We have many fathers, of the different orders, who go about *preaching and baptizing,* by which means the knowledge of the holy Evangile is firmly planted in the hearts of the *natives,* who confess yearly. . . . The churches and their altars are richly adorned with all requisites for holy worship. . . . [I]t is edifying and wonderful to see the *devotion of the natives at the holy mass.* . . . *[A]ll the natives, men, women, and children, are taught the holy prayers in their own tongue.* (Kerr, Vol. IV, p. 321)

In the land of Zarahemla, Alma, the son of Alma, went about the land preaching and then baptizing:

> . . . he began to establish a Church in the land which was in the borders of Nephi; yea, the land of Mormon; yea, and he did *baptize* his brethren in the waters of Mormon. (Alma 3: p. 232)

Other prophets also had success with the Nephites and Lamanites:

> and [the sons of Helaman] went forth . . . to *teach the word of God among all the people of Nephi, beginning at the city of Bountiful . . . and from thence into the land of Zarahemla among the Lamanites.*

dissenters . . . came forth . . . and *were baptized* unto repentance . . . eight thousand of the Lamanites which were in the land of Zarahemla and round about, *baptized* . . . (Helaman 2: p. 419)

After baptism, the Indian women were given new Christian names:

But the present which we considered as most valuable, was twenty women; among whom was the excellent Donna Marina, *so called after her baptism.* (Kerr, Vol. IV, p. 472)

Here the ladies who were destined to be the *brides of our officers,* having been instructed in the principles of the Christian religion *were baptized.* The daughter of Xicotencatl *was named Donna Luisa.* (Kerr, Vol. IV, p. 20–21)

For the Lamanites, after baptism, the converted ones changed the name of their tribe to a Nephite name:

Now these are they which were converted unto the Lord: The people of the Lamanites which were in the land of Ishmael, and also of the people of the Lamanites which were in the land of Middoni . . . the city of Nephi . . . land of Shilom . . . land of Shemlon . . . city of Lemuel . . . city of Shimnilom . . . .

And now it came to pass that the king and those people which were converted, *were desirous that they might have a name, that thereby they might be distinguished from their brethren* . . . they called their name Anti-Nephi-Lehies . . . and *were no more called Lamanites* . . . and they were friendly with the Nephites . . . (Alma 14: p. 290 [23:8–17]).

Friendly, indeed! Many noble Indian women were given as wives to the Spaniards by tribal chiefs:

In Tabasco, the twenty Indian women presented to Cortes by the chiefs were baptized by our chaplain, Olmedo, who preached to them many good things of our holy faith. . . . Cortes gave one of these women to each of his captains. These were the *first Christian women* in New Spain. (Kerr, Vol. IV, p. 473)

Next day the chiefs brought five daughters of their principal caciques, who were much handsomer than the other women of the country, each attended by a female slave. On this occasion Xicotenatl *presented his own daughter to Cortes,* and desired him to *assign the others among his principal officers.* (Kerr, Vol. IV, p. 19–20)

In the "Book of Mosiah," Nephites intermarried with Lamanite women:

. . . those which were the children of Amulon (note: priest of King Noah but still technically a Nephite) and his brethren, *which had taken to wife the daughters of the Lamanites,* they were displeased with the conduct of their fathers, and they would no longer be called by the names of their fathers; *therefore they took upon themselves the name of Nephi, that they might be called the children of Nephi,* and be numbered among those which were called Nephites. (Mosiah 11: p. 208 [25:12])

Traveling to temples, preaching to Indians, conversion to Christianity, baptism, changing to Christian names: is it all an amazing coincidence? It's no miracle. The Smiths used the spiritual conversion of the Mexicans from idolators to Roman Catholicism as the story for saving the Lamanites.

Whore of the Earth

The Book of Mormon authors wrote extreme language condemning non-Nephite and hence non-Mormon churches as "the whore" of the earth whose own swords will cut their own heads and "drink its own blood." This was clearly targeting the modern-day Protestant sects in America. If an individual didn't belong to Joseph Smith's Church of Christ (as it was originally named), then he or she belonged to that "other" church:

And it came to pass that he saith unto me, Look, and behold that great and abominable church, which is the mother of abominations, whose foundation is the Devil. And he saith unto me, Behold there is, save it be, two churches: the one is the church of the Lamb of God, and the other is the church of the Devil; wherefore, whoso belongeth not to the church of the Lamb of God, belongeth to that great church, which is the mother of abominations; and she is the whore of all the earth. (1 Nephi 3: p. 33 [14:9–10])

And the blood of that great and abominable church, which is the whore of all the earth, shall turn upon their own heads: for they shall war among themselves, and the sword of their own hands shall fall upon their own heads, and they shall be drunken with their own blood. (1 Nephi 7, p. 57 [22:13])

In his preaching, Joseph Jr. never hid his contempt for Christians:

What is it that inspires the professors of Christianity generally with a hope of salvation? It is that smooth, sophisticated influence of the devil, by which he deceives the whole world.[218]

The only principle upon which they judge me is by comparing my acts with the foolish traditions of their fathers and nonsensical teachings of hireling priests, whose object and aim were to keep the people in ignorance for the sake of filthy lucre; or as the prophet says, to feed themselves, not the flock.[219]

Since the Smiths copied the establishment of the Roman Catholic Church in New Spain as the Nephites' ancient church, their motives require thoughtful analysis. Perhaps their disdain for Christians in scripture and sermon has an additional meaning. A few pages out of "The Book of Alma" may provide some insight.

The apostate Nephite Korihor is spreading the word in Zarahemla that all the Nephite/Christian prophecies are false. High Priest Giddonah asks why "Do ye go about perverting the ways of the Lord? Why do you teach people that there shall be no Christi. . . ." (Alma 16: p. 306 [30:22]) Korihor replies:

. . . Because I do not teach the foolish traditions of your fathers, and because I do not teach this people to bind themselves down under the foolish ordinances and performances which are laid down by ancient priests, to usurp power and authority over them, to keep them in ignorance, that they may not lift up their heads, but be brought down according to thy words. Ye say that this people is a free people. Behold, I say they are in bondage. Ye say that those ancient prophecies are true. Behold, I say that ye do not know that they are true. Ye say that this people is a guilty and a fallen people, because of the transgression of a parent. Behold, I say that a child is not guilty because of its parents.

And ye also say that Christ shall come. But behold, I say that ye do not know that there shall be a Christ. And ye say also, that he shall be slain for the sins of the world; and thus ye lead away this people after the foolish traditions of your fathers, and according to your own desires; and ye keep them down, even as it were, in bondage, that ye may glut yourselves with the labors of their hands, that they durst not look up with boldness, and that they durst not enjoy their rights and privileges; yea, they durst not make use of that which is their own, lest they should offend their priests, which do yoke them according to their desires, and hath brought them to believe by their traditions, and their dreams, and their whims, and their visions, and their pretended mysteries, that they should, if they did not do according to their words, offend some unknown being, which they say is God; a being which never hath been seen nor known, which never was nor never will be. (Alma 16: pp. 306–307)

Korihor's sermon might have been a message to the Smiths' latter-day followers to let go of their rigid Christian beliefs and follow the *The Book of Mormon*. Or could this be the Smiths' honest opinion about God and all religion? Their motives were to secretly write in their book what they were thinking: that foolish ideas of Jesus and God were misused by cunning priests to profit from and enslave an otherwise free people in bondage and ignorance. To show how it could be done, the Smith family accomplished this exact feat for their own "filthy lucre."

Mexico

18

GOLD PLATES AND TABLETS

When God gave Moses the Ten Commandments, the inscriptions were made on stone tablets. For the Latter-day Saints, the holy scripture was engraved on plates of gold. While historians may argue about whether Moses really had stone tablets from God, we can state with certainty that the Mormon tablets never existed.

Here is the Smiths' story: Sometime after 420 AD, Moroni (the son of Mormon, not Captain Moroni) buried a stone box filled with the gold plates, the liahona, a breastplate, the sword of Laban, and magic spectacles called Urim and Thummim, which had been passed down from the ancient prophet Abraham. Moroni's stone box was hidden in the Camorah hillside in Upstate New York for 1,400 years. Moroni appeared to Joseph Jr. in a vision and showed him the location. Four years later, Smith dug up the box and took the plates, spectacles, and breastplate home.

Imagine if a treasure trove of ancient religious artifacts from the Holy Land was found buried in New York State. What if a holy scripture written by the biblical prophets of Israel were buried there, too? What a sensation that would cause around the world! If Smith's gold plates were so divinely obtained, what happened to them? Why weren't they housed in a museum for proof of *The Book of Mormon*? Because they existed only in words taken from the pages of *The Travels of Marco Polo* and in the imagination of Joseph Smith, Jr.

Marco Polo's Golden Tablets of Authority

The idea for "gold plates" that Joseph Smith Jr. pretended to discover with an angel's help sprang from two sources. One was a story printed in the 1818 *Travels of Marco Polo*, and the other was in geography and travel books published around that time which, transformed through plagiarism, became *The Book of Mormon*. The Smiths adapted stories from these sources to use in the original, secret *Book of Mormon* manuscript.

We believe he favored the term *plate* for a couple of reasons. In each of the reference books, illustrations were engraved on copper plates, which were used to print the pages for insertion into a book. Each copper plate was assigned a name such as "plate 1, plate 2," etc. Second, Cortes had discovered "gold plate" in Mexico, which either meant actual plates or the Aztecs' gold bullion. Either way, "gold plates" existed in name and shape in ancient Mexico, and these two meanings made the word *plates* Smith's final choice.

The idea of engraved writing on golden *tablets* would have been less ambiguous and historically appealing. This word also came from Marco Polo. At the beginning of *The Travels of Marco Polo*, his father, Nicolo, and uncle, Maffio, visited Kublai Khan on their first trip. The khan gave these two favored, medieval merchants a golden tablet that acted as both a passport and a royal "credit card" wherever they traveled within the khan's empire[220] (Figures 81 and 82).

The khan also used gold and silver tablets to issue orders, record events, and provide rewards for military officers or members of the court[221] (Figure 83).

After Marco, his father, and his uncle spent several years with Kublaï Khan, they wished to return home to Venice. Before the Polos left the khan's palace, he gave them another gold tablet, or "royal chop"[222] (Figure 84).

Recognizing the impressiveness of the tablets as well as the value of this part of Polo's story, the authors of *The Book of Mormon* used metallic tablets as the true God.[23] Having heard these commands addressed to them by the Grand *Khan,* they humbly prostrated themselves before him, declaring their willingness and instant readiness to perform, to the utmost of their ability, whatever might be the royal will. Upon which he caused letters, in the Tartarian language,[24] to be written in his name to the Pope of Rome, and these he delivered into their hands. He likewise gave orders that they should be furnished with a golden tablet displaying the imperial cipher,[25] according to the usage established by his majesty ; in virtue of which the person bearing it, together with his whole suite, are safely conveyed and escorted from station to station by

the governors of all places within the imperial dominions, and are entitled, during the time of their residing in any city, castle, town, or village, to a supply of provisions and every thing necessary for their accommodation.

Figures 81 & 82. Marsden, *Marco Polo,* 12 & 13

as a recurring symbol throughout the Nephite history. This also applied to their personal story about Camorah, with Mormon's gold plates.

Gold Plates or Tablets? Both are in *The Travels of Marco Polo*

William Marsden described "large golden plates" found in Tartar burial tombs in footnote 878 on page 451 (Figure 85).

On page 449, Marco Polo was in the city of Mien looking at a grand sepulcher of the king. It was a pyramid covered "with a plate of gold, an inch in thickness. . . ." So either above ground or underground, we find "gold plates" in Marco Polo.

In the early section of the Marco Polo book is the account of Nicolo's and Maffio's leaving Kublai Khan's palace and returning to Venice. This was the brothers' *first* trip, which did not include Marco (he wasn't born yet). The Polo brothers received a generous reward from the khan: a tablet of pure gold, or "royal chop":

Of the kind of rewards granted to those who conduct themselves well in fight, and of the golden tablets which they receive.

THE Grand *khan* appoints twelve of the most intelligent amongst his nobles, whose duty it is to make themselves acquainted with the conduct of the officers and men of his army, particularly upon expeditions and in battles, and to present their reports to his majesty,[515] who, upon being apprised of their respective merits, advances them in his service; raising those who commanded an hundred men, to the command of a thousand, and presenting many with vessels of silver, as well as the customary tablets or warrants of command and of government.[516] The tablets given to those commanding an hundred men are of silver, to those commanding a thousand, of gold or of silver gilt; and those who command ten thousand receive tablets of gold, bearing the head of a lion;[517] the former being of the weight of an hundred and twenty *saggi*,[518] and these with the lion's head, two hundred and twenty. At the top of the inscription on the tablet is a sentence to this effect : " By the power and might of the great God, " and through the grace which he vouchsafes to our empire, be the " name of the *Kaan* blessed; and let all such as disobey (what is " herein directed) suffer death and be utterly destroyed." The officers who hold these tablets have privileges attached to them, and in the inscription is specified what are the duties and the powers of their respective commands. He who is at the head of an hundred thousand men, or the commander in chief of a grand army, has a golden tablet weighing three hundred *saggi*, with the sentence abovementioned, and at the bottom is engraved the figure of a lion, together with representations of the sun and moon.[519] He exercises also the privileges of his high command, as set forth in this magnificent tablet. Whenever he

Figure 83. Marsden, *Marco Polo*, 278

He ... gave orders that they should be furnished with a golden tablet displaying the imperial cipher.[223]

When they took their leave he furnished them with four golden tablets, each of them a cubit in length, five inches wide, and weighing three or four marks of gold.[224]

service. He sent for them, however, and addressed them with much kindness and condescension, assuring them of his regard, and requiring from them a promise that when they should have resided some time in Europe and with their own family, they would return to him once more. With this object in view he caused them to be furnished with the golden tablet (or royal *chop*) which contained his order for their having free and safe conduct through every part of his dominions with the needful supplies for themselves and their attendants. He likewise gave them authority to act in the capacity of his ambassadors to the Pope, the Kings of France and Spain, and the other Christian princes.[59]

Figure 84. Marsden, *Marco Polo*, 29

Although the great Khan was not a Christian, he respected Christianity and was familiar with its teachings. In his Tartar religion, he believed in one most high God. The Khan had an engraving on his gold plates giving honor to the Almighty for keeping the empire safe. Their inscription began with invoking the blessing of the Almighty.[225]

At the top of the *inscription* on the tablet is a sentence to this effect: '*By the power and might of the great God, and through the grace which he vouchsafes to our empire.*'[226]

878. This laudable respect shewn by the Tartar tribes to the sanctity of the grave, has been the occasion of the Russians discovering in the burial places of these people a great number and variety of undisturbed articles, as well as large deposits of the precious metals, which former conquerors had not presumed to violate. " In these tombs " says Strahlenberg " are found all sorts of vessels, urns, " wearing-apparel, ornaments and trinkets, cimetars, daggers, horse-trappings, " knives, all sorts of little idols, medals of gold and silver, chess-boards, and " chess-men of gold; as also large golden plates on which the dead bodies have " been laid." P. 364. " The surprising quantity " says Coxe " of golden orna- " ments found in the tombs of Siberia, were they not evident to sight, would " exceed all belief."

Figure 85. Marsden, *Marco Polo*, 451

417

The Khan's gold tablet invoked the "most high" God and the khan's law. In Second Nephi, Nephi mentions engraving the laws of the "Mighty God" for his people:

And *I engraved that which is pleasing unto God.* (2 Nephi 4, p. 73 [5:32]) . . . the *Mighty God shall deliver his covenant people.* (2 Nephi 5: p. 75 [6:17])

In these quotes, the khan's order is compared to the Lord's law. The verse from First Nephi is Nephi himself writing about the plates of brass that he and his brothers took when they raided Laban:

With this object in view he caused them to be furnished with the golden tablet (or royal *chop*) which *contained his order* for their having free and safe conduct.[227]

And from First Nephi:

Yea, and I also thought that they could not keep the *commandments of the Lord* according to the law of Moses, save they should have the law. And I also knew that the *law was engraven upon the plates of brass.* . . . I knew that the Lord had delivered Laban into my hands. (1 Nephi 1: p. 12–13 [4:15–17])

Both stories of gold tablets describe the language used for the engravings. From *The Travels of Marco Polo*:

Upon which he caused letters, in the Tartarian language, to be written in his name to the Pope of Rome, and these he delivered into their hands.[228]

And from *The Book of Mormon*:

. . . we have written this record according to our knowledge, in the characters, which are called among us the reformed Egyptian, being handed down and altered by us, according to our manner of speech. (Mormon 4: p. 538 [9:32])

Some engravings on the khan's gold tablets were warnings. If anyone disobeyed the orders on the tablet, that person would "suffer death and be utterly destroyed." In "The Book of Alma," the commandments of that prophet, passed to his son, Helaman, warn that those who disobey will either "be destroyed" or will "be utterly destroyed."

The Travels of Marco Polo Bk. II, Ch. III, p. 278	The Book of Mormon Alma Ch. XVII, p. 328 [37:21, 22]
. . . and those who command ten thousand receive	And now, I will speak unto you concerning those
tablets of gold, bearing the head of a lion.	twenty-four plates, that ye keep them.
At the top of the inscription on the tablet is a sentence to this effect:	
"By the power and might of the great God,	the Lord said,
and through the grace which he vouchsafes to our empire, be the name of the *Kaan* blessed;	
and let all such as disobey [what is herein directed] suffer	If they did not repent, they
death and be	should be
utterly destroyed."	destroyed from off the face of the earth.

The Big Picture: The Real Mormon Plates

To the plagiarists, the 1818 book *The Travels of Marco Polo was* the gold plates. It was a literary treasure that, they believed, nobody would ever connect to their book. The Smiths treated parts of the pre-1830 *Marco Polo*, along with travel and geography books, as if they were sacred writings, or "records," engraved on metal plates. The many examples we've led you through so far are the details. Now you are ready for the big picture.

Below is a chart of the real plates made by Kendal Sheets. The Smiths may have drawn up such a chart as an organizing device and kept it hidden or memorized it. Either way, it provides an important overview by showing what parts of the real-life published books were used for which parts of *The Book of Mormon*.

Here's one example: the explorer Ludivico Verthema traveled through Arabia in the 1500s and wrote his own story about it. This would be the "record" of Verthema from 1503 AD. His story was also published in English by Robert Kerr in 1812 AD. This would be a "plate" of Kerr's, which contained the ancient "record" of Verthema's. The Smiths plucked details from his travelogue to compose the story of Lehi's trek across the desert wilderness in Arabia. This was part of the rewritten "gold plates of Mormon," which incorporated abridgements of ancient "records." Because of the percentage-through-the-text comparisons, we know that *The Travels of Marco Polo* served as the template for the Smiths' method of inserting stories from other books (Figures 86 and 87).

This is the *private* story of the plates—the untold story of the Smiths' forgery, which they kept locked up and hidden from the public for 180 years. Now that you know what the Smiths knew in the beginning, let's investigate the family's *public* story of the plates and what they told their gullible church flock.

The Most Amusing Recitals

The first time Joseph Smith wrote down the story of his childhood miracles was in 1832. He was assisted by a scribe, as with *The Book of Mormon* creations, but he also penned some with his own hand. These he wrote down on a few pages of a notebook that is known as the *Joseph Smith Letterbook*. He begins with a grand introduction of himself as befitted God's most important prophet.[229]

A History of the life of Joseph Smith jr. an account of his marvilous experience and all the mighty acts which he doeth in the name of Jesus Christ
the son of the living God of whom he beareth record and also an account
of the rise of the church of Christ in the eve of time according as the
Lord brought forth and established by his hand firstly he receiving the
testamony from on high seccondly the ministering of Aangels thirdly the
reception of the holy Priesthood by the ministring of Aangels to adminster
the letter of the Gospel the Law and commandments as they were given
unto him and the ordinences, fourthly a confirmation and reception of
the high Priesthood after the holy order of the son of the living God power
and ordinence from on high to preach the Gospel in the administration
and demonstration of the spirit the Kees of the Kingdom of god confered
upon him and the continuation of the blessings of God to him &c.

Smith claimed that it was between his twelfth and fifteenth year that his
mind turned to the thoughts of religion, and he figured out that the different church denominations were apostates. When he was sixteen, he saw a
"pillar of fire," but in the *Letterbook* the word *fire* was crossed out and *light*
placed there in its stead. He saw heaven, and God told Joseph his sins were
forgiven. When he was seventeen he again called on the Lord, but this time
the angel Moroni appeared. This begins the written tale of Joseph, Moroni,
and the gold plates. He wrote,

> . . . it came to pass when I was seventeen years of age that I again called
> upon the Lord and he shewed unto me a heavenly vision for behold an
> angel of the Lord came and stood before me and it was by night he called
> me by name and he said the Lord had forgiven me my sins and he revealed
> unto me that in the Town of Manchester Ontario County N.Y. there was
> plates of gold upon which there was engravings which was engraven by
> Maroni & his fathers the servants of the living God in ancient days and
> deposited by the commandments of God . . . and it was on the 22d day of
> Sept. AD 1822 and thus he appeared unto me three times in one night and
> once the next day.

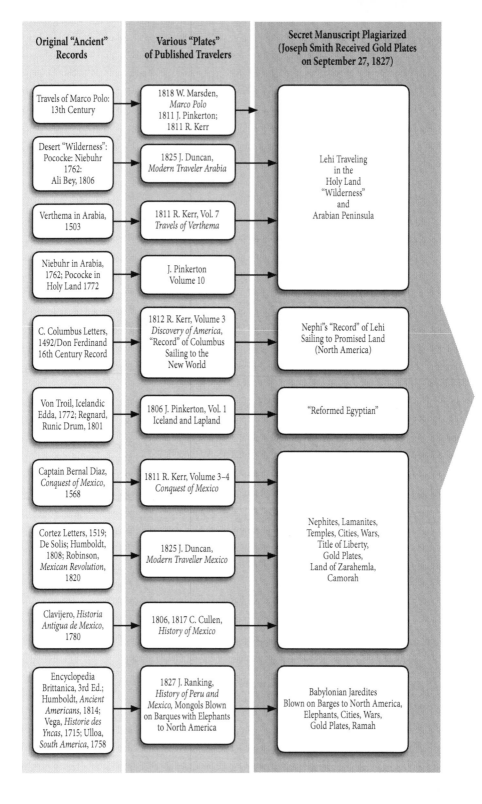

Original "Ancient" Records	Various "Plates" of Published Travelers	Secret Manuscript Plagiarized (Joseph Smith Received Gold Plates on September 27, 1827)
Travels of Marco Polo: 13th Century	1818 W. Marsden, *Marco Polo* 1811 J. Pinkerton; 1811 R. Kerr	Lehi Traveling in the Holy Land "Wilderness" and Arabian Peninsula
Desert "Wilderness": Pococke: Niebuhr 1762: Ali Bey, 1806	1825 J. Duncan, *Modern Traveler Arabia*	
Verthema in Arabia, 1503	1811 R. Kerr, Vol. 7 *Travels of Verthema*	
Niebuhr in Arabia, 1762; Pococke in Holy Land 1772	J. Pinkerton Volume 10	
C. Columbus Letters, 1492/Don Ferdinand 16th Century Record	1812 R. Kerr, Volume 3 *Discovery of America*, "Record" of Columbus Sailing to the New World	Nephi"s "Record" of Lehi Sailing to Promised Land (North America)
Von Troil, Icelandic Edda, 1772; Regnard, Runic Drum, 1801	1806 J. Pinkerton, Vol. 1 Iceland and Lapland	"Reformed Egyptian"
Captain Bernal Diaz, *Conquest of Mexico*, 1568	1811 R. Kerr, Volume 3–4 *Conquest of Mexico*	Nephites, Lamanites, Temples, Cities, Wars, Title of Liberty, Gold Plates, Land of Zarahemla, Camorah
Cortez Letters, 1519; De Solis; Humboldt, 1808; Robinson, *Mexican Revolution*, 1820	1825 J. Duncan, *Modern Traveller Mexico*	
Clavijero, *Historia Antigua de Mexico*, 1780	1806, 1817 C. Cullen, *History of Mexico*	
Encyclopedia Brittanica, 3rd Ed.; Humboldt, *Ancient Americans*, 1814; Vega, *Historie des Yncas*, 1715; Ulloa, *South America*, 1758	1827 J. Ranking, *History of Peru and Mexico*, Mongols Blown on Barques with Elephants to North America	Babylonian Jaredites Blown on Barges to North America, Elephants, Cities, Wars, Gold Plates, Ramah

Jospeh Smith Dictated Secret Manuscript from behind a Curtain to Martin Harris (July, 1828) or Out of a Hat to Oliver Cowdery (April, 1829)

The First Book of Nephi, His Reign and Ministry

The Second Book of Nephi

The Book of Jacob, the Brother of Nephi

The Book of Enos

The Book of Jarom

The Book of Omni

The Words of Mormon

The Book of Mosiah

The Book of Alma, the Son of Alma

The Book of Helaman

The Book of Nephi, the Son of Nephi, which was the Son of Helaman

The Book of Nephi, Which is the Son of Nephi, One of the Disciples of Christ

Book of Mormon

Book of Ether

Book of Moroni

Printed Copy of
The Book of Mormon
(1830)

THE

BOOK OF MORMON:

AN ACCOUNT WRITTEN BY THE HAND OF MOR-
MON, UPON PLATES TAKEN FROM
THE PLATES OF NEPHI.

Wherefore it is an abridgment of the Record of the People of Nephi; and also of the Lamanites; written to the Lamanites, which are a remnant of the House of Israel; and also to Jew and Gentile; written by way of commandment, and also by the spirit of Prophecy and of Revelation. Written, and sealed up, and hid up unto the Lord, that they might not be destroyed; to come forth by the gift and power of God unto the interpretation thereof; sealed by the hand of Moroni, and hid up unto the Lord, to come forth in due time by the way of Gentile; the interpretation thereof by the gift of God; an abridgment taken from the Book of Ether.

Also, which is a Record of the People of Jared, which were scattered at the time the Lord confounded the language of the people when they were building a tower to get to Heaven: which is to shew unto the remnant of the House of Israel how great things the Lord hath done for their fathers; and that they may know the covenants of the Lord, that they are not cast off forever; and also to the convincing of the Jew and Gentile that Jesus is the Christ, the ETERNAL God, manifesting Himself unto all nations. And now if there be fault, it be the mistake of men; wherefore condemn not the things of God, that ye may be found spotless at the judgment seat of Christ.

BY JOSEPH SMITH, JUNIOR,
AUTHOR AND PROPRIETOR.

PALMYRA:
PRINTED BY E. B. GRANDIN, FOR THE AUTHOR.
1830.

Figures 86 & 87.

The angel directed Joseph to find the final set of metal plates engraved and buried by the Nephites: the gold plates of Mormon. After the vision, Joseph did as commanded.

> . . . and then I immediately went to the place and found where the plates was deposited as the angel of the Lord had commanded me and straightway made three attempts to get them and then being excedingly frightened I supposed it had been a dreem of Vision but when I considered I knew that it was not therefore I cried unto the Lord in the agony of my soul why can I not obtain them behold the angel appeared unto me again and said unto me you have not kept the commandments of the Lord which I gave unto you.

Another record-keeping work began in 1838. It was called *History of the Church*, and in it the "prophet" recalled events that transpired in 1827 on the Camorah hillside. He retells the story of his 1832 visions but with richer detail and a better-developed storyline. This time the angel that spoke to him was "Moroni," who also led the young boy to the hillside. Joseph pried open a stone box in the ground that held the treasures.

> I made an attempt to take them out, but was forbidden by the messenger, and was again informed that the time for bringing them forth had not yet arrived, neither would it, until four years from that time; but he told me that I should come to that place precisely in one year from that time, and that he would there meet with me, and that I should continue to do so until the time should come for obtaining the plates.[230]

Although Joseph did not mention the reasons for the delay in getting the plates, his mother seemed to know why. Junior had other purposes in mind; he was tempted to profit financially from digging up the gold plates. In her 1853 book, on pages eighty-four to eighty-six, Mother Smith wrote:

> On the twenty-second of September, 1824, Joseph again visited the place where he found the plates the year previous; and supposing at this time

that the only thing required, in order to possess them until the time for their translation, was to be able to keep the commandments of God—and he firmly believed he could keep every commandment which had been given him—he fully expected to carry them home with him. Therefore, having arrived at the place, and uncovering the plates, he put forth his hand and took them up, but, as he was taking them hence, *the unhappy thought darted through his mind that probably there was something else in the box besides the plates, which would be of some pecuniary advantage to him.*

So, in the moment of excitement, he laid them down very carefully, for the purpose of covering the box, lest some one might happen to pass that way and get whatever there might be remaining in it. After covering it, he turned round to take the Record again, but behold, it was gone, and where he knew not, neither did he know the means by which it had been taken from him; upon which the angel of the Lord appeared to him, and told him that he had not done as he had been commanded, for in a former revelation he had been commanded not to lay the plates down, or put them for a moment out of his hands, until he got into the house and deposited them in a chest or trunk, having a good lock and key, and, contrary to this, he had laid them down *with the view of securing some fancied or imaginary treasure that remained.*

In the moment of excitement, Joseph was overcome by the powers of darkness, and forgot the injunction that was laid upon him.

Having further conversation with the angel on this occasion, Joseph was permitted to raise the stone again, when he beheld the plates as he had done before. He immediately reached forth his hand to take them, but instead of getting them, as he anticipated, *he was hurled back upon the ground with great violence.* When he recovered, the angel was gone, and he arose and returned to the house, weeping for grief and disappointment.

Nevertheless, in September 1827, when he was twenty-one years old, he was finally allowed to lift the plates and other priceless artifacts from Moroni's box and take them home.

According to Smith:

At length the time arrived for obtaining the plates, the Urim and Thummim, and the breastplate. On the twenty-second day of September, one thousand eight hundred and twenty-seven, having gone as usual at the end of another year to the place where they were deposited, the same heavenly messenger delivered them up to me with this charge: that I should be responsible for them; that if I should let them go carelessly, or through any neglect of mine, I should be cut off; but that if I would use all my endeavors to preserve them, until he, the messenger, should call for them, they should be protected.[231]

Let's discuss the night when Joseph Smith purportedly brought the plates home from the hill Camorah. He wrote:

I soon found out the reason why I had received such strict charges to keep them safe and why it was that the messenger had said that when I had done what was required at my hand, he would call for them, for no sooner was it known that I had them than the most strenuous exertions were used to get them from me. Every stratagem that could be invented was resorted to for that purpose.[232]

In her book, Lucy wrote a strange account of Joseph's being attacked on his way home with the plates. He wrapped the plates in his shirt and hid them in a birchtree log a few miles from home. Nobody knows what happened to the magic spectacles, Urim and Thummim, and the breastplate that night, but according to Lucy's book, they show up later.

The plates were secreted about three miles from home, in the following manner: Finding an old birch log much decayed, excepting the bark, which was in a measure sound, he took his pocket knife and cut the bark with some care, then turned it back, and made a hole of sufficient size to receive the plates, and laying them in the cavity thus formed, he replaced the bark; after which he laid across the log, in several places, some old stuff that happened to lay near, in order to conceal, as much as possible, the place in which they were deposited.

Joseph, on coming to them, took them from their secret place, and wrapping them in his linen frock, placed them under his arm and started for home.[233]

Does that story make any sense? Who would hide the key to humankind's redemption inside a decayed log under "some old stuff"? And who would place it miles from home, with no easy access for checking on it or watching for thieves? This seems foolhardy.

Marco Polo didn't write about hiding things in tree logs. Our search for the meaning of all these peculiar acts led us to John Pinkerton's *General Collection of the Best and Most Interesting Voyages and Travels*, Volume the First, which was published in London in 1808.[234] It was also published in Philadelphia in 1810.[235] In this volume, the learned editor concentrated on travels to the northern regions from Iceland to Russia (Figure 88).

About one-third of the way into the volume is a discussion about hieroglyphic characters as well as stories of birch trees and things put into hollowed-out birch logs. We will get to the hieroglyphics in the next chapter. For now let's see if we can figure out what happened with this book in the Smith household.

Beginning on page 131 is the chapter titled "A Journey Through Flanders, Holland, &c. by M. Regnard," which Pinkerton then titled "Regnard's Journey to Lapland, &c." On page 184, the traveler visited an altar of the pagan Laplanders:

We approached this altar, and perceived rather a large heap of rein-deer's horns, [and] the gods. . . . The first was the thickest and the largest . . . it was not at all shaped in the human form and I cannot well say what it resembled; but this I can say, that it was very greasy and very dirty, in consequence of the blood and fat with which it was covered. This one was called Seyta. . . . All these stones, and particularly that which represented Seyta, were *placed upon branches of the birch-tree* which had been lately cut; and there was to be seen on one side of a mast of carved pieces of wood, upon which *some characters were engraved.*[236]

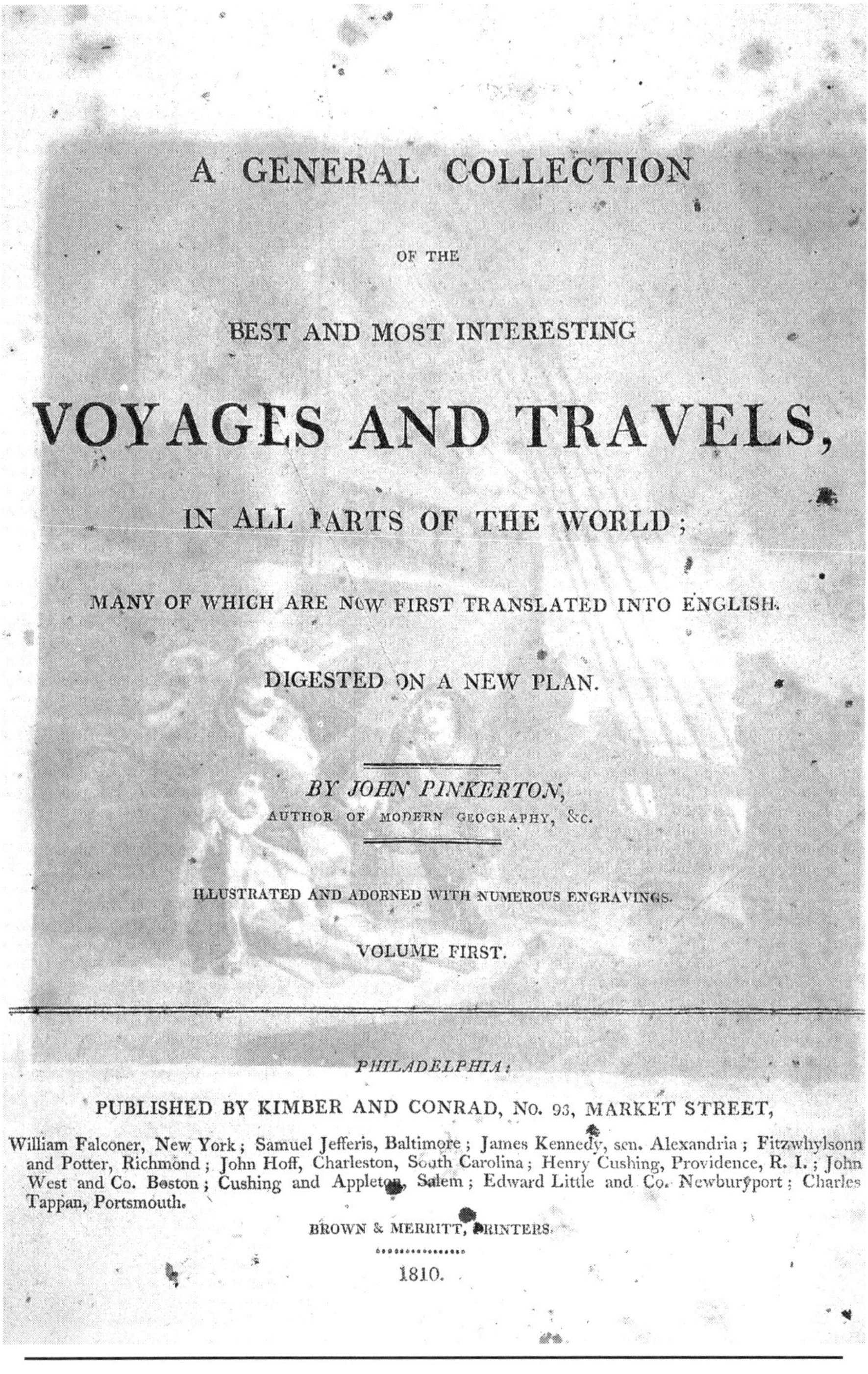

A GENERAL COLLECTION

OF THE

BEST AND MOST INTERESTING

VOYAGES AND TRAVELS,

IN ALL PARTS OF THE WORLD;

MANY OF WHICH ARE NOW FIRST TRANSLATED INTO ENGLISH.

DIGESTED ON A NEW PLAN.

BY JOHN PINKERTON,
AUTHOR OF MODERN GEOGRAPHY, &c.

ILLUSTRATED AND ADORNED WITH NUMEROUS ENGRAVINGS.

VOLUME FIRST.

PHILADELPHIA:

PUBLISHED BY KIMBER AND CONRAD, No. 93, MARKET STREET,

William Falconer, New York; Samuel Jefferis, Baltimore; James Kennedy, sen. Alexandria; Fitzwhylsonn and Potter, Richmond; John Hoff, Charleston, South Carolina; Henry Cushing, Providence, R. I.; John West and Co. Boston; Cushing and Appleton, Salem; Edward Little and Co. Newburyport; Charles Tappan, Portsmouth.

BROWN & MERRITT, PRINTERS.

1810.

Figure 88. Pinkerton, *Voyages and Travels*, Vol. 1, Philadelphia, Title Page

On page 190, where Regnard writes about preserving meat, he says, "Their salting tub consists of the trunk of a *tree hollowed out by the hands of nature, which they cover in the best manner they are able, to prevent the bears from stealing it.*" And on page 192, Regnard observed a Laplander house with mother and child in it:

> The cradle was at the end of the hut, hanging in the air; it was made out of a *hollow tree,* and full of fine moss, which supplied the place of *linen,* mattrass (sic), and coverlid."

In her book, Lucy wrote about the gold plates, hieroglyphics, a linen wrapping, a wooden chest, a hollowed-out birch tree log, tree bark, cutting wood, and covering material. Let's compare Lucy's and Mr. Regnard's content:

Pinkerton, Vol. I, "Regnard's Journey to Lapland" (1808)	Lucy Smith, *History of the Prophet Joseph Smith Jr.,* p. 104 (1853)
All these stones, and particularly that which represented Seyta, were placed upon branches of the **birch-tree** which had been lately cut (p. 184)	Finding an old **birch log** much decayed, excepting the bark, which was in a measure sound,
	he took his pocket knife and **cut the bark** with some care, then
tree hollowed out by the hands of nature (p. 190)	turned it back, and **made a hole of sufficient size** to receive the plates
which they cover in the best manner they are able,	. . . laying them in the cavity thus formed, he **replaced the bark** . . . after which he laid across the log, in several places, some old stuff that happened to lay near, in order to conceal, as much as possible, the place in which they were deposited.
	We supposed that Joseph has taken the plates, and hid them somewhere, and we were **apprehensive that our enemies might discover their place of**

Pinkerton, Vol. I, "Regnard's Journey to Lapland" (1808)	Lucy Smith, *History of the Prophet Joseph Smith Jr.,* p. 104 (1853)
to prevent the bears from stealing it. (p. 190)	deposit.
it was made out of a hollow tree, and full of fine moss, which	
supplied the place of linen,	wrapping them in his
mattrass [sic], and coverlid. (p. 192)	linen frock

Another chapter in Pinkerton's first volume is "Account of Danish Lapland by Leems." It, too, contains keywords that are similar to those in Lucy's story. Leems wrote about a magic drum of the Laplanders called a *kannus* or *tabor* drum. Leems said that the drums were of wood and resembled a box. Let's compare his material to Lucy's:

"Account of Danish Lapland by Leems"	Lucy Smith, *Biographical Sketches,* p. 102
Runic drums . . . resembled a kind of large box.	When he came, Joseph requested him to get a chest. And after giving
That as the common boxes are made to open and shut. (p. 474, line 11–18)	these instructions, Joseph started for the plates. (line 23)
The wizard kept his Runic drum, as a secret, not to be revealed. (line 46)	The plates were secreted about three miles from home, in the following manner . . .
at a distance from cottages in the woods. (p. 474, lines 27–28)	Finding an old birch log (lines 28–30)
(p. 474, line 21) on the bark of the alder-tree.	much decayed, excepting the bark . . . he took his pocket knife and cut the bark with some care.
(p. 457, lines 15–18) It was a custom too in the time past, to lay on the body, the outward bark of	
the birch tree, which the Norwegians call, *Naever,* and use in place of laths,	he replaced the bark; then turned it back, and made a hole of sufficient size to receive the plates, and laying them

"Account of Danish Lapland by Leems"	Lucy Smith, *Biographical Sketches,* p. 102
	in the cavity thus formed, he replaced the bark; after which
covered with heaps of stones gathered and raised up for this purpose.	he laid across the log, in several places, some stuff that happened to lay near,
	in order to conceal, as much as possible, the place in which they were deposited.
p. 474, lines 46–48	line 39
The wizard kept his Runic drum as a secret not to be revealed, covered and	Joseph, on coming to them took them from their secret place, and,
rolled up in fillets or bandages	wrapping them in his linen frock, placed them under his arm and started for home.
lest it should be exposed to the eyes of every one.	line 37, in order to conceal as much as possible.
p. 457, lines 21, In funerals of the rustic Laplanders . . . that	[See above:
the end of the sepulchral linen, while the procession is moving, for greater solemnity and ornament, projects a little from the bier.	wrapping them in his linen frock, placed them under his arm and started for home.]

Keeping the drums wrapped and secretly stashed away from the home was a common practice of the wizards, and keeping the plates wrapped and secreted in a birch tree away from home was Joseph's method of hiding them.

Flipping through the pages of Regnard's record, we found more material about hollow logs on page 180.

This instrument, with which they perform all their charms, and which they call *Kannus,* is made of the trunk of a pine and a *birch-tree,* and the veins of which ought to proceed from east to west. This *kannus* is made of a single *piece of wood, hollowed* in its thickest part in an oval

form, the under part of which is convex, in which they make two aper-
tures long enough to suffer the fingers to pass through, for the purpose of
holding it more firmly. The upper part is covered with the skin of a rein-
deer, on which they paint in red, a number of figures, and from whence
several brass rings are seen hanging, and some pieces of the bone of the
rein-deer.

So the runic drum *itself* is a hollowed-out section of birch tree! To recap,
Joseph hid the gold plates with hieroglyphics in a birch log; Laplanders
used birch logs to store things in and write hieroglyphics on for pagan ceremonies; and a runic drum was made of a birch tree with painted figures
on it. This drum was something important to Lucy Smith. We assumed it
had something to do with the gold plates, but what?

In the next chapter we will investigate the authenticity of the Nephite
writing system of "reformed Egyptian" hieroglyphics. You will have the rare
opportunity to study an actual sample of the hieroglyphics copied by the
hand of Joseph Smith Jr. from the gold plates. Think about this: if Junior's
hand-copy was a forgery, then it would prove that Joseph *himself* had par-
ticipated in the family conspiracy. And if *that* was true, then the young
boy who became the Latter-day Prophet himself would be exposed as an
imposter.

19

STRANGE CARACTORS

When Marco Polo, his father, and his uncle Maffio returned to Venice from their epic adventure, their relatives barred them from their own home. The Polos were unrecognizable. Even their language had changed to include the Tartars' accents.

Nobody believed their accounts of their travels, so they decided to show proof. They organized a gathering of all their relatives. After eating, Marco retrieved their tattered, threadbare Tartar clothes. The three proceeded to cut open these garments to reveal a large quantity of costly jewels, such as rubies, sapphires, garnet cabochons, diamonds, and emeralds that had been sewn into them. The Polos had converted all their gold from Kublai Khan into gemstones for ease of travel and concealment during their long voyage to Italy. The spectacle of extreme wealth convinced the disbelievers of their journey.

The Smiths would have read this story. They well knew that most people would not believe their fantastical stories of angels, ancient Jews in America, and golden plates. Like the Polos, they needed proof. But the Smiths were desperately poor. They couldn't even pay their own debts. Buying enough gold to make the plates was out of the question.

The Smiths hatched a plan that proved hugely successful. The Latter-day prophet pretended to copy hieroglyphics from gold plates onto a piece of paper. With this, he planned to hoodwink a prospective backer into believing that the symbols were the Nephites' "reformed Egyptian."

Here is how Lucy Mack Smith explained away her son's scheme:

> Joseph began to make arrangements to accomplish the translation of the Record. The first step that he was instructed to take in regard to this work, was to make a fac-simile of some of the characters, which were called reformed Egyptian, and to send them to some of the most learned men of this generation, and ask them for the translation thereof.[238]

Why would God and his angel Moroni appear on Earth and choose the young boy as their latter-day prophet but force him to depend on others for the all-important task of translation? Joseph himself was supposed to translate the hieroglyphics using the power of God, wasn't he?

The "instruction" (request) for making the facsimile came from Martin Harris. Harris, Joseph's first scribe, considered selling his farm to fund the printing of *The Book of Mormon*. According to Joseph, he was "a farmer of respectability. . . ."[239] Harris wanted to confirm that the unseen gold plates—and Joseph's claims—were authentic before he handed over proceeds from the property sale.

The problem facing Smith was that there *were* no gold plates, so he couldn't give them to Harris to verify their existence. He badly needed the farmer's money. So what could he do but copy symbols from his reference books and hope for the best? Nothing.

Where would he go for the reformed-Egyptian characters? The Mexican Indians had hieroglyphics such as in this illustration of Aztec numbers (Figure 89).

Perhaps using known Mexican characters would have been too obvious. Instead, the Smiths went to John Pinkerton's *General Collection of the Best and Most Interesting Voyages and Travels, Volume the First* which was published in London and Philadelphia in 1808. In that volume, the editor concentrated on travels in the northern regions from Iceland to Russia. In the

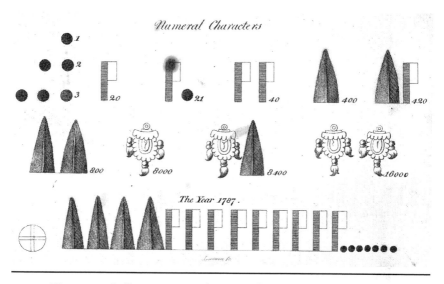

Figure 89. Cullen, *History of Mexico,* "Numerical Characters"

previous chapter about the gold plates we learned that in Lapland, wizards used a drum made from a hollow birch tree to practice magic, and the skin stretched across the drum was emblazoned with runic symbols. Included in Pinkerton's volume is a section written by Professor Knud Leems:

> Runic drums are found covered with a very extended skin, after the manner of common drums. On the outside of the parchment are *painted various characters.*[240]

After page 180, Editor Pinkerton included an engraved plate of a Laplander and his magic drum (Figure 90).

What do the drum's symbols mean? From the Pinkerton book:

> In the first place [the Laplanders] mix Jesus Christ indifferently with their false gods, and they make only one being of God and the devil, whom they believe they may worship in the manner most agreeably to their taste. This mixture is particularly to be remarked on their tabors, where they place Storiunchar and his family above Jesus Christ and his

Figure 90. Pinkerton, *Voyages and Travels*, Vol. 1, "Magical Drum"

apostles. They have three principal gods; the first is called Thor, or the god of thunder; the second Storiunchar; and the third *Parjutte*, which means the fun. These three gods are worshipped only by the Laplanders of Lula and Pitha; for those of Kimiet and of Torno . . . know of one only, whom they call *Seyta*. . . . (Pinkerton Vol. 1, p. 179)

Professor Leems also reported on the magic tabor drums:

> ... various characters, on the bark of the alder-tree, of which some are to signify the deity; some Radien, or chief god, Jupiter, of the Pagan Laplanders; some the angels; some evil spirits; some *Noaadie-Gadze*, or the associates of the magician; some the sun; some Phosphorus, and the evening star, some temples; some the habitations of the Norwegian people, some *Passe-Varek*, or sacred mountains, where sacrifices were offered ... some small sheds, propped on pillars ... some birds, some fishes; and others to represent bears and foxes, with some difference. Some of the characters are of happy omen, others unlucky and inauspicious: to the one the evil spirits and wolf are usually applied; to the other god and the angels, *Noaadie-Gadze*, the bear, fox, &c.[241]

One drum seen personally by Leems included symbols for the Laplander god Diermes, which name signifies thunder, the reindeer called Godde; the sun; image of Son of God, the Father; the Holy Spirit; Mary, mother of God; a church temple; a little man signifying the devil killing men as Disease; the devil freely ranging about; Helva-dola, meaning hellfire; a circular figure, Helvet Tarve-Geume, which is the cauldron of Hell; Helvet-Haude, the sepulchre of hell; and a bound devil.[242]

Additional material, written by Mr. M. Regnard, states:

> They usually paint the following figures ... the gods whom they hold in the greatest veneration, as Thor, with his underlings, and Seyta. . . . Jesus Christ, with two or three apostles are to be seen.[243]

This leads us back to the story of Joseph Smith and the "reformed Egyptian" writing. You will see that the "caractors" he copied for Martin Harris—and any other person with the blind faith to believe him—look suspiciously like the Laplanders' pagan symbols on the tabor drum. Joseph Smith's *Caractors* document from 1828 is followed closely below by a cutout of the runic drum (Figures 91 and 92).

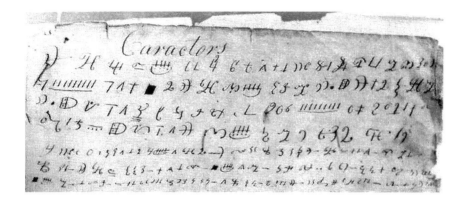

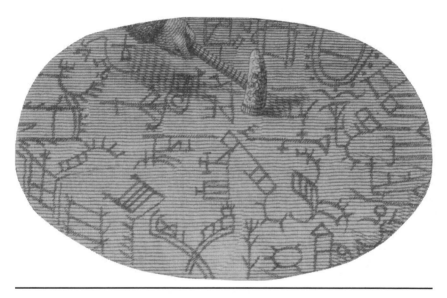

Figures 91 & 92. Joseph Smith, "Caractors," and Pinkerton, *Voyages and Travels,* Vol. 1, "Magical Drum"

Copied below is an advertising poster called "Stick of Joseph," which the Mormon Church distributed in 1844. The characters on the broadside were purported to be those copied by Smith from *The Book of Mormon's* gold plates[244] (Figure 93).

Comparing the markings on the tabor drum to Smith's document is somewhat tedious, so we made it easier by numbering some of the symbols on the drum that correspond to the reformed Egyptian symbols in the table below (Figure 94).

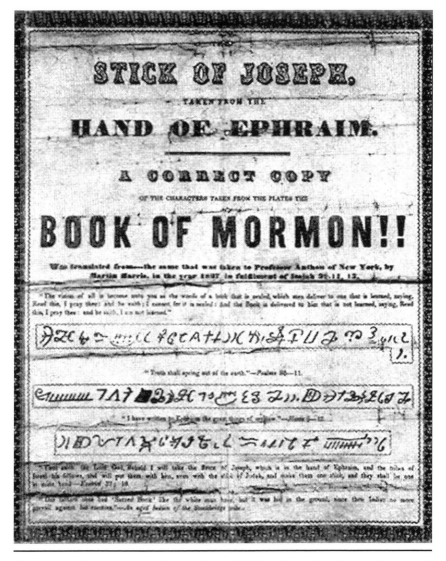

Figure 93. Advertisement, "Stick of Joseph Taken from the Hand of Ephraim"

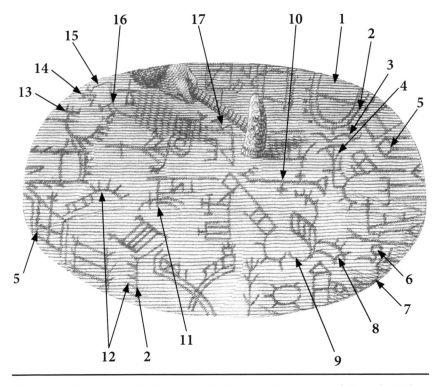

Figure 94. Numerical Callouts on Pinkerton, *Voyages and Travels*, Vol. 1, "Magical Drum"

Sami Shaman Rune Drum (Lapland *Kannus* Drum)	"Caractors"	"Stick of Joseph"
1.	Caractors Rows 2, 3, 4	Stick of Joseph
2.	Caractors Rows 1, 4–6	Stick of Joseph

Sami Shaman Rune Drum (Lapland *Kannus* Drum)	"Caractors"	"Stick of Joseph"
3.	Caractors Rows 2, 3, 4	Stick of Joseph
4.	Caractors Rows: 5, 6*	
5. p. 476[1] A square signifies *Helvet-Haude*, that is, the sepulcher of hell, into which all believing in Satan are said to be thrown.	Caractors Rows 2 6, 7	Stick of Joseph
6. A circle, *Helvet Tarve-Geune*, is said to signify the pitchy cauldron of hell, in which it is thought souls are said to be thrown. (Pinkerton Vol. I, p. 476)	Caractors Rows 1, 3, 4, 5	
7.	Caractors Rows 4, 7	

Sami Shaman Rune Drum (Lapland *Kannus* Drum)	"Caractors"	"Stick of Joseph"
8.	Caractors Rows 1, 2, 4, 7	Stick of Joseph
9.	Caractors Rows 2, 3, 7	Stick of Joseph
10.	Caractors Rows 1, 2, 4, 7	Stick of Joseph
11.	Caractors Rows 3, 5	
12. (p. 476) This figure on the skin of the Runic drum has been interpreted, *Helvet-dola*, that is, hell fire.	Caractors Rows 2, 3	Stick of Joseph
13.	Caractors Rows 1, 6, 7	Stick of Joseph

Sami Shaman Rune Drum (Lapland *Kannus* Drum)	"Caractors"	"Stick of Joseph"
14.	Caractors Rows 1, 3, 6	Stick of Joseph
15.	Caractors Rows 4, 7	
16.	Caractors Rows 1, 2, 3, 4, 5	Stick of Joseph
17.	Caractors Row 1	

*This symbol was the first recognized by Kendal Sheets as being copied from the tabor drum.

Joseph also used some Arabic-looking characters for his writing, such as these (Figure 95).

Figure 95. Joseph Smith, Individual "Caractors"

Such lettering can be found in many books of the time, but let's go back to one of the Smiths' favorites—Marsden's *Marco Polo*. Here are a few examples (Figures 96, 97, and 98).

Martin Harris was satisfied with Smith's reformed-Egyptian hieroglyphics on a piece of paper as a substitute for the prophet's producing the actual plates for inspection. The farmer took the "fac-simile" to New York City and presented it for evaluation to Professor Charles Anthon at Columbia College (later known as Columbia University). Anthon was not Harris's first choice. The initial expert to whom Harris presented his request seems to have been stymied by what he saw and sent the farmer to Anthon.

There are two conflicting accounts of what happened next. Joseph Smith, writing his *History* for the church's *Times and Seasons* newspaper, reported Martin Harris's version.[245] It seems suspicious to us that the newspaper didn't just interview Harris himself. We pick up his account mid-story, where Joseph tells about the time when he and Emma had to leave Manchester and move to Pennsylvania. They had just met Harris, who donated fifty dollars to help Smith with his expenses in translating the plates:

Many conjectures have been offered with regard to its origin, amongst which the most plausible is that of Mr. Langlès, who considers it as the word شرقين *sharekīn*, signifying "eastern people," i. e. " eastern Arabs," from شرق *shark*, the " east," or " rising sun," in contradiction to غربين *gherbīn* or مغربين *mughrebīn* " western " people," from غرب *gharb* the " west," or " setting sun."

Figure 96. Marsden, *Marco Polo*, 44

as from other authorities, that *Sis* سيس was the capital of the Lesser Armenia

Figure 97. Marsden, *Marco Polo*, 43

" tempore Justini (Justiniani يوستينيانوس in the Arabic text) Romanorum impera-

Figure 98. Marsden, *Marco Polo*, 147

Mr. Harris was a resident of Palmyra Township Wayne county, in the State of New York and a farmer of respectability; by this timely aid (fifty dollars) was I enabled to reach the place of my destination in Pennsylvania, and immediately after my arrival there I commenced copying the characters of the plates. I copied a considerable number of them, and by means of the Urim and Thummim I translated some of them, which I did between the time I arrived at the house of my wife's father in the month of December, and the February following. Some time in this month of February the aforementioned, Mr. Martin Harris came to our place, got the characters which I had drawn off the plates and started with them to the city of New York. For what took place relative to him and the characters, I refer to his own account of the circumstances as he related them to me after his return which was as follows.

I went to the city of New York and presented the characters which had been translated, with the translation thereof to Professor Anthony [sic], a gentleman celebrated for his literati attainments;—Professor Anthony stated that the translation was correct, more so than any he had before seen translated from the Egyptian. I then showed him those which were not yet translated, and he said that they were Egyptian, Chaldeac, Assyriac, and Arabac [Arabic], and he said that they were true characters. He gave me a certificate certifying to the people of Palmyra that they were true characters, and that the translation of such of them as had been translated was also correct. I took the certificate and put it into my pocket, and was just leaving the house, when Mr. Anthony called me back, and asked me how the young man found out that there were gold plates in the place where he found them. I answered that an angel of God had revealed it unto him.

He then said to me, let me see that certificate, I accordingly took it out of my pocket and gave it to him, when he took it and tore it to pieces, saying that there was no such thing now as ministering angels, and that if I would bring the plates to him, he would translate them. I informed him that a part of the plates were sealed, and that I was forbidden to bring them, he replied, 'I cannot read a sealed book.' I left him and went to Dr.

Mitchel who sanctioned what Professor Anthony has said respecting both the characters and the translation."

Thus, according to Smith's version of Harris's encounter with the professor, Smith's translation was correct, but Anthon responded by tearing up his written certification of translation of the reformed Egyptian.[246]

The professor, however, had a very different recollection of the event. In a letter to Mr. E. D. Howe, the leading Mormon antagonist of the day, Mr. Anthon wrote:

New York, Feb. 17, 1834.

Dear Sir—I received this morning your favor of the 9th instant, and lose no time in making a reply. The whole story about my having pronounced the Mormonite inscription to be "reformed Egyptian hieroglyphics" is perfectly false. Some years ago, a plain, and apparently simple-hearted farmer, called upon me with a note from Dr. Mitchell of our city, now deceased, requesting me to decypher, if possible, a paper, which the farmer would hand me, and which Dr. M. confessed he had been unable to understand.

Upon examining the paper in question, I soon came to the conclusion that it was all a trick, perhaps a hoax. When I asked the person, who brought it, how he obtained the writing, he gave me, as far as I can now recollect, the following account: A "gold book," consisting of a number of plates of gold, fastened together in the shape of a book by wires of the same metal, had been dug up in the northern part of the state of New York, and along with the book an enormous pair of "gold spectacles"! These spectacles were so large, that, if a person attempted to look through them, his two eyes would have to be turned towards one of the glasses merely, the spectacles in question being altogether too large for the breadth of the human face. Whoever examined the plates through the spectacles, was enabled not only to read them, but fully to understand their meaning. All this knowledge, however, was confined at that time to a young man, who had the trunk containing the book and spectacles in his sole possession. This young man was placed behind a curtain, in the garret of a farm house, and being thus concealed from view, put on the spectacles occasionally, or rather, looked through one of the glasses, decyphered [sic] the characters in the book, and, having committed some of them to paper, handed copies from behind the curtain, to those who stood on the outside. Not a word, however, was said about the plates having been decyphered "by the gift of God." Everything, in this way, was effected by the large pair of spectacles. The farmer added, that he had been requested to contribute a sum of money towards the publication of the "golden book," the contents of which would, as he had been assured, produce an entire change in the world and save it from ruin.

So urgent had been these solicitations, that he intended selling his farm and handing over the amount received to those who wished to publish the plates. As a last precautionary step, however, he had resolved to come to New York, and obtain the opinion of the learned about the meaning of the paper which he brought with him, and which had been given him as a part of the contents of the book, although no translation had been furnished at the time by the young man with the spectacles.

On hearing this odd story, I changed my opinion about the paper, and, instead of viewing it any longer as a hoax upon the learned, I began to regard it as part of a scheme to cheat the farmer of his money, and I communicated my suspicions to him, warning him to beware of rogues.

He requested an opinion from me in writing, which of course I declined giving, and he then took his leave carrying the paper with him. This paper was in fact a singular scrawl. It consisted of all kinds of crooked characters disposed in columns, and had evidently been prepared by some person who had before him at the time a book containing various alphabets. Greek and Hebrew letters, crosses and flourishes, Roman letters inverted or placed sideways, were arranged in perpendicular columns, and the whole ended in a rude delineation of a circle divided into various compartments, decked with various strange marks, and evidently copied after the Mexican Calendar given by Humboldt, but copied in such a way as not to betray the source whence it was derived.

I am thus particular as to the contents of the paper, inasmuch as I have frequently conversed with my friends of the subject, since the Mormonite excitement began, and well remember that the paper contained any thing else but 'Egyptian Hieroglyphics.'

Some time after, the same farmer paid me a second visit. He brought with him the golden book in print, and offered it to me for sale. I declined purchasing. He then asked permission to leave the book with me for examination. I declined receiving it, although his manner was strangely urgent. I adverted once more to the roguery which had been in my opinion practised upon him, and asked him what had become of the gold plates. He informed me that they were in a trunk with the large pair of spectacles. I advised him to go to a magistrate and have the trunk examined. He said the 'curse of God' would come upon him should he do this. On my pressing him, however, to pursue the course which I had recommended, he told me that he would open the trunk, if I would take the "curse of God" upon myself. I replied that I would do so with the greatest willingness, and would incur every risk of that nature, provided I could only extricate him from the grasp of rogues. He then left me.

I have thus given you a full statement of all that I know respecting the origin of Mormonism, and must beg you, as a personal favor, to publish this letter immediately, should you find my name mentioned again by these wretched fanatics.

Yours respectfully, CHAS. ANTHON.[247]

Who was telling the truth, Anthon or Harris? If the characters Smith copied were a mishmash of symbols derived from various sources, some turned on their side to be unrecognizable, then Professor Anthon's learned suspicions were correct: it was a rogue's scheme to cheat the farmer out of his money. If the characters were a derivation of Egyptian by tribes of Jews in ancient America, then Joseph Smith was right, and the professor was the fool.

Did Joseph Smith use the Mexican or Mayan calendar in his facsimile? We'll never know for sure. The original paper, known as the "Anthon Transcript" disappeared, and no copy had been made.

Jews Writing in Reformed Egyptian

Lucy Smith reminded us that the name of the Nephites' writing is called "reformed Egyptian." This unique language has never been confirmed by any Egyptian-hieroglyphics scholar. It has never been proven to exist by any Mormon. Nor will it ever be.

The Nephites were supposedly ancient Jews. Why did they not engrave the golden plates in their own Hebrew language? In his eponymous chapter, the prophet Mormon says:

> And now behold, we have written this record according to our knowledge in the characters, which are called among us the reformed Egyptian, being handed down and altered by us, according to our manner of speech. And if our plates had been sufficiently large, we should have written in the Hebrew; but the Hebrew hath been altered by us also; and if we could have written in the Hebrew, behold, ye would have had none [sic] imperfection in the record. (Mormon 4: p. 538 [9:32–33])

But why did the Nephite writing bear the name *Egyptian*? Why might Smith have chosen hieroglyphics rather than Hebrew? The ancient Americans wrote in hieroglyphics but did not have an alphabet. This fact was included in the 1825 book *Modern Traveller . . . Mexico and Guatimala* by the author and editor James Duncan, who wrote (Figure 99).

> The Toltecs first appeared in the year 648. . . . they were acquainted with the art of hieroglyphic writing. . . .[248] None of these nations were acquainted with alphabetic characters; and this circumstance will serve to account for the astonishing variety of the American dialects.[249]

> On the north-west coast . . . the natives display a decided taste for hieroglyphic paintings. The Iroquois and the Hurons also, made hieroglyphic paintings on wood, strikingly resembling those of the Mexicans.

We have already discussed Clavigero's and others' theories about how the ancient Americans either came from Egypt or had cultural connections.

undated the country of Anahuac. The Toltecs first appeared in the year 648; the Chichimecs in 1170; the Nahuatlacs in 1178; the Acolhuans and Aztecs in 1196. The Toltecs introduced the cultivation of maize and cotton; they built cities, made roads, and constructed those great pyramids which are among the most interesting remains in this country. They were acquainted with the art of hieroglyphic writing, could found metals, and their tools were sufficiently tempered to cut the hardest stones. They had a solar year more perfect than that of the Greeks and Romans.* Humboldt supposes that the Toltecs, or Aztecs, (both of these tribes being of the same family,) might be a part of those Hiong-nues who, according to the Chinese historians, emigrated under their leader Punon, and were lost in the northern parts of Siberia, from whence they might easily reach the north-western coast of the new continent. † This

---

* Their complicated method of computing cycles of years, was identically the same with that made use of by the Hindoos, Thibetans, Chinese, and Japanese.—HUMBOLDT's *Researches*, vol. i. p. 301.

† On the north-west coast, between Nootka Sound and Cook's River, especially under the parallel of 57° N., the natives display a decided taste for hieroglyphic paintings. The Iroquois and the Hurons also, made hieroglyphic paintings on wood, strikingly resembling those of the Mexicans. On the American coast nearest to Asia, along Behring's Straits, between lat. 67° and 64° 10′, we find a great number of huts frequented by Siberian hunters, which

---

Figure 99. Duncan, *Modern Traveller, Mexico,* 189

Using the name *Egyptian* for the new hieroglyphic writing meshed well with the prominent theories of Joseph Smith's day.

So did ancient Nephite writing come from the Egyptians? The Babylonians? The Mexicans? The Jews? No, it was from the Laplanders' runic drums.

Magic Spectacles: The Urim and Thummim

It is astonishing that Martin Harris apparently accepted Joseph Smith's scribbled characters as examples of "reformed Egyptian." With that precedent, perhaps we should not be amazed that he swallowed another hard-to-believe claim: that of the "Urim and Thummim."

The next scripture written after the "The Book of Mormon" was "The Book of Abraham." In it Smith wrote:

> AND I, Abraham, had the Urim and Thummim, which the Lord my God had given unto me, in Ur of the Chaldees. (Abraham 3:1)

According to Joseph, the Urim and Thummim allowed the wearer to visualize a translation of the reformed Egyptian into his own language. He claimed they were packed in the box with the gold plates:

> Also, that there were two stones in silver bows—and these stones, fastened to a breastplate, constituted what is called the Urim and Thummim—deposited with the plates; and the possession and use of these stones were what constituted "seers" in ancient or former times; and that God had prepared them for the purpose of translating the book. (*History of the Church*, 1:35)

He also said:

> Through the medium of the Urim and Thummim I translated the record by the gift and power of God.[250]

To translate the characters engraved on the gold plates, Joseph claimed he had used "seer" stones. (He allegedly found a rock locally, at the bottom of a well that he was hired to dig, as he obviously couldn't produce the Urim and Thummin.)

He placed a common rock into his hat and pulled the hat over his face. He said God did the rest, and Martin Harris believed that, too.

Joseph found many more rocks to use when he performed the hat trick. Each of the Latter-day Saints churches headquartered in Salt Lake City, Utah, and Independence, Missouri, keep some of Joseph's magic rocks as part of their church archives.

Joseph called the Urim and Thummim a "key" for deciphering the hieroglyphics. This word leads us back to John Pinkerton and a manuscript called the *Edda*.

In the first volume of Pinkerton's *Collection of Travels* there is a chapter called "Von Troil's Letters on Iceland."[251] The Letters were written by Uno Von Troil and others in and around 1776.

Von Troil was the archbishop of Uppsala, Sweden. He and several companions traveled to Iceland in 1772 and wrote "observations on the civil, literary, ecclesiastical, natural history" and other aspects of the country in *Letters on Iceland*, published in 1780. The Smiths would have found Von Troil's writings in John Pinkerton's 1808 publication.

Among Von Troil's letters was a discussion of the *Edda*, a thirteenth-century work written on parchment in "ancient characters" in the Icelandic language. It is the source of most of what is known about Norse mythology. Its stories include gods, superhuman heroes, warrior-queens, giants, dwarves, and elves. The *Edda* begins with the Creation and ends with the world's cataclysmic destruction in the battle of Ragnarok.

Included in the Pinkerton collection is letter from Chevalier Ihre to Dr. Troil "Concerning the *Edda*."[252] The scholars debate in their letters about how "to know if this codex is not a magazine of all kinds of Icelandic works, which have been accidentally collected in one volume, and bound together?"[253]

The description of the *Edda* fits so neatly into the Smiths' concept of the gold plates that they were able to incorporate the Pinkerton chapter into

The Book of Mormon. More importantly, Joseph and Lucy Smith both used it in their own writings.

The Smiths skillfully mined Pinkerton's to invent the mythical reformed Egyptian writing system on gold plates. Not only the characters themselves but the descriptions *about* the ancient Nephite language were copied from stories in Pinkerton's book of travels to the northern countries.

Von Troil described the *Edda*[254]:

> ... it was written in ancient characters, in the Icelandic language, on parchment ...

and Smith's story says:

> They were filled with engravings, in Egyptian characters ...

In this part, the *Edda* had "holes," "leaves," and a certain "thickness":

> It is true, there are some *round holes* in the parchment, but these seem to have been there at first, as no part of the text is lost by them. The size is a small quarto, *one finger in thickness*, containing fifty four *leaves* and a half, or one hundred and nine pages ...

We compared this to "leaves of a book," the "three rings," and "thickness" of the Smiths' gold plates:

> ... bound together in a volume as the leaves of a book, with three rings running through the whole. The volume was something near six inches in thickness ...

Part of the writing on the Icelandic *Edda* could not be interpreted:

> ... another hand has patched in a stenographical writing, of which I did not know what to make during a long time, and indeed *I did not take great pains to decipher it.*

As for the gold plates:

> ... a *part of which was sealed.*

The *Edda* looked old:

> ... which may proceed partly *from its old age,* and partly perhaps from its having been long kept, and made use of in Icelandic smokey [sic] rooms. It is in very good preservation, and in *general legible.* ... The *characters are old* ...

> I clearly perceived that the manuscript was *very old.*

And the plates?

> The whole book exhibited many *marks of antiquity* in its construction ...

The *Edda* contained a genealogy of ancestors.

> [The *Edda*] contained a list of Icelandic lagmen, and a lang*f*edgatal or *genealogy of Sturleson's ancestors.*

And from Smith:

> For behold, *Laban hath the record of the Jews, and also a genealogy of my forefathers,* and they are engraven upon plates of brass. (1 Nephi 1: p. 9 [3:3])

We noticed that Smith equivocates when describing his plates. In a text from *Joseph Smith*[237],

> These records were engraven on plates which had the appearance of gold ...

Smith commented only on the plates as having "the *appearance* of gold"; he did not write that they were *actually made of gold*. Most people don't realize that.

Below is a side by side table that compares the *Edda* to the Nephite writing system in *The Book of Mormon*.

"Von Troil's Letters on Iceland," Pinkerton, p. 708–709	"The Book of Mormon" Mormon 4: p. 538
it was	And now behold, we have written
written in ancient	this record according to our knowledge in the
characters . . .	characters,
Perhaps what we call among us	which are called among us
belsinge runes . . .	the reformed Egyptian, being handed down and
differ from the common runes, by having the staff taken away.	altered by us, according to our manner of speech.
. . . in the Icelandic language, on parchment.	

The Smiths imitated the phrase *what we call among us*, which described the runic symbols by writing "which are called among us" to introduce the Nephites' different form of writing. The "handed down and altered by us, according to our manner of speech" verse also has its origins in the belsinge-runes discussion.

The writer explains an interesting piece of history where a group of monks in Iceland invented its own secret way of writing so those who learned to read the common language would still be unable to read the new one, thus having to rely on the monks' religious interpretations of it.

After letters became more universally known among the people, the subtle monks however, desirous of knowing something which the vulgar were unacquainted with, *invented various mysterious ways of writing in this manner,* which they not only make use of among themselves, but introduced into public writings. This taste met with admirers among our ancestors in Sweden, and thence we find so many kinds of what are called *villerunes*, which were unintelligible to the vulgar.[255]

Writing so that it was "unintelligible to the vulgar" is a good way to create an ancient alphabet that nobody else could understand. This is what Smith did with the gold plates: no one in the world but he could decipher them.

On page 708 of the Pinkerton text, Mr. Ihre gave an example of the runic writing system in the *Edda* (Figure 100).

Ihre wrote that a "key" was found to interpret the characters of runic writing. The explanation of the Urim and Thummim, therefore, begins with that discussion about the Icelandic *Edda*.

Here is Lucy's quote using the word *key* as Joseph's term for the Urim and Thummim:

> That of which I spoke, which *Joseph termed a key*, was indeed, nothing more nor less than the Urim and Thummim, and it was by this that the angel showed him many things which he saw in vision; by which he could also ascertain, at any time, the approach of danger, either to himself or the Record, and on account of which he always kept the Urim and Thummim about his person.[256]

Other similarities emerge among the runic drum, gold plates, and the Urim and Thummim:

I will however give a specimen of it : dfxtfrb scrkptprks bfnfdktb skt pmnkbxs hprks. As I was reading in Vanly's Bibliotheca Anglo Saxonica, I accidentally met with a similar collection of consonants, with a key affixed to it, which shewed that the whole secret consisted in placing, instead of each vowel, that consonant which in the alphabet followed next to it ; also instead of a, e, i, o, u, y, the letters b, f, k, p, x, z, were put ; and according to this rule the afore-mentioned riddle signified, Dextera scriptoris benedicta sit omnibus horis.

Figure 100. Pinkerton, *Voyages and Travels*, Vol. 1, 708

The Laplanders, preparing for a longer journey, for hunting, and other matters of greater account, before they enter on it, *usually consulted their Runic drums.*[257]

The wizards also consulted their drums to warn of danger from a trespasser finding gold on their land:

28. Item, *if people shall appear gathering of stones, gold, metal, or other like, on the land,* your pinnaces may draw nigh, marking what things they gather, using or *playing upon the drum,* or such other instruments, as may allure them to hearkening, to fantasy, *or desire to see,* and hear your instruments and voices, *but keep you out of danger,* and shew to them no point or sign of rigour and hostility.[258]

The Mormon prophet used his Urim and Thummim for similar purposes. He consulted them to receive warnings before any thieves tried to steal the gold plates:

Joseph kept the Urim and Thummim constantly about his person, by the use of which he could in a moment tell whether the plates were in any danger.[259]

Hollow birch trees become Lucy Smith's expose' of the story about reformed Egyptian and the runic drum; writing of an Icelandic lagman becomes a description of the gold plates; and the Urim and Thummim are giant spectacles in a trunk. The Smiths truly never cease to amaze us with their imagination and ingenuity. Ironic, is it not, that Joseph Smith passed off the symbols as a lost record of God's restoration of truth and salvation, when in actuality they were derived from the Laplanders' pagan symbols of Lapland gods, hell, divination, and a means of communication with the devil. Perhaps Professor Anthon is the only true prophet in Mormon history. His warning to beware of rogues is just as true today as it was when he gave it to the pitiful, duped Mr. Harris.

Michmalojan

20

How to
Fool a Witness

Despite all the clever writing, testimony, and theatrics about gold plates, the fact remains that no one has physically, objectively, or scientifically verified the existence of small tablets of metal "that had the appearance of gold" engraved with a verified ancient language called "reformed Egyptian hieroglyphics" used by pre-Columbian Jews who had civilized the American continents, with elephants.

In effect, the Smiths were performing a new and much more ambitious version of their old looking-glass and gold-digging con games. The Smiths knew that no gold plates or magic spectacles existed; it was all a ruse to accomplish their schemes. Professor Charles Anthon of Columbia College recognized the hoax right away. Others weren't so savvy.

In pre-Mormon days, ingenuous farmers paid Joseph and his father to look into the spirit world and dig for gold and silver on their property. These landowners believed that treasure lay hidden on their acreage, although none was ever found.

The Smiths now played a similar scheme, claiming the existence of gold plates and artifacts even though none existed—no inscribed plates, no sword, no breastplate, no liahona, and no Urim and Thummim that God had given to the prophet Abraham.

Nor did the younger Smith unearth a stone box on Camorah Hill, supposedly hidden there by Moroni (the son of Mormon) 1,500 years before. If the box had been in the hillside for so many hundreds of years, why wouldn't Joseph show that archaeological treasure to anyone or request that learned professors examine it and declare its authenticity? Moroni never instructed Joseph not to show that box to anyone. He was free to do so but chose not to. Oddly, none of his early followers challenged his secrecy. That in itself is proof of the Smiths' genius for holding sway over people and fooling them.

The gold treasure existed only in the mind of those who were overwhelmed by the power of Joseph's persuasion. If the plates had been real and Martin Harris had taken one to Professor Anthon at Columbia College for examination and analysis, just about everyone in the civilized world would have heard of the momentous discovery. We could view them today in a museum in Utah, perhaps, or in a glass case next to the Rosetta Stone.

If the plates had in fact existed, we could study them and learn about the rich Jewish history of the Nephites and Jaredites in ancient America, who rode around on horses and elephants, and the cursed Lamanites, who eventually became the Native Americans.

The Smiths believed, rightly, that their histrionics, yarns about angels, and claims of a written manuscript would be enough to gain converts. Martin Harris was their first convert. He wanted to verify that the Egyptian hieroglyphics were authentic and the plates were real before he gave money to the Smiths. The father and son knew that other people might want further proof. They might want to see and handle the plates.

Thus, even with the written manuscript, Joseph realized he had to provide something more. His parents knew it, too. To give his family a platform from which to operate, they needed to bamboozle people into testifying that they had seen and handled the tablets. Ah, but how to accomplish that when the plates weren't real? We already know that the Smiths couldn't afford to buy that much gold and fashion phony plates. Besides, anything they could manage to forge could never be presented to someone like Professor Anthon. Such a forgery inspected by learned men would expose the whole scam.

To solve their dilemma, the Smiths took their inspiration from Dr. Uno Von Troil, the archbishop of Uppsala, who had himself faced skepticism while dealing with an extremely old manuscript written in an unfamiliar language.

What would have been of particular interest to the Smiths is that Von Troil believed the *Edda* to be authentic and penned by Samundur Sigfusson. Von Troil's assessments were doubted by "Mr. Schloczer," and in "Letter XXIII," Von Troil defends his position. The Smiths borrowed the archbishop's logic and arguments to defend their *Book of Mormon*. If Von Troil could assert that Sigfusson was the author of a manuscript written sometime around the year 1200 AD, couldn't they claim that Moroni had inscribed the gold plates in the distant past?

The Smiths' next step was to persuade a small group of fledgling Mormon converts—the most fanatical and thus most easily duped—to sign declarations saying that they had seen the hieroglyphics and handled the plates, even if they had not. Once Joseph convinced this inner circle that the plates were real, he would have them sign letters that used Von Troil's reasoning as the template. To his credit, Joseph worked the plan and persuaded witnesses to sign his letters.

In the *General Collection of the Best and Most Interesting Voyages and Travels*, Mr. Pinkerton began his chapter on page 621 of *Volume the First*[260] (Figure 101).

Pinkerton began by complaining about the writings of prior investigators in Iceland. Their reports, he stated, "do not exactly correspond with the truth."

He goes on to say:

It can therefore by no means be thought superfluous, that Dr. Von Troil has favoured the literary world with his interesting Letters on Iceland; a work which, on account of its varied matter, and the great learning displayed everywhere, for the instruction of the curious reader, deserves the warmest approbation of the public.

LETTERS ON ICELAND,

CONTAINING OBSERVATIONS ON THE CIVIL, LITERARY, ECCLESIASTICAL, AND NATURAL HISTORY; ANTIQUITIES, VOLCANOES, BASALTES, HOT SPRINGS ; CUSTOMS, DRESS, MANNERS OF THE INHABIT-ANTS, &C. &C. MADE DURING A VOYAGE UNDERTAKEN IN THE YEAR 1772, BY JOSEPH BANKS, ESQ. F. R. S. ASSISTED BY DR. SOLANDER, F. R. S. DR. J. LIND, F. R. S. DR. UNO VON TROIL, AND SEVERAL OTHER LITERARY AND INGENIOUS GENTLEMEN.

WRITTEN BY UNO VON TROIL, D. D.

First chaplain to his Swedish majesty, almoner of the Swedish orders of knighthood, and member of the academy of sciences at Stockholm.

TO WHICH ARE ADDED,

The Letters of Dr. Ihre and Dr. Bach to the Author, concerning the Edda and the Elephantiasis of Iceland: also, Professor Bergman's curious Observations and Chemical Examination of the Lava and other Substances produced on the Island.

INTRODUCTION.

THE accounts of Iceland, which have hitherto made their appearance in the English language, are of such a nature, that it would betray ignorance or partiality to recommend them to the public as satisfactory and faithful.

The first writer of any known history of Iceland in the present century was John Andersson, afterwards burgomaster of Hamburgh, who undertook a voyage to this not much frequented island in a Greenland ship; but the authenticity of his performance is far from being such as may be relied on with confidence.

Niels Horrebow, a Danish astronomer, was sent to Iceland by the court of Denmark, on purpose to contradict Andersson's account : he published some observations on Iceland, but, from too great a desire to please his employers, he fell into the opposite error, and paints all his objects with a glow of colouring, that does not exactly correspond with the truth.

In Richer's Continuation of Rollin's History is a history of Iceland, a most pitiful compilation, and full of the grossest errors that ever disgraced the historical page.

Under the authority of the Royal Society of Sciences at Copenhagen, Eggert Olafsen and Biarne Povelsen, two men of learning, natives of Iceland, and residing in the country, travelled all over that island, and gave, in two volumes in quarto, a faithful and ample account of all that deserves the attention of the learned and curious, illustrated by numerous engravings; but though the performance is accurate and circumstantial, yet it is unfortunately clogged with repetitions, and the facts are recounted in so tedious and uninteresting a manner, that it requires a most phlegmatic temper, and a large fund of patience, to go through the whole of this work, for it is filled with a long and dull recital of events, methodized in the most formal manner possible. It can therefore by no means be thought superfluous, that Dr. Von Troil has favoured the literary world with his interesting Letters on Iceland ; a work which, on account of its varied matter, and the great learning displayed everywhere, for the instruction of the curious reader, deserves the warmest approbation of the public.

Men of talents and learning will, we flatter ourselves, think highly of this present performance by Dr. Von Troil, though perhaps it may be sometimes a little deficient in point of language.

Figure 101. Pinkerton, *Voyages and Travels*, Vol. 1, 621

Pinkerton believed that Dr. Troil's letters were authentic and deserved to be well received by the public. Pinkerton tells us that the present letters are a translation from German and can be "safely stated as a faithful translation from the original, and a work of real merit and utility." He declares:

> *We leave it to the unprejudiced reader to form a judgment of this performance* which is replete with variety of matter, treated in an instructive and satisfactory manner; and likewise on the great learning relative to natural history, historical, antiquarian, and philological subjects, which are every where blended in the context of the following letters; and we are of opinion, that in respect to these points, *this work requires no apology for offering it to the impartial public.*

There it was! The Smiths' solution! They would go on the offensive. They would offer letters from witnesses saying that, regarding the points of history and subjects of the plates and translation of *The Book of Mormon*, they needed "no apology for offering it to the impartial public." The "unprejudiced readers" could "form a judgment." They could imply that anyone who dared question them was biased and close-minded.

They could draft letters to sound like the description of the history of Iceland and the *Edda*, but theirs would announce to the public the existence of the gold plates and then persuade people to sign them. Getting that first signature was crucial; once one person took the plunge, others would follow. Smith Junior had already made a believer of Martin Harris and could count on him to commit. His next target was Oliver Cowdery.

Cowdery, a schoolteacher like Joseph Smith, Sr., was boarding at the Smith homestead in 1828 when he converted to Mormonism. Junior's parents or brother Hyrum must have converted Cowdery, because Joseph and wife Emma were living in Pennsylvania with Emma's parents at the time. Cowdery met the prophet when Joseph visited the family farm in Palmyra, New York, in 1829. Joseph hired Cowdery as his scribe after he had divested Martin Harris of that responsibility. Harris had "lost" the first 116 pages of the manuscript called "The Book of Lehi" after an argument with his wife over Harris's mortgaging their farm and giving the proceeds to Joseph. When Joseph offered the position to Cowdery, he accepted.

Cowdery wrote down most of the newly scripted *Book of Mormon* from Joseph's translation-in-a-hat act. Joseph was so convincing, or Cowdery so gullible, that many years later, even after a falling-out with Joseph and being excommunicated from the church, he declared:

> I wrote with my own pen the entire Book of Mormon (save a few pages) as it fell from the lips of the Prophet, as he translated it by the gift and power of God, by means of the Urim and Thummim, or as it is called by that book, Holy Interpreters. I beheld with my eyes, and handled with my hands, the gold plates from which it was translated. I also beheld the Interpreters. That book is true.[261]

Before Cowdery traveled to Harmony, Pennsylvania, to become the new *Book of Mormon* scribe, Joseph wrote the following, which, as other writings he called "revelations," he framed as if God were dictating and he was God's scribe. He would dangle an opportunity—an honor!—before Harris and Cowdery, so they would ask to be witnesses rather than have to be asked:

> . . . yea, and the testimony of three of my servants shall go forth with my words unto this generation. Yea, three shall know of a surety that these things are true, for I will give them power, and that they may behold and view these things as they are, and to none else will I grant this power to receive this same testimony among this generation.

Joseph didn't have to look far for that third witness. David Whitmer was a friend and in-law of Cowdery's. Whitmer knew that Cowdery performed Smith's work of conversion and testimony about the gold plates and translations.

After running into trouble with the locals in Harmony, Joseph and Cowdery moved into the Whitmer homestead in Fayette, New York. They completed the translation there in June 1829.[262]

Whitmer watched Joseph put the seer stone in his hat, place the hat over his face, and dictate the words to Cowdery, who served as scribe. Some reports say Whitmer took Cowdery's place as scribe for few pages of the burgeoning manuscript.

Like Cowdery, Whitmer was convinced that Joseph's claims were true and that he was indeed a chosen prophet of God. The whole Whitmer household believed in the new manuscript, the new religion, and, more important to Smith's plans, they believed in Joseph Smith, Jr.

While in the Whitmer residence, Joseph prepared his most fervent converts—Martin Harris, Oliver Cowdery, and David Whitmer—to be his flunkies. Imagine how ecstatic they must have felt when Joseph showed the three men this revelation:

> Where at that day when the book shall be delivered unto the man of whom I have spoken, the book shall be hid from the eyes of the world, that *the eyes of none shall behold it save it be that three witnesses shall behold it, by the power of God,* besides him to whom the book shall be delivered; *and they shall testify to the truth of the book and the things therein.*
>
> And *there is non [sic] other which shall view it, save it be a few according to the will of God, to bear testimony of his word unto the children of men; for the Lord God hath said that the words of the faithful should speak as if it were from the dead.*
>
> Wherefore, the Lord God will proceed to bring forth the words of the book; *and in the mouth of as many witnesses as seemeth him good will he establish his word; and wo be unto him that rejecteth the word of God.*[263]

Pretty heady stuff, being selected by God to be one of only three witnesses sanctioned by God! And God is clear about the witnesses' duties: "testify to the truth of the book and the things therein." And if they didn't perform as directed? ". . . wo be unto him that rejecteth the word of God."

Joseph recorded in his own writings how he had worked the trio into such fervor that they *asked him* to pray and see if God would allow them to be the witnesses:

Almost immediately after we had made this discovery, it occurred to *Oliver Cowdery, David Whitmer, and the aforementioned Martin Harris* (who had come to inquire after our progress in the work) that *they would have me inquire of the Lord, to know if they might not obtain of him to be these three special witnesses. And finally they became so very solicitous, and teased me so much, that at length I complied,* and through the Urim and Thummim, I obtained of the Lord for them the following revelation.[264]

God's answer, or revelation, came to Joseph right on cue:

Behold I say unto you, that you must rely upon my word, which if you do with full purpose of heart, you shall have a view of the plates, and also the breastplate, the sword of Laban, and Urim and Thummim, which were given to the brother of Jared upon the mount, when he talked with the Lord face to face, and the miraculous directors which were given to Lehi while in the wilderness on the borders of the Red Sea. And it is by your faith that you shall obtain a view of them, even by that faith which was had by the prophets of old.

And *after that you have obtained faith, and have seen them with your eyes, you shall testify of them by the power of God. And this you shall do that my servant Joseph Smith, Jr., may not be destroyed, that I may bring about my righteous purposes unto the children of men in this work.*[265]

Most likely feeling that they themselves had been touched by God, Harris, Cowdery, and Whitmer followed Joseph into the woods to pray. Martin separated from the other three. What happened next comes from David Whitmer:

We went out into the woods nearby, and sat down on a log and talked awhile. We then kneeled down and prayed. Joseph prayed. We then got up and sat on the log and were talking, when all at once a light came down from above us and encircled us for quite a little distance around, and the angel stood before us. . . . [The angel] was dressed in white, and spoke and called me by name and said, "Blessed is he that keepeth His commandments." That is all I heard the angel say.

[The angel] showed us the plates, the sword of Laban, the Directors, the Urim and Thummim, and other records. Human language could not describe heavenly things and that which we saw.

I did not handle the plates—only saw them. . . . Joseph, and I think Oliver and Emma told me about the plates, and described them to me, and I believed them, but did not see except at the time testified of.[266]

That was from an interview with David years *after* Joseph excommunicated him from the church. The interview continued:

Q: Is it possible that you imagined this experience?

A: [O]ur testimony is true. And if these things are not true, then there is no truth; and if there is no truth, there is no God; and if there is no God, there is no existence. But I know there is a God, for I have heard His voice and witnessed the manifestation of his power.[267]

Oliver Cowdery had a similar recollection of the event. He was also later excommunicated, as was Martin Harris. Splinter groups were already forming from Joseph's church, and each man joined a different one. Both came back to the mainstream sect, however, and never denied they had seen the angel and the plates. Whitmer left and never came back, but he, too, emphatically declared his whole life that he had seen the angel and heard God.[268]

If they had reneged, they might have seemed like lying fools guilty of sacrilege. If they had had any doubts about what they had seen and heard while in a heightened, excitable state, they might have remembered the revelation's warning: "and wo be unto him that rejecteth the word of God."

How To Forge a Letter

The first letter Smith's followers signed is called "The Testimony of Three Witnesses," and the second letter is titled "And Also the Testimony of Eight Witnesses." Both were printed on the final two pages of the 1830 *Book of Mormon*. The first letter, which is longer than the second, was signed by Oliver Cowdery, David Whitmer, and Martin Harris.

It states outright that although they all "saw the engravings on the plates," it was because "an Angel of God came down from heaven, and he brought and laid before our eyes, that we beheld and saw the plates, and the engravings thereon. . . ." This refers not to *physical* plates but only to spiritual ones.

After we read the two letters a number of times, what became apparent was how Joseph Smith used the Iceland and Lapland chapters from John Pinkerton to draft the declarations, especially the one about the Icelandic *Edda* and its introduction by Pinkerton. Meredith Sheets made this discovery after realizing that wording in the letters was just like some of the wording that Joseph and his mother copied from Professor Knud Leems and Von Troil to forge the Egyptian hieroglyphics and the description of the gold plates, as we explained in the previous chapter.

At this point we felt disappointed in the young prophet. He could have written testimonials in his own words, with original thoughts. No one could have exposed original letters as fakes if created by Smith based only on the text of the letters themselves. Instead he seems to have strived for a consistency in his verbiage of the testimonies, history, letters, and *The Book of Mormon*. The multiple paths all led back to the same source: the John Pinkerton chapter on Iceland. Because of this decision, Joseph left a trail for analysts to follow.

Shown below is the text of "The Testimony of Three Witnesses" (Figure 102).

We placed the comparison of Von Troil's *Letters on Iceland* in a table next to Smith's letter to show the plagiarized text or the inspirational text for the copied testimonials. The numbers within each phrase on the left column are page numbers from the 1808 Pinkerton chapter.[269]

The same chapter informed Joseph's writing about the plates and reformed Egyptian. The first letter, in our opinion, is of better quality than the second because it contains more original writing about angels and God.

THE TESTIMONY OF THREE WITNESSES.

BE it known unto all nations, kindreds, tongues, and people, unto whom this work shall come, that we, through the grace of God the Father, and our Lord Jesus Christ, have seen the plates which contain this record, which is a record of the people of Nephi, and also of the Lamanites, his brethren, and also of the people of Jared, which came from the tower of which hath been spoken; and we also know that they have been translated by the gift and power of God, for his voice hath declared it unto us; wherefore we know of a surety, that the work is true. And we also testify that we have seen the engravings which are upon the plates; and they have been shewn unto us by the power of God, and not of man. And we declare with words of soberness, that an Angel of God came down from heaven, and he brought and laid before our eyes, that we beheld and saw the plates, and the engravings thereon; and we know that it is by the grace of God the Father, and our Lord Jesus Christ, that we beheld and bear record that these things are true; and it is marvellous in our eyes: Nevertheless, the voice of the Lord commanded us that we should bear record of it; wherefore, to be obedient unto the commandments of God, we bear testimony of these things.— And we know that if we are faithful in Christ, we shall rid our garments of the blood of all men, and be found spotless before the judgement seat of Christ, and shall dwell with him eternally in the heavens. And the honor be to the Father, and to the Son, and to the Holy Ghost, which is one God. Amen.

OLIVER COWDERY,
DAVID WHITMER,
MARTIN HARRIS.

Figure 102. Book of Mormon, "The Testimony of Three Witnesses"

"Von Troil's Letters on Iceland" Pinkerton, Vol. 1	"The Testimony of Three Witnesses" *The Book of Mormon*
Dr. Von Troil has **favoured the literary world** with his interesting Letters on Iceland . . . deserves the warmest approbation of the public (p. 621) this work requires no apology for **offering it to the impartial public** (p. 621)	Be it known unto **all nations, kindreds, tongues, and people, unto whom this work shall come,**
	. . . that we, through the grace of God the Father, and our Lord Jesus Christ, have seen the plates which contain this
That this catalogue was the **work of several hands** may, in my opinion, be perceived by more than one indication (p. 712),	record, which is a **record of the people** of Nephi, and also of the Lamanites, his brethren, and also of the people of Jared
	. . . which came from the tower of which hath been spoken; and
. . . together with a **translation of my letter**	we also know that they have been **translated by the gift and power**
(p. 707)/I did not take great pains to decypher it (p. 708)	**of God,**
	. . . for his voice hath
I therefore now **declare**	**declared it unto us;**
that there is nothing else in it, but what has already been mentioned (p. 708)]	
. . . it may however be safely stated as a faithful translation from the original, and a work of real merit and utility (p. 622) . . . and paints all his objects with a glow of colouring, that does not exactly correspond with **the truth.**	. . . **wherefore we know of a surety, that the work is true**

The latter half of the letter refers to the episode in the woods where the witnesses said the angel displayed the spiritual plates:

. . . it was **written in ancient characters,** in the Icelandic language, on parchment (p. 708)	And we also testify that we have **seen the engravings** which are upon the plates

I clearly perceived that the manuscript was very old (p. 709);

illustrated by numerous

engravings (p. 621)

. . . but though the performance is accurate and circumstantial (p. 621)

Mr. Schloczer's first objection is, that I have not given a complete description of the manuscript (p. 707)/Though I now resume the pen, it is not so

much with any immediate designs to refute those objections which have been made against me, as to

give those accounts and explanations which have been required of me (p. 707)]

. . . and they have been shewn unto us by the power of God, and not of man. And we declare with words of soberness, that an Angel of God came down from heaven, and he brought and laid before our eyes, that we beheld and saw the plates, and the

engravings thereon;

. . . and we know that it is by the grace of God the Father, and our Lord Jesus Christ, that we

beheld and bear record that these things are true;

. . . and it is marvellous in our eyes: Nevertheless,

the voice of the Lord commanded us that we should bear record of it;

The closing contains flowery language with the illustrious intent to make the letters sound like serious oaths to God.

. . . wherefore, to be obedient unto the commandments of God, we bear testimony of these things. And we know that if we are faithful in Christ, we shall rid our garments of the blood of all men, and be found spotless before the judgement seat of Christ, and shall dwell with him eternally in the heavens. And the honor be to the Father, and to the Son, and to the Holy Ghost, which is one God. Amen.

OLIVER COWDERY,
DAVID WHITMER,
MARTIN HARRIS.

Perhaps Joseph recognized the weaknesses of the first letter or received some criticism for it. The second letter was signed by eight people and seems like an attempt to correct the shortcomings of the first: the lack of seeing physical plates (Figure 103).

It says the witnesses "did handle with our own hands" the plates and that "we saw the engravings thereon." No references to angels or visions. The signers of the second letter are

Christian Whitmer

Jacob Whitmer

Peter Whitmer, Jr.

John Whitmer

Hiram Page

Joseph Smith, Sen.

Hyrum Smith

Samuel H. Smith

Three were members of Joseph's own family: Smith Sr. was Joseph's father and co-conspirator, so he can be ruled out as a reliable source. Hyrum Smith was his older brother, and Samuel Smith was his next-younger brother. Both of these brothers worked with Joseph Jr. to build and manage the church and convert people to the Mormon faith. The remaining witnesses were all members of the Whitmer family.

David Whitmer signed the first letter but not the second. In the second letter, the witnesses stated that they had seen and handled plates, but what had really transpired? Joseph had a wooden box made to hold the alleged plates. He let people lift the box and shake it to feel how heavy it was. He allowed the people to see a cloth in the box with what looked like sheets of metal underneath. The witnesses could touch the cloth, but none was permitted to raise it and look underneath; if they saw the plates with their physical eyes, Moroni would destroy Joseph and probably the witness, too.

So there they were, Joseph's first converts hefting and shaking a box with something metal hidden underneath a tablecloth and believing that

AND ALSO THE TESTIMONY OF EIGHT WITNESSES.

BE it known unto all nations, kindreds, tongues, and people, unto whom this work shall come, that Joseph Smith, Jr. the Author and Proprietor of this work, has shewn unto us the plates of which hath been spoken, which have the appearance of gold; and as many of the leaves as the said Smith has translated, we did handle with our hands; and we also saw the engravings thereon, all of which has the appearance of ancient work, and of curious workmanship. And this we bear record, with words of soberness, that the said Smith has shewn unto us, for we have seen and hefted, and know of a surety, that the said Smith has got the plates of which we have spoken. And we give our names unto the world, to witness unto the world that which we have seen : and we lie not, God bearing witness of it.

CHRISTIAN WHITMER,
JACOB WHITMER,
PETER WHITMER, JR.
JOHN WHITMER,
HIRAM PAGE,
JOSEPH SMITH, SEN.
HYRUM SMITH,
SAMUEL H. SMITH.

Figure 103. Book of Mormon, "And Also The Testimony of Eight Witnesses"

the gold treasure was just under that fabric. Joseph had perfected his con game. He no longer needed to say the gold was under the ground; he could simply claim it was under the tablecloth, and they believed him.

To intensify their experience, the second letter says the witnesses "hefted" the plates. This refers to their picking up the wooden box that held cloth-covered items and then raising it and lowering it. Joseph wrote the letter for the witnesses to declare that they had handled the plates and seen the engravings. Joseph showed his witnesses the "Caractors," or hieroglyphics, that he had ostensibly copied from the plates. He placed his handwritten copy next to the covered plates so that his witnesses could "see" the engravings at the same time as "handling" the plates.

John Whitmer later testified that he lifted the box with the covered plates. He said it was as heavy as lead or gold, "and I knew that Joseph had not credit enough to buy so much lead."[270] He meant to convey the idea that the Smiths were very poor. He continued:

> I now say, I handled those plates; there were fine engravings on both sides. I handled them.[271]

Joseph's wife and youngest brother made similar claims—that they either saw or touched the plates through a covering of some sort. In an interview with Mr. J. W. Peterson about the plates, William said:

> I did not see them uncovered, but I handled them and hefted them while wrapped in a tow frock (ed: a shirt) and judged them to have weighed about sixty pounds. I could tell they were plates of some kind and that they were fastened together by rings running through the back.[272]

Emma, Joseph's wife, was interviewed at a different time about the plates:

> Q: Are you sure that he had the plates at the time you were writing for him?

> A: The plates often lay on the table without any attempt at concealment, wrapped in a small linen table cloth, which I had given him to fold them in. I once felt the plates as they thus lay on the table, tracing their outline and shape. They seemed to be pliable like thick paper, and would rustle with a metallic sound when the edges were moved by the thumb, as one does sometimes thumb the edges of a book. . . . I moved them from place to place on the table, as it was necessary in doing my work."[273]

How can Emma say the plates were not concealed when she states in the *same sentence* that they were concealed? If Joseph could use his powers to confuse his own wife to such a degree that she made these absurd statements, then there must have been no limit to what he could get others to say or do for him. Below is the full text of the second letter with the original or inspirational text from the Von Troil *Letters on Iceland* inserted on the left side:

"Letters on Iceland" Pinkerton, Vol. 1	"And Also the Testimony of Eight Witnesses" *The Book of Mormon*
Dr. Von Troil has favoured the literary world with his interesting Letters on Iceland . . . deserves the warmest approbation of the public (p. 621)/this work requires no apology for offering it to the impartial public (p. 622)]	Be it known unto all nations, kindreds, tongues, and people, unto whom this work shall come,
together with a translation of my letter (p. 707)/I did not take great pains to decypher it (p. 708)	that Joseph Smith Jr., the translator of this work,
	has shown unto us the plates of which hath been spoken

From this point in the letter, the wording imitates Joseph Smith's own writing in his "History of the Church" and Mormon church newspaper articles describing the plates as having the "appearance of gold," "leaves," "engravings," "old age," etc., which were the same descriptions that Joseph copied from the Icelandic *Edda* letter to Von Troil written by Chevalier Ihre. The original page 708 is partially reproduced in the following[274] (Figure 104), and a partial copy of page 709 appears as[275] (Figure 105).

This is how we discovered that Smith's letters were not original. Joseph wrote them based on his own forgeries describing the plates. Let's continue:

. . . this codex . . . is written on parchment, the colour of which is dark brown (p. 708) The size is a small quarto, one	. . . which have the appearance of gold;

But to oblige Mr. Schloczer, and perhaps many others, I will inform them that this codex, as I said before, is written upon parchment, the colour of which is dark brown, which may proceed partly from its old age, and partly perhaps from its having been long kept, and made use of in the Icelandic smokey rooms. It is in very good preservation, and in general legible. It is true, there are some round holes in the parchment, but these seem to have been there at first, as no part of the text is lost by them. The size is a small quarto, one finger in thickness, containing fifty four leaves and a half, or one hundred and nine pages, besides a white leaf before, and one behind, on which there are however some bad figures, of which these on the first represent Gangleri, with Herjafu-har and Thridi, who resolve questions. The characters are old, and when compared with many others, seem to prove that the copier lived about the beginning of the four-teenth century : but all this is of very little importance. Mr. Schloczer believes his subsequent questions may give more light in settling the principal point, as they tend to discover who was the author of the Edda, and what really belongs to it.

Figure 104. Pinkerton, *Voyages and Travels*, Vol. 1, 708

finger in thickness, containing	. . . and as
fifty four leaves	many of the leaves as the said
(p. 708)	Smith has translated,
. . . who had frequently had this	. . . we did handle with
manuscript in his own hands, and examined it (p. 708)	our hands;
. . . the Rubric was written in a	
later hand . . . no reasonable eye-witness could believe it was written in 1541 . . . (p. 709)/	. . . and we also saw the
illustrated by numerous engravings; (p. 621)/	engravings thereon
it was written in ancient characters, in the Icelandic language, on parchment (p. 708)	
. . . may proceed from its old age (p. 708)/	
I clearly perceived that the manuscript was very old	. . . all of which has the appearance of an ancient work
(p. 709)	
curious and complete catalogue	. . . and of curious workmanship
(p. 624)	

I mentioned in my letter to Mr. Lagerbring, that the Rubric was written in a later hand; which is right so far as has been added after the Edda itself was begun, which may be seen by the narrow space left for it, so that it has forced the copier to bring the last line into that immediately preceding it. Besides, I clearly perceived that the manuscript was very old, and that no reasonable eye-witness could believe it was written in 1541, as Mr. Schloczer conjectures. But as it had been written with red ink, which had preserved its colour better than the black, I then believed the hand had been somewhat younger; but as I have now very minutely compared the writing in the Rubric with that of the Edda, I think I may safely affirm, that they are both written by one and the same hand. From hence it follows, that he who copied the Edda considered the above-mentioned articles, and no others, as essential parts of it.

Figure 105. Pinkerton, *Voyages and Travels*, Vol. 1, 709

The end of the letter is meant to be a declaration of truth of its statements, such as Ihre's declarations to Dr. Von Troil about the *Edda*:

I think I may safely affirm (p. 709)/I therefore now declare that there is nothing else in it (p. 708)

And this we **bear record,**

... it may however be safely stated as a faithful translation from the original, and a work of real merit and utility (p. 622)

... **with words of soberness, that the** said Smith has shown unto us, for we have seen and hefted, and know of a surety, that the said Smith has got the plates of which we have spoken

It gives me great pleasure to find that my thoughts on these subjects have been examined by men of learning in Germany

And **we give our names unto the** world, to witness unto the world that which we have seen:

... by which means **a number of false notions which had been formed on the subject and design of this book have been removed** (p. 707)

and **we lie not** God bearing witness of it.

BY JOSEPH BANKS, ESQ., F.R.S. ASSISTED BY DR. SOLANDER, F.R.S., DR. J. LIND., F.R.S., DR. UNO VON TROIL, AND SEVERAL OTHER LITERARY AND INGENIOUS GENTLEMEN ... The Letters of Dr. IHRE and Dr. BACH to the AUTHOR ... also, Professor BERGMAN's curious Observations.

(p. 621)

CHRISTIAN WHITMER,
JACOB WHITMER,
PETER WHITMER, JR.
JOHN WHITMER,
HIRAM PAGE,
JOSEPH SMITH, SEN.
HYRUM SMITH,
SAMUEL H. SMITH.

Notice above that eight witnesses signed the letter, and yet there are only seven men, including the author Von Troil, listed in the title, page 621. One name was left out: Mr. Chevalier Ihre, who wrote the section "Concerning the *Edda*," beginning on page 707. That brings the total writers of *Letters on Iceland* to eight.

It doesn't really matter what *The Book of Mormon* witnesses said or didn't say or saw or didn't see. Whatever stories, letters, declarations, sermons, or church histories were written or spoken by the Smiths or others about gold plates do not matter, either. All of it was based on a forgery. Joseph Smith's own "Caractors" of reformed Egyptian, which he stated were copied from the plates, betrayed him. He drafted most of them from an 1808 illustration of a magical runic drum. The learned professor Anthon was not quite correct in his evaluation. The Smiths' behavior wasn't just a scheme to cheat the farmer Martin Harris out of his money. It was an attempt to cheat the entire world.

Smith was counting on what Von Troil said about Mr. Schloczer, who was skeptical of the archbishop's assessment: "It is highly proper to be well-acquainted with a subject before one ventures to treat of it." Smith was so secretive that he made sure no one could fit that description.

⟫ 21 ⟪

THE NEW RELIGION (IS THE SAME AS THE OLD RELIGION?)

On April 7, 1844, the prophet Joseph Smith said:

> I am learned, and know more than all the world put together.

A day later he said:

> God made Aaron to be the mouth piece for the children of Israel, and He will make me be god to you in His stead, and the Elders to be mouth for me; and if you don't like it, you must lump it.[276]

How could the man make such bold claims when he didn't have any gold plates, no sword of Laban, breastplate, or magic spectacles, and certainly no liahona to prove his claims? It was because he could hold up a printed copy of *The Book of Mormon*, which Joseph called the "keystone" of their religion, and the reformed Egyptian characters for everyone to know that he was telling the truth. This made him appear credible enough so that he could articulate extravagant, exaggerated, and far-fetched lies, and many people believed him.

Consider this: Joseph said he saw heaven and met and talked to God the Father and Jesus Christ, Moses, John the Baptist, and Peter and John, the disciples of Jesus . . . and the list goes on and on of the who's who of the Bible. Joseph used the written stories of visions from Laplanders, activities of Tartar lords, and many other recorded items to create the reports of each miraculous encounter. He was meticulous and disciplined in copying visions and phenomena from the history books so everything he preached or wrote would sound authentic. Nothing was left to chance. It was all scripted and acted out in the theater of the Latter-day Church.

He also had a plan to keep this facade intact and his church prosperous for a lifetime. The latter-day prophet said he would recreate all the lost and corrupted doctrines and rituals, which he was going to restore by his miraculous dispensation.

Outsiders to the religion do not realize that most of the rituals and beliefs are not actually in *The Book of Mormon*. His strategy was to use a continuous flow of orders and directions from God that could be revealed to the faithful believers only by the prophet himself. In this way, Joseph would never forfeit his position as the unchallenged and unquestioned leader of the new church. A year before *The Book of Mormon* was published he convinced Oliver Cowdery through one of these revelations that working a divining rod meant that God was speaking to Oliver and that ongoing supernatural power was present with Joseph:

A Revelation given to Oliver,

in Harmony, Pennsylvania, April, 1829.

Oliver, verily, verily I say unto you, that assuredly as the Lord liveth, which is your God and your Redeemer, even so sure shall you receive a knowledge concerning the engravings of old records, which are ancient, which contain those parts of my scripture of which have been spoken, by the manifestation of my Spirit; yea, behold I will tell you in your mind and in your heart by the Holy Ghost, which shall come upon you and which shall dwell in your heart.

O remember, these words and keep my commandments. Remember this is your gift. Now this is not all, for you have another gift, which is the gift of working with the rod: behold and it has told you things: behold there is no other power save God, that can cause this rod of nature, to work in your hands, for it is the work of God; and therefore whatsoever you shall ask me to tell you by that means, that will I grant unto you, that you shall know.[277]

Oliver must have taken this revelation to heart, because apparently he attempted his own translation from the ancient characters. God, through Joseph's revelation, blocked Oliver's attempts to translate. This would have been problematic for Joseph if someone else could claim to be God's seer and translator. This was Joseph's role alone. Using these revelations, Smith was able to muster control over his new converts while pretending to provide them with all the lost doctrines of ancient Christianity. With a stroke of Smith's pen, God took away any powers that Oliver thought he possessed through this new dispensation:

> Be patient my son, for it is wisdom in me, and it is not expedient that you should translate at this present time. Behold the work which you are called to do, is to write for my servant Joseph; and behold it is because you did not continue as you commenced, when you begun to translate, that I have taken away this privilege from you. Do not murmur my son, for it is wisdom in me that I have dealt with you after this manner.[278]

In 1831, Joseph held a church conference where he asked leaders to verify that his commandments really *did* come from God. It was recorded:

> The testimony of the witnesses to the book of the Lord's commandments, which He gave to His Church through Joseph Smith, Jun., who was appointed by the voice of the Church for this purpose; we therefore feel willing to bear testimony to all the world of mankind, to every creature upon the face of all the earth . . . that these commandments were given by inspiration of God, and are profitable for all men, and are verily true.[279]

For Better or for Worse

For better or for worse, the Latter-day Saints of all different sects have attracted notoriety because of their tradition of polygamy.

Because Joseph Smith Jr. wanted his *Book of Mormon* to sound like the Bible and because he plagiarized *The Travels of Marco Polo*, seemingly incompatible concepts occupy the same gospel as doctrine. The most infamous custom is polygamy. Strictly defined, *polygamy* is a marriage in which a spouse of either sex may have more than one mate at the same time.

Some Mormon sects still practice polygamy as one of Joseph Smith's fundamental revelations, and they stand in judgment of the Utah-based church, which abandoned the practice in 1890. The Latter-day Saints church that did not move to Utah but remained in Ohio included Smith's widow, Emma, and his mother, Lucy. That group never practiced polygamy, and they denied that Joseph Jr. taught the doctrine. Then why all the confusion? Weren't Joseph's revelations supposed to repudiate the corrupted doctrines and restore the ancient beliefs once and for all?

This doctrine is said to be a commandment from God to Joseph Smith Jr. in July 1843, long after *The Book of Mormon* was completed and published. That means it was not engraved on Moroni's golden plates.

Smith created new revelations to convince his wife Emma, as well as other members, that polygamy was ordered by God so that she would not object to being one of several women with whom he mated. The writing is titled "For Time and for All Eternity, Revelation received at Nauvoo, Illinois, on 12 July 1843 concerning biblical men having wives and concubines, adultery, a commandment for Emma Smith, the law of the priesthood" and begins with God's ordering the adherents to obey His laws:

> Verily thus Saith the Lord, unto you my servant Joseph, that inasmuch as you have inquired to know and understand wherein I the Lord justified my Servants, Abraham Isaac and Jacob . . . as touching the principle and doctrine of their having many wives and concubines; Behold and lo, I am the Lord thy God, and will answer thee as touching this matter:

Therefore, prepare thy heart to receive and obey the instructions which I am about to give unto you, for all those, who have this law revealed unto them, must obey the Same; for behold I reveal unto you a new and everlasting covenant, and if ye abide not that covenant, then are ye damned; for no one can reject this covenant and be permitted to enter into my glory . . .[280]

It continues with Smith as the chosen one—the only and the ultimate authority in the church:

. . . through the medium of mine anointed whom I have appointed on the earth to hold this power, (and I have appointed unto my Servant Joseph to hold this power in the last days, and there is never but one on the earth at a time on whom this power and the keys of this priesthood is confered [sic]). . .

& again, as pertaining the Law of priesthood; if any man espouse a virgin, & desire to espouse another, & the first give her consent, & if he espouse the second, & they are virgins & have vowed to no other man, then is he justified; he cannot Commit adultery . . . & if he have ten virgins given unto him by this Law, he Cannot Commit adultery, for they belong to him. . . [281]

Let's assume that God did not command Smith to have more than one wife. Then where did the latter-day prophet get the idea of polygamy? Certainly not from accepted Christian doctrine, although many of the teachings in *The Book of Mormon* do come from the Old Testament.

The idea of polygamy came from the 1818 edition of *The Travels of Marco Polo*.[282] There, Smith found some unusual religious practices and beliefs of the Tartars, a huge nomadic tribe whose values were based on Buddhism and shamanism. Smith copied the Tartar beliefs and practices and integrated them into the gospel of the Latter-day Saints Church. That is why many of the Mormon beliefs resemble Eastern, not Western, religions.

The wandering Tartar herders and warriors provided the inspiration for many of Smith's *missing and so-called corrupted doctrines* that God, through his prophet, would restore on Earth.

The following information compares Mormon religious doctrines with the Tartar religion, as described by Marco Polo in the 1818 *Travels of Marco Polo*.

Sample of Twelve Common Tartar and Mormon Beliefs

1. Polygamy is permitted: "ten (or twenty) virgins"
2. There is more than one god.
3. There is a high, celestial, and sublime god.
4. There is a god over terrestrial things.
5. Gods can have wives and children.
6. After death, man shall receive the same body or a natural body in heaven.
7. Dead Children can be married together in Heaven through a wedding performed on Earth.
8. Man is immortal, but if unworthy, he cannot ascend to higher levels of existence.
9. Heaven has several levels, including Celestial . . .
10. Terrestrial level . . . and
11. Telestial.
12. Blood atonement is an acceptable practice (not among Tartars but described in detail by Marco Polo).

When Smith read *The Travels of Marco Polo*, he inevitably came upon the description of "ten wives." Mix in his need to sound biblical, and the ten wives became the "ten virgins" in his revelation.

Smith redefined polygamy as "plural marriage," probably based on the following from Marsden's Marco Polo translation: ". . . polygamy is not in use in Tibet; but that it exists . . . in the *plurality* of husbands. . . ."[283] and "It is among the upper rank only . . . where a *plurality* of wives are to be found. Every great office of state has his *haram* consisting of six, eight, or ten women. . . ."[284]

Marco Polo described the practice of the Tartars to keep multiple wives:

> ... whilst on the other hand it is admirable to observe the loyalty of
> the husbands towards their wives; amongst whom, although there are
> perhaps ten or twenty, there prevails a degree of quiet and union that is
> highly laudable. No offensive language is ever heard, their attention being
> fully occupied with their traffic . . .[285]

> And the more praiseworthy are the virtues of modesty and chastity in
> the wives, because the men are allowed the indulgence of taking as many
> as they chuse . . . The wife who is the first espoused has the privilege of
> superior attention, and is held to be the most legitimate; which extends
> also to the children borne by her. In consequence of this unlimited num-
> ber of wives, the offspring is more numerous than amongst any other
> people. . . .[286]

Joseph Smith Jr. and Emma Hale married on January 18, 1827. He practiced polygamy secretly for many years. The revelation is dated 1843, but
his first documented mating outside marriage took place in 1836.[287] Plural
marriages could be sanctified by means of what Smith termed *sealings*.

> And Verily, verily, I say unto you, that whatsoever you Seal on Earth Shall
> be Sealed in heaven, and whatsoever you bind on earth in my name, and by
> my word, Saith the Lord, it Shall be eternally bound in the heavens . . .[288]

This meant he could be "sealed" with as many women as he chose. The
revelation would remain in effect "for time and for all eternity." Ironically,
the practice of polygamy was condemned on the gold plates in *The Book of
Mormon*'s "Book of Jacob."

Reportedly, when Emma learned of the "plural wives" revelations, she
asked Joseph to bring them to her for examination. According to eyewitness reports, "Hyrum took the revelation to Emma and returned some time
later angry and crestfallen. In all his life, he said, he had never been so
abused by a woman . . . although she stormed at Hyrum, Emma was terribly

shaken by the sight of the manuscript. Sorrowfully she said to William Law: 'The revelation says I must submit or be destroyed. Well, I guess I'll have to submit....'" According to Heber Kimball, Emma now threatened to leave her husband altogether.[289]

In the revelation, Emma Smith was on the receiving end of divine death threats from "the Lord your God."

> ... and I command mine handmaid, Emma Smith, to abide and cleave unto my Servent [sic] Joseph, and to none else. But if She will not abide this commandment; She Shall be destroyed, said the Lord; for I am the Lord thy God, and will destroy her, if She abide not in my law; but if She will not abide this Commandment, then Shall my Servent Joseph, do all things for her, even as he hath said, and I will bless him, and multiply him, and give unto him an hundred fold in the world, of fathers and mothers, brothers and Sisters, houses and lands, wives and children, and crowns of eternal lives in the eternal worlds.[290]

"God" even called Emma "the transgressor" if she did not support Joseph's polygamy. Emma felt she had no choice but to obey:

> Therefore, it Shall be lawful in me, if She receive not this law, for him to receive all things, whatsoever I, the Lord, his God, will give unto him, because She did not believe & administer unto him according to my word; & She then becomes the transgressor, & he is exempt from the law of Sarah, who administered unto Abraham according to the law, when I Commanded Abraham to take Hagar to wife.[291]

Having dispensed with the menace of wifely objections or a possible public outcry, Smith composed the revelation that repeats three times that "he cannot commit adultery."

Although the Utah Church of Jesus Christ of Latter-day Saints abandoned the practice and the Independence, Missouri, Community of Christ never endorsed the practice, these verses about Smith's "revelations" to practice polygamy are still regarded as Holy Scripture.

Fanny Alger, a sixteen- or seventeen-year-old girl and live-in house-guest of the Smiths, was the first of many celestial "sealings" for Joseph Smith. Fanny Alger's sealing took place in 1836, when the prophet was in his early thirties. The forty-nine wives who were sealed to Smith suggest that he had many more.[292] After all, in *The Travels of Marco Polo*, ". . . the men are allowed the indulgence of taking as many as they chuse. . . ." Joseph added most of his celestial wives between 1842 and 1844.

In May 1843, when Smith was thirty-eight, he "married" fifteen-year-old Helen Mar Kimball. Sometime in the spring of that same year he married sixteen-year-old Flora Ann Woodworth. Still abiding by God's revelations, Smith married five pairs of sisters as well as Patty and Sylvia Sessions, who were mother and daughter. Many of Joseph's women were already married, and their husbands willingly shared them with their prophet.[293]

Smith thus redefined adultery so he could commit the act with impunity. He also made sure the new wives and Emma too would not be unfaithful to him:

> But if one, or either of the ten virgins, after she is espoused, Shall be with another man, she has Committed adultery, & Shall be distroyed [sic]; for they are given unto him to multiply & replenish the Earth, according to my Commandment.[294]

In an attempt to hide his plagiarism regarding polygamy, Smith systematically worked to reverse Polo's story sequence and used it for his own revelations. Let's compare Smith's version with Polo's original, both in terms of specific concepts and the sequence of ten subjects. We labeled the organization of these ten comparison items below. For example, *The Travels of Marco Polo* notes "for love and duty to their husbands" as the "No. 1" in the text. Smith made it the last of his commandments as "No. 10": ". . . shall she believe and administer unto him." The same reversal holds true for numbers two and nine, etc. The summary of numbers two and nine are: Polo's *"Infidelity to the marriage bed"* versus Smith's *"she has committed adultery."*

Polo's quotes in the following are from the 1818 edition of *The Travels of Marco Polo* within pages 204–205. The Smith quotes are from the *Doctrines and Covenants*, which came from Joseph Smith's 1843 revelation "For Time and Eternity," already referenced.

Polo, No. 1:   . . . for love and **duty to their husbands**

Smith, No. 10:   . . . shall she believe and **administer unto him**

Polo, No. 2:   . . . **Infidelity to the marriage bed** is regarded by them as a vice not merely dishonourable, but of the **most infamous nature**

Smith, No. 9:   . . . if . . . she . . . shall be with another man, **she has committed adultery**

Polo, No. 3:   . . . **loyalty of the husbands towards their wives**

Smith, No. 4:   . . . then shall **my servant Joseph do all things for her**

Polo, No. 4:   . . . . . there are perhaps **ten** (*wives*)

Smith, No. 8:   And if he have **ten virgins** given unto him

Polo, No. 5:   And the more praiseworthy are the **virtues of modesty and chastity** in the **wives**

Smith, No. 2:   And let mine handmaid, Emma Smith, receive all **those** (*wives*) that have been given unto my servant, Joseph, and who are **virtuous and pure**

Polo, No. 6:   . . . **the men** are allowed the indulgence of **taking as many** (*wives*) **as they chuse**

Smith, No. 7:   . . . **if any man** espouse a virgin, and **desire to espouse another** . . . **they are given unto him**

Polo, No. 7:   . . . when he receives a **young woman in marriage**, he pays a dower ("property") to her parent*.

Smith, No. 6:   . . . let not my servant Joseph put his **property** out of his hands, lest an enemy come and distroy [sic] him

Polo, No. 8:   . . . The **wife who is first espoused** has the privilege of superior attention

Smith, No. 3:   . . . I give unto **mine handmaid, Emma Smith, your wife, whom I have given unto you,** that She Stay herself . . . to prove you all, as I did Abraham, and that I might require an offering at your hand by covenant and Sacrifice: and let **mine handmaid, Emma Smith,** receive all those that have been given unto my Servent Joseph

Polo, No. 9:   . . . In the consequence of this unlimited number of wives, the offspring is **more numerous** than amongst any other people

Smith, No. 5: . . . I will . . . multiply him, and give unto him an hundred fold in this world

Polo, No. 10: . . . Every marriage is solemnized with great ceremony.

Smith, No. 1: . . . whatsoever you seal (marry) on earth shall be sealed in heaven; and whatsoever you bind on earth . . . by my word, saith the Lord, it shall be eternally bound in the heavens

We wonder what all of the polygamist Mormon wives throughout history would say if they were alive today and knew the truth about Marco Polo and the Tartars.

The Book of Mormon and Polygamy

The great Kublai Khan had multiple wives by whom he fathered many offspring. In *The Book of Mormon*, kings in and around Zarahemla also had "wives and concubines," a phrase copied from *The Travels of Marco Polo*. To add another dimension to the plagiarism, the quotes below are just a sample of many and are organized by percentage-through-the-text of both books, *The Travels of Marco Polo* and *The Book of Mormon*:

Smith, 21.09%: And now it came to pass that the people of Nephi, under the reign of the second king, began to grow hard in their hearts, and indulge themselves somewhat in wicked practices, such as like unto David of Old, desiring *many wives and concubines,* and also Solomon, his son . . . (Jacob 1: p. 124 [1:15])

Smith, 21.60%: Behold, David and Solomon truly had many wives and concubines, which thing was abominable before me, saith the Lord. (Jacob 2: p. 127 [2:24])

Polo, 23.94%: The laity (of Kampion) take to themselves as many as thirty wives . . . (Marsden, 181)

Polo, 38.23%: Here are likewise the apartments of his *wives and concubines* . . . (Marsden, 289)

Smith, 30.27%: For behold, he did not keep the commandments of God, but he did walk after the desires of his own heart. And he had many wives and concubines. And he did cause his people to commit sin, and do that which was abominable in the sight of the Lord. (Mosiah 7: p. 178 [11:2])

Smith, 30.44%: And it came to pass that he placed his heart upon his riches, and he spent his time in riotous living with his wives and his concubines; and so did also his priests spend their time with harlots. (Mosiah 7: p. 179 [11:14])

Polo, 37.83%: The Grand khan has had twenty sons by his four legitimate wives, the eldest of whom, named Chingis . . . Besides these, his majesty has twenty-five sons by his concubines . . . (Marsden, 286)

Polo, 38.23%: Here are likewise the apartments of his wives and concubines . . . (Marsden, 289)

Polo, 83.60%: He [the king] has at least one thousand *wives and concubines* . . . (Marsden, 632)

Smith, 94.90%: And it came to pass that Riplakish did not do that which was right in the sight of the Lord, for he did have *many wives and concubines* . . . (Ether 4: p. 558 [10:5])

Looking at only the percentages, many of the polygamy quotes in *The Book of Mormon* appear relative to *The Travels of Marco Polo*. In the following table, for example, Polo's first reference is 23.94 percent into his book, and Smith's is 21.09 percent, a difference of fewer than three percentage points.

Polo:	Smith:	Difference:
23.94%	21.09%	2.85%
27.12%–8.23%	21.60%–30.44%	5.52%–7.79%
83.60%	94.90%	11.30%

End Goal: Becoming Gods

Marco Polo stated that the Tartars believed those who had gone through the proper marriage ceremony on Earth, which included marriage contracts, and had properly ascended, would remain married in heaven. His memoir was written in the year 1298. Then, 545 years later, Joseph Smith taught this belief in the 1843 "For Time and for All Eternity" revelation.[295]

> ... if a man marry a wife by my word, which is my law, and by the new and everlasting covenant ... shall be of full force when they are out of the world; and they shall pass by the angels; and the Gods ...

When Latter-day Saints become deities, according to Smith, they will be gods in heaven:

> Then shall they (husband and wife) be Gods, because they have no end ... Then they shall be Gods, because they have all power, and the angels are subject to them.

Unmarried Children Who Die Can Be Married in Heaven by a Ritual Performed on Earth

Joseph Smith Jr. also plagiarized some of the Tartars' unusual child-care practices. So bizarre are these and all of the other comparisons from *Marco Polo*, they could not have come from any other place.

For example, what happens when children die before they are married? The infant and child mortality rates in the early 1830s were high. Being able to conceptualize one child united in a spiritual marriage with another was a comforting thought.

In this anecdote from *The Travels of Marco Polo*, the Tartars practiced the marriage of dead children.

Travels of Marco Polo, Book I, Chapter XLIX, Pages 217–218.
Of the rules of justice observed by these people; and of an imaginary kind of marriage contracted between the deceased children of different families.

491

When one man has had a son, and another man a daughter, although both may have been dead for some years, they have a practice of contracting a marriage between their deceased children, and of bestowing the girl upon the youth. They at the same time paint upon pieces of paper human figures to represent attendants with horses and other animals, dresses of all kinds, money, and every article of furniture; and all these, together with the marriage-contract, which is regularly drawn up, they commit to the flames; in order that through the medium of the smoke (as they believe) these things may be conveyed to their children in the other world, and that they may become husband and wife in due form. After this ceremony the fathers and mothers consider themselves as mutually related, in the same manner as if a real connexion had taken place between their living children.

We can compare the "marriage of dead children" beliefs not just from the text but from personal experience. In July 1992, Meredith Sheets observed and photographed a sign on a large baptismal font replica in the South Visitor's Center, Temple Square, Salt Lake City, Utah. The sign read:

SACRED ORDINANCES ON BEHALF OF THE DEAD ARE PERFORMED FOR THOSE WHO DID NOT HAVE THE OPPORTUNITY IN THIS LIFE FOR BAPTISM AND ETERNAL MARRIAGE.

When Sheets visited Temple Square again in July 1993, the sign on the baptismal font replica had been changed, and the reference to "eternal marriage" had been removed. The reasons for hiding the quote are ripe for speculation. Perhaps the temple owners did not want the public to know about Joseph Smith's revelation that said,

All ordinances of the temple that are done for the living, including marriage, can also be done for the Dead . . .[296]

There Is More Than One God

First the Tartars and then Mormons believed in separate celestial and terrestrial gods. The Tartars also believed, as do the Mormons, that they could ascend to be united with the divinity.

> . . . each person has a tablet fixed up against a high part of the wall of his chamber, upon which is written a name, that serves to denote the high, celestial, and sublime God. . . . they have a statue which they name *Natigai* [Natigay], which they consider as the God of all terrestrial things. . . . (Marsden, 381)

Joseph Smith taught:

> I will preach on the plurality of Gods. I have selected this text for that express purpose. I wish to declare I have always and in all congregations when I have preached on the subject of the Deity, it has been the plurality of Gods. It has been preached by the Elders for fifteen years.
>
> I have always declared God to be a distinct personage, Jesus Christ a separate and distinct personage from God the Father, and that the Holy Ghost was a distinct personage and a Spirit: and these three constitute three distinct personages and three Gods. If this is in accordance with the New Testament, lo and behold! we have three Gods anyhow, and they are plural: and who can contradict it?[297]
>
> I have it from God & get over it if you can—I have a witness of the *H.G—& a test. that Paul had no allusion to the . . . text—Twice I will shew from the Heb. Bible & the 1st. word shews a plurity [sic] of Gods—& I want the apostate & learned men to come here—& prove to the contrary *an unlearned boy* must give you a little Hebrew . . . (*Holy Ghost. **Heathen God)[298]

This next story about the religion of the Tartars leads us to more areas of common beliefs. One finds that the Tartars believed in one high god of heaven and one on the earth, that there are three levels of heaven, and that one can rise or fall to a level depending on how he or she acts on Earth. We learn from the Tartars that ultimately a man can ascend to become a god himself.[299] For spiritual beliefs, this is perhaps the most controversial aspect of the Mormon religion to many outsiders: that God used to be a man and eventually became a god and that man on Earth today can become a god just like the high God.

On April 7, 1844, Smith gave a sermon at the funeral for "Elder King Follett," where he proclaimed:

> . . . you have got to learn how to be gods yourselves . . . the same as all gods have done before you, namely, by going from one small degree to another . . . from grace to grace . . . to sit in glory, as do those who sit enthroned in everlasting power.[300]

A High, Celestial, and Sublime God

As you read earlier, each Tartar had a tablet on his wall with a name of "the high, celestial, and sublime God." The Tartars had a single "high" God, and the Mormons also have a single "high" God. The Mormon high god was appointed for the Mormons by "The heads of the Gods."

According to the *History of the Church*, on June 16, 1844, the prophet Smith stated: ". . . In the beginning the head of the Gods brought forth the Gods, or as others have translated it, 'the head of the Gods called the Gods together . . .'" (HC 6:475), and "The head God organized the heavens and the earth." (HC 6:475) With reference to the one high or great Mormon God, Smith stated:

> The heads of the Gods appointed one God for us. . . . (HC 6:476)

Another of Smith's statements from the funeral sermon is:

> . . . the father to preside as the Chief or President—Jesus as the Mediator & Holy Ghost as the testator or witness . . . the Great God has a name . . . By which He will be Called which is Ahman . . .[301]

Smith most likely invented the name *Ahman* for his Great God by removing *Br* from *Brahman*. The word *Brahman* is used many times in Marsden's *Marco Polo* for the followers of *Brahma*, the high God of the Hindus who came from a certain region:

> Bramins or brahmans, originally from the province of Lac or Lar—are most honourable merchants—abhor an untruth—remarkable for continence. . . . (Marsden, p. 759)

> People are gross idolaters and addicted to sorcery. . . . (Marsden, P. 768)

> Rosaries or chaplets, the use of which is to assist the memory in counting the repetition of prayers, are employed for this purpose by followers of Brahma, Buddha or Fo, and Mahomet, as well as by part of the Christian church. (Marsden, 634 n. 1272)

The Mormon doctrine "The Rise of the Church of Christ" reads:

> Wherefore by these things we know that there is a god in heaven who is infinite & eternal, from everlasting to everlasting the same unchangable [sic] God the maker of heaven & Earth & all things that in them is & that he created man male & female & after his own image . . .[302]

Three Degrees of Heaven

Joseph Smith taught that there are three heavens or degrees of heaven:

> A man may be saved, after the judgment, in the terrestrial kingdom or in the telestial kingdom, but he can never see the celestial kingdom of God, without being born of the water and the Spirit. He may receive a glory like unto the moon . . . or a star . . . but he can never come unto Mount Zion, and unto the city of the living God, the heavenly Jerusalem, and to an innumerable company of angels . . . (HC 1:283)

Paul ascended into the third heavens, and he could understand the three principal rounds of Jacob's ladder—the telestial, the terrestrial, and the celestial glories or kingdoms . . . (HC 5:402)

Celestial Level of Heaven

The word *celestial* is found in the King James version of the Bible, and it is used several times in the writings of Marco Polo regarding the religion of the Tartars. Examples of the celestial levels of heaven are as follows:

Tartar Beliefs:
". . . these people are idolaters, and for deities, each person has a tablet fixed up against a high part of the wall of his chamber, upon which is written a name, that serves to denote the high, celestial, and sublime God . . ." (Marsden, 381)

The Mormons also believe in the same kind of high God:

. . . these are they whose bodies are celestial, which glory is that of the Son, even the glory of God, the highest of all . . .

And thus we saw the glory of the celestial, which excelleth in all things where God, even the Father, reigneth upon his throne forever and ever.[303]

Joseph Smith's teachings of April 2, 1843, differ from the Tartar religion in that in the end, those in the celestial degree of glory receive a white "seer" stone, whereas in the Tartar religion no award is given. Smith's instructions were as follows:

Then the white stone mentioned in Rev. c 2 v 17 is the Urim and Thummim whereby all things pertaining to an higher order of kingdoms even all kingdoms will be made known and a white stone is given to each of those who come into this celestial kingdom. . . .[304]

Terrestrial Level of Heaven

Joseph Smith taught that the "terrestrial" level was reserved for those who died "without the law." The bodies in the terrestrial heaven cannot go to the celestial heaven to be with God. Marco Polo observed of the Tartars that:

> They worship another likewise, named *Natigay* . . . Him they consider as the <u>divinity who presides over their terrestrial concerns</u>. . . . . (Marsden, '*Of the . . . terrestrial deities of the Tartars, and their modes of worship* . . .', 209–210,).

Some of Smith's teachings about the terrestrial level are found in the 1832 Vision "The Eyes of Our Understanding":

> And again, we saw the <u>Terrestrial world</u> . . . these are they who are of the terrestrial, whose glory differeth from that of the church of the first born, who have received the fulness of the Father, even as that of the Moon differeth from the Sun of the firmament.

> Behold, these are they who died without law . . .

> Who received not the testimony of Jesus in the flesh, but afterwards received it. . . . who received not the testimony of Jesus in the flesh, but afterwards received it: these are they who are honorable men of the earth, who were blinded by the craftiness of men . . . who are thrust down to hell: these are they who shall not be redeemed from the devil, until the last resurrection.[305]

Smith also taught that there is a god over terrestrial matters and said that it was Jesus Christ, the son of the most high God. Christ will rule in the terrestrial level of glory:

> . . . these are they who receive of the presence of the Son, but not of the fulness of the Father: wherefore, they are bodies terrestrial, and not bodies celestial . . .

I [Joseph Smith] said, Christ and the resurrected Saints will reign over the earth during the thousand years. They will not probably dwell upon the earth, but will visit it when they please, or when it is necessary to govern it. (HC 5:212,1842)

"Telestial" Level of Heaven

The *telestial* level of heaven was something new to the church members. The word *telestial* is not in the Bible or in *The Travels of Marco Polo*. However, on page 209 of *Marco Polo*, the title of Chapter XLVII begins with "*Of the celestial and terrestial deities of the Tartars . . .*" The word *terrestial* is misspelled; it should have been *terrestrial*. Using the technique that Smith employed throughout his use of Polo's work, he could have easily derived from the misspelled *terrestial* his new word *telestial*.

In the Tartar religion, a man never dies spiritually, no matter how sinful. He would simply descend into lower states without any (or very much) hope of rising to the "celestial" level of glory. This is quite similar to Joseph Smith's teachings where those in the telestial level ". . . will not be gathered with the saints . . . ." The Tartars believed that once a person has "descended" he would not be eligible for a higher level of existence:

. . . but if on the contrary, being the son of a gentleman, he has behaved unworthily, he will, in his next state, be a clown, and at length a dog; continually descending to a condition more vile than the preceding. (Marsden, p. 381)

According to Joseph Smith's revelation, which he published in the church newspaper in 1832, people placed in the Telestial level of glory will never be able to rise to the Celestial level but are like stars in the heaven compared to the Sun (celestial glory) and moon (terrestrial glory): ". . . but where God and Christ dwell they cannot come . . . ." "God" through Joseph Smith, said:

. . . for these are they who are of Paul, and of Apollos, and of Cephas: they are they who say, there are some of one and some of annother [sic]; some of

Christ; and some of John; and some of Moses . . . last of all, these all are they who will not be gathered with the saints, to be caught up into the church of the first born, and received into the cloud; these are they who are liars, and sorcerers, and adulterers, and whoremungers [sic], and whosoever loveth and maketh a lie: these are they who suffer the wrath of Almighty God until the fulness of times, when Christ shall have subdued all enemies . . .[306]

Man Can Ascend through Various Levels to Reach Godhead or Be United with Divinity

The Tartar belief for becoming gods is:

If he . . . has conducted himself worthily and decently, he will be re-born, in the first instance . . . *thus continually ascending in the scale of existence, until he be united to the divinity.* (Marsden, p. 381)

The belief of ascension of a human to become a god was preached by Joseph Smith Jr. in June of 1844. He said that God is merely an exalted man, and that this was the great secret of God:

God himself *was once as we are now, and is an exalted man*, and sits enthroned in yonder heavens! That is the great secret. . . . I say, if you were to see him today, you would see him like a man in form—like yourselves in all the person, image, and very form as a man. . . . It is the first principle of the gospel to know for a certainty the character of God, and to know that we may converse with Him as one man converses with another, and that *He was once a man like us; yea, that God himself, the Father of us all, dwelt on an earth, the same as Jesus Christ himself did* . . . (HC 6:305)

Smith preached the Tartar belief of "*continually ascending in the scale of existence*" most clearly when he said:

. . . and you have got to learn how to be gods yourselves, and to be kings and priests to God, the same as all gods have done before you . . . *by going*

. . . from a small capacity to a great one . . . to sit in glory as do those who sit enthroned in everlasting power. (HC 6:306)

He also wrote, on June 16, 1844, regarding how to become a God in the celestial kingdom:

Go and read the vision in the Book of Covenants. There is clearly illustrated glory upon glory—one glory of the sun, another glory of the moon, and a glory of the stars; and as one star differeth from another star in glory, even so do they of the telestial world differ in glory, and every man who reigns in celestial glory is a God to his dominions. (HC 6:477)

Gods Can Have Wives and Children

The Tartar god *Natigay* had wives and children:

They Worship another likewise, named *Natigay*. . . . To this deity they associate a wife and children. . . . (Marsden, 209)

They give him a wife and children, and worship him. . . . (Marsden, 381)

The Mormons believe in the same concept of gods—that they are married with children! We learned earlier that Mormons believe they can become gods, and now we learn in context that when they are gods, their families will be together:

. . . if a man marry a wife by my word . . . and it shall be said unto them, ye shall come forth in the first resurrection . . . shall be of full force when they are out of the world, and they shall pass by the angels, and the Gods . . . Then they shall be Gods.[307]

A question may be asked-"Will mothers have their children in eternity?" Yes! Yes! Mothers, you have your children: for they shall have eternal life, for their debt is paid. . . . It will never grow; it will still be the child, in the same precise form as it appeared before it died out of its mother's arms, but possessing all the intelligence of God. Children dwell in the mansions of glory and exercise power, but appear in the same form as when on earth.[308]

Blood Atonement

Blood atonement was not a Tartar practice, but Marco Polo described it. In the province of Malabar, the people had a horrible custom for penance by condemned criminals:

> The following extraordinary custom prevails at this place. When a man who has committed a crime, for which he has been tried and condemned to suffer death, upon being led to execution, declares his willingness to sacrifice himself in honour of some particular idol, his relations and friends immediately place him in a kind of chair, and deliver to him twelve knives of good temper and well sharpened. In this manner they carry him about the city, proclaiming with a loud voice, that this brave man is about to devote himself to a voluntary death, from motives of zeal for the worship of the idol. Upon reaching the place where the sentence of the law would have been executed, he snatches up two of the knives, and crying out, "I devote myself to death in honour of such an idol," hastily strikes one of them into each thigh, then one into each arm, two into the belly, and two into the breast. Having in this manner thrust all the knives but one into different parts of his body, repeating at every wound the words that have been mentioned, he plunges the last of them into his heart, and immediately expires. . . . (Marsden, 633)

Joseph Smith's "revelations" introduced the idea of suffering a physical death for spiritual crimes.

> . . . I say unto you, if a man marry a wife . . . and they are sealed by the Holy Spirit . . . and he or She Shall Commit any sin or transgression of the new and everlasting covenant whatever, and all manner of blasphemies,

and if they commit no murder . . . yet they Shall come forth in the first resurrection, and enter into their exaltation; but *they Shall be destroyed in the flesh, and Shall be delivered unto the buffetings of Satan unto the day of redemption, said the Lord God.*[309]

Blood Atonement as Taught by Joseph Smith Jr. Reported by Joseph Fielding Smith Jr.

Joseph Fielding Smith Jr., the grandson of Hyrum Smith, became president of the Utah-based Latter-day Saints Church. Although what follows was published after Joseph Smith's death, Fielding Smith informed the believers that his great-uncle Joseph's teaching on blood atonement was still alive as church doctrine. He wrote:

> Joseph Smith taught that there were certain sins so grievous that man may commit, that they will place the transgressors beyond the power of the atonement of Christ. If these offenses are committed, then the blood of Christ will not cleanse them from their sins even though they repent. *Therefore their only hope is to have their own blood shed to atone, as far as possible, in their behalf. This is scriptural doctrine, and is taught in all the standard works of the Church . . .*[310]

Melchizedek, the Holy Priesthood

To organize their new church, the Smiths created an ecclesiastical structure with distinct purposes and privileges for church members. They called the privileges "priesthoods," and only male church members could receive such honors. Even today, Mormon women cannot join the priesthood. The Smiths borrowed concepts from the Bible and put ink to paper by developing a story about how Jesus had personally approved the priesthoods for Joseph Jr. We begin with an account of the prophet's hearing the voice of Jesus with a message for the church. By 1835 Smith expanded the revelation to include the apostles "Peter, and James and John," who were sent to ordain the church and also included himself within the prophecy:

Listen to the Voice of Christ.
A Commandment to the Church of Christ,
Given in Harmony, Pennsylvania, September 4, 1830.
Listen to the voice of Jesus Christ, your Lord, your God and your Redeemer, whose word is quick and powerful. . . . which John I have sent unto you, my servants, Joseph Smith, jr. and Oliver Cowdery, to ordain you unto this first priesthood which you have received, that you might be called and ordained even as Aaron . . . And also with Peter, and James, and John, whom I have sent unto you, by whom I have ordained you and confirm you to be apostles . . . unto whom I have committed the keys of my kingdom, and a dispensation of the gospel for the last times.[311]

Smith discussed the priesthood with more holy statements directly from God to the church, which were published in the 1835 "Covenants and Commandments of the Lord."

Hearken, O ye people of my church, saith the voice of him who dwells on high, and whose eyes are upon all men . . .
Section III. On Priesthood. There are, in the church, two priesthoods, namely: the Melchizedek, and the Aaronic . . . Melchizedek was such a great high priest: before his day it was called *the holy priesthood, after the order of the Son of God.* . . . The Melchizedek priesthood holds the right of presidency, and has power and authority over all the offices in the church . . . to administer in spiritual things . . . The power . . . of the lessor, or Aaronic priesthood is . . . to administer in outward ordinances . . . agreeably to the covenants and commandments.[312]

In *The Book of Mormon*, Smith's story about Melchizedek did not come from "him who dwells on high." It actually was copied from a story about a Tartar New Year festival described by Marco Polo. "Melchizedek" replaced "Kublai khan" as the master of ceremonies. The first comparisons track at least thirty-five words or phrases from *The Travels of Marco Polo* that were plagiarized in the *Book of Mormon* section "Book of Alma," where the high priest Melchizedek is described as a king during biblical times.

The Nephite record discusses the priesthood soon after the description of Nephite money (copied from the Tartars, remember?). A debate begins between the prophet Amulek and a certain businessman named Zeezrom, who, along with a number of Nephite lawyers, was "expert in the devises of the Devil." Amulek's speech to the Nephites is another mishmash from the New and Old Testaments, which causes Zeezrom to "tremble" and repent. The prophet Alma takes over the preaching, and in chapter ten the story becomes Alma's teaching about the "holy order of this High Priesthood," which you will see in the table below. It is more sophisticated plagiarism than many of the other stories in *The Book of Mormon*; therefore we added highlighting in the table and show a keyword list after the text. The percentages into the text for these two stories match beautifully with a difference of less than one percent:

Marco Polo: 43.39 to 43.78%
Book of Mormon: 44.05 to 44.22%
Difference: 0.56 to 0.44%

Travels of Marco Polo "Of the White-feast held on the first day . . . of February"	*Book of Mormon* "holy order of this High Priesthood"
(43.78%, n. 619, p. 331)	(44.05%, Alma 10, p. 259, lines 9–12)
The superstition of considering	. . . sanctified by the Holy Ghost,
	having their garments made
white,	white,
which is naturally the emblem of	
purity,	being pure
as having an influence in	and
producing good fortune,	spotless before God . . . there
has been	
very prevalent	were many,

Travels of Marco Polo "Of the White-feast held on the first day . . . of February"	*Book of Mormon* "holy order of this High Priesthood"
throughout the world;	exceedingly great many,
	which were made pure . . .
	(44.22%, p. 260, lines 15–23)
	Now this Melchizedek was a king
as black, on the contrary, from its	over the land of Salem; and his
connexion with	people had waxed strong in
impurity, darkness,	iniquity and abominations;
and the grave, has been thought the	yea, they had all gone astray: they were full of
forboder of ill-luck,	all manner of wickedness;
and become the type of sadness.	but Melchizedek having exercised mighty faith, and received the office of High Priesthood, according to the holy order of God,
	[(p. 260, lines 15–23)
. . . Kublaï,	Now this Melchizedek
although he adopted most of the	was a king over the land
civil institutions of	of Salem; and
his . . . subjects,	his people . . .]
did not,	did
and possibly could not, even if he had wished it,	
oblige	preach repentance unto
his own people	his people.
	—And behold,
to change their ancient	they did repent;
superstitions.	and
[". . . he adopted most of the civil institutions of	Melchizedek did establish peace in the land

Travels of Marco Polo "Of the White-feast held on the first day . . . of February"	Book of Mormon "holy order of this High Priesthood"
his . . . subjects . . .	
	in his days; therefore he was called the Prince of **Peace** . . .
	(p. 260, lines 4–7):
It accordingly appears that	. . . yea, humble yourselves even as the people
during his reign	in the days of Melchizedek,
at least, and probably	who was also a High Priest after this same order which I have spoken, who also
so long as his dynasty held the throne,	took upon him the High Priesthood forever.
	(44.05%, P.259, lines 6–7)
	. . . therefore they were called
The **festival**	after this **holy order,** and were
of the New year was	sanctified, and their
celebrated in white dresses	garments were washed white . . .
	(p. 260, lines 7–9)
	And it was this same
and white horses were amongst the most acceptable	Melchizedek to whom Abraham paid tithes;
	yea even our father Abraham paid
presents to the emperor.	tithes of one tenth part of all he possessed.
(43.65%, p. 330, lines 3–12)	(44.22%, p. 260, lines 30–43)
	And it came to pass that when
. . . a person of high dignity . . .	Alma had said
	these words unto them,
a great prelate,	he
rises	stretched forth his hand unto them

506

Travels of Marco Polo "Of the White-feast held on the first day . . . of February"	Book of Mormon "holy order of this High Priesthood"
	and
and says with a loud voice:	cried with a mighty voice, saying,
"Bow down and do reverence;"	Now is the time to repent,
when instantly all bend their bodies until their foreheads touch the floor. Again	for the day of salvation draweth nigh; yea, and
the prelate cries:	the voice of the Lord,
"God bless our lord,	by the mouth of angels, doth
and long preserve him in the	declare it unto all nations;
	yea, doth declare it, that they may have
	glad tidings of great joy;
enjoyment of felicity*[1]"	yea, and he doth sound these glad tidings
The people again reply:	among all his people,
"God grant it."	yea,
(43.52%, p. 329, lines 3–6)	
. . . embracing each other with demonstrations of	
	[See Above: ". . . that
joy and festivity . . . through the coming year . . .	they may have glad tidings of great joy . . ."]
(43.39%, P. 328, Lines 2–13): . . . it is customary for the Grand khan,	
as well as all	even to them
who are	that are . . .
subject to him,	
in their several countries. . . .	upon the face of the earth . . .
inhabitants of all	our being wanderers
the provinces and kingdoms who hold	in a strange

Travels of Marco Polo "Of the White-feast held on the first day . . . of February"	Book of Mormon "holy order of this High Priesthood"
lands	land;
or rights of jurisdiction under the Grand *khan*,	therefore
send him valuable presents . . .	we are thus highly favored,
that his majesty may experience throughout the year,	for we have these
uninterrupted felicity* . . .	glad tidings declared unto us in
[all the provinces and kingdoms]	all parts of our vineyard.

¹*felicity* means happiness, blessedness, or *joy*.

The keywords pulled out of the two stories are compelling evidence of how the Grand khan's and his New Year festival ended up as the High Priesthood of Melchizedek in the "Book of Alma."

	Marco Polo (pp. 328–331)	Book of Mormon (pp. 259–260)
1	superstition	the Holy Ghost
2	white	white
3	purity	pure
4	very prevalent	were many
5	throughout the world	exceedingly great many
6	impurity, darkness	iniquity and abominations
7	*Kublaï*	Melchizedek
8	his subjects	his people
9	did not oblige	did preach repentance unto
10	his people	his people
11	to change their ancient superstitions	they did repent
12	during his reign	in the days of Melchizedek
13	so long as his dynasty held the throne	took upon him the High Priest- hood forever

	Marco Polo (pp. 328–331)	Book of Mormon (pp. 259–260)
14	celebrated in white dresses	garments were washed white
15	white horses acceptable presents	Melchizedek to whom Abraham paid tithes
16	presents to the emperor	one tenth
17	Mungals,	having their
18	the use of white	garments made white
19	a person of high dignity	Alma
20	a great prelate, rises	he stretched forth his hand
21	and says with	and cried with
22	a loud voice	a mighty voice
23	Bow down and do reverence	Now is the time to repent
24	the prelate cries:	the voice of the Lord
25	God bless our lord	angels, doth declare
26	enjoyment of felicity	glad tidings of great joy
27	people again reply	among all his people
28	as well as all	even to them
29	who are	that are
30	in their several countries	scatter abroad upon the face of the earth
31	inhabitants of all	our being wanderers
32	lands	land
33	send him valuable presents	we are thus highly favored
34	uninterrupted felicity	glad tidings declared unto us
35	all the provinces and kingdoms	all parts of our vineyard

The Aaronic Priesthood

Imagine this: in August of 1830, about four months after the whole *Book of Mormon* went public, Jesus Christ visited Joseph Smith Jr. in Upstate

New York to discuss what Joseph should do next. Jesus told Joseph, ". . . unto the first Priesthood which you have received, that you might be called and ordained even as Aaron (Aaronic Priesthood)." (HC 1:107). Jesus also sent *John the Baptist* for a follow-up meeting. They decided that the Aaronic priesthood was to be subservient to the Melchizedek priesthood. This Aaronic "minor priesthood" included those saintly men who performed work as teachers, bishops, deacons, or priests.

A connection exists between the Aaronic priesthood story at 36.39 percent in *The Book of Mormon* and a *Marco Polo* story at 36.24 percent, the difference being only 0.15 percent. In the Bible, Aaron is the older brother of Moses, but in *The Book of Mormon*, Aaron is the son of Mosiah. The Smiths used Marco Polo to introduce *The Book of Mormon*'s Aaron. This connection is shown below, first with keywords because of the significance of how they both follow the same sequence, meaning the Mormon scripture follows the Polo version sentence by sentence. On the Polo side, there are four prophets: Jesus, Mahomet, Moses, and Sogomombar-kan (Buddha), and on the Mormon side there are also four prophets: Ammon, Aaron, Omer, and Himni. The Smiths replaced the second-listed prophet Mahomet with the Nephite prophet Aaron.

36.24%; *Travels of Marco Polo* "Of the return of the Grand khan to the city of Kanbalu," Page 274.	36.39–36.56%; *Book of Mormon* "Sons of Mosiah" Page 214, Lines 38–40
"There are	And the
four great Prophets	four of them
who are reverenced and worshipped by the	were the sons of Mosiah:
different classes of mankind.	and their names were
The Christians regard	
Jesus Christ as their divinity;	Ammon, and
the Saracens, Mahomet;	Aaron,
the Jews, Moses;	and Omer,
and the idolaters,	and

36.24%; *Travels of Marco Polo* "Of the return of the Grand khan to the city of Kanbalu," Page 274.	36.39–36.56%; *Book of Mormon* "Sons of Mosiah" Page 214, Lines 38–40
Sogomombar-kan,	Himni:
the most eminent amongst their idols."	these were the names of the sons of Mosiah.
	(36.56%, p. 215, lines 1–9):
he (Grand *khan*) assigned to	after the
Nicolo and Maffio Polo,	sons of Mosiah . . .
when upon the occasion of	
sending them	returned
as his ambassadors	
to the Pope (father),	to their father, the king,
they ventured to address	and desired of him that he would
a few words to him	grant unto them,
	that they might . . . go up to the land of Nephi . . .
on the	that they might impart
subject of Christianity.	the word of God
	to their brethren, the Lamanites . . .
(36.24%, p. 274, line 6)	(36.73%, p. 216, line 7)
. . . the (Grand *khan*)	Now king Mosiah . . .
commanded all the Christians to attend him, and to	
bring with them their Book,	took the records
	which were engraven upon the plates of brass, and also the plates of
which contains	Nephi, according to
the four Gospels of the	the commandments of God,
Evangelists.	and after having translated and caused to be written the records which were on the plates of gold, which had been found by the people of Limhi. . . .

36.24%; *Travels of Marco Polo* "Of the return of the Grand khan to the city of Kanbalu," Page 274.	36.39–36.56%; *Book of Mormon* "Sons of Mosiah" Page 214, Lines 38–40
(p. 275, ln. 32)	And now he translated them
"... whilst the idolaters, who	
by means of	by the means of
their profound art can effect such wonders ..."	those two stones which was fastened into the rims of a bow.
You are witnesses that their idols have the faculty of speech, and	... and they have been kept and preserved by the hand of the Lord, that he
predict to them	should discover
whatever is required.	to every creature which should possess the land,
(line 28): "the idolaters declare	
that what they exhibit is performed through their own sanctity and	the iniquities and abominations of his people; and
the influence of their idols."	whosoever has these things,
	is called seer ...

Can there be any question about whether Melchizedek is Kublai Khan or that the four great prophets in *The Travels of Marco Polo* are the same four sons of Mosiah? At a fraction of a percent difference between the locations in the text, we think not.

Regardless of his deeds, Joseph Smith's religious beliefs, which he copied from the Eastern shamanistic religion of the Tartars, live on in Latter-day Saints temples and churches around the world, where Smith is heralded as a religious prophet second only to Jesus Christ.

22

SPECTRES AND VISIONS

I n the 1832 memoir of his extraordinary childhood, Joseph Smith claimed that back in 1822,

> ... an angel of the Lord came an stood before me an it was night and he called me by name and he said the Lord had forgiven me my sins and he revealed unto me that in the Town of Manchester Ontario County N.Y. there was plates of gold upon which there was engravings which was engraven by Maroni & his fathers the servants of the living God in ancient days and deposited by the commandments of God and kept by the power thereof.[313]

Over the years Smith had revised his tale about the vision enough times until, in 1838, he finally made the serious effort to document his early visions of God, Jesus, and the angel Moroni. Instead of describing the visit of a single heavenly visitor, the 1838 transcription includes two personages: God the Father *and* Jesus.

How would you like to play the role of plagiarist this time? Pretend to be Joseph Smith Jr. for a few minutes. You need to invent a story that details your early visions, but its specifics have to be so obscure that no one will suspect a fraud. Your task: to page through various reference books and find inspiration for your spiritual visions.

Imagine you are seated at the Smith family kitchen table. The source-books you used to create *The Book of Mormon* years ago are spread out in front of you once again. You have a quill pen and blank paper. Your plan is to read as many pages as necessary and then combine the material, just as you had done with your wildly successful *Book of Mormon*.

The first book you crack is James Duncan's 1825 publication of *Modern Traveller, Arabia.*[314] You used this resource to create "The First Book of Nephi" and "The Book of Abraham," which pinpointed *Kolob* as the planet where God lives. You stop at pages fifty-two and fifty-three, where the author discusses the confused state of Christianity in Arabia and laments the resulting rise of the "Koreishite imposter" (Figures 106 and 107).

Duncan's book does not have much to report about visions, spirits, or even strange events. Reading all the way to page 326, however, you read about a phenomenon that occurs at sunset along the Arabian coast. It's the same material you used for "The First Book of Nephi," but you mark the page nonetheless; it might be a good idea to tie some parts of your new writing to visions described by the ancient Nephites (Figure 108).

So far, so good. Your next resource is John Ranking's book about the Mongols invading Peru and Mexico with elephants, published in 1828.[315] You copied from this book for "The Book of Ether," and now you recall something in it about a woman having a vision with bright light in her bedroom. You flip through the book, and . . . there it is! On pages 177 to 179, in a footnote. It's about the queen mother of Genghis Khan having a vision. It continues with a footnote about visiting a city with engravings on stone, including some about "great personages, or kings" (Figures 109, 110, and 111).

That sounds interesting. You keep the page open on the table.

Pushing those books aside and continuing to look for more material, you remember that you used the tabor drum from John Pinkerton's *General Collection* volume[316] about Lapland to draw the runic symbols and pass them off to the impressionable Martin Harris as "reformed Egyptian." This

anity, were, Hamyar, Ghassân, Rabia, Taghlab, Bah-
rah, Tonouch, part of the tribes of Tay and Koddâah,
the inhabitants of Najrân (Nedjeraun), and the Arabs
of Heirah......The Jacobites had two bishops subject
to their *mafriân*, or metropolitan of the East : óne
was called the bishop of the Arabs absolutely, whose
seat was for the most part at Akula ; * the other had
the title of the Bishop of the Scenite Arabs, of the
tribe of Thaaleb, in Hira, whose seat was in that
city. The Nestorians had but one bishop, who pre-
sided over both these dioceses of Hira and Akula, and
was immediately subject to their patriarch." Whatever place be meant by Akula, the see was evidently
in Arabian Irak ; and that of Heirah could only include the western shore of the Persian Gulf. Thus,
in fact, the larger part of the peninsula does not
appear to have been under the ecclesiastical rule of
either Jacobite or Nestorian bishop.† How is it that
we do not read of a bishop of Saba or of Saana, of
Mascat or of Mekka ? A bishop of *Tephra*, which
Sale supposes to be Dhafâr, is mentioned as disputing
with the Jews of Hamyar ; and Nedjeraun is also
said to have been an episcopal see. These bishops
we presume to have been of the orthodox communion,
if they existed ; but Gregentius, bishop of Tephra,
might be a foreigner, possibly an Abyssinian prelate.

At all events, it is admitted that the state of the
eastern churches, more especially of the Arabian, were

---

* Abulfaragius makes Akula to be Kûfah; others make it a different town near Bagdad.—See SALE.

† Gibbon says, " The sects whom they (the Catholics) oppressed, successively retired beyond the limits of the Roman empire. The Marcionites and Manicheans dispersed their fantastic
opinions and apocryphal gospels ; the churches of Yemen, and the
princes of Hira and Ghassan were instructed in the purer creed of
the Jacobite and Nestorian bishops."

Figure 106. Duncan, *Modern Traveller, Arabia,* 52

in a deplorable state of declension and ignorance when the Koreishite impostor first conceived the bold project of uniting the jarring creeds of Jew, Christian, and Magian, in a new religion adapted to the clime and to the people. " If," says Sale, " we look into the ecclesiastical historians even from the third century, we shall find the Christian world to have then had a very different aspect from what some authors have represented ; and so far from being endued with active grace, zeal, and devotion, and established within itself with purity of doctrine, union, and firm profession of the faith, — that, on the contrary, what by the ambition of the clergy, and what by drawing the abstrusest niceties into controversy, and dividing and subdividing about them into endless schisms and contentions, they had so destroyed that peace, love, and charity from among them, which the Gospel was given to promote, and, instead thereof, continually provoked each other to that malice, rancour, and every evil work, that they had lost the whole substance of their religion, while they thus eagerly contended for their own imaginations concerning it ; and in a manner quite drove Christianity out of the world, by those very controversies in which they disputed with each other about it. In these dark ages it was, that most of those superstitions and corruptions we now justly abhor in the church of Rome, were not only broached, but established, which gave great advantages to the propagation of Mohammedism. The worship of saints and images, in particular, was then arrived at such a scandalous pitch, that it even surpassed whatever is now practised among the Romanists.

" After the Nicene council, the eastern church was engaged in perpetual controversies, and torn to pieces by the disputes of the Arians, Sabellians, Nes-

---

Figure 107. Duncan, *Modern Traveller, Arabia,* 53

326   ARABIA.

for the whole year, though the prevailing one is generally from the same point in which the monsoon blows
in the lower part of the gulf. Above Cosseir, an extraordinary change takes place; from thence to Suez, the
wind blows for rather more than eight months from
the N.W. At Mocha, during the prevalence of the
S.E. wind, a thick haze covers the opposite coast;
but the moment the north-wester commences, the
opposite mountains and islands gradually appear.
The high land of Assab is visible from Mocha,
although its distance was ascertained to be seventy
miles, by a set of cross bearings taken from the
island of Perim. This proves that there is a great
degree of refraction in the atmosphere, of which indeed we had still more positive proof, by the appearance of several other headlands at the same time, and
which we knew were much too low to be seen directly
at the distance they actually were. A very singular
phenomenon also occurred, which has been taken
notice of by the ancients;—the sun set like a pillar of
fire, having totally lost its usual round form,—a
splendid testimony in favour of Agatharchides, who
says, the sun rose like a pillar of fire.

Figure 108. Duncan, *Modern Traveller, Arabia*, 326

These claims of descent were occasionally renewed. " Those who were most interested in the advancement of Genghis Khan, have had the insolence to make him pass for the Son of God; but his mother, more modest, said only that he was the son of the Sun. But not being bold enough to aver that she was personally beloved by that glorious luminary, she pretended to derive this fabulous honor from Buzengir, his ninth predecessor; and his partisans reported, that Buzengir was the son of the Sun. His mother, having been left a widow, lived a retired life; but some time after the death of her husband, Douyan-Byan, she was suspected to be pregnant. The deceased husband's relations forced her to appear before the chief judge of the tribe, for this crime. She boldly defended herself, by declaring that no man had known her; but that one day, lying negligently upon her bed, a light appeared in her dark room, the brightness of which blinded her, and that it penetrated three times into her body; and that if she

Figure 109. Ranking, Conquest of Peru, Mexico, 177

brought not three sons into the world, she would submit to the most cruel torments. The three sons were born, and the princess was esteemed a saint.

Buzengir was married to Alancoua, from whom Genghis Khan was descended in the ninth degree.

The Moguls regard this fable as a sacred truth; and are persuaded that, by this miracle, a prince should one day be born, to avenge God on mankind for the injustice committed by them on earth; and they believed Genghis Khan to be that prince."—*Petis de la Croix, Book* i. *Ch.* i.

Figure 110. Ranking, Conquest of Peru, Mexico, 178

northern, brought all the divine benefit of his presence. We find allusions to the Sun and Lion in the capital of the Moguls.—" We reached Taimingzing, (Oloug-yourt), in Mongolia, an old ruined city. There are in it two towers, or turrets; the largest was an octagon, very high, the front of which was built with brick. About ten fathoms from the ground, there was, on each of the eight sides, stones placed, on which were carved several histories. Upon some of them are exhibited great personages, or kings, as big as the life, sitting with their feet under them, and attendants at each side of them. Others show us several figures, which seem to represent queens folding their hands together, with their servants on each side; the queens having crowns on their heads, and the others being adorned with *rays* or lustres. Other parts represent warriors in the Chinese manner, and the king, bare-headed, in the middle, with a sceptre in his hand. All the by-standers have hideous diabolical visages. A great many stone statues, as large as life, of men, idols, great stone *lions*, and tortoises of an uncommon largeness, were lying in the city. The proportion of many of the images is so exactly observed, that they are like the performances of European masters.—*Isbrandt's Ides in Harris, Vol.* ii. *p.* 937.

Figure 111. Ranking, *Conquest of Peru, Mexico*, 179

book is from your set that was published in Philadelphia. The Laplanders used a lot of magic, so you'll see if Mr. Pinkerton included anything else you can use. Browsing through the book, you find a couple of stories about Laplander visions in the record of Mr. Leems's chapter. You read the pages and see if this book has what you need (Figures 112, 113, and 114).

CHAP. XXI.....OF THE MAGIC ARTS OF THE LAPLANDERS, EXERCISED BY MEANS OF RUNIC SYMBOLS, FLIES: IN THE CURE OF DISORDERS BY MEANS OF THE JUOIGEN, OR A CERTAIN MAGIC SONG, AND IN THE RESTITUTION OF THINGS TAKEN BY THEFT.

IT is my intention in this chapter, agreeably to its title, to speak of the magic arts of the Laplanders, by means of Runic symbols; yet the reader kindly will pardon me

Figure 112. Pinkerton, *Voyages and Travels*, Vol. 1, 469

ACCOUNT OF DANISH LAPLAND BY LEEMS. 471

They further confessed, that while they fastened three knots on a linen towel in the name of the devil, and had spit on them, &c. they called the name of him they doomed to destruction. One confessed that she had raised a tempest, by means of wind she had shut up

Figure 113. Pinkerton, *Voyages and Travels*, Vol. 1, 471

As they related, Satan appeared to them under a variety of unufual and moft horrible appearances: one time like a black man, without a head; at another like a tall man, clothed in black, and a horned forehead; now as a rough and horned man, and afterwards as a black man, whofe knees were horned, his hands and feet defended with nails, and his hair and beard black: another time he took the fhape of a man with large and burning eyes, his hands black and covered with hair, and with a flame of fire coming from his mouth; then in the likenefs of a cat, handling them from their feet to their mouth, and counting their teeth; and laftly, in the fhape of a dog, a little bird, and a crow.

On their relation, the devil, when they are dedicating themfelves to his fervice, impreffes on them a certain fign, as on his flaves: he is faid to have laid hold of the arm of one in fuch a manner that blood would flow from it; to have bitten the left arm of another; to have marked the left thigh with his nails to a third, and to have torn the left knee of a fourth with his talons.

That they fhould be more ready and eafy to enter into league and amity with him, he affigns various innocent and agreeable names, as they fay; fuch as Chriftian, Chriftopher, Jacob, Zacharias, Peter, Samuel, Mark, Angel of Light, Dominic, Abraham, Ifaac, John, Martin, Olaus, Giermund, Afmodus, Frufius, Peace, and Saclumbus.

It is true that all thefe and more the witches had confeffed on trial, and to this confeffion they were properly brought at the ftake; but their witchcraft for the greateft part confifted, in my opinion, in fancy, in imaginings, and in dreams. It is even probable

VOL. I.   3 P

Figure 114. Pinkerton, *Voyages and Travels*, Vol. 1, 473

Those stories of the devil and magic arts may come in handy. Next is something eminently useful: a vision by a Laplander about meeting an angel (Figures 115 and 116).

CHAP. XXII.—*On the various Superstitions of the Laplanders.*

THAT the Laplanders were formerly addicted to a variety of superstitions is sufficiently well known. With some Thursday was kept holy; at least it was thought impious to handle wool on that day. Almost all held Saturday, some Friday as holidays, calling this latter *Fasto-Beive*, that is the day of fasting above the rest.

A maritime Laplander of the name of Peter Peterson, dwelling in one of the bays of west Finmark, and parish of Kielvig, commonly called Smorfiord, told me that when he once went out to hunt hares on a Saturday, and was from fatigue seated on the ground, that a spectre with a human visage and dark garment, appeared to him, asking him what he did there, and on his answering that he came to hunt hares, which he intended to give to his priest, the spectre replied, what do you think that hares taken on the Saturday, which should be observed with the greatest veneration, can be acceptable to your priest? And then subjoined in caution, that he should carefully guard against violating Saturday, or any other holy day for the future, by any profane exercise. He added that from this profanation of the ancient festivals, that the wild beasts, birds, and fishes, abhorring and detesting the impiety of irreligious men, quitting their haunts, had fled away and hastened into other countries. That the same spectre, which hitherto presented itself in ragged garments, had soon after appeared to him in a more sumptuous habit, addressing him in words of this kind: you will sacrifice a cow to me, when this is done, the sea, the air, and earth will bring forth again fishes, fowl, and beasts. When this conversation was ended, the Laplander, you will suppose in consternation and disorder, returned home, sat a little, but soon drew his knife in a rage, and in the midst of these agitations of mind and body fell like to a dying man to the ground. His servants faithfully attended on him under this loss of his understanding and senses, striving now and then to awaken him, by slight blows, but in vain. Meantime the apparition which appeared to him in hunting, presented itself to him in his vision, using these words: you will never recover from this disease, unless you sacredly promise, when you get well, that you will, with due right sacrifice a cow to me. The unhappy man made this promise, and immediately awoke from his trance, but so weak that he could not walk; and as he fancied even still to see the spectre walking up and down before him, he cried out with a loud voice to those present to help him, and drive off the spectre left he should rush in upon him. Restored at last to himself, he sincerely laid open all he saw and heard, gravely and severely injoining, that none of his people should attempt to profane the Saturday, or any other day that was sacred and festive. He ended here, and instantly recited the Lord's Prayer, and part of the catechism. On the next day, this said Laplander was visited by a great many who had accidentally heard these matters, to whom he gave a sincere explanation of all that happened to him, and attempted to persuade them to bring back and restore Saturday, and all the other festivals of old, which through time were brought into disuse, and should for that purpose sacrifice lambs in order that the former plenty with which the country abounded should be restored. Some obeyed his monitions, while others took the whole vision for a mere illusion and juggle of the malign spirit.

Figure 115. Pinkerton, *Voyages and Travels*, Vol. 1, 481

For my part, what to think of this vifion, whether it may be true or falfe, I leave to perfons of refleƈtion to determine. This at leaft I can fuggeft, that the Laplander to whom it happened was a fimple and honeft man, free from fraud of any kind. Be-fides, when it is remembered tnat the infernal fpirit can change himfelf into a thou-fand forms, it was eafy for him, who did not fcruple to tempt the fon of God, in whom were hidden fuch treafures of wifdom, thus to attempt and circumvent with his wiles, a poor fimple man, incredibly weak and helplefs in himfelf, that he might lead him with others out of the true way to his deftruƈtion. -

It was a cuftom with them folemnly to keep the Nativity of Chrift, and the facred days of the holy Virgin. A Laplander of the coaft from a bay in the parifh of Alten, called *Lerrets-Fiorden*, of the name of Andrew Peterfon related a certain objeƈt had pre-fented itfelf to him, when once he was bringing a load of hay, from the fhed called Loaawe, on which we treated more at large in another place, as fodder for the cattle, on which according to the old ftyle the Chriftmas was to be celebrated. The ftory is thus. When overcome with fatigue, the Laplander had fat down on his way, he heard a hifs-ing noife three times repeated, on which in difmay he exclaimed, O God come to my affiftance I pray you! He rofe inftantly on this, and laying afide, or diffembling his fears, he haftened home, but on his way addreffed by a clear fhrill voice; ftop friend, I wifh to fpeak a few words with you, on which he ftopped, and turning about he perceived a figure oppofite to him of human fhape, in a fplendid drefs feverely reproving him, becaufe on that day, on which the feftival of Chrift had fallen, he was not afhamed to undertake fuch a bufinefs, ferioufly affirming himfelf to be the meffenger of God, fent from heaven for this purpofe, to inftruƈt him and others, that the Na-tivity of Chrift, and other holydays old ftile, were to be kept holy, and that the innova-tion of violating this, as well as other feftivals was rafhly introduced, and that fuch an inftitution was merely human, and therefore of no authority and obligation: that Thurfday from twelve o'clock to evening, and alfo Saturday were to be religioufly ob-ferved, and that the reafon of the diftrefs of grain, and other calamities with which men are affliƈted, is chiefly to be found in that irreligious profanation of ancient fefti-vals. He fpoke and inftantly difappeared in air. The Laplander haftened home as faft as he could, but before he came there his fpeech failed him, and he fell as if lifelefs to the ground, and no doubt would have died in that fituation, had not fome perfons been at hand, who feeing the danger of the man, took him home to his cot, after lift-ing him up juft dead in their arms. After remaining fome time in this ftate he awoke, related what happened, and ferioufly admonifhed his friends, according to the mandate of the angel who appeared to him, to be obfervant of all the old feftivals, particularly Thurfdays and Saturdays, all of which fhould be facredly and religioufly revered. Let the reader make his own refleƈtions on this ftory as on the former.

The day before Chriftmas the eating of meat was forbidden. A young Laplander told me that on attempting to eat a piece of meat, that he had taken from off the fire, he was not only reproved by his father, but the meat was taken even out of his mouth by him, after he was feverely chaftifed for attempting to eat it.

The evenings preceding the birth of the Saviour, and the feaft of the Virgin Mary old ftyle, were alfo fafts; the one for the good education of boys, the other in honour of the *Joulo-Gadze*, or affembly of the Yules of whom we fpoke in Chapter XIX., on the gods of the Laplanders. On the birth of Chrift it was a cuftom, that the women fhould pile up boiled meats of various kinds in their aprons, and fhould carry them to the cow-houfe to be hung up in it for three days, and on the third day to return, folemnly to confume the provifions they had laid up. It was alfo a cuftom to fet food on the fame day before the crows.

4   For

Figure 116. Pinkerton, *Voyages and Travels*, Vol. 1, 482

That looks like a treasure trove of visions! Lots of spectres, action, and religion. You pick up your quill pen and get started. You need to keep track of what was copied from where. Phrases from James Duncan's *Modern Traveller, Arabia* you will tag with a star "*". If text comes from John Ranking's story of the queen of the Tartars, you will use a plus sign "+". For quotes from page 481 of Pinkerton, you'll use parentheses "()" and material from page 482 you'll enclose in brackets "[]". You won't mark extracted quotes from other pages in Pinkerton's *Account of Danish Lapland by Leems* because those are easy to remember.

You need to build a framework for the vision. What circumstances surround the event? You really like the idea of various religions being in chaos. You can elevate yourself and simultaneously discredit the other religions— your competition. Now create a vision of God talking to you about the corruption of other belief systems. Start with James Duncan and the confused state of Christianity in the ancient Middle East and the rise of Islam.

Quotes from Historic Literature Books	Plagiarized Phrases to Use For Your New Vision Story
it is admitted that the state of eastern churches, more especially of the Arabian, were in a deplorable state of declension and ignorance when the Koreishite imposter first conceived the bold project of uniting the jarring creeds of Jew, Christian, and Magian, in a new religion adapted to the clime and to the people.	the whole district of country seemed affected by it, and great multitudes united themselves to the different religious parties, which created no small stir and division amongst the people. Some were contending for the Methodist faith, some for the Presbyterian, and some for the Baptist.
*If . . . we look into the ecclesiastical historians even from the third century, we shall find the Christian world to have then a very different aspect from what some authors have represented; *what by the ambition of the clergy,* *and so far from being ensued with	
active grace,	the great
zeal, and devotion,	zeal manifested by the respective clergy,

Quotes from Historic Literature Books	Plagiarized Phrases to Use For Your New Vision Story
	who were active in
established within itself with purity of doctrine, union and firm profession of the faith,	getting up and promoting this extraordinary scene of religious feeling, . . . it was seen that the seemingly good feelings of both
that,	the priests and the converts were
on the contrary*	more pretended than real; for a scene of great confusion and bad feeling ensued—
*while they thus eagerly	priest
contended for their own imaginations	contending against priest,
concerning it; and in a manner drove Christianity out of the world, by those very controversies in which they disputed with each	
other about it.*	and convert against convert;
*and what by drawing the abstrusest niceties into controversy, and dividing and subdividing about them into endless schisms and contentions, they had so destroyed	
that peace, love, and charity from among them, which the Gospel was given to promote, and, instead thereof, continually provoked each other to that malice, rancour, and every evil work*	so that all their good feelings one for another, if they ever had any,
*that they had	
	were entirely
lost the whole substance of their religion,*	lost in a strife of words and a contest about opinions.
(A maritime Laplander . . . when he	
once went out to hunt hares on a Saturday, and was from fatigue	having looked around me, and finding myself alone,
seated on the ground)	kneeled down

Quotes from Historic Literature Books	Plagiarized Phrases to Use For Your New Vision Story
(in the midst of these agitations of mind and body fell like to a dying man to the ground)	I was seized upon by some power which entirely overcame me, and had such an astonishing influence over me
[his speech failed him, and he fell life-less to the ground]	as to bind my tongue so that I could not speak
"p. 471, line 1–3: witches . . . fastened three knots on a linen towel in the name of the devil, and	
spit on them, &c. they called the name of him they	it seemed to me for a time as if I were
doomed to destruction"	doomed to sudden destruction.
(His servants faithfully attended on him under this loss of his understanding and senses, striving now and then to awaken him, by slight blows, but in vain.)	But, exerting all my powers to call upon God to deliver me out of the power of this enemy which had seized upon me, and at the very moment when I was ready to sink into despair and abandon myself to destruction—
	not to an imaginary ruin, but to
(Meantime	the power of
the apparition which appeared to him in hunting, presented itself to him in his vision)	some actual being from the unseen world, who had such marvelous power as I had never before felt in any being—just at this moment of great alarm
*At Mocha, during the prevalence of the S.E. wind,	
a thick haze covers the opposite coast*	Thick darkness gathered around me
*A very singular phenomenon occurred, which has been taken notice by the ancients; the sun set	
like a	I saw a
pillar of fire,	pillar of light
having totally lost its usual round form,*	exactly over my head, above the brightness of the sun, which

Quotes from Historic Literature Books	Plagiarized Phrases to Use For Your New Vision Story
	descended gradually until it fell upon me.
	–or–
	(in the 16th year of my age a
	pillar of fire above the
pillar of fire	brightness of the
sun set like a	sun at noon day came down from above and rested upon me and I was filled with the spirit of god and the Lord opened the heavens upon me and I saw the Lord and he spake unto me saying Joseph my son thy sins are forgiven thee)[317]
(a spectre with a human visage and dark garment, appeared to him . . .)	I saw two Personages, whose brightness and glory defy all description,
(that the same spectre, which hitherto presented itself in ragged garments, had soon after appeared to him in a more sumptuous habit, addressing him in words of this kind . . .)	
(he fancied even still to see the	
spectre walking up and down before him)	standing above me in the air.
(asking him what he did there,	One of them spake unto me,
and on his answering that he came to hunt hares, which he intended to give to his priest)	No sooner, therefore, did I get possession of myself, so as to be able to speak,
The sects whom they (the Catholics) oppressed, successively retired beyond the limits of the Roman empire.	then I asked the Personages . . . which of all the sects was right, that I might know which to join.
*The Marcionites and Manicheans dispersed their fantastic opinions and apocryphal gospels; the churches of Yemen, and the princes of Hira and Ghassan were instructed	I was answered that I must join none of them, for they were all wrong; and the Personage who addressed me said that all their

Quotes from Historic Literature Books	Plagiarized Phrases to Use For Your New Vision Story
in the purer creed of the Jacobite and Nestorian bishops.*	creeds were an abomination in his sight;
*In these dark ages it was, that	
most of those superstitions and corruptions we now justly abhor in the church of Rome, were not only broached, but established, which gave great advantages to the propagation of Mohammedism.*	that those professors were all corrupt;
This corruption of doctrine and morals in the princes and clergy, was necessary followed by a general depravity of the people; those of all conditions making it their sole business to get money by any means, and then to squander it away, when they had got it, in luxury and debauchery. (Duncan, *Arabia*, p. 55)	
(the spectre replied, what do you think that hares taken on the Saturday, which should be observed with the greatest veneration, can be acceptable to your priest?)	He again forbade me to join with any of them; and many other things did he say unto me, which I cannot write at this time
(And then subjoined in caution, that he should carefully guard against violating Saturday, or any other holy day for the future, by any profane exercise.)	
(He added that from this profanation of the ancient	
festivals, that the wild beasts, birds, and fishes, abhorring and detesting the impiety of irreligious men, quitting their	all their creeds were an abomination in his sight;
haunts, had fled away and hastened to other countries. That the same spectre . . . addressing him in words of this kind: you will sacrifice a cow to me,	that those professors were all corrupt;

Quotes from Historic Literature Books	Plagiarized Phrases to Use For Your New Vision Story
when this is done, the sea, the air, and earth will again bring forth fishes, fowl, and beasts.)	
(you will never recover from this disease, unless you sacredly promise, when you get well, that you will, with due right sacrifice a cow to me.)	
(The unhappy man made this promise,	
and immediately awoke from his trance, but	When I came to myself again, I found myself lying on my back, looking up into heaven.
	When the light had departed,
so weak that he could not walk . . .)	I had no strength;
(When this conversation was ended, the Laplander, you will suppose in	
	but soon
consternation and disorder,	recovering in some degree,
returned home.)	I went home.

Now you look across the Pinkerton book to the next page, 482, for more of Leems's *Superstitions of the Laplanders* and finish the table.

[For my part, what to think of this vision, whether it may be true or false, I leave to persons of	It caused me serious
reflection to determine.]	reflection then, and often has since,
[This at least I can suggest, that	
the Laplander to whom it happened	how very strange it was that an
was a simple and honest man, free from fraud of any kind. Besides, when it is remembered that the infernal spirit can change himself into a	obscure boy, of a little over fourteen years of age, and one, too,

thousand forms, it was easy for him, who did not scruple to tempt the son of God, in whom were hidden such treasures of wisdom, thus to attempt to circumvent with his wiles,

a poor simple man, incredibly weak and helpless in himself,

who was doomed to the necessity of obtaining a scanty maintenance by his daily labor,

that he might lead him with others out of the true way to his destruction.]

should be thought a character of sufficient importance to attract the attention of the great ones of the most popular sects of the day

after I had retired to my bed for

(He ended here, and instantly recited the Lord's prayer, and part of the catechism)

the night, I betook myself to prayer and supplication to Almighty God for forgiveness of all my sins and follies,

he treated my communication not

(Some obeyed his monitions, while others took the whole vision for a mere illusion and juggle of the malign spirit)

only lightly, but with great contempt, saying it was all of the devil, that there were no such things as visions or revelations in these days.

[This at least I can suggest, that

the Laplander to whom it happened was a simple and honest man

and though I was an obscure boy, only between fourteen and fifteen years of age, and my circumstances

a poor simple man, incredibly weak and helpless in himself]

in life such as to make a boy of no consequence in the world,

Are you ready to put it all together now? This will be your first vision of God while praying to him in the woods. He will appear and tell you that all present creeds and religions are corrupt.

Your writing needs drama and details, but they can't have been dreamed up by just anyone. You need the poor, simple, and honest Laplander with his spectre vision to transform this event into a true miracle. You like the Laplander's characterization as "simple." As explained by the learned author Mr. Leems, you raise your own credibility, and consequently that of the vision, if you're just a simple, honest, and helpless soul searching for the truth.

Knowing that your many enemies will accuse you of arrogance, you build in self-deprecation. Then you'll repeat over and over throughout your life that you, like the Laplander, are but an obscure, uneducated, poor, and innocent boy. Now people will surely believe you.

One more thing: you almost forgot to change the "pillar of fire" quote to "pillar of light." Saying "fire" might be too obvious; you already used it for Lehi's vision in "The First Book of Nephi." Since the report stated that it is a famous phenomenon in Arabia, someone might trace it to Duncan's book about Arabia, which would be a disaster. You were sloppy with your editing, though, and merely crossed it out in your 1832 Letterbook, so it's still there in the papers. Luckily, you remembered now and changed it to "light" in the 1838 version, which you finished below:

Some time in the second year after our removal to Manchester, there was in the place where we lived an unusual excitement on the subject of religion. It commenced with the Methodists, but soon became general among all the sects in that region of country. Indeed, the whole district of country seemed affected by it, and great multitudes united themselves to the different religious parties, which created no small stir and division amongst the people, some crying, "Lo, here!" and others, "Lo, there!" Some were contending for the Methodist faith, some for the Presbyterian, and some for the Baptist.

For, notwithstanding the great love which the converts to the different faiths expressed at the time of their conversion, and the great zeal manifested by the respective clergy, who were active in getting up and promoting this extraordinary scene of religious feeling, in order to have everybody converted, as they were pleased to call it, let them join what sect they pleased; yet when the converts began to file off, some to one party and some to another, it was seen that the seemingly good feelings of both the priests and the converts were more pretended than real; for a scene of great confusion and bad feeling ensued—priest contending against priest, and convert against convert; so that all their good feelings one for another, if they ever had any, were entirely lost in a strife of words and a contest about opinions.

I was at this time in my fifteenth year. My father's family was proselyted to the Presbyterian faith, and four of them joined that church, namely, my mother, Lucy; my brothers Hyrum and Samuel Harrison; and my sister Sophronia.

During this time of great excitement my mind was called up to serious reflection and great uneasiness; but though my feelings were deep and often poignant, still I kept myself aloof from all these parties, though I attended their several meetings as often as occasion would permit. In process of time my mind became somewhat partial to the Methodist sect, and I felt some desire to be united with them; but so great were the confusion and strife among the different denominations, that it was impossible for a person young as I was, and so unacquainted with men and things, to come to any certain conclusion who was right and who was wrong.

My mind at times was greatly excited, the cry and tumult were so great and incessant. The Presbyterians were most decided against the Baptists and Methodists, and used all the powers of both reason and sophistry to prove their errors, or, at least, to make the people think they were in error. On the other hand, the Baptists and Methodists in their turn were equally zealous in endeavoring to establish their own tenets and disprove all others.

In the midst of this war of words and tumult of opinions, I often said to myself: What is to be done? Who of all these parties are right; or, are they all wrong together? If any one of them be right, which is it, and how shall I know it?

While I was laboring under the extreme difficulties caused by the contests of these parties of religionists, I was one day reading the Epistle of James, first chapter and fifth verse, which reads: If any of you lack wisdom, let him ask of God, that giveth to all men liberally, and upbraideth not; and it shall be given him.

Never did any passage of scripture come with more power to the heart of man than this did at this time to mine. It seemed to enter with great force into every feeling of my heart. I reflected on it again and again, knowing that if any person needed wisdom from God, I did; for how to act I did not know, and unless I could get more wisdom than I then had, I would never know; for the teachers of religion of the different sects understood the same passages of scripture so differently as to destroy all confidence in settling the question by an appeal to the Bible.

At length I came to the conclusion that I must either remain in darkness and confusion, or else I must do as James directs, that is, ask of God. I at length came to the determination to "ask of God," concluding that if he gave wisdom to them that lacked wisdom, and would give liberally, and not upbraid, I might venture.

So, in accordance with this, my determination to ask of God, I retired to the woods to make the attempt. It was on the morning of a beautiful, clear day, early in the spring of eighteen hundred and twenty. It was the first time in my life that I had made such an attempt, for amidst all my anxieties I had never as yet made the attempt to pray vocally.

After I had retired to the place where I had previously designed to go, having looked around me, and finding myself alone, I kneeled down and began to offer up the desires of my heart to God. I had scarcely done so, when immediately I was seized upon by some power which entirely overcame me, and had such an astonishing influence over me as to bind my tongue so that I could not speak. Thick darkness gathered around me, and it seemed to me for a time as if I were doomed to sudden destruction.

But, exerting all my powers to call upon God to deliver me out of the power of this enemy which had seized upon me, and at the very moment when I was ready to sink into despair and abandon myself to destruction—not to an imaginary ruin, but to the power of some actual being from the unseen world, who had such marvelous power as I had never before felt in any being—just at this moment of great alarm, I saw a pillar of light exactly over my head, above the brightness of the sun, which descended gradually until it fell upon me.

It no sooner appeared than I found myself delivered from the enemy which held me bound. When the light rested upon me I saw two Personages, whose brightness and glory defy all description, standing above me in the air. One of them spake unto me, calling me by name and said, pointing to the other—This is My Beloved Son. Hear Him!

My object in going to inquire of the Lord was to know which of all the sects was right, that I might know which to join. No sooner, therefore, did I get possession of myself, so as to be able to speak, than I asked the Personages who stood above me in the light, which of all the sects was right (for at this time it had never entered into my heart that all were wrong)—and which I should join.

I was answered that I must join none of them, for they were all wrong; and the Personage who addressed me said that all their creeds were an abomination in his sight; that those professors were all corrupt; that: "they draw near to me with their lips, but their hearts are far from me, they teach for doctrines the commandments of men, having a form of godliness, but they deny the power thereof."

He again forbade me to join with any of them; and many other things did he say unto me, which I cannot write at this time. When I came to myself again, I found myself lying on my back, looking up into heaven. When the light had departed, I had no strength; but soon recovering in some degree, I went home. And as I leaned up to the fireplace, mother inquired what the matter was. I replied, "Never mind, all is well—I am well enough off." I then said to my mother, "I have learned for myself that Presbyterianism is not true." It seems as though the adversary was aware, at a very early period of my life, that I was destined to prove a disturber and an annoyer of his kingdom; else why should the powers of darkness combine against me? Why the opposition and persecution that arose against me, almost in my infancy?

Some few days after I had this vision, I happened to be in company with one of the Methodist preachers, who was very active in the before mentioned religious excitement; and, conversing with him on the subject of religion, I took occasion to give him an account of the vision which I had had. I was greatly surprised at his behavior; he treated my communication not only lightly, but with great contempt, saying it was all of the devil, that there were no such things as visions or revelations in these days; that all such things had ceased with the apostles, and that there would never be any more of them.

I soon found, however, that my telling the story had excited a great deal of prejudice against me among professors of religion, and was the cause of great persecution, which continued to increase; and though I was an obscure boy, only between fourteen and fifteen years of age, and my circumstances in life such as to make a boy of no consequence in the world, yet men of high standing would take notice sufficient to excite the public mind against me, and create a bitter persecution; and this was common among all the sects—all united to persecute me.

It caused me serious reflection then, and often has since, how very strange it was that an obscure boy, of a little over fourteen years of age, and one, too, who was doomed to the necessity of obtaining a scanty maintenance by his daily labor, should be thought a character of sufficient importance to attract the attention of the great ones of the most popular sects of the day, and in a manner to create in them a spirit of the most bitter persecution and reviling. But strange or not, so it was, and it was often the cause of great sorrow to myself.

However, it was nevertheless a fact that I had beheld a vision. I have thought since, that I felt much like Paul, when he made his defense before King Agrippa, and related the account of the vision he had when he saw a light, and heard a voice; but still there were but few who believed him; some said he was dishonest, others said he was mad; and he was ridiculed and reviled. But all this did not destroy the reality of his vision. He had seen a vision, he knew he had, and all the persecution under heaven could not make it otherwise; and though they should persecute him unto death, yet he knew, and would know to his latest breath, that he had both seen a light and heard a voice speaking unto him, and all the world could not make him think or believe otherwise.

So it was with me. I had actually seen a light, and in the midst of that light I saw two Personages, and they did in reality speak to me; and though I was hated and persecuted for saying that I had seen a vision, yet it was true; and while they were persecuting me, reviling me, and speaking all manner of evil against me for so saying, I was led to say in my heart: Why persecute me for telling the truth? I have actually seen a vision; and who am I that I can withstand God, or why does the world think to make me deny what I have actually seen? For I had seen a vision; I knew it, and I knew that God knew it, and I could not deny it, neither dared I do it; at least I knew that by so doing I would offend God, and come under condemnation.

Don't rest yet. You are only half finished. You need to work with Leems's second vision story on page 482 and John Ranking's book to introduce another heavenly visitor. Remember, Ranking's quotes will be marked with plus signs "+". This time the spectre makes a "hissing sound" to get the Laplander's attention.

+She boldly defended herself, by declaring that no man

had known her; but that one day,

lying negligently upon

her bed,

a light

appeared in her dark room,

the brightness of which blinded her,+

[and turning about he perceived a

figure opposite him of human shape . . .']

Upon some of them are exhibited great personages, or kings, as big as the life,

*(p. 184) "At the white feast, at the beginning of the year, the Grand Khan, and all his subjects

clothe themselves in white

when, on the evening of the above-mentioned

twenty-first of September,

after I had retired to

my bed for the night,

I discovered a light

appearing in my room,

which continued to increase until the room was lighter than at noonday . . .

when immediately a

personage appeared at my bed side, standing in the air, for his feet did not touch the floor.

Not only was his

robe exceedingly

garments." *

white, but his whole person was glorious beyond description,

*Upon some of them are exhibited great **personages,** or kings, as big as the life, sitting with their

His **hands were naked** and his arms also, a little above the wrist, so, also were

feet under them, and attendants at each side of them. Others show us several figures, which seem to represent queens **folding their hands** together, . . . and the king,

his feet naked, as were his legs, a little above the ankles. His

bare-headed, in the middle, with a

sceptre in his hand.*

head and neck were also bare. I could discover that he had no other

All the bystanders have hideous diabolical visages.

clothing on but this robe, as it was open, so that I could see into his bosom

[the Laplander had sat down on his way,

he **heard a hissing noise**

He called me by name, and said unto me that he was a messenger sent from the presence of God to me, and **that his name was Moroni;** that God had a work for me to do; . . .

when again I beheld the **same messenger** at my bedside, and heard him rehearse or repeat over again to me the same things as before; and added a caution to me, telling me that Satan would try to tempt

three times repeated]

me . . . After this **third visit,** . . . when almost immediately after the heavenly messenger had **ascended**

+ and that it penetrated **three** times into her body +

from me the third time,

[on which in dismay **he exclaimed,** O God come to my assistance I pray you!]

While I was thus in the act of **calling** upon God

[on his way he was addressed by a clear shrill voice; stop friend, I wish to speak a few words with you, on which he stopped,

and turning about he perceived a

figure opposite him of human shape,

in a splendid dress]

[severely reproving him, because on that day, on which the festival of Christ had fallen, he was not ashamed to undertake such a business,]

[seriously affirming himself to be the

messenger of God, sent from heaven for this purpose,

to instruct him and others,

that the Nativity of Christ, and other holydays old stile, were to be kept holy, and that the innovation of violating this, as well as other festivals was rashly introduced, and that such an institution was merely human, and therefore of no authority and obligation . . .]

[He spoke and

instantly

disappeared in air.]

+ "He that is at the head of a hundred thousand men, has a golden

He called me by name, and said unto me that he was a messenger sent from the presence of God to me, and that his name was Moroni

when

immediately a personage appeared at my bedside, standing in the air, for his feet did not touch the floor.

He had on a loose robe of most exquisite whiteness. It was a whiteness beyond anything earthly

He also said that the fulness of the everlasting Gospel was contained in it, as delivered by the Savior to the ancient inhabitants;

He called me by name, and said unto me that he was a

messenger sent from the presence of God to me, and that his name was Moroni;

that God had a work for me to do . . .

He said there was a book deposited, written upon gold plates . . . He also said that the fulness of the

everlasting Gospel was contained in it, as delivered by the Savior to the ancient inhabitants;

After this communication, when

instantly I saw, as it were, a conduit open right up into heaven, and he

ascended till he entirely disappeared,

He said there was a book deposited, written upon

tablet, with an inscription—'By the power and might of the great God, be the name of the Kaan

gold plates.

(kublai), blessed; and let all such as disobey suffer death." Under this is engraved the figure of a lion, with representations of the sun and moon. (Ranking, pp. 179–180)+

only to those to whom I should be commanded to show them; if I did I should be destroyed.

*There are in it two towers, or turrets; About ten fathoms from the

ground, there was, on each of eight sides, stones placed on which were carved several histories.*

giving an account of the former inhabitants of this continent, and the sources from whence they sprang.

[The Laplander hastened

I started with the intention of

home as fast as he could, but before he came there

going to the house . . .

my strength entirely

his speech failed him, and

failed me, and

he fell as if lifeless to the

I fell helpless on

ground,

the ground,

and no doubt would have died in that situation, had not some persons been at hand, who seeing the danger of the man, took him home to his cot, after lifting him

and for a time was

up just dead in their arms.]

quite unconscious of anything.

[After remaining some time in this state he awoke, related what happened, and seriously admonished his friends, according to the mandate of the angel who appeared to him, to be observant of all the old festivals.]

The first thing that I can recollect was a voice speaking unto me . . . com-manded me to go to my father and tell him of the vision and commandments which I had received.

That was a lot of work but worth the effort. Are you ready to write the vision of a hissing messenger coming three times into your bedroom?

While I was thus in the act of calling upon God, I discovered a light appearing in my room, which continued to increase until the room was lighter than at noonday, when immediately a personage appeared at my bedside, standing in the air, for his feet did not touch the floor.

He had on a loose robe of most exquisite whiteness. It was a whiteness beyond anything earthly I had ever seen; nor do I believe that any earthly thing could be made to appear so exceedingly white and brilliant. His hands were naked, and his arms also, a little above the wrist; so, also, were his feet naked, as were his legs, a little above the ankles. His head and neck were also bare. I could discover that he had no other clothing on but this robe, as it was open, so that I could see into his bosom.

Not only was his robe exceedingly white, but his whole person was glorious beyond description, and his countenance truly like lightning. The room was exceedingly light, but not so very bright as immediately around his person. When I first looked upon him, I was afraid; but the fear soon left me.

He called me by name, and said unto me that he was a messenger sent from the presence of God to me, and that his name was Moroni; that God had a work for me to do; and that my name should be had for good and evil among all nations, kindreds, and tongues, or that it should be both good and evil spoken of among all people.

He said there was a book deposited, written upon gold plates, giving an account of the former inhabitants of this continent, and the source from whence they sprang. He also said that the fulness of the everlasting Gospel was contained in it, as delivered by the Savior to the ancient inhabitants;

Also, that there were two stones in silver bows—and these stones, fastened to a breastplate, constituted what is called the Urim and Thummim—deposited with the plates; and the possession and use of these stones were what constituted "seers" in ancient or former times; and that God had prepared them for the purpose of translating the book.

After telling me these things, he commenced quoting the prophecies of the Old Testament. He first quoted part of the third chapter of Malachi;

and he quoted also the fourth or last chapter of the same prophecy, though with a little variation from the way it reads in our Bibles. Instead of quoting the first verse as it reads in our books, he quoted it thus:

For behold, the day cometh that shall burn as an oven, and all the proud, yea, and all that do wickedly shall burn as stubble; for they that come shall burn them, saith the Lord of Hosts, that it shall leave them neither root nor branch.

And again, he quoted the fifth verse thus: Behold, I will reveal unto you the Priesthood, by the hand of Elijah the prophet, before the coming of the great and dreadful day of the Lord.

He also quoted the next verse differently: And he shall plant in the hearts of the children the promises made to the fathers, and the hearts of the children shall turn to their fathers. If it were not so, the whole earth would be utterly wasted at his coming.

In addition to these, he quoted the eleventh chapter of Isaiah, saying that it was about to be fulfilled. He quoted also the third chapter of Acts, twenty-second and twenty-third verses, precisely as they stand in our New Testament. He said that that prophet was Christ; but the day had not yet come when "they who would not hear his voice should be cut off from among the people," but soon would come.

He also quoted the second chapter of Joel, from the twenty-eighth verse to the last. He also said that this was not yet fulfilled, but was soon to be. And he further stated that the fulness of the Gentiles was soon to come in. He quoted many other passages of scripture, and offered many explanations which cannot be mentioned here.

Again, he told me, that when I got those plates of which he had spoken—for the time that they should be obtained was not yet fulfilled—I should not show them to any person; neither the breastplate with the Urim and Thummim; only to those to whom I should be commanded to show them; if I did I should be destroyed. While he was conversing with me about the plates, the vision was opened to my mind that I could see the place where the plates were deposited, and that so clearly and distinctly that I knew the place again when I visited it.

After this communication, I saw the light in the room begin to gather immediately around the person of him who had been speaking to me, and it continued to do so until the room was again left dark, except just around him; when, instantly I saw, as it were, a conduit open right up into heaven, and he ascended till he entirely disappeared, and the room was left as it had been before this heavenly light had made its appearance.

I lay musing on the singularity of the scene, and marveling greatly at what had been told to me by this extraordinary messenger; when, in the midst of my meditation, I suddenly discovered that my room was again beginning to get lighted, and in an instant, as it were, the same heavenly messenger was again by my bedside.

He commenced, and again related the very same things which he had done at his first visit, without the least variation; which having done, he informed me of great judgments which were coming upon the earth, with great desolations by famine, sword, and pestilence; and that these grievous judgments would come on the earth in this generation. Having related these things, he again ascended as he had done before.

By this time, so deep were the impressions made on my mind, that sleep had fled from my eyes, and I lay overwhelmed in astonishment at what I had both seen and heard. But what was my surprise when again I beheld the same messenger at my bedside, and heard him rehearse or repeat over again to me the same things as before; and added a caution to me, telling me that Satan would try to tempt me (in consequence of the indigent circumstances of my father's family), to get the plates for the purpose of getting rich. This he forbade me, saying that I must have no other object in view in getting the plates but to glorify God, and must not be influenced by any other motive than that of building his kingdom; otherwise I could not get them.

After this third visit, he again ascended into heaven as before, and I was again left to ponder on the strangeness of what I had just experienced; when almost immediately after the heavenly messenger had ascended from me for the third time, the cock crowed, and I found that day was approaching, so that our interviews must have occupied the whole of that night.

I shortly after arose from my bed, and, as usual, went to the necessary labors of the day; but, in attempting to work as at other times, I found my strength so exhausted as to render me entirely unable. My father, who was laboring along with me, discovered something to be wrong with me, and told me to go home. I started with the intention of going to the house; but, in attempting to cross the fence out of the field where we were, my strength entirely failed me, and I fell helpless on the ground, and for a time was quite unconscious of anything.

The first thing that I can recollect was a voice speaking unto me, calling me by name. I looked up, and beheld the same messenger standing over my head, surrounded by light as before. He then again related unto me all that he had related to me the previous night, and commanded me to go to my father and tell him of the vision and commandments which I had received.

I obeyed; I returned to my father in the field, and rehearsed the whole matter to him. He replied to me that it was of God, and told me to go and do as commanded by the messenger. I left the field, and went to the place where the messenger had told me the plates were deposited; and owing to the distinctness of the vision which I had had concerning it, I knew the place the instant that I arrived there.

Well done! You just wrote the first few pages of the official *History of the Church* record.

There will be a problem, though. Your mother, Lucy Mack Smith, will write her own history long after you publish yours. In fact, she will write it long after you are dead. She'll claim that you got it wrong. It was an angel named "Nephi," not "Moroni," that visited your bedroom three times in a white robe and told you about the gold plates.

Lucy Smith's version is on the left side of the table below, and the version written by Joseph Jr. is on the right.

He called me by name, and	He called me by name, and
said unto me that he was	said unto me that he was
a messenger sent from the presence of God to me, and that	a messenger sent from the presence of God to me, and that
his name was Nephi.[318]	his name was Moroni.[319]

Why the discrepancy? The next chapter will explain *why* the mother wrote that "Nephi" made the supernatural visit to her home. Her message here is only a hint about a greater story she wants to tell. She's going to expose their whole scheme.

Macuilxochitl

23

THE PROPHET'S
MOTHER
AND THE YEAR 1811

Over the first decade of growth of the Latter-day Saints church, the Smith family's plans surely met with greater success than they had ever imagined. Many immigrants from Europe converted to the exciting new religion after their arrival in America. Joseph Smith Jr.'s flock had many successes and had grown to more than ten thousand members.

But with success came setbacks. Mormons had been chased out of nearly every town where they had set up a church. After a series of violent skirmishes and near extermination in Missouri, the Mormons finally found peace in Illinois.

Nauvoo, Illinois, was different from any other city in America. It was rough and bustling like other frontier cities, but it was a religious community planned and administered according to Joseph's vision. He was mayor, general of the Nauvoo legion, and president of the church.

By 1844 Nauvoo was nearly the size of Chicago, but Joseph wasn't satisfied. He launched a campaign for the presidency of the United States. The largest voting bloc in Illinois was ready to cast every ballot for him.

In 1844 eyewitnesses recalled Joseph's powerful preaching:

> . . . brother Joseph arose like a lion about to roar; and being full of the
> Holy Ghost, spoke in great power, bearing testimony of the visions he

had seen, the ministering of angels which he had enjoyed; and how he had found the plates of the Book of Mormon, and translated them by the gift and power of God. He commenced by saying if nobody else had the courage to testify of so glorious a message from Heaven, and of the finding of so glorious a record, he felt to do it in justice to the people, and leave the event with God.[320]

But just as he hit his peak, everything came undone. He had been through a series of skirmishes with state militias and the law. His next act was the final straw. According to some rumors, a local independent newspaper was about to expose his polygamy, so Joseph, along with the city council, ordered its office and printing press destroyed. A mob of Mormons executed the order. Whether or not Smith ordered the mob's attack, that act inflamed the Illinois press and enraged the state's governor. When a warrant was issued for his arrest, Joseph and his brother Hyrum turned themselves in at the county jail. Shortly thereafter, in June 1844, a lynch mob broke in (or more likely was allowed in by local authorities) and murdered the two brothers. Now they were martyrs.

A month later, Joseph's younger brother, Samuel, a prominent missionary and elder of church, died from illness he had caught while trying to escape the same authorities in the cold weather.

A year later the prophet's mother, Lucy Mack Smith, attended the church's annual conference in the Nauvoo Temple. The new president, Brigham Young, granted Lucy's request to speak before the more than five thousand attendees.

Hers was a solemn sermon that asked the congregation to search their souls for the truth about why they were in the church. Her address included strange questions, one of which asked the members "whether [they] were willing to receive stolen goods or not." Apparently reflecting on her family's past, she warned them not to keep secrets or "do in secret as you would do in the presence of millions." Below is part of her transcribed speech, with our grammatical revisions to make it more readable.

Hello brothers and sisters. I have been looking round upon this congregation. I have long been waiting for the time when the Lord would give me strength to look upon you and my children. I feel solemn. I want everyone to look into their hearts to see why they have come to this place, for whether they have come to follow Christ through evil and good report or for any other cause. I want to have time to talk about my husband, and my sons Hyrum and Joseph and want to give you all my advice. . . .

For a long time I have been wanting to ask whether you were willing to receive stolen goods or not. I want to know if you believe in such things. . . .

God gives us our children and we are accountable. In the fear of God I warn you I want you to take your little children and teach them in the fear of God. I want you to teach them about Joseph in Egypt and such things and when they are four years old they will love to read their bible. I presume there never were a family that were so obedient as mine. . . . I want the young men to remember that I love children . . . I want them to be obedient to their parents and do every thing just right. I want them to be good and kind and do in secret as you would do in the presence of millions. . . .

Don't suppose that one-third of this people ever saw or knew anything of Joseph, Hyrum, Samuel, William, or my family. Now they are all gone and none left but poor William.[321]

After Lucy lost her husband, Joseph Jr., Hyrum, and Samuel, something seems to have snapped inside her. We can perhaps call it a change of heart. Perhaps it was guilt she had been struggling with since at least 1811, watching her husband as he hatched the scheme, took action, and drew not only herself into it but their young son Joseph as his protégé. Her husband's acts had endangered the whole family and led to pointless deaths.

Lucy wrote her own book as a combined memoir, family record, and early church history. Titled *Biographical Sketches of Joseph Smith the Prophet, and His Progenitors for Many Generations* (*History*), it was printed for Orson Pratt while he was on a mission to England in 1853[322].

Lucy's book carries far more meaning than anyone could have imagined. For the first time, Kendal Sheets deciphered her writing. It hid the deepest, darkest family secrets. She confessed how and why *The Book of*

Mormon was written, who knew about the deception, and who was its mastermind.

She seemed to know that one day someone would discover the truth about Marco Polo, the Mexicans, the Laplanders, the Tartar doctrines, and the hissing spectre. Whoever did so, she thought, would also be able to decipher her own book in the same way.

Mrs. Smith was a brilliant woman. In her book she leads us through a literary maze rife with word clues, double meanings, and revelations to explain her reasons for exposing *The Book of Mormon* conspiracy. This is Lucy's story.

By the time she published her book, the church and religion the Smiths had fabricated subjected her to unimaginable suffering. She had endured an arduous relocation from Missouri because mobs drove the Mormons from the state. Some of her closest relatives died from illnesses caused by the move. She endured continual harassment by creditors and lawsuits filed by her husband's and son's enemies. She lived through the death of her husband in 1840 and the murder of two sons by a mob. For her to feel intense grief and resentment about the many tragedies and disappointments was only natural.

Burdening her conscience was a deep truth about *The Book of Mormon*, and she wanted to free herself. To comprehend her confession, we need to understand her stories and the clues in her book. To tell her story, Lucy used the same methods that concealed the *Marco Polo* references in *The Book of Mormon*.

Lucy dictated her book after her husband and eldest sons were dead. No one survived who could refute what she wrote or stop her from publishing it. Mother Smith wrote strange, puzzling, and often nonsensical stories about her husband and Joseph Jr.

As we explained in the chapter about the Tree of Life, she stated that her husband, not Joseph Jr., first experienced the visions similar to those in *The Book of Mormon*. She emphasized in particular the year 1811; after the beginning of that year she and her husband began having these visions. And in 1811 the father, *not* the son, was looking for the correct form of a religion that was truly in accord with the teachings of the ancient apostles. On page fifty-six she stated:

> About this time [1811] my husband's mind became much excited
> upon the subject of religion; yet he would not subscribe to any particular
> system of faith, but contended for the ancient order, as established by our
> Lord and Saviour Jesus Christ, and his Apostles.[323]

Deemphasizing her son Joseph the Prophet as the pioneer who searched
for a better religion, she attributed this all-important act to her husband.

What led us to investigate Mrs. Smith's book? We felt that one important aspect of the whole *Book of Mormon* scheme was missing. We had
focused on the book itself. Now we wanted to know about the events surrounding the writing of the book. How and why did a young man named
Joseph Smith Jr. turn *The Travels of Marco Polo* into *The Book of Mormon*
and a new made-up religion?

If Joseph actually did copy *Marco Polo* and other texts, then other family members must have known about it and probably seen him working
on it. Surely his mother and father would have been well aware of such
activities.

We have no account of Senior's life and early spiritual experiences, but
the one person who knew a lot about him, his wife, wrote extensively about
her husband. This is what piqued our interest.

The most well-known and controversial material in Mrs. Smith's book
concerns the visions she and her husband ostensibly had nineteen years
before *The Book of Mormon* was published. Mrs. Smith stated that in 1811
she and Joseph Sr. began to think deeply about religion and had astonishing
dreams and visions. She wrote on page fifty-seven:

> One night my husband retired to his bed, in a very thoughtful state of
> mind, contemplating the situation of the Christian religion, or the confu-
> sion and discord that were extant. He soon fell into a sleep, and before
> waking had the following vision, which I shall relate in his own words,
> just as he told it to me the next morning.

In 1811, Joseph Smith Jr., the official "author" of *The Book of Mormon*, was only six years old and could not possibly have been a part of

this religious episode in the Smith family's life. The description of Senior's visions begins on page fifty-six with a conspicuous historical account of where the family lived and when the spiritual events took place. Prior to the first vision she wrote:

> ... then moved to Royalton, where Ephraim was born, March 13, 1810. We continued here until we had another son, born March 13, *1811,* whom we called William.
>
> One night my husband retired to his bed. . . . He soon fell into a sleep, and before waking, had the following vision.

Mrs. Smith began the story of her husband's second vision like this:

> In 1811 we moved from Royalton, Vermont, to the town of Lebanon, New Hampshire. Soon after arriving here, my husband received another very singular vision, which I will relate . . .

Why would Mrs. Smith backdate her husband's Tree of the Sun/ coconut-tree visions a full *seven years* before William Marsden published his translation of *Marco Polo* in 1818?

Senior's visions may have occurred after 1811, but Mrs. Smith wanted to put that particular date "on the table." Why? She could have chosen any year she wanted for her book; no one was alive to dispute or verify it.

During his research, Kendal Sheets discovered by chance that more than one Marco Polo translation was published in 1811. When British author John Pinkerton created his multi-volume set of accounts of various explorers, he placed *The Travels of Marco Polo* in Volume VII. Pinkerton's 1811 translation into English was based on the same Italian manuscript by Ramusio that Marsden translated in 1818. Likewise, Robert Kerr published a version in 1811.

Curiously, the 1811 *Marco Polo* by Pinkerton was published in London by the same company, Longman, that published Marsden's *Marco Polo* in 1818. At this point, to us, nothing was a coincidence. Copies of the title pages are shown below (Figures 117 and 118).

A

GENERAL COLLECTION

OF THE

BEST AND MOST INTERESTING

VOYAGES AND TRAVELS

IN ALL PARTS OF THE WORLD;

MANY OF WHICH ARE NOW FIRST TRANSLATED INTO ENGLISH.

DIGESTED ON A NEW PLAN.

BY JOHN PINKERTON,

AUTHOR OF MODERN GEOGRAPHY, &c. &c.

ILLUSTRATED WITH PLATES.

VOLUME THE SEVENTH.

LONDON:

PRINTED FOR LONGMAN, HURST, REES, ORME, AND BROWN, PATERNOSTER-ROW ;
AND CADELL AND DAVIES, IN THE STRAND.

1811.

Figure 117. Pinkerton, *Voyages and Travels*, Vol. 7, Title Page

(101)

THE

CURIOUS AND REMARKABLE VOYAGES AND TRAVELS

OF

MARCO POLO, *A GENTLEMAN OF VENICE*,

Who in the Middle of the thirteenth Century paſſed through a great part of Aſia, all the Dominions of the Tartars, and returned Home by Sea through the Iſlands of the Eaſt Indies.

[Taken chiefly from the accurate Edition of Ramuſio, compared with an original Manuſcript in His Pruſſian Majeſty's Library, and with moſt of the Tranſlations hitherto publiſhed.]

1. *A ſuccinct Introduction to this Work.*— 2. *An Account of the Author from Ramuſio and other Writers.*— 3. *The ſeveral Editions and principal Tranſlations that have been publiſhed of theſe Travels.*— 4. *An Account of the Objections that have been raiſed againſt them.*— 5. *The Characters given of this Performance by ſeveral eminent Critics.* — 6. *The Author's introductory Account, containing an Abridgment of his Travels to the Time of his Return to Venice.*— 7. *A Deſcription of Armenia the Leſſer, of the Country of the Turks, of Armenia the Greater, of the Province of Zorzania, the Kingdom of Moſul, of the City of Baldach, or Bagdat, of the City of Tauris, with an Account of a remarkable Earthquake.*—8. *Of the Country of Perſia, the City of Jaſdi, the City of Cerman, of the Town of Camandu, and of the Country where Rhubarb grows.*— 9. *Of ſeveral other Countries, and the principal Curioſities in them.*— 10. *The Hiſtory of the Aſſaſſins, and of the Manner in which their Prince was killed, together with the Deſcription of many other Countries.*— 11. *Of the City of Samarcand, the Town of Lop, and of the great Deſart in its Neighbourhood, with other remarkable Paſſages.*— 12. *Of the Province of Camul, and ſeveral other Countries to the City of Ezina, and another great Deſart.*— 13. *Of the City of Caracarum, and of the Tartars, with a complete Hiſtory of that Nation, and of their Monarchs.*— 14. *Of the vaſt Countries to the Northward of Tartary, and many other curious Particulars.*— 15. *Of the great Power of Cublai-Khan, of his Government, Family, Dominions, &c.*— 16. *Of his Palace in the City of Cambalu, a particular Deſcription of that City, and other remarkable Obſervations.*— 17. *Of the Magnificence of the Court of the Grand Khan, and of the Manners and Cuſtoms of his Subjects.*— 18. *A copious Account of the Countries between the Place of his Reſidence, and the Country of Thibet.*— 19. *A large Deſcription of the laſt mentioned Province, and of many others, with an Account of the Obſervations made by the Author in his Progreſs through them.*— 20. *Of the Province of Mangi, and of the Manner in which it was reduced under the Power of the Tartars, together with an Account of the Provinces and Cities afterwards reduced under their Dominion.*— 21. *Of the noble City of Quinſai, and of the vaſt Revenues drawn from thence by the Emperor of the Tartars.*— 22. *Of the Iſland of Zipangri, and of the Attempt made by the Tartars to conquer it, and their Miſcarriage in them.* — 23. *A large Account of various Countries, Provinces, Cities, and Iſlands in the Eaſt Indies.*— 24. *Of the great Iſland of Ceylon, of the Kingdom of Malabar, and the State of other Countries viſited by the Author.*— 25. *Of the Kingdom of Murſili, the Diamond Mines there, and other Countries adjacent.*— 26. *Of the Iſland of Madagaſcar*

Figure 118. Pinkerton, *Voyages and Travels*, Vol. 7, 101

You will find Senior's vision in the next table, where we compare it to Pinkerton's *Marco Polo*.

Pinkerton's 1811 edition *The Curious and Remarkable Voyages* *and Travels of Marco Polo*, pp. 113–115	*History of Joseph Smith the Prophet* Chap. XIV, pp. 58–59
you meet with another	. . . I was traveling in an open,
desert . . .	desolate field, which appeared to
grievously barren . . .	be very barren. . . .
There is	beyond me, was
a great plain,	a . . . valley,
in which	in which
a great tree grows,	stood a tree,
called the Tree of the Sun,	such as I, had never seen before
which the Christians call the Dry Tree.	[great tree]. . . .
There is no tree within one hundred miles.	It was exceedingly handsome, insomuch that I looked
	upon it with wonder and admiration.
That country [Reobarle and Ormus] abounds with rivers and	Its beautiful
	branches spread themselves . . .
palm-trees . . .	like an umbrella, and
It produceth	It bore
prickly husky shells,	a kind of fruit, in shape much
like those of	like a
chesnuts . . .	chestnut bur, and
This tree is very thick, and hath	
leaves which on one side,	as white as snow, or, if
are white.	possible, whiter.

The most remarkable thing is that Mrs. Smith told us the *exact date* of the 1811 *Marco Polo* book that contained the tree with the shells like chestnuts.

We are not merely comparing Senior's vision with *Marco Polo*; we are also comparing it with *The Book of Mormon* text. The description of "dazzling white" fruit by the father is similar to *was white, to exceed all the whiteness that I had ever seen* in the fruit described in *The Book of Mormon*. Senior eats the fruit and finds it "delicious beyond description," which is similar to Lehi's finding it to be "most sweet, above all that I had ever before tasted" in *The Book of Mormon*.

Senior's vision story is found in both the 1811 *and* the 1818 Polo books. A major difference that Lucy inserted into the vision is that instead of using only the 1818 *Marco Polo* story of a coconut tree, she also used the 1811 *Marco Polo* story that had a "Tree of the Sun."

Mrs. Smith skillfully tied her husband to the *1811 Marco Polo* and therefore to *The Book of Mormon* at a date too early for any participation by Joseph Jr.

Mrs. Smith purposefully inserted the exact date of Pinkerton's book with Marco Polo's description of the "shells . . . of chestnuts" on the tree and the date of her husband's vision that described the "chesnut bur" and "burs or shells" on the tree. This was her revelation to us: the mother of the Mormon prophet, the supposed author of *The Book of Mormon*, pointed a finger at her husband. She buried Marco Polo's words in her own book to show us that her husband was the one who used an *1811 Marco Polo translation* to begin writing *The Book of Mormon*.

The deeper we investigated, the more secrets we unearthed.

Now that we had discovered Mrs. Smith's strategy, we looked again at her and her husband's visions and wondered what other secrets she dared to share. Lucy records their "dreams" in her *History* to show us their combined early efforts in developing a procedure to invent *The Book of Mormon* and the Mormon religion. The tables below lists parts of her "dream" and her husband's first two "visions." Notice that she was very careful when she developed her dream and used some creativity to hide the source. At the end of her dream, however, she said the tree's branches were "as lively as the dancing of a sunbeam," which uses the same word, *sun*, that Polo used when he named the tree the Tree of the *Sun*. In the following table are excerpts from Mrs. Smith's dream compared to parts of the 1811 *Marco Polo* story:

Pinkerton's 1811 edition *The Curious and Remarkable Voyages and Travels of Marco Polo*, pp. 113–114	Lucy Smith's "1811 dream" *Biographical Sketches of Joseph Smith*, 1853 edition, Chap. VIII, pp. 54, 55
At length you come to	I thought that I stood in a **large**
very good plains	**and beautiful meadow**
That country abounds with	in this magnificent meadow, was a
rivers	. . . **stream of water**
There is a great plain, in which	I discovered **two trees** . . . These
a **great tree grows,**	**trees** . . . **towered** . . . **to a great height**
called the	I saw one of them was
	surrounded with a bright belt, that shone like burnished gold, but far more brilliantly . . . the tree encircled with this golden zone. . . ./. . . the branches danced . . . as lively as the dancing of a
Tree of the Sun	sunbeam.

Since Mrs. Smith wanted us to know her husband's source for his visions, she made no effort to hide the words of Marco Polo. In the table below are excerpts from Senior's first vision compared to parts of Marco Polo's story:

John Pinkerton's Translation, 1811 ed. *The Curious and Remarkable Voyages and Travels of Marco Polo*, p. 114, 115	Joseph Smith Sr. 1811 First Vision *Biographical Sketches of Joseph Smith* 1853 ed., Chap. XIV, p. 57
But having	
	I seemed to be
passed over this desert	traveling in . . . this gloomy

John Pinkerton's Translation, 1811 ed. *The Curious and Remarkable Voyages and Travels of Marco Polo*, p. 114, 115	Joseph Smith Sr. 1811 First Vision *Biographical Sketches of Joseph Smith* 1853 ed., Chap. XIV, p. 57
you . . . meet with another desert	desert.
grievously barren; it hath not	. . . Not a vestige of life,
either trees, or fruits,	either animal or vegetable,
or water . . .	could be seen . . .
. . . The wood is solid and strong, in colour yellow, like box . . .	. . . travel on, and . . . you will find on a certain log a box . . .
	all manner of beasts, horned cattle,
Lions also are found there.	roaring animals, rose up on every side.

Mrs. Smith also revealed through her husband's visions that he is the one who conceived the idea of *The Book of Mormon* and brought the whole family along with him. The clue to this is in Senior's second "vision," recorded by Mrs. Smith, where he begins to eat the white fruit in the "chestnut . . . burs or shells" and says, "I must bring my wife and children that they may partake with me."[324]

This is Lucy's way of telling us that since the "chestnut bur" fruit represents the 1811 *Marco Polo* book that her husband used in the initial creation of *The Book of Mormon*, then the family's father is the one responsible for getting his wife and children involved in the endeavor to write and sell *The Book of Mormon*.

Mrs. Smith wanted to drive this point home. She recalled again in her book how her *entire family*, "father, mother, sons, and daughters," would sit and listen to Joseph, Jr., tell his stories. What was really going on in this family? Lucy revealed it to us with the chestnut bur and the Tree of Life. Joseph was given "instructions from the Lord"; in other words, he was practicing reading and speaking about their secret manuscript.

In the beginning of her book, Lucy Smith does *not* introduce her son, the "prophet" Joseph Smith, for whom her book is named. Instead she waits until page fifty-six, where she *still* does not introduce him as a "prophet." His introduction is surprisingly short and unremarkable.

In the meantime we had a son, whom we called Joseph, after the name of his father; he was born December 23, 1805. I shall speak of him more particularly by and by.

Why would Lucy introduce God's latter-day prophet, the one who brought true salvation to mankind, in such muted, matter-of-fact prose?

We believe Mrs. Smith was clever. Her startling lack of deference was not an oversight or a sign of disrespect. It was meant to place the responsibility, or the blame, for the deception where it belonged—with her husband.

We believe the whole Smith family made a pact: to keep secret their plan to convert the text of *Marco Polo* into *The Book of Mormon*. They were afraid—and justifiably so—that once their scheme was set in motion, exposure would outrage the believers they had hoodwinked. Their fury and sense of betrayal could result in violence.

On page eighty-four of her book, Mrs. Smith tells us that her son Joseph got the entire family to keep the secret suppressed or else they would face dire consequences. Although we quoted this before, read it again with a new insight from Lucy and from all of our prior chapters:

> Accordingly, by sunset the next day we were all seated, and *Joseph commenced telling us* the great and glorious things which God had manifested to him; but, before proceeding, *he charged us not to mention out of the family that which he was about to say to us,* as the world was so wicked that when they came to a knowledge of these things *they would try to take our lives;* and that when we should obtain the plates, *our names would be cast out as evil by all people.*

> *Hence, the necessity of suppressing these things as much as possible,* until the time should come for them to go forth to the world.

Lucy revealed that in 1822, Junior already knew many things about the subjects in *The Book of Mormon*, long before he claimed to have obtained the gold plates in 1827. This means that he was reading sourcebooks already in his possession, perhaps ones that his father had provided for him.

Let's revisit the quote on page eighty-five of her text, where Mrs. Smith said that after September 21, 1823, the Smith family would sit and listen to her son Joseph:

> During our evening conversations, Joseph would occasionally give us some of the most amusing recitals that could be imagined. He would describe the ancient inhabitants of this continent, their dress, mode of travelling, and the animals upon which they rode; their cities, their buildings, with every particular; their mode of warfare; and also their religious worship. This he would do with as much ease, as if he had spent his whole life with them.

How fascinating: Lucy noted that Joseph's "most amusing recitals" concerned the same topics to be included in the then-unpublished *Book of Mormon*. The significance of this cannot be overstated, nor can her remark about the ease with which he recited these tall tales. Four or five years before he had claimed to possess the gold plates, Joseph Jr. was apparently well-versed in subjects that would appear in *The Book of Mormon*.

Just prior to this quote, Lucy included her son's alleged visions in 1822. In essence, it duplicated the church history that Joseph had dictated in 1838, which included the "pillar of light" vision and Moroni's telling him about the gold plates. Through her crafty writing, Lucy was once again sending us a message.

Recall that in 1832, Joseph Jr. recorded memories of his childhood in an official *History of the Church* document, the Joseph Smith *Letterbook*. He claimed to have had the visions when he was sixteen years old, which would have been in 1822. Why then does Lucy say that in 1823, one year *after* the visions, her son was entertaining the family with "amusing recitals" of *The Book of Mormon*? If he had already seen the visions, wouldn't he have told them about seeing God in a forest and being visited by the angel Moroni, or Nephi, in his bedroom?

Immediately following the "evening conversations" quote, Lucy wrote: "On the twenty-second of September, 1824, Joseph again visited the place where he found the plates." By writing this, she connected Joseph's "amusing recitals" to the then-buried gold plates.

Next we wanted to know whence the Smiths obtained the sourcebooks. The family had lived in New York, New Hampshire, and Pennsylvania. The Smiths didn't live on the wilderness frontier; they were in civilized New England. According to Lucy Smith's memoir, they traveled around the northeastern United States, including New York City and Boston. Our country had many bookstores then: in Philadelphia (the city where Pinkerton's volumes I through VII were republished) and in New York City, for example. Libraries at state and private universities could have had Marsden's book, Pinkerton's and Kerr's collections, and the rest of the geography books we have discussed.

Mrs. Smith hinted at where she and her husband may have acquired the *Marco Polo* books. Although we can't show it in Lucy's text explicitly, we strongly believe that Jason Mack, her brother, visited the Smith family during this time. Jason owned a schooner, and on page fifty-two of Lucy's book you will find:

> Owning a schooner himself, he took their produce to Liverpool [England], as it was then the best market.

Surely Jason could have purchased books and brought them back to his sister and her family.

We also know from Lucy that Joseph Senior occasionally conducted business in New York City during these years. Senior traveled around the Northeast, including the largest cities in America. Her chapter twelve was titled "Joseph Smith, Senior, Loses His Property and Becomes Poorer—Receives a Visit from Jason Mack—the History of the Latter Concluded."

> My husband, in a short time, went to the city of New York, with the view of shipping his gensang, and finding a vessel in port which was soon to set sail, he made arrangements with the captain to this effect—that he was to sell the gensang in China, and return the avails thereof to my husband;

and this captain bound himself to do, in a written obligation. . . . he was owing eighteen hundred dollars in the city of Boston, for store goods.[325]

This business colleague could have been another source of books.

People do not commit a crime without a motive. In her history of Joseph Jr., Lucy Smith subtly reveals why she and her husband started writing *The Book of Mormon* in 1811. To tell this story, she describes two different types of work the family performed. One was called work to "sustain ourselves" on page sixty-eight and work "to provide for our present necessities" on page sixty-six. These descriptions included detailed accounts of farming, crops, selling fruit, etc.

The second type of work lacked any description at all. She called it "making arrangements for the future" or, as she states on page sixty:

> Meanwhile, myself and companion were doing all that our abilities would admit *for the future welfare and advantage of the family,* and were greatly blessed in our labours.

Once we had decoded her allusions to *The Book of Mormon* and *Marco Polo,* we could read her history through a new filter. In the very next chapter after the story of the "chestnut bur" vision, Mrs. Smith told us why she committed to helping her husband create *The Book of Mormon.* On pages fifty-nine and sixty, when she wrote about that description-less endeavor, it was her way of saying they were working on *The Book of Mormon*:

> We moved, as before-mentioned, to the town of Lebanon, New Hampshire. Here we settled ourselves down, and began to contemplate, with joy and satisfaction, the prosperity which had attended our recent exertions; and *we doubled our diligence, in order to obtain more of this world's goods,* with the view of assisting our children, when they should need it; and, as is quite natural, we looked forward to the decline of life, and *were providing for its wants, as well as striving to procure those things which contribute much to the comfort of old age.*

Thus, Mrs. Smith confesses that "we," meaning herself and her husband, wrote *The Book of Mormon* manuscript to obtain "more of this world's goods," to retire comfortably, and to provide for their children. In short, they wrote it for profit.

They were interrupted many times by the problems of raising a family in the 1800s. On page sixty-six she said that instead of working on their unidentified project, they had to stop because of hardship:

> We were compelled to strain every energy to *provide for our present necessities, instead of making arrangements for the future,* as we had previously contemplated.

Young children do not think about supporting their parents; it is the other way around. Since financial security was a major factor in the motivation to write, we can look to the family's provider, Joseph Sr., as the culprit.

How did Lucy Smith broach the subject of supernatural occurrences or mystical experiences such as the visions and the gold plates? She did so in a way that would make us pay attention to double meanings. The only way to detect and decipher these hidden messages was to be aware of *The Book of Mormon* plagiarism. This is what she was counting on.

Besides the tale of the chestnut bur, Mrs. Smith included a story that exposed a second fundamental piece of evidence in her confession. At first read, the story seems strange, even absurd, and out of place. It is about an ancient breastplate and a handkerchief.

In chapter twenty-seven, Lucy wrote that Joseph brought home the "treasure." This treasure was the "plates," the "Urim and Thummim," and one more item: the "breastplate." Mrs. Smith stated on page 101 that she saw, handled, and discussed these items allegedly found with the gold plates:

> Joseph . . . said, 'Do not be uneasy mother, all is right—see here, I have got a key.' I knew not what he meant, but took the article of which he spoke into my hands, and, upon examination, found that it consisted of two smooth, three cornered diamonds set in glass, and the glasses were set in

silver bows, which were connected with each other in much the same way as old fashioned spectacles.

On page 106, she wrote, "That of which I spoke, which Joseph termed a key, was indeed, nothing more nor less than the Urim and Thummim, and it was by this that the angel showed him many things which he saw in vision."

At this point, an astute investigator should ask, "If Lucy Smith is exposing the family's conspiracy and showing us that her husband began writing *The Book of Mormon*, why would she include a story of her handling obviously nonexistent items that her son claimed to have found with the gold plates?" Isn't Mrs. Smith contradicting herself with this testimony of handling items that were part of the family's plans for writing and selling *The Book of Mormon*? No, not if she felt conflicted about the family's scheme.

Far from penning a contradiction, Mother Smith is putting us on alert to investigate this story. Since the whole section is important, we provide it below, beginning on page 107:

> When he returned, he requested me to come down stairs. I told him, that I could not leave my work just then, yet, upon his urgent request, I finally concluded to go down, and see what he wanted, upon which he handed me the breastplate spoken of in his history.
>
> It was wrapped in a thin muslin handkerchief, so thin that I could see the glistening metal, and ascertain its proportions without any difficulty.
>
> It was concave on one side, and convex on the other, and extended from the neck downwards, as far as the centre of the stomach of a man of extraordinary size. It had four straps of the same material, for the purpose of fastening it to the breast, two of which ran back to go over the shoulders, and the other two were designed to fasten to the hips. They were just the width of two of my fingers, (for I measured them,) and they had holes in the end of them, to be convenient in fastening.
>
> The whole plate was worth at least five hundred dollars: after I had examined it, Joseph placed it in the chest with the Urim and Thummim.

The breastplate and the Urim and Thummim that Joseph claimed to have brought home were supposed to be the ancient items worn by priests from the Old Testament in the days of the prophet Abraham when they went into the temple.

Why is each mundane detail important enough to be placed in the historical account of the "greatest prophet since Jesus"? What could possibly be important about "straps" with "holes in the end of them" two fingers wide that attached to an ancient Hebrew breastplate? The answer is simple: nothing.

There is absolutely nothing important about these absurd details. So what's the point? Lucy was trying to get our attention and tell us that something in this story is important enough to investigate.

One specific description of the breastplate demanded our attention. She said it was "wrapped in a *muslin* handkerchief." What is a "muslin handkerchief" and what would it be doing wrapped around an ancient breastplate found with the gold plates? Also, how could she expect anyone to believe that a handkerchief would be large enough to cover such a relic of "extraordinary size"?

Perhaps she intended to convey another message. With that in mind, Kendal searched the 1818 *Marco Polo* translation. On page sixty of Marsden's 1818 translation, the traveler describes the province of *Mosul* and its inhabitants, which included Arabians, Nestorian Christians, Jacobite Christians, Armenian Christians, and a race called the Kurds. It was noteworthy enough for Polo to describe "All those cloths of gold and of silk which we call *muslins* are of the manufacture of Mosul." Thus, the same word *muslin* used to identify a handkerchief cloth wrapped around the breastplate was described on page sixty of the 1818 *Marco Polo*.

Was this a coincidence? If Lucy wanted someone to discover the truth about why she was confessing the use of *both* the 1818 *and* 1811 *Marco Polo* translations, then she would be giving us something more to go on than just a "muslin handkerchief." If she was quoting from the 1818 version, she not only had full knowledge of the 1811 edition translated by John Pinkerton but also the 1818 translation by William Marsden. So far, she had not disappointed us. We reread the details about the breastplate.

Mrs. Smith said that the straps on the breastplate were "just the width of two of my fingers (for I had measured them)." Why would she measure the width of the straps with two fingers? Was this a clue?

Kendal searched the 1818 *Marco Polo* forward and backward from page sixty. Marco Polo did not measure anything with two fingers. If she wanted to specify the use of the 1818 *Marco Polo* version, she could use something written by William Marsden in the footnotes, something that would distinguish it from Pinkerton's volume, which had no footnotes. Directly linking the muslin cloth of Marco Polo to editor William Marsden's book to the breastplate she said she had measured would be an amazing feat. But this is exactly what the clever Lucy Smith led us to discover.

On the same page in the 1818 *Marco Polo* as the muslin-cloth reference, footnote 129 is inserted before the reference to the Nestorians, the Jacobites, and the Maronites. In the footnote, William Marsden informs us regarding the nation of Georgia that:

> The people of this nation . . . have retained amongst them the Christian faith, as it is thought from the time of the Apostles; but at this day it is spotted with many absurdities. They hold with the church in Rome in the use of the cross, affirming it to be meritorious if they make the same with *two fingers*, as the Papists use, but idle and vain *if with one finger,* as the Jacobites.

This was more than we expected. Lucy had just confirmed the specific reference to the "two fingers" in Marsden's footnotes. She is deliberately linking *muslin* and *two fingers* in the *same story on a single page in both her writing about the breastplate and Marsden's* 1818 *Marco Polo*. Here are the comparisons:

Polo	Lucy Smith
Polo, p. 60: All those cloths of gold and of silk which we call **muslins** are of the manufacture of **Mosul.**	Lucy Smith, p. 107: It was wrapped in a thin **muslin** handkerchief.

Polo	Lucy Smith
Polo, Note 129 (numbered in text on page 60, full note printed on page 61): They hold with the church of Rome in the use of the cross, affirming it to be meritorious if they make the same with **two fingers**, as the Papists use, but idle and vain if with one finger, as the Jacobites.	Lucy Smith, p. 107: They [the straps] were just the width of **two of my fingers**, (for I measured them).

So far we have been led to a solid reference to the 1818 *Marco Polo's* mention of the muslin cloth and the two fingers, plus an equally substantial reference to the now-famous chestnut bur in the 1811 *Marco Polo* that is found in Joseph Senior's 1811 vision. We believe Mrs. Smith is telling us, through her obscure message in her book, that her husband, and not her son, hatched this conspiracy of *The Book of Mormon* in 1811 and continued it through 1818. She used much of her biography to leave behind a picture of what really transpired in the Smith household in those days.

This was not all; she had more to tell.

After reading the 1818 *Marco Polo* footnote for the "two fingers" reference, we noticed something else: in the same footnote is a discussion of the different Christian denominations at the time of Marco Polo. The main story by Marco Polo on page sixty mentions the Christian denominations of "Nestorians, Jacobites, and Armenians." William Marsden quotes one priest as saying:

> The people of this nation . . . have retained amongst them the *Christian faith,* as it is thought *from the time of the Apostles;* but at this day it is *spotted with many absurdities.*

This comment is strikingly similar to one Mrs. Smith attributes to her husband in her book on page fifty-six.

> About this time [1811, after the birth of their son William] my husband's mind became much excited upon the *subject of religion;* yet he

would not subscribe to any particular system of faith, but contended for the *ancient order,* as established by our Lord and Saviour Jesus Christ, and his *Apostles.*

Immediately before the visions story of the chestnut bur and the Tree of the Sun/Tree of Life, Mrs. Smith states that starting in 1811, her "husband's mind became much excited upon *the subject of religion.* What was her point?

In this case she led us to the Polo text that sums up the alleged rationale behind her son's seeing the need for *The Book of Mormon*: the Christian church was now practicing a corrupted faith by following Holy Writ that had become bastardized since the time of the first apostles. *The Book of Mormon*, he thought, would restore the true gospel and doctrines of the Bible.

Since the time of the apostles, the *Polo* footnote says, the Christian Church had formed many sects (e.g., Nestorian, Armenian, Roman Catholic, Jacobite), and thus had become impure or, as Marsden wrote, "spotted with absurdities." In effect, Lucy Mack Smith exonerates her son Joseph from originating the idea of replacing a contaminated gospel with *The Book of Mormon.*

Prior to the breastplate story, Mrs. Smith wrote that her son Joseph worked on the family farm "in order to be as near as possible to the *treasure* which was confided to his care."[326] Lucy says that the breastplate was not particularly valuable because it was "worth at least five hundred dollars."[327]

To any sensible person, this statement is nonsense. Why would anyone who lived in the nineteenth century, or any other time, believe that such an invaluable historical item from the time of the Old Testament to be worth only five hundred dollars? If the breastplate really existed, and if Lucy believed it was an authentic artifact, it would have been a "Lost Ark of the Covenant" type of discovery, a monumental find of profound historical significance to Christians and Jews alike. It would be priceless, even in 1827. How could Lucy not have realized that? Surely her son Joseph would have impressed the significance upon her.

But Mrs. Smith was not trying to appraise the value of the ancient relic. Instead she wrote something ridiculous, an utter devaluation of what Junior supposedly possessed, as a way to enlighten us.

Once again, Mrs. Smith is speaking to us with allegories, clues, and riddles. We took her statement about the five hundred dollars as another mystery to solve.

Because her story with *muslin* and *two fingers* in it took us to page sixty in the 1818 *Marco Polo*, we started our investigation there. We already knew that Polo's numbers were used extensively in *The Book of Mormon*, so we thought that Mrs. Smith might have done the same thing. We found no mention of *five hundred* in the Marco Polo "muslin cloth" story or in any of the footnotes. The 1818 *Marco Polo* has 756 pages, but nothing on page five hundred relates to her story. The 1811 *Marco Polo* does not even have five hundred pages. One book, though—one that she had not yet referenced— had more than five hundred pages. To be exact, it had 588 pages—*The Book of Mormon*.

Turning to page five hundred, we looked for anything linking that page to the stories in her book or a message that was meant for us. We read the very first line:

> . . . *be a sign unto them, that they may know the work of the Father.*

Lucy Smith spoke to us through *The Book of Mormon* so that we would know the truth. She wanted to tell her story so that "they may know the work of the father." The text on this page speaks of God, but in Lucy Smith's code, it means only one thing: the mastermind behind *The Book of Mormon* was her husband, Joseph Smith Sr.

⚭

It seems fitting that Mrs. Smith used words from *The Book of Mormon* to clarify the conspiracy created by her husband and her son. She must have known that someday someone would figure out the truth behind *The Book of Mormon*. When that day inevitably arrived, she wanted to set the record straight and express her opinion about what would happen once the truth came out. Mrs. Smith's pathetic and prophetic message from page five hundred of the 1830 *Book of Mormon* talks about the end of the world. She was speaking of the time when her family's deception comes to light:

And when that day shall come, it shall come to pass that kings shall shut their mouths: for that which had not been told them shall they see; and that which they had not heard shall they consider.

I will cut off witchcrafts out of thy hand, and thou shalt have no more soothsayers: thy graven images I will also cut off . . . and thou shalt no more worship the works of thy hands. . . .

And it shall come to pass that all lyings, and deceivings, and envyings, and strifes, and priestcrafts, and whoredoms, shall be done away.

THE END

Epilogue

Joseph Smith Jr. became the prophet and military leader of a religion with well over ten thousand members. He had convinced the gullible with his multiple religious books and revelations. As the self-styled brigadier general of his Mormon militia, he wore a military uniform, carried a cavalry sword, rode a white horse, and was addressed as "General Smith." He reportedly had up to 49 polygamous wives. He was in his glory and in total control.

In 1841 Smith held a private meeting with several of his church elders. He admonished them, saying, ". . . we do not keep our own secrets, but reveal our difficulties to the world, even to our enemies." Then he claimed, ". . . I can keep a secret till Doomsday."[328]

His mother, Lucy Mack Smith, also had to keep her son's and husband's secret. She loved her family and defended *The Book of Mormon* and their church. But she suffered from a guilty conscience and grew weary of the burden of her secret. After the murder of her sons Joseph and Hyrum, she decided she could not to keep it any longer. Her book was her confession or, more accurately, her mea culpa. Mother Smith knew she was partly responsible for the suffering of many Mormon families and for the loss of life.

Trouble dogged Joseph Jr. Some was self-induced, such as the inevitable backlash over his polygamy, but some was undeserved. The worst persecution began in 1838 in Missouri. Governor Lilburn Boggs issued Executive Order 44, "to exterminate the Mormons, by God."[329] Later known as the "Execution Order," it unleashed the Missouri army and mobs to burn Mormon houses, destroy their farms, and starve them out. When those attacks didn't rid the state of Mormons, Boggs sent a fresh military contingent of six thousand men to the city of Far West to massacre the Mormon survivors.[330] Men's heads were bashed in with rifle butts, and the victims were left for dead.[331] What happened next was tragic:

Immediately after this there came into the city a messenger from Haun's Mill, bringing the intelligence of an awful massacre of the people who were residing in that place . . . a force of two or three hundred, detached from the main body of the army . . . who, the day previous, had promised them peace and protection, but on receiving a copy of the Governor's order, 'to exterminate or to expel,' . . . returned upon them the following day, and surprised and massacred the whole population of the town. . . . The messenger informed us, that he . . . collected the dead bodies of the people, cast them into a well; and there were upwards of twenty who were dead, or mortally wounded, and there are several of the wounded, who are now living in this city.[332]

Joseph and Hyrum were arrested and tried in court. Hyrum testified in a different trial later that:

. . . [the guard] boasted over us of their great achievements at Haun's Mill and other places, telling us how many houses they had burned, and how many sheep, cattle, and hogs they had driven off, belonging to the 'Mormons,' and how many rapes they had committed, and what kicking and squealing there was among the d – – d bitches, saying that they lashed one woman upon one of the d – – d 'Mormon' meeting benches, tying her hands and her feet fast, and sixteen of them abused her as much as they had a mind to, and then left her bound and exposed in that distressed

condition. These fiends of the lower region boasted of these acts of bar-
barity, and tantalized our feelings with them for ten days.[333]

Starving, with no food for traveling, no money, and walking in the
snow, most of the Mormons, including the Smith family, had to flee Missouri and take refuge in Illinois. Lucy, Joseph Sr., and much of the family
became ill from the trip. With help from a sympathetic jailer, Joseph and
Hyrum escaped from incarceration. By 1840, Joseph and his church had
recovered and were settled in Nauvoo, Illinois.[334]

Tragedy soon struck again, however, when Joseph Sr. became ill and
died. Lucy recorded a series of his final blessings on each of his children.
Lucy seemed intent on disrespecting her husband and her son with the
publication of these alleged blessings. She claims her husband's last words
to her son the prophet were:

> Joseph, my son, you are called to a high and holy calling. You are even
> called to do the work of the Lord. You shall even live to finish your work."
> At this Joseph cried out, weeping, "Oh! my father, shall I?" "Yes," said his
> father, "you shall live to lay out the plan of all the work which God has
> given you to do."[335]

Oh! my father, shall I?

Is that a response one would expect from God's highest prophet? Joseph
Sr., the patriarch of the Latter-day Saints, offered his last blessing that God
would keep his son alive to finish their work. But Senior was no seer. He
could not deliver any blessing from God to his son. Instead he delivered
a curse. Joseph did not survive. Because of his machinations, Senior was
indirectly responsible for Joseph's and Hyrum's death at the hands of a
bloodthirsty mob four years later.

Mrs. Smith's amazing story, which places her family at the foundation
of the largest and most controversial American-born religion, was not written in vain. Now the truth is known.

Joseph Smith Sr. and Lucy Mack Smith started their *Book of Mormon*
project using the 1811 *Marco Polo* Pinkerton translation and continued,

using the 1818 Marsden translation and numerous other history books. Joseph Jr. was the flamboyant storyteller who sold it to the congregations using the con-game skills he had honed in the treasure-hunting ventures. The whole family knew about the grand deception and agreed to keep it secret.

All these schemes might have seemed like a good idea, but then they careened out of control.

Lucy retaliated as best she could. She still had to worry about her own well-being and that of Emma and her grandchildren, so she cloaked the truth in ambiguity. In the end, the Latter-day prophet's own mother turned against the family, cast aside her vows of secrecy, and exposed them all.

If the world judges the Smiths harshly for their sins, we hope it feels some compassion for Lucy. She was wrong for conspiring to create false scripture and a phony religion to deceive thousands—and now millions—of souls who thought they believed in something real when it was all just a fairy tale spun for profit. But in her memoirs, she gave the world an honest testimony. She wanted "all lyings, and deceivings" to end.

In her grand finale, she left it up to God to judge her, no doubt hoping that her confession, left for someone like us to discover, would be enough to save her soul. Out of respect, we close this book, concluding our part in this American odyssey, with a quote from Lucy Mack Smith:

> Here ends the history of my life, as well as that of my family, as far as I intend carrying it for the present. And I shall leave the world to judge, as seemeth them good, concerning what I have written.
>
> But this much I will say, that the testimony which I have given is true, and will stand for ever; and the same will be my testimony in the day of God Almighty, when I shall meet them, concerning whom I have testified, before angels, and the spirits of the just made perfect, before Archangels and Seraphims, Cherubims and Gods; where the brief authority of the unjust man will shrink to nothingness before Him, who is the Lord of lords, and God of gods.[336]

NOTES

¹ Joseph Smith, Jr., *The Book of Mormon* (Palmyra, N.Y.: E.B. Grandin, for the author, 1830).

² Marco Polo, *The Travels of Marco Polo, A Venetian, In the Thirteenth Century, Being A Description of Remarkable Places and Things, in The Eastern Parts of the World, Translated from the Italian, with Notes, With a Map*, trans. William Marsden (London: Cox and Baylis, 1818).

³ Originally named the "Reorganized Church of Jesus Christ of Latter Day Saints."

⁴ Joseph Smith, Letterbook I. History (Handwriting of Frederick G. William, 1832). Reprinted in: Dean Jesse, editor, *The Personal Writings of Joseph Smith* (Salt Lake City: Deseret Book, 2002), 10.

⁵ Richard Neitzel Holzapfel and T. Jeffery Cottle, *Old Mormon Palmyra and New England, Historic Photographs and Guide* (Santa Ana, CA: 1991), 60.

⁶ Ibid., 60.

⁷ Lucy Smith, *Biographical Sketches of Joseph Smith, and His Progenitors for many Generations* (Liverpool: pub. for Orson Pratt by S.W. Richards, 1853), 51.

⁸ Ibid.

⁹ Ibid., 56–57.

¹⁰ Edward L. Queen, Stephen R. Prothero, Gardiner H. Shattuck, *Encyclopedia of American Religious History*, Vol. 1, 3d ed. (New York: Facts on File, Inc., 1996 and 2009), 232–233.

¹¹ *Ibid.*, 416.

¹² Joseph Smith, Letterbook I. Joseph Smith, *Personal Writings*, 12–13.

¹³ Lucy Smith, *Biographical Sketches*, 85.

14 Editorial, *"Money digging,"* *Wayne Sentinel*, Vol. II, No. 21, Whole No. 73, Feb. 16, 1825, Palmyra, N.Y. edition, reprinted from the *Windsor (Vermont) Jour.*, Jan. 17, 1825.

15 Fawn M. Brody, *No Man Knows My History: The Life of Joseph Smith The Mormon Prophet*, (New York: Vintage Books, 1971), 20: "Joseph's wife once described it as 'not exactly black but rather dark in color . . .'"; fn: "Emma Smith letter to Mrs. Pilgrim from Nauvoo, Illinois, March 27, 1871. It is now in the library of the Reorganized Church in Independence, Missouri. Martin Harris's statement [that Joseph could see wondrous sites in it, 'ghosts, infernal spirits, mountains of gold and silver'] was published in *Tiffany's Monthly, 1859, pp. 163–170.* [Harris] said further: 'There was a company there in that neighborhood, who were digging for money supposed to have been hidden by the ancients. Of this company were old Mr. Stowel—I think his name was Josiah—also old Mr. Beman, also Samuel Lawrence, George Proper, Joseph Smith, jr., and his father, and his brother Hiram Smith. They dug for money in Palmyra, Manchester, also in Pennsylvania and other places.'"

16 Ibid., 28–29.

17 Editorial, *The Reflector*, (Palmyra, N.Y.) Vol. II., Ser. I.—No. 12, February 1, 1831.

18 Lucy Smith, *Biographical Sketches*, 84.

19 Ibid., 85.

20 Brodie, *No Man Knows My History*, 14.

21 Lucy Smith, *Biographical Sketches*, 77.

22 Alma P. Burton, editor, *Discourses of the Prophet Joseph Smith* (Salt Lake City: Deseret Book Co., 1970), 36–37.

23 Marquardt, H. Michael, editor, "Thou Shalt Be Obedient" from *Book of Covenants* 30, in *The Joseph Smith Revelations: Text and Commentary* (Salt Lake City: Signature Books, 1999), 83.

24 Marsden, *Marco Polo*, i.

25 Marsden, *Marco Polo*, v, fn. "In different versions his age is stated at fifteen, seventeen, and nineteen years. It has elsewhere been shewn to be probable that his birth did not take place at an earlier period than the year 1254, and consequently about the latter part of 1269 he was in his sixteenth year."

26 Ibid., xxvi.

27 Ibid.

28 Ibid., xxi.

29 Joseph Smith, Jr., *The Wentworth Letter* (1842): "March 1, 1842.—At the request of Mr. John Wentworth, Editor and Proprietor of the *Chicago Democrat*, I have written the following sketch of the rise, progress, persecution, and faith of the Latter-day Saints, of which I have the honor, under God, of being the founder. Mr. Wentworth says that he wishes to furnish Mr. Bastow, a friend of his, who is writing the history of New Hampshire, with this document As Mr. Bastow has taken the proper steps to obtain correct information, all that I shall ask at his hands, is, that he publish the account entire, ungarnished, and without misrepresentation." Reprinted in: Joseph Smith, *History of The Church of Jesus Christ of Latter-day Saints*, 7 vols. 4:537–38.

30 Authors' note: the name *Camorah* was changed to *Cumorah* in the 1837 *Book of Mormon* edition. Because the present book compares the *Book of Mormon* that was first published in 1830 to the 1818 *Travels of Marco Polo* by William Marsden, the original spellings of words from each printed source are used.

31 Joseph Smith, Jr., *The Book of Mormon* (Palmyra, N.Y., 1830), iv.

32 Joseph Smith, *History of The Church of Jesus Christ of Latter-Day Saints*, 7 vols. 6:74.

33 Authors' note: When quoting from *The Book of Mormon*, text from the original 1830 chapter and page is used. Citation in brackets [] refers to chapter and verse from the version printed by the Church of Jesus Christ of Latter Day Saints that is headquartered in Salt Lake City, Utah.

34 Marsden, *Marco Polo*, 67.

35 Lucy Smith, *Biographical Sketches*, 58.

36 *Ibid.*

37 John Pinkerton, Author of Modern Geography, "The Curious and Remarkable Voyages and Travels of Marco Polo, a Gentleman of Venice, Who in the Middle of the thirteenth Century passed through a great part of Asia, all the Dominions of the Tartars, and returned Home by Sea through the Islands of the East Indies [Taken chiefly from the accurate Edition of Ramusio, compared with an original Manuscript in His Prussian Majesty's Library, and with most of the Translations hitherto published.] " in *A General Collection of the Best and Most Interesting Voyages and Travels in All Parts of the World; Many of Which Are Now First Translated Into English, Digested on a New Plan, Illustrated with Plates, Volume the Seventh*, (London: Longman, Hurst, Rees, Orme, and Brown, Paternoster-Row; and Cadell and Davies, in the Strand, 1811), 101.

38 *Ibid*, 114.

39 James Duncan, *The Modern Traveller, a Popular Description, Geographical, Historical, and Topographical, of the Various Countries of the Globe, Arabia* (London: Printed for James Duncan; Oliver and Boyd, Edinburgh; M. Ogle, Glasgow; and R.M. Tims, Dublin, 1825), 289.

40 Robert Kerr, *Ed.*, "Voyages and Travels in Egypt, Syria, Arabia, Persia, and India, By Ludovico Verthema in 1503," in *A General History and Collection of Voyages and Travels, Arranged in Systematic Order: Forming a Complete History of the Origin and Progress of Navigation, Discovery, and Commerce, by Sea and Land, From the Earliest Ages to the Present Time*, Vol. 7 (Edinburgh: George Ramsey and Company, 1812), 66. (Kerr's Introduction states, "We learn from the *Bibliotheque Universelle des Voyages I*, 264, that this itinerary was originally published in Italian at Venice, in 1520. The version followed on the present occasion was republished in old English, in 1811, in an appendix to a reprint of Hakluyt's *Early Voyages, Travels, and Discoveries*; from which we learn that it was translated from *Latine into Englishe*, by Richarde Eden, and originally published in 1576 . . . of Verthema . . . we only know . . . he was a gentleman of Rome; and we learn, at the close of his itinerary, that he was knighted by the Portuguese viceroy of India, and that his patent of knighthood was confirmed in Lisbon, by the king of Portugal.)

41 John Pinkerton, Ed., "Travels in Arabia, by Carsten Niebuhr," in *A General Collection of the Best and Most Interesting Voyages and Travels in All Parts of the World; Many of Which Are Now First Translated Into English, Asia, Volume the Tenth* (London: Longman, Rees, Orme, and Brown, 1811), 50.

42 Robert Kerr, Ed., "History of the Conquest of Mexico, Written in the Year 1568, by Captain Bernal Diaz Del Castillo, One of the Conquerors," in *A General History and Collection of Voyages and Travels, Arranged in Systematic Order: Forming a Complete History of the Origin and Progress of Navigation, Discovery, and Commerce, by Sea and Land, From the Earliest Ages to the Present Time*, Vol. 4 (Edinburgh: George Ramsey and Company, 1812), 6–7.

43 John Pinkerton, Ed., "A Journey from Aleppo to Jerusalem by Henry Maundrell," *A General Collection of the Best and Most Interesting Voyages and Travels in All Parts of the World; Many of Which Are Now First Translated Into English, Asia*, Vol. 10 (London: Longman, Rees, Orme, and Brown, 1811), 359.

44 John Pinkerton, Ed., "A Description of the East, &c. by Richard Pococke, LLD. F.R.S. Book the First. Of Palestine, or the Holy Land," in *A General Collection of the Best and Most Interesting Voyages and Travels in All Parts of the World; Many of Which Are Now First Translated Into English, Asia*, Vol. 10 (London: Longman, Rees, Orme, and Brown, 1811), 415. (Pinkerton added footnote to the title referencing the original publication of the account and *plates* along with it: "London 1745, folio. His account of Egypt, 1743, folio, belongs to Africa. The plates are very numerous, ill chosen, and ill executed; and have become useless since the far superior engravings published by latter travellers." [Authors' Note: We believe Pinkerton's and other references to *plates* and *engravings* in the history books may have inspired the Smiths to use the same term throughout *The Book of Mormon* and their own stories.]

45 John Pinkerton, Ed., "A Journey from Aleppo to Jerusalem by Henry Maundrell," *A General Collection of the Best and Most Interesting Voyages and Travels in All Parts of the World; Many of Which Are Now First Translated Into English, Asia*, Vol. 10 (London: Longman, Rees, Orme, and Brown, 1811), 314.

46 John Pinkerton, Ed., "A Journal From Grand Cairo to Mount Sinai, and Back Again, in Company With Some Missionaries De Propaganda Fide at Grand Cairo, Translated From a Manuscript Written by the Prefetto of Egypt, by the Right Rev. Robert Clayton, Lord Bishop of Clogher, to the Society of Antiquaries, London, ('An Exact Journal From Cairo to Mount Sinai, Begun the First of September, 1722')," in *A General Collection of the Best and Most Interesting Voyages and Travels in All Parts of the World; Many of Which Are Now First Translated Into English, Asia*, Vol. 10 (London: Longman, Rees, Orme, and Brown, 1811) 404.

47 Brodie, *Life of Joseph Smith*, 293.

48 In Brodie, *Life of Joseph Smith*, 170, the author notes, "By now (1835) Champollion had worked out the entire system from the Rosetta stone, but his scholarship was not made available to the British public until 1837, with the publication of John G. Wilkinson's *Manners and Customs of the Ancient Egyptians* (1837)."

[49] Rt. Reverend F.S. Spalding, D.D., Bishop of Utah, *Joseph Smith, Jr., As a Translator* (Salt Lake City: The Arrow Press, 1912) ("To sum up then, these three fac-similes of Egyptian documents in the 'Pearl of Great Price' depict the most common objects in the mortuary of Egypt. Joseph Smith's interpretation of them as part of a unique revelation through Abraham, therefore, very clearly demonstrates that he was totally unacquainted with the significance of these documents and absolutely ignorant of the simplest facts of Egyptian writing and civilization . . . Joseph Smith represents portions of a unique revelation through Abram things which were commonplaces and to be found by many thousands in every-day life of the Egyptians. We orientalists could publish scores of these 'fac-similes from the Book of Abraham' taken from other sources. For example, any visitor in a modern museum with an Egyptian collection can find for himself plenty of examples of four jars with animal heads—the jars depicted under the couch in fac-simile number one. It should be noted further that the hieroglyphics in the two fac-similes from the 'Book of Abraham' (Nos. 2 and 3), though they belong to a very degenerate and debased age in Egyptian civilization, and have been much corrupted in copying, contain the usual explanatory inscriptions regularly found in such funerary documents." James H. Breasted, Ph.D., Haskell Oriental Museum, University of Chicago. "I return herewith, under separate cover, the 'Pearl of Great Price.' The 'Book of Abraham,' it is hardly necessary to say, is a pure fabrication. Cuts 1 and 3 are inaccurate copies of well known scenes on funeral papyri, and cut 2 is a copy of one of the magical discs which in the late Egyptian period were placed under the heads of mummies. There were about forty of these latter known in museums and they are all very similar in character. Joseph Smith's interpretation of these cuts is a farrago of nonsense from beginning to end. Egyptian characters can now be read almost as easily as Greek, and five minutes' study in an Egyptian gallery of any museum should be enough to convince any educated man of the clumsiness of the imposture." Dr. Arthur C. Mace, Assistant Curator, Metropolitan Museum of Art, New York, Department of Egyptian Art.), 26–28

[50] Duncan, *Modern Traveller, Arabia*, 145.

[51] Pinkerton, *Voyages and Travels, Volume the Tenth*.

[52] Pinkerton, "Travels in Arabia, by Carsten Niebuhr," 1

[53] Robert Kerr, Ed., *A General History and Collection of Voyages and Travels, Arranged in Systematic Order: Forming a Complete History of the Origin and Progress of Navigation, Discovery, and Commerce, by Sea and Land, From the Earliest Ages to the Present Time, Vol. 7* (Edinburgh: George Ramsey and Co., 1812).

[54] Kerr, "Voyages and Travels in Egypt, Syria, Arabia, Persia, and India, by Ludovico Verthema, in 1503," in *Voyages and Travels, Vol. 7*, 41.

[55] Duncan, *Modern Traveller, Arabia*.

[56] Kerr, *Voyages and Travels, Volume 7*, 66–67.

[57] Robert Kerr, Ed., "History of the Conquest of Mexico, Written in the Year 1568, by Captain Bernal Diaz Del Castillo, One of the Conquerors," in *A General History and Collection of Voyages and Travels, Arranged in Systematic Order:*

Forming a Complete History of the Origin and Progress of Navigation, Discovery, and Commerce, by Sea and Land, From the Earliest Ages to the Present Time, Volume 4 (Edinburgh: George Ramsey and Co., 1812), 254.

[58] Pinkerton, "Travels in Arabia, by Carsten Niebuhr," in *Voyages and Travels,* 167.

[59] John Pinkerton, Ed., "Memoirs of North America; Containing a Geographical Description of That Vast Continent, the Customs and Commerce of the Inhabitants, &c." in *A General Collection of the Best and Most Interesting Voyages and Travels in All Parts of the World; Many of Which Are Now First Translated Into English, Volume the Thirteenth* (London: Longman, Rees, Orme, and Brown, 1812), 371.

[60] Duncan, *Modern Traveller, Arabia,* 7–9. (Authors' note: James Duncan also included an abridged version of Niebuhr's travels.)

[61] Duncan, *Modern Traveller, Arabia,* 99.

[62] Kerr, *Voyages and Travels,* Vol. 7, 70.

[63] Duncan, *Modern Traveller, Arabia,* 331.

[64] Pinkerton, *Voyages and Travels,* Vol. 10, 113.

[65] *Ibid.,* 116.

[66] *Ibid.,* 117.

[67] Kerr, *Voyages and Travels,* Vol. 7, 73.

[68] *Ibid.,* 75.

[69] Duncan, *Modern Traveller, Arabia,* 342–343.

[70] Kerr, *Voyages and Travels,* Vol. 7, 66, n. 6.

[71] *Ibid.,* 73.

[72] Pinkerton, *Voyages and Travels,* Vol. 10, 97.

[73] *Ibid.,* 68.

[74] Duncan, *Modern Traveller, Arabia,* 15.

[75] Pinkerton, *Voyages and Travels,* Vol. 10, 119.

[76] Marsden, *Marco Polo,* 100–101.

[77] Marsden, *Marco Polo* (1818).

[78] Robert Kerr, Ed., "History of the Discovery of America, by Christopher Columbus; Written by His Son Don Ferdinand Columbus," in *A General History and Collection of Voyages and Travels, Arranged in Systematic Order: Forming a Complete History of the Origin and Progress of Navigation, Discovery, and Commerce, by Sea and Land, From the Earliest Ages to the Present Time,* Vol. 3 (Edinburgh: George Ramsey and Co., 1812).

[79] John Pinkerton, Ed., "The History of the Life and Actions of Admiral Christopher Colon, and of His Discovery of the West Indies, Called the New World, Now in Possession of His Catholic Majesty, Written by His Own Son Don Ferdinand Colon," in *A General Collection of the Best and Most Interesting Voyages and Travels in All Parts of the World; Many of Which Are Now First Translated Into English, Volume the Twelfth* (London: Longman, Rees, Orme, and Brown, Pasternoster-Row; and Cadell and Davies, in the Strand, 1812), 4.

[80] Kerr, *Voyages and Travels,* Vol. 3, 7.

[81] Joseph Smith, *The Personal Writings of Joseph Smith,* compiled and edited by Dean C. Jessee (Deseret Books: Salt Lake City, 1984), 273–274.

[82] Marsden, *Marco Polo*, 112.

[83] *Ibid.*, 669–670.

[84] *Ibid.*, 671, n. 1354.

[85] "None Shall Be Exempt from the Justice and the Laws of God," *Revelation Received at Hiram, Ohio in November 1831 to the Church of Christ in the Land of Zion*, (LDS Doctrine and Covenants 107; RLDS Doctrine and Covenants 104), in Marquardt, *Joseph Smith Revelations*, 177.

[86] Pinkerton, *Voyages and Travels*, Vol. 10, 171–173. (Authors' Note: Joseph Smith would have learned from Niebuhr that "Sihhr" is a practice of "open sorcery" and that a "philosopher's stone" was used for alchemy. Other pretended practices used by Arabs that mix religion with occult include visions of angels and God, seeing distant items or events, and pretended miracles would have all been helpful to Joseph Smith to fool the naive and accomplish his schemes. The following contains portions copied from the 1811 Niebuhr account titled *Of the Occult Sciences of the Arabians*:

> To speak of the occult sciences, of any people, is to describe their ignorance, weakness of understanding, and wildness of imagination. Such a description would be too humiliating to human pride, did it not at the same time afford us consolation, by shewing from what endless absurdities we are saved by the study of sound philosophy, particularly of physics.
>
> Those pretended occult sciences are in high estimation among the Arabians. None dare practice them, unless previously authorised by a master in the art, after serving a sort of apprenticeship; or, as the Arabians say, without having for some time spread the carpet for prayer before the feet of a famous master. A certain proof of their veneration for these sciences, is, that one of the first men in Mecca, and of the highest nobility in Arabia, Schiech Mohammed el Dsjandsjeni, is not the most celebrated master of the science of Ism Allah.
>
> This science of Ism Allah, or the name of God, is the most sublime of all; for God is the lock, as Mahomet is the key; and consequently none but Musselmans can acquire it. It enables its possessor to discover what is passing in the most distant countries, to make himself familiar with genii, and to oblige them to obey his pleasure; to dispose of the winds and seasons as he chooses; and to cure the bites of serpents, and many other diseases or infirmities . . .
>
> The art of procuring sublime visions is not unknown to these Arabians; they use the same means which are employed by the devotees of certain societies in Europe. They shut themselves up for a long time without eating or drinking, in a dark place, and continue to repeat their prayers aloud till they faint away. After recovering from the swoon, and leaving the cave, they relate what they have seen in their trance. The common pretences are, that they have

beheld God in his glory, angels, and spirits of all sorts, heaven and hell.

The second of these sciences, called Simia, is not of so exalted a nature, but has something human in it. It only teaches juggling tricks. Although the most sensible of the Mahometan clergy disapprove of this science, some orders of dervises, however, apply to it, and practice it, as they say, to prove the truth of their religion, and the sanctity of the founder of their order. These pretended miracles are no where oftener performed than at Basra, where I have seen a company of dervises, of the order of Bed-reddin, walk all day about in the streets, leaping, dancing, beating the drum, and making gesticulations with sharp pointed irons, which they seemed to strike into their eyes.

ᗯ

The science of Ramle is properly the art of fortune telling. Jews, as well as Musselmans, deal in it. When a man falls sick, his friends, in order to learn whether he will recover, send to consult a Mullah, who returns an answer, after examining his book, and receives for his pains a cock or a sheep . . .

A science truly occult, and which every Arabian of worth must hold in abhorrence, is what they call Sihhr, or pure open sorcery. The end of this science is rather to do mischief to another person than to do good to the person who practices it. It is sometimes employed, however, to seduce a wife from the arms of her husband into those of a stranger. All that is required for this is to fix a certain billet on her door. The inhabitants of Oman are peculiarly skilled in this execrable science: yet they are certainly inferior to our European sorcerers; for they know nothing of the art of riding through the air on a broomstick, or of nocturnal assemblies under the presidency of the devil.

I found in Arabia more votaries than I expected of an occult science of a different sort, the pursuit of the philosopher's stone. The Arabians are so passionately addicted to this science, which is the object of their highest wishes, and most eager researches, that they often ruin their fortunes by it, as with the alchymists of Europe have been accustomed to do. They suppose the secret of making gold to be known in Europe, especially among the Venetians. They have books in their own language which talk of that science, and inspire them with wild hopes. It should seem, that the idea of the philosopher's stone is originally oriental, and has been brought westward, like many other foolish fables.)

[87] Robert Kerr, "History of the Discovery and Conquest of Mexico, Written in the Year 1568, by Captain Bernal Diaz Del Castillo, One of the Conquerors," in *A General History and Collection of Voyages and Travels, Arranged in Systematic*

Order, Forming a Complete History of the Origin and Progress of Navigation, Discovery, and Commerce, by Sea and Land, From the Earliest Ages to the Present Time, Vol. III (Edinburgh: George Ramsay and Co., 1811).

88 *Ibid.*, 488.

89 Duncan, *Modern Traveller, Mexico*, 39–40.

90 Kerr, *Voyages and Travels*, Vol. 4, 124–125.

91 *Ibid.*, 43.

92 Duncan, *Modern Traveller, Mexico*, 34.

93 Kerr, *Voyages and Travels*, Vol. 4, 299.

94 Duncan, *Modern Traveller, Mexico*, 80.

95 Robert Kerr, *A General History and Collection of Voyages and Travels, Arranged in Systematic Order: Forming a Complete History of the Origin and Progress of Navigation, Discovery, and Commerce, by Sea and Land, From the Earliest Ages to the Present Time*, "History of the Conquest of Mexico, Written in the Year 1568, by Captain Bernal Diaz Del Castillo, One of the Conquerors," Vol. 3–4, (Edinburgh: George Ramsey and Co.,1812.

96 James Duncan, *The Modern Traveller, A Popular Description, Geographical, Historical, and Topographical, of the Various Countries of the Globe. Mexico and Guatimala*. Vol. I, II (Edinburgh: Oliver and Boyd, 1825).

97 Dean C. Jessee, *The Personal Writings of Joseph Smith*, (Salt Lake City: Deseret Books, 1984), 243.

98 John Lloyd Stephens, *Incidents of Travels in Central America, Chiapas, and Yucatan and Incidents of Travel in Central America* (New York: Harper and Bros., 1841).

99 *Joseph Smith, History of The Church of Jesus Christ of Latter-day Saints*, Vol. 6, 53 (copied from *Times and Seasons*).

100 Kerr, *Voyages and Travels*, Vol. 4, 36.

101 *Ibid.*, 37.

102 *Ibid.*, 168.

103 Duncan, *Modern Traveller, Mexico*, 28.

104 *Ibid.*, 33.

105 Kerr, *Voyages and Travels*, Vol. 4, 149–150.

106 *Ibid.*, 154

107 John Pinkerton, "A Description of the East &c, by Richard Pococke, LLD. F.R.S., Book the First, of Palestine, or the Holy Land, London, 1745," in *A General Collection of the Best and Most Interesting Voyages and Travels in All Parts of the World, Volume the Tenth* (London: Longman, Hurst, Rees, Ormes, and Brown, 1811), 472.

108 Kerr, *Voyages and Travels*, Vol. 4, 261.

109 *Ibid.*, 6–7.

110 *Ibid.*, 36.

111 Neither are the cities of the Mayans. As we noted in the prior chapter, Joseph Smith, Jr. publicly used the Stephens book, published in 1841 and which documented Mayan ruins in the Yucatan and other areas of Mesoamerica, as incontrovertible evidence of Nephite cities and therefore confirmation of *The Book*

of Mormon. Obviously, Smith's unlearned flock did not realize that he secretly possessed pre-1830 Mexican history books that he used to write *The Book of Mormon.*

[112] Charles Cullen, Esq., *The History of Mexico. Collected From Spanish and Mexican Historians, From Manuscripts, and Ancient Paintings of the Indians. Together with the Conquest of Mexico by the Spaniards, Illustrated by Engravings, with Critical Dissertations on the Land, Animals, and Inhabitants of Mexico by Abbe D. Francesco Saverio Clavigero. Translated from the Original Italian by Charles Cullen. In Three Volumes* (Philadelphia: Thomson Dobson, 1806 and 1817), map of "Lakes of Mexico."

[113] Kerr, *Voyages and Travels*, Vol. 4, 168.

[114] Duncan, *Modern Traveller, Mexico*, Vol. 1, 10.

[115] *Ibid.*, 21.

[116] *Ibid.*, 37.

[117] Kerr, *Voyages and Travels*, Vol. 4, 36.

[118] Duncan, *Modern Traveller, Mexico*, Vol. 1, 202.

[119] Kerr, *Voyages and Travels*, Vol. 4, 38.

[120] Kerr, *Voyages and Travels*, Vol. 3, 495.

[121] Cullen, *History of Mexico*, Vol. 1, 67.

[122] Cullen, *History of Mexico*, Vol. 1, 68. (Authors' note: One interesting aspect of Joseph Smith Jr.'s contemporary history is the use of carved "sun stones" in the former Latter-day Saints temple at Nauvoo, Illinois built in 1844. The temple was destroyed later by vandals. Each stone had a face in the middle with sunbeams emanating from around the top half of the face. Smith allegedly told his flock that he saw the face in a vision from God, and it represented the Celestial Kingdom.

[123] Cullen, *History of Mexico*, Vol. 1, 369.

[124] *Ibid.*, 373.

[125] *Ibid.*, 377–378.

[126] Kerr, *Voyages and Travels*, Vol. 4, 37–38.

[127] Duncan, *Modern Traveller, Mexico*, Vol. 1, 7.

[128] John Pinkerton was not the only geographer or scholar with a theory about how the Mexicans came from China, or Tartary. Duncan reported that "Humboldt supposes that the Toltecs, or Aztecs, (both of these tribes being of the same family,) might be a part of those Iliong-nues who, according to the Chinese historians, emigrated under their leader Punon, and were lost in the northern parts of Siberia, from when they might easily reach the north-western coast of the new continent," in *Modern Traveller, Mexico*, pp. 189–190. Duncan's footnote reads, " 'However,' says Humboldt, 'in order to conceive that Asiatic tribes established on the table-land of Chinese Tartary should pass from the old to the new continent, it is not necessary to have recourse to a transmigration at such high latitudes. A chine of small islands stretches from Corea and Japan to the southern cape of the peninsula of Kamschatka . . . Another Archipelago, by which the great basin of Behring is terminated on the sound, advances from the peninsula of Alaska 400 leagues towards the west . . . Asiatic tribes might have

gone, by means of these islands, from one continent to the other, without going higher on the continent of Asia than the parallel of 55°, and by a passage of not more than 24 or 36 hours. The north-west winds which, during a great part of the year, blow in these latitudes, favour the navigation from Asia to America between lat. 50° and 60° N.'"

[129] Duncan, *Modern Traveller, Mexico*, Vol. 1, 182.

[130] Editor Robert Kerr commented on the prophesied return of the "god of the air," Quetzalcoatl:

> According to Clavigero, there was an ancient tradition current among the Mexicans that <u>Quetzalcoatl, their god of the air</u>, had disappeared long ago, promising to return after a certain period, and to govern them in peace and happiness; and on the first appearance of the Spaniards on their coast, observing certain marks of resemblance between them and their mythological notions about this god, <u>they believed their god of the air had returned</u>, and was about to resume the government. (Vol. III, p. 477, fn. 5)

> The appearance, strength of arms, and strange beasts made all the Indians believe they were gods, or "teules" as Diaz recorded. Robert Kerr commented again:

> By Clavigero this expression is made Teuetin, which he says signifies lords or gentlemen as applied to all the Spaniards; and that this word having some resemblance to Teteo, <u>the Mexican term for gods, made them believe they were considered as gods by the Mexicans</u>. (Vol. III, p. 478, fn. 8)

[131] Kerr, *Voyages and Travels*, Vol. 3, 468.

[132] Kerr, *Voyages and Travels*, Vol. 4, 6.

[133] Kerr, *Voyages and Travels*, Vol. 4, 251.

[134] A. V. B. Norman, "Swords," *Encyclopedia Americana, U.S. Constitutional Bicentennial Commemorative Edition*, 988, XXVI, p. 157. A. V. B. Norman is the author of *Arms and Armor and History of War and Weapons, 449–1660 AD*.

[135] Noah Webster, *A Dictionary of the English Language; Compiled for the Use of Common Schools in the United States* (Hartford: George Goodwin and Sons, 1817), 55.

[136] Marsden, *Marco Polo*, 210.

[137] *Ibid.*, 270.

[138] *Ibid.*, 443.

[139] Kerr, *Voyages and Travels*, Vol. 4, 21.

[140] *Ibid.*, 45.

[141] Marsden, *Marco Polo*, 210.

[142] *Ibid.*, 269.

[143] Marsden, *Marco Polo*, 443.

[144] Kerr, *Voyages and Travels*, Vol. 4, 242.

[145] *Ibid.*, 233.

[146] *Ibid.*, 178.

[147] John Pinkerton, *Voyages and Travels, South America.*, Vol. XIV, plate 5, p. 548.

[148] Pinkerton, *A General Collection of Voyages and Travels. South America.*, Vol. XIV, p. 548, "A Voyage to South America, which was undertaken by Don Antonio De Ulloa, Captain of the Spanish Navy."

[149] *Second American Edition of Nicholson's British Encyclopedia a Dictionary of Arts & Sciences* (Philadelphia: Mitchell Amos White , 1818).

[150] Kerr, *Voyages and Travels*, Vol. 4, 260.

[151] *Ibid.*, 5.

[152] *Ibid.*, 120.

[153] *Ibid.*, 174.

[154] *Ibid.*, 182–183.

[155] Alexander the Great could not even conquer the entire area because of the difficulty of proceeding upward through a certain narrow pass in the mountains. A few local forces could defend the pass against an entire army. Since he could not proceed, Alexander had a wall constructed to seal off the pass and keep the native forces in the mountains, away from the remainder of the province. In footnote 115, page 56, William Marsden wrote: "This is the celebrated Pass between the foot of mount Caucasus and the Caspian sea, where stands the small but strong city of Derbend, called . . . by the Turks . . . the 'Gate of Iron' . . .

[156] Marsden, *Marco Polo*, 52.

[157] William Marsden, *The Travels of Marco Polo* (1818).

[158] Robert Kerr, *Voyages and Travels*, Vol. 3 (1811).

[159] James Duncan, *The Modern Traveller, Arabia* (1825).

[160] James Duncan, *The Modern Traveller, Mexico* (1825).

[161] Kerr, *Voyages and Travels*, Vol. 4, 8.

[162] Kerr, *Voyages and Travels*, Vol. 4, 133.

[163] Kerr, *Voyages and Travels*, Vol. 4, 24.

[164] Kerr, *Voyages and Travels*, Vol. 4, 37. (Note: In Kerr, Vol. 3, p. 461 Diaz refers to the initial troop number as "508, besides the seamen." Some difference in numbers of the Spanish army was the result of a contingent remaining as a rear guard along the Atlantic coast. The troop count grew after defeating General Narvaez whereupon Cortez conscripted the Narvaez army into his own.)

[165] Duncan, *Modern Traveller*, Arabia, 127.

[166] Duncan, *Modern Traveller, Mexico*, 131.

[167] Robert Kerr, Ed., "Spanish Discoveries Subsequent to Columbus," in *A General History and Collection of Voyages and Travels, Arranged in Systematic Order: Forming a Complete History of the Origin and Progress of Navigation, Discovery, and Commerce, by Sea and Land, From the Earliest Ages to the Present Time*, Vol. 3 (Edinburgh: George Ramsey and Co., 1812), 427

[168] *Ibid.*, 427.

[169] Duncan, *Modern Traveller, Mexico*, 103.

[170] *Ibid.*, 108.

[171] *The Holy Bible by the Special Command of King James I, of England*, including *The New Testament of our Lord and Saviour Jesus Christ.* (Walpole, New Hampshire: Anson Whipple, 1815).

[172] Robert Kerr, Ed., "History of the Conquest of Mexico, Written in the Year 1568, by Captain Bernal Diaz Del Castillo, One of the Conquerors." in *A General History and Collection of Voyages and Travels*, Vol. 3-4 (Edinburgh: George Ramsey and Co., 1812).

[173] Kerr, *Voyages and Travels*, Vol. 4, 108-109.

[174] Duncan, *Modern Traveller, Mexico*, Vol. 1, 56.

[175] Kerr, *Voyages and Travels*, Vol. 4, 40.

[176] John Ranking, *Historical Researches on the Conquest of Peru, Mexico, Bogota, Natchez, and Talomeco, in the Thirteenth Century by The Mongols, Accompanied with Elephants; and the Local Agreement of History and Tradition, With the Remains of Elephants and Mastodontes, Found in The New World.* (London: Longman, Rees, Orme, Brown, and Green, 1827).

[177] Marsden, *The Travels of Marco Polo*, 1818.

[178] Duncan, *Modern Traveller, Mexico*, Vol. 1, 166.

[179] "Book of Nephi, the Son of Nephi, Which was the Son of Helaman," Ch. 6, p. 484.

[180] John Ranking, *Historical Researches*.

[181] *Ibid.*, 463-464.

[182] Most articles the authors could locate relating to the Tower of Babel estimate its construction (and destruction) to have occurred somewhere between 2,400 BC and 3,500 BC The latest estimated date of construction was 1,500 BC.

[183] Ranking, *Historical Researches*, 268.

[184] *Ibid.*, 1.

[185] *Ibid.*, 21-22.

[186] *Ibid.*, 21, footnote.

[187] *Ibid.*, 285, 289.

[188] *Ibid.*, 374.

[189] *Ibid.*, 48.

[190] *Ibid.*, 203.

[191] *Ibid.*, 47-48.

[192] *Ibid.*, 48-49.

[193] *Ibid.*, 306.

[194] *Ibid.*, 53.

[195] Ivan T. Sanderson, "Elephants," *in Encyclopedia Americana*, International Edition, (Grolier, Inc., Danbury, CT., 1988) Vol. 10, p. 213.

[196] Louis A. Brennan's *Beginners Guide to Archaeology* (Stackpole Books, Harrisburg, PA, 1973), p. 49.

[197] Marsden, *Marco Polo*, page 227, note 436.

[198] Turner, Samuel. *An Account of an Embassy to the Court of the Teshoo Lama, in Tibet; Containing a Narrative Journey Through Bootan, and Part of Tibet.* (London: W. Bulmber & Co., 1800).

[199] Ranking, *Historical Researches*, 293-294.

[200] *Ibid.*, 268-269.

[201] *Ibid.*, 58-59.

[202] *Ibid.*, 350.

[203] *Ibid.*, 119–121.

[204] *Ibid.*, 118–119.

[205] *Ibid.*, 122.

[206] *Ibid.*, 120.

[207] *Ibid.*, 12 and footnote.

[208] *Ibid.*, 24.

[209] *Ibid.*, 122.

[210] *Ibid.*, 122–123.

[211] *Ibid.*, 122–124.

[212] *Ibid.*, 119.

[213] Charles Cullen, Esq., *The History of Mexico. Collected From Spanish and Mexican Historians, From Manuscripts, and Ancient Paintings of the Indians. Together with the Conquest of Mexico by the Spaniards, Illustrated by Engravings, with Critical Dissertations on the Land, Animals, and Inhabitants of Mexico by Abbe D. Francesco Saverio Clavigero. Translated from the Original Italian by Charles Cullen. In Three Volumes* (Philadelphia: Thomson Dobson, 1806) Plate IX, "The Greater Temple of Mexico."

[214] James Duncan, *The Modern Traveller, A Popular Description, Geographical, Historical, and Topographical, of the Various Countries of the Globe. Mexico and Guatimala.* (London: Oliver and Boyd, 1825) Vol. I, 35–36.

[215] *Ibid.*, 36.

[216] W. Bullock, *Six Months Residence and Travels in Mexico: Containing Remarks on the Present State of New Spain, Its Natural Productions, State of Society, Manufactures, Trade, Agriculture, Antiquities, &c.* 2d Ed. (London: John Murray, Albemarle Street, 1825).

[217] Robert Kerr, "History of the Conquest of Mexico, Written in the Year 1568, by Captain Bernal Diaz Del Castillo, One of the Conquerors," in *A General History and Collection of Voyages and Travels, Arranged in Systematic Order: Forming a Complete History of the Origin and Progress of Navigation, Discovery, and Commerce, by Sea and Land, From the Earliest Ages to the Present Time*, Vol. 4 (Edinburgh: George Ramsey and Company, 1812), 41.

[218] Joseph Fielding Smith, *Teachings of the Prophet Joseph Smith* (Salt Lake City: Deseret Book, 1938), 270.

[219] *Ibid.*, 315.

[220] Marsden, *Marco Polo*, 12–13.

[221] *Ibid.*, 278.

[222] *Ibid.*, 29.

[223] *Ibid.*, 12.

[224] *Ibid.*, 34.

[225] *Ibid.*

[226] *Ibid.*, 278.

[227] *Ibid.*, 29.

[228] *Ibid.*, 12.

[229] The original text had numerous misspellings, edits, and corrections, some of which are reproduced here on purpose.

[230] Joseph Smith, *History of the Church*, 1:51–53.

[231] Joseph Smith, *History of the Church*, 1:59.

[232] Joseph Smith, *History of the Church*, 1:60 (1838).

[233] Lucy Smith, *Biographical Sketches*, p. 104.

[234] John Pinkerton, *A General Collection of the Best and Most Interesting Voyages and Travels in All Parts of the World; Many of Which Are Now First Translated Into English, Illustrated with Plates, Volume the First, Europe* (London: Longman, Hurst, Rees and Orme, 1808).

[235] Pinkerton, *A General Collection of the Best and Most Interesting Voyages and Travels in All Parts of the World; Many of Which Are Now First Translated Into English, Illustrated with Plates, Volume the First, Europe* (Philadelphia: Kimber and Conrad, 1810).

[236] Pinkerton, *General Collection*, Vol. 1, 184.

[237] *Encyclopedia of Joseph Smith's Teachings*, edited by Larry E. Dahl and Donald Q. Cannon.

[238] Lucy Mack Smith, *Biographical Sketches*, 109.

[239] *History of Joseph Smith., Times and Seasons*, vol. 3 (November 1841–October 1842), Vol. No. 13, May 2, 1842, p. 773.

[240] John Pinkerton, *A General Collection of the Best and Most Interesting Voyages and Travels in All Parts of the World; Many of Which Are Now First Translated Into English, Illustrated with Plates, Volume the First, Europe* (London: Longman, Hurst, Rees and Orme, 1808), 474.

[241] *Ibid.*, 474.

[242] *Ibid.*, 476.

[243] *Ibid.*, 180.

[244] BYU Studies, vol. 20, no. 4, p. 325 (1980).

[245] *History of Joseph Smith, Times and Seasons*, vol. 3 (November 1841–October 1842), Vol. No. 13, May 2, 1842, p. 772–773

[246] *History of Joseph Smith, Times and Seasons*, vol. 3 (November 1841–October 1842), Vol. No. 13, May 2, 1842, p. 773.

[247] Eber D. Howe, *Mormonism Unvailed*, (Painesville: printed and published by the author, 1834), 270.

[248] Duncan, *Modern Traveller, Mexico*, 189.

[249] *Ibid.*, 193.

[250] Alma P. Burton, *Joseph Smith, Discourses*, 276.

[251] John Pinkerton, " Von Troil's Letters on Iceland," in *A General Collection of the Best and Most Interesting Voyages and Travels in All Parts of the World; Many of Which Are Now First Translated Into English, Illustrated with Plates, Volume the First, Europe* (London: Longman, Hurst, Rees and Orme, 1808), 621.

[252] *Ibid.*, 708.

[253] *Ibid.*

[254] *Ibid.*, 708–709.

[255] *Ibid.*, 709.

[256] Lucy Mack Smith, *Biographical Sketches*, 106.

[257] Pinkerton, Vol. 1, 474.

[258] *Ibid.*, 5.

[259] Lucy Mack Smith, *Biographical Sketches*, 103.

[260] Pinkerton, "Letters on Iceland by Uno Von Troil," in *General Collection, Volume the First*, 621.

[261] Richard Lloyd Anderson, *Investigating the Book of Mormon Witnesses* (Salt Lake City: Deseret Book Co., 1981), 61.

[262] Anderson, *Witnesses*, 6–9, 32.

[263] *Ibid.*, 8–9, n. 13.

[264] *Ibid.*, 9–10; Book of Commandments 4:8, with the Whitney manuscript reading "the things which he desireth to view," now D&C 5:24, Cp. n. 11.

[265] Anderson, *Witnesses*, 10; D&C 17, 1–4, first published in the 1835 edition with the dating: June, 1829, given previous to their viewing the plates containing the Book of Mormon."

[266] Anderson, *Witnesses*, 80–81.

[267] *Ibid.*, 82.

[268] *Ibid.*, 182–187.

[269] Pinkerton, *General Collection*, Vol. 1, 621.

[270] Anderson, *Witnesses*, 107–108.

[271] *Ibid.*, 131.

[272] Interview of William Smith with E. C. Briggs and J. W. Peterson, (*Zion's Ensign*, Jan. 13, 1894), 6.

[273] Anderson, *Witnesses*, 29.

[274] Pinkerton, *General Collection*, Vol. 1, 708.

[275] *Ibid.*, 709.

[276] Joseph Smith, *History of the Church of Jesus Christ of Latter-Day Saints, Period I, History of Joseph Smith, the Prophet by Himself* [7 vols.] (Salt Lake City: Deseret Book Company, 1978), Vol. 6, 308, 319–320.

[277] *The Book of Commandments*, 7, "Spirit of Revelation. Revelation received at Harmony, Pennsylvania, in April 1829 for Oliver Cowdery," (September, 1830) in *The Joseph Smith Revelations: Text and Commentary*, ed. Michael H. Marquardt (Salt Lake City, Signature Books, 1999), 35–37.

[278] *The Book of Commandments*, 8, "Be Patient My Son. Revelation received at Harmony, Pennsylvania, in April 1829 for Oliver Cowdery," in Marquardt *Joseph Smith Revelations*, 37.

[279] Smith, *History*, Vol. 1, 226.

[280] Revelation, "For Time and for All Eternity, Revelation received at Nauvoo, Illinois, on 12 July 1843 concerning biblical men having wives and concubines, adultery, a commandment for Emma Smith, the law of the priesthood," ed. Marquardt, 323.

[281] *Ibid.*, 324.

[282] Marco Polo, *The Travels of Marco Polo, A Venetian, In The Thirteenth Century*, ed. William Marsden (London: Cox and Baylis, 1818).

283 *Ibid.*,185, n. 356.

284 *Ibid.*, 367 n. 691.

285 *Ibid.*, 204–205.

286 *Ibid.*, 205.

287 Fawn M. Brodie, *No Man Knows My History—The Life of Joseph Smith*, Second Edition (New York: Vintage Books, 1995), 335.

288 Revelation, "For Time and for All Eternity," ed. Marquardt, 327.

289 Brodie, *No Man Knows My History*, 341–342 and fn., "The Journal history in the Mormon Church library in Salt Lake City states that Kimball asserted this in a speech in Salt Lake City, July 12, 1857."

290 Revelation, "For Time and for All Eternity," ed. Marquardt, 327.

291 *Ibid.*, 328.

292 Brody, *No Man Knows My History*, 335–336.

293 *Ibid.*, 336.

294 Revelation, "For Time and for All Eternity," ed. Marquardt, 328.

295 *Ibid.*, 324–235.

296 Joseph Smith, *The Words of Joseph Smith: The Contemporary Accounts of the Nauvoo Discourses of the Prophet Joseph*, ed. Andrew Ehat and Lyndon Cook (Salt Lake City: Bookcraft, 2d. ed., 1981), 385.

297 Joseph Smith, *History of the Church* (1844), Vol. 6, 474.

298 "16 June 1844 [Sunday Morning], Grove East of Temple, Thomas Bullock Report," in Ehat, *The Words of Joseph Smith*, 378–379.

299 Marsden, *Marco Polo*, 383, Note 726: "This is the Hindu doctrine of the metempsychosis, which along with the schismatic religion of *Buddha*, was introduced into China (as the annals of that country inform us) about the year 65 of our era. It had not, however, (according to the elder De Guignes) made any considerable progress until the year 335, when the emperor then reigning took it under his protection. . . ." (Hist. gén. des Huns, t. i, p. 11, liv. iii, p. 223). Note 727, pp. 383–384: "According to the Hindu belief the souls of men reanimate new bodies, until by repeated regenerations, all their sins are done away, and they attain such a degree of perfection as will entitle them to what is called *mukti*, eternal salvation, by which is understood a release from future transmigration, and an absorption in the nature of the Godhead." (Wilkins, notes to *Bhagvat Gītā*, p. 140).

300 Joseph Smith, *History of the Church*, Vol. 6, 306.

301 Instruction at Lyceum at Nauvoo, Ill., on Tuesday, March 9, 1841. McIntire Minute Book.

302 "The Rise of the Church of Christ" in *The Articles and Covenants of the Church of Christ composed at Fayette, New York, in [1–9] June 1830* (Zebedee Coltrin Journal) in Marquardt, 63.

303 *Vision of Joseph Smith, Jr., and Sidney Rigdon received at Hiram, Ohio, on 16 February 1832*, "The Eyes of Our Understanding," from *The Evening and Morning Star 1*, (July 1832): [2–3], ed. Marquardt, 186–190.

304 William Clayton, *Diary, Sunday Afternoon, Ramus Illinois* (1843), in Ehat, *The Words of Joseph Smith*, 169.

[305] *Vision of Joseph Smith, Jr.*, Marquardt, 186–190.

[306] Vision of Joseph Smith, Jr. and Sidney Rigdon received at Hiram, Ohio, on 16 February 1832, "The Eyes of Our Understanding," from *The Evening and Morning Star* I (July 1832): [2–3], ed. Marquardt, 186–193.

[307] Revelation, "For Time and for All Eternity," ed. Marquardt, 324–325.

[308] Joseph Smith, "King Follet Sermon," in *History of the Church*, Vol. 6, 302–17.

[309] Revelation, "For Time and for All Eternity," ed. Marquardt, 325.

[310] Joseph Fielding Smith, Doctrines of Salvation in *Sermons and Writings of Joseph Fielding Smith, Compiled by* Bruce R. McConkie (Salt Lake City, Utah: Bookcraft, 1955) Vol. I, 135.

[311] *Doctrine and Covenants*, "Part Second. Covenants and Commandments of the Lord, to his servants of the church of the Latter Day Saints," Section 50, verses 1–3 (1835).

[312] *Ibid.*, Section 3, "On Priesthood," verses 1–3.

[313] Smith, Jr., Joseph. History, 1832, Joseph Smith Letterbook 1, p. 1. Handwriting of Frederick G. Williams and Joseph Smith.

[314] Duncan, *Modern Traveller, Arabia* (1825).

[315] Ranking, *History of Peru and Mexico* (1828).

[316] Pinkerton, *General Collection, Volume the First* (Philadelphia: Kimber and Conrad, 1810).

[317] Smith Jr., Joseph. History, 1832, Joseph Smith Letterbook 1, p. 1. Handwriting of Frederick G. Williams and Joseph Smith.

[318] Lucy Smith, *Biographical Sketches*, 79.

[319] Smith Jr., Joseph. *History of the Church*, Vol. 1, Verse 34.

[320] Joseph Smith, *Encyclopedia of Joseph Smith's Teachings*, edited by Larry E. Dahl and Donald Q.Cannon.

[321] Ronald W. Walker, *The Historians' Corner* BYU Studies, Vol. 32, pp. 278–282, Num. 1 and 2—Winter and Spring 1992.

[322] Joseph F. Smith stated, "Lucy Smith died near Nauvoo, May 5, 1855, but years prior to this date some of her effects were left in the hands of her son, William Smith, among them being the manuscript copy of this history. From William (who was the last surviving brother of the Prophet, and whose death occurred at Osterdock, Clayton county, Iowa, November 13, 1893,) the document fell (surreptitiously it was declared by George A. Smith) into the hands of Isaac Sheen, who was at one time a member of the Church in Michigan. When in September, 1852, Apostle Orson Pratt went on a mission to England, he called on Mr. Sheen on his way East and being shown the manuscript copy, he purchased it for a certain sum of money, took it to Liverpool with him, where, without revision and without the consent or knowledge of President Young or any of the Twelve, it was published under his direction in 1853." (*History of Joseph Smith by his Mother*, Introduction VIII, 1954 edition)

[323] Lucy Smith, *Biographical Sketches*.

[324] *Ibid.*, 58.

[325] *Ibid.*, 49–51.

[326] *Ibid.*, 107.

[327] *Ibid.*

[328] Joseph Smith, History of The Church of Jesus Christ of Latter-day Saints, 7 Vols. 4:479; sermon delivered at Smith home on Dec. 19, 1841.

[329] Lucy Smith, *Biographical Sketches*, 234.

[330] *Ibid.*, 230.

[331] *Ibid.*, 232.

[332] *Ibid.*, 234–235.

[333] *Ibid.*, 245–246.

[334] *Ibid.*, 254–258.

[335] *Ibid.*, 267.

[336] *Ibid.*, 281–282.

Nepohualco

Made in the USA
Charleston, SC
18 October 2012